Itsuwaribito・空・

YUUKI IINUMA

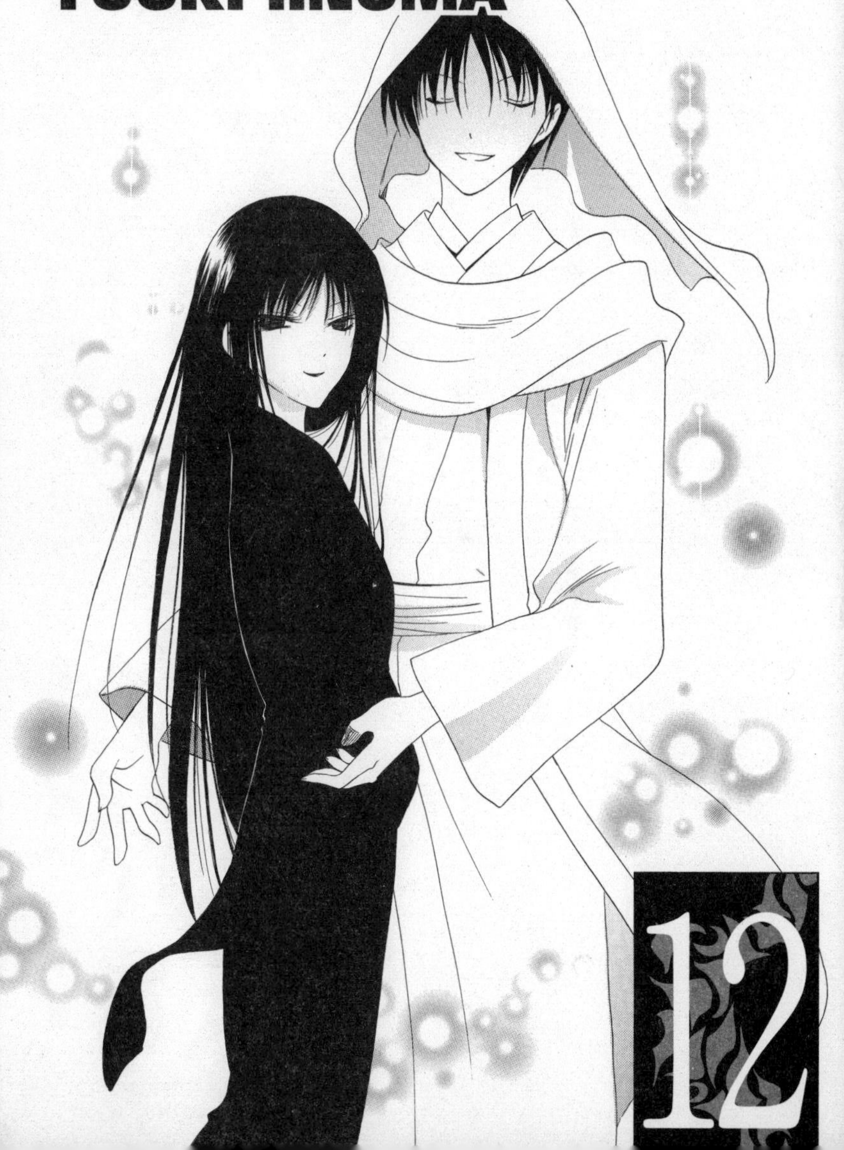

12

Contents

Chapter 108
People and the World

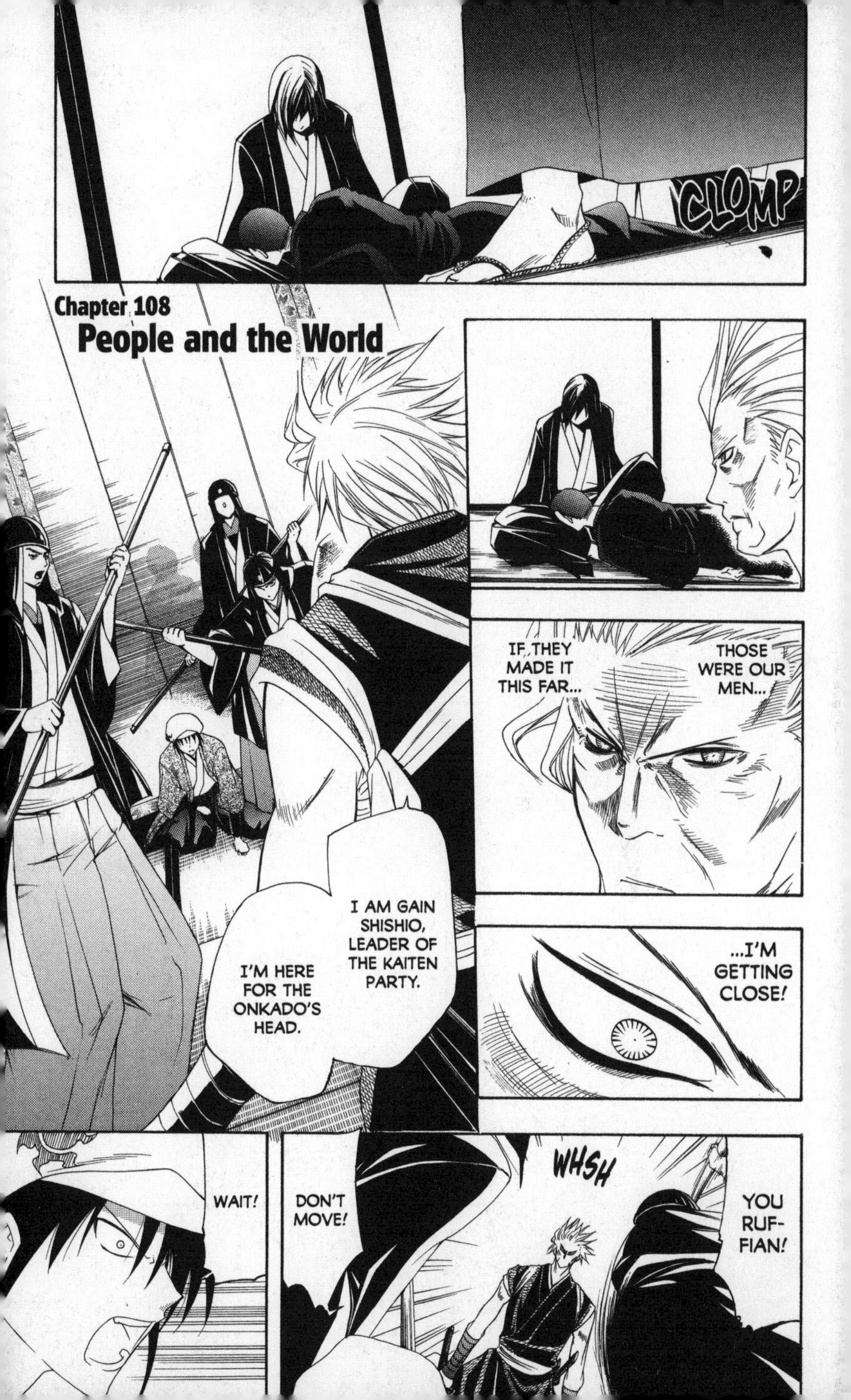
CLOMP
THOSE WERE OUR MEN...
IF THEY MADE IT THIS FAR...
...I'M GETTING CLOSE!
I AM GAIN SHISHIO, LEADER OF THE KAITEN PARTY.
I'M HERE FOR THE ONKADO'S HEAD.
WHSH
YOU RUF-FIAN!
DON'T MOVE!
WAIT!

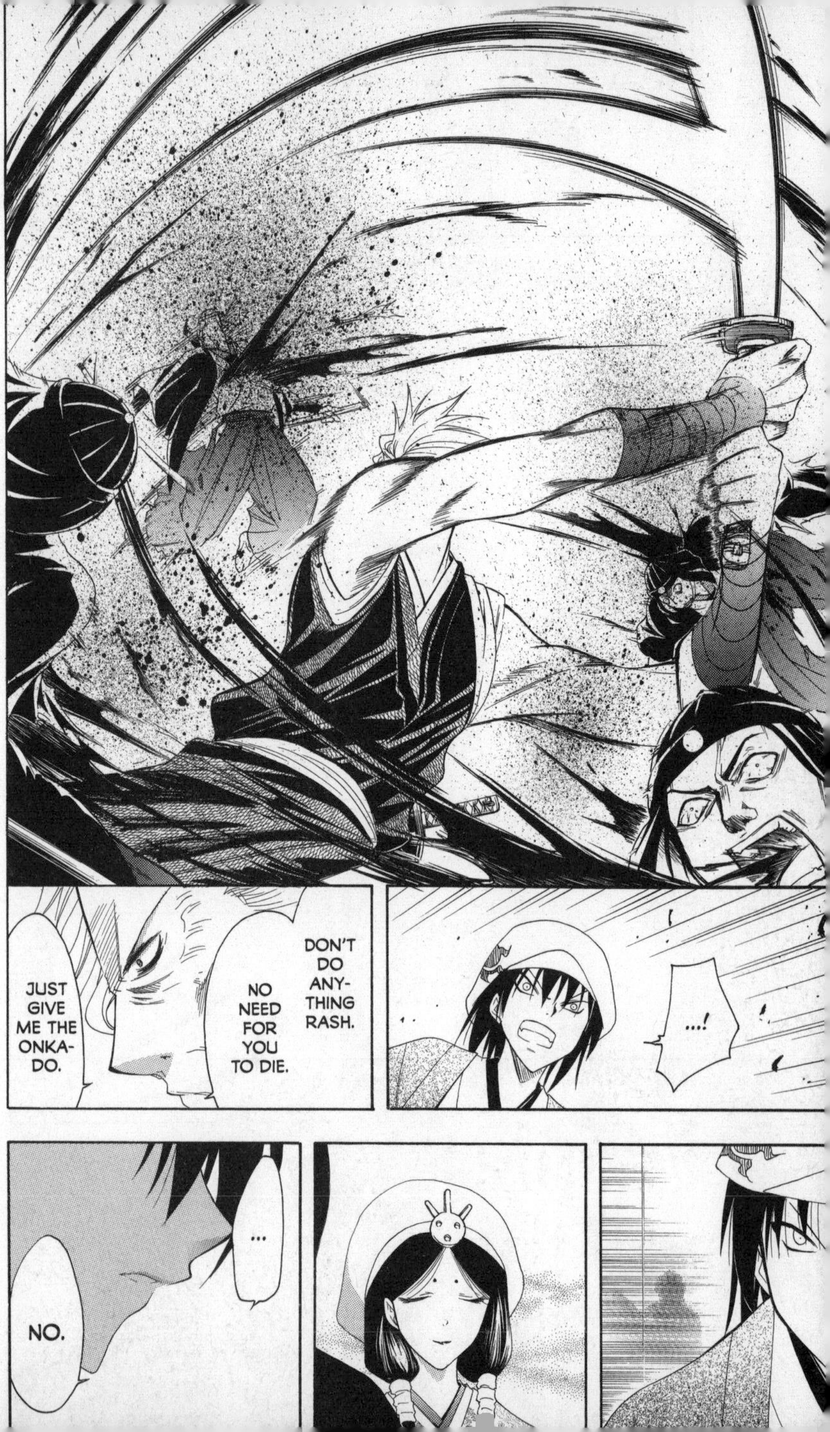
...!
DON'T DO ANYTHING RASH.
NO NEED FOR YOU TO DIE.
JUST GIVE ME THE ONKA-DO.
...
NO.

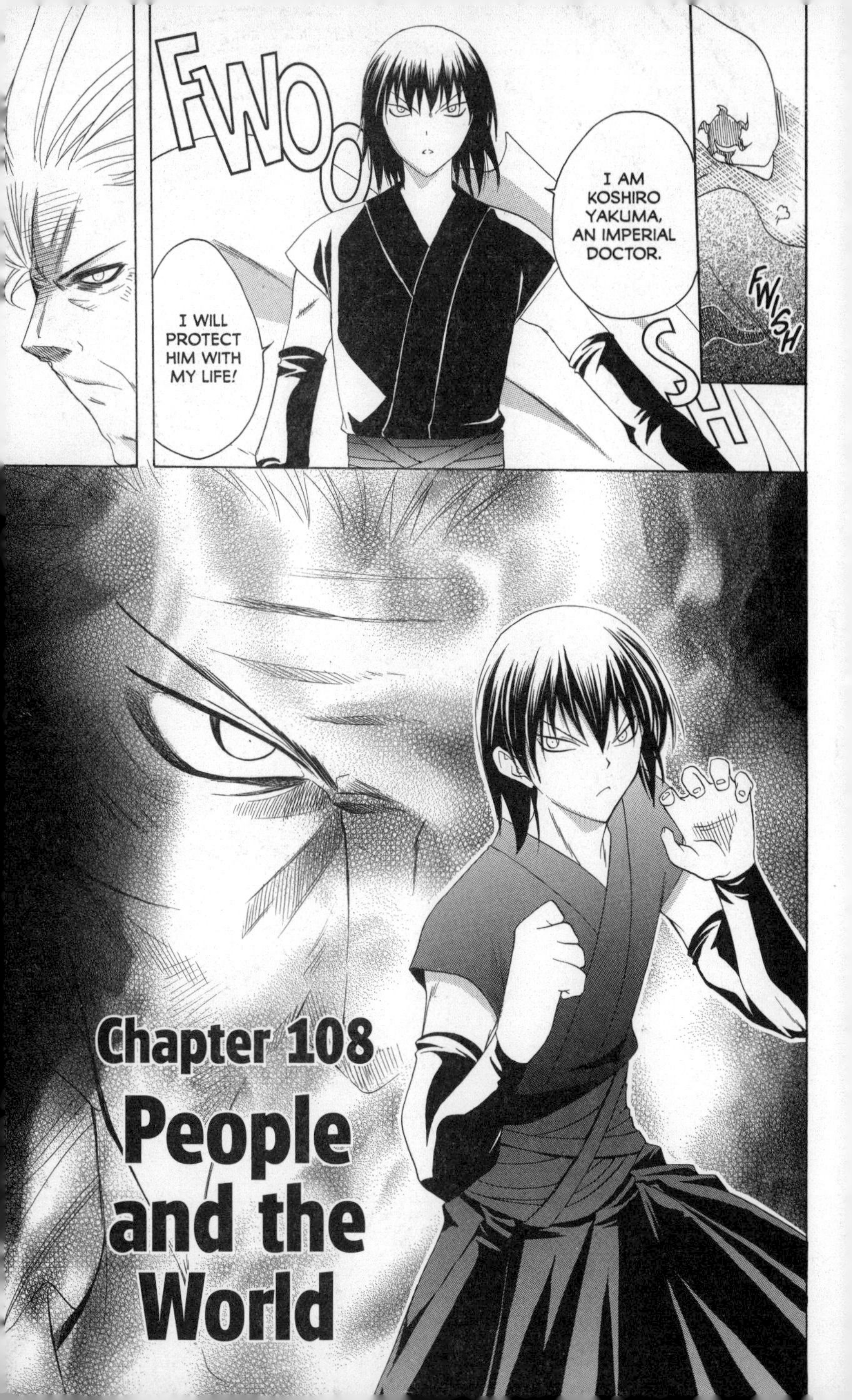
FWISH
I AM KOSHIRO YAKUMA, AN IMPERIAL DOCTOR.
FWOOO
SH
I WILL PROTECT HIM WITH MY LIFE!
Chapter 108
People and the World

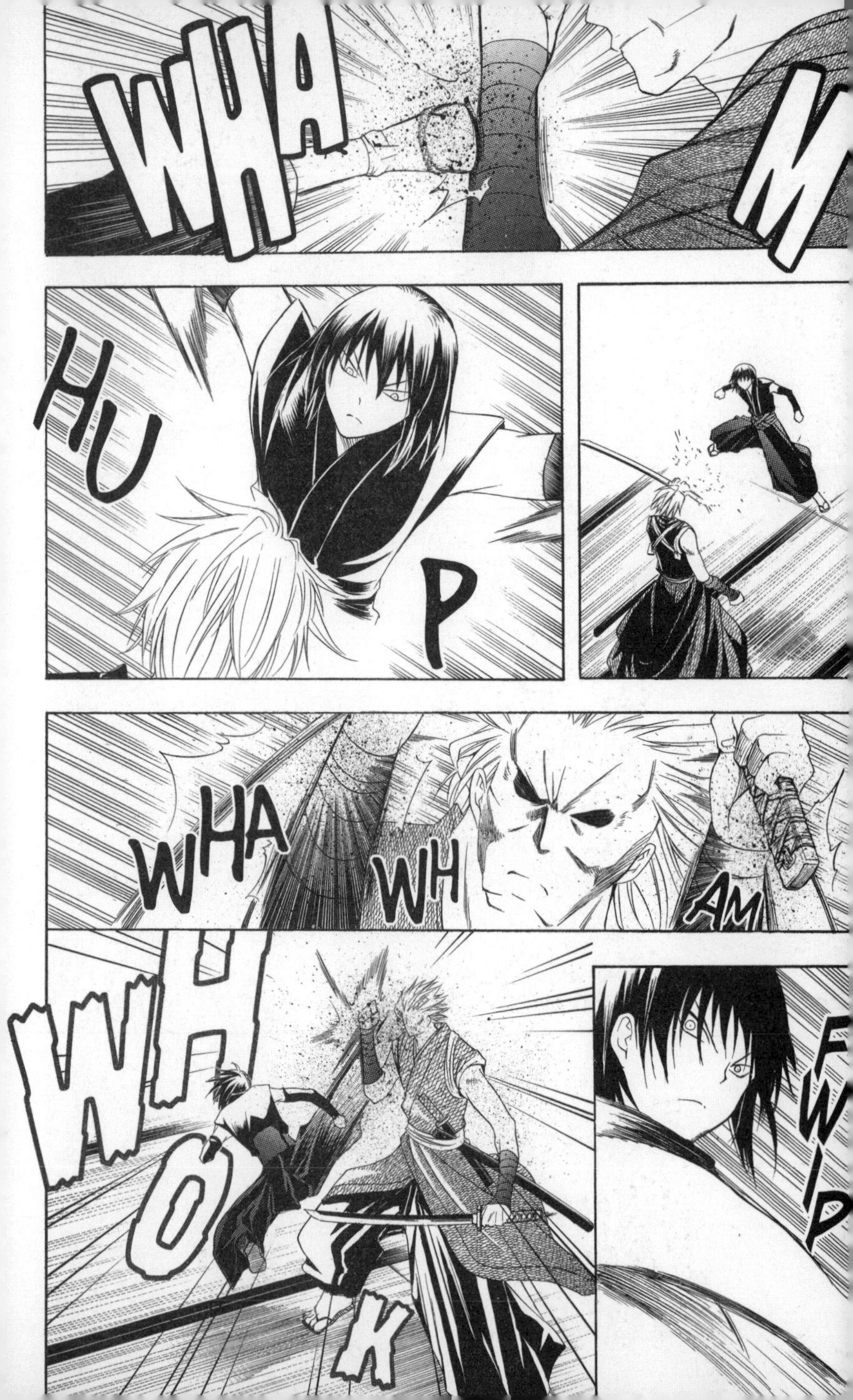
WHA
M
HU
P
WHA
WH
AM
FWIP
WH
O
K

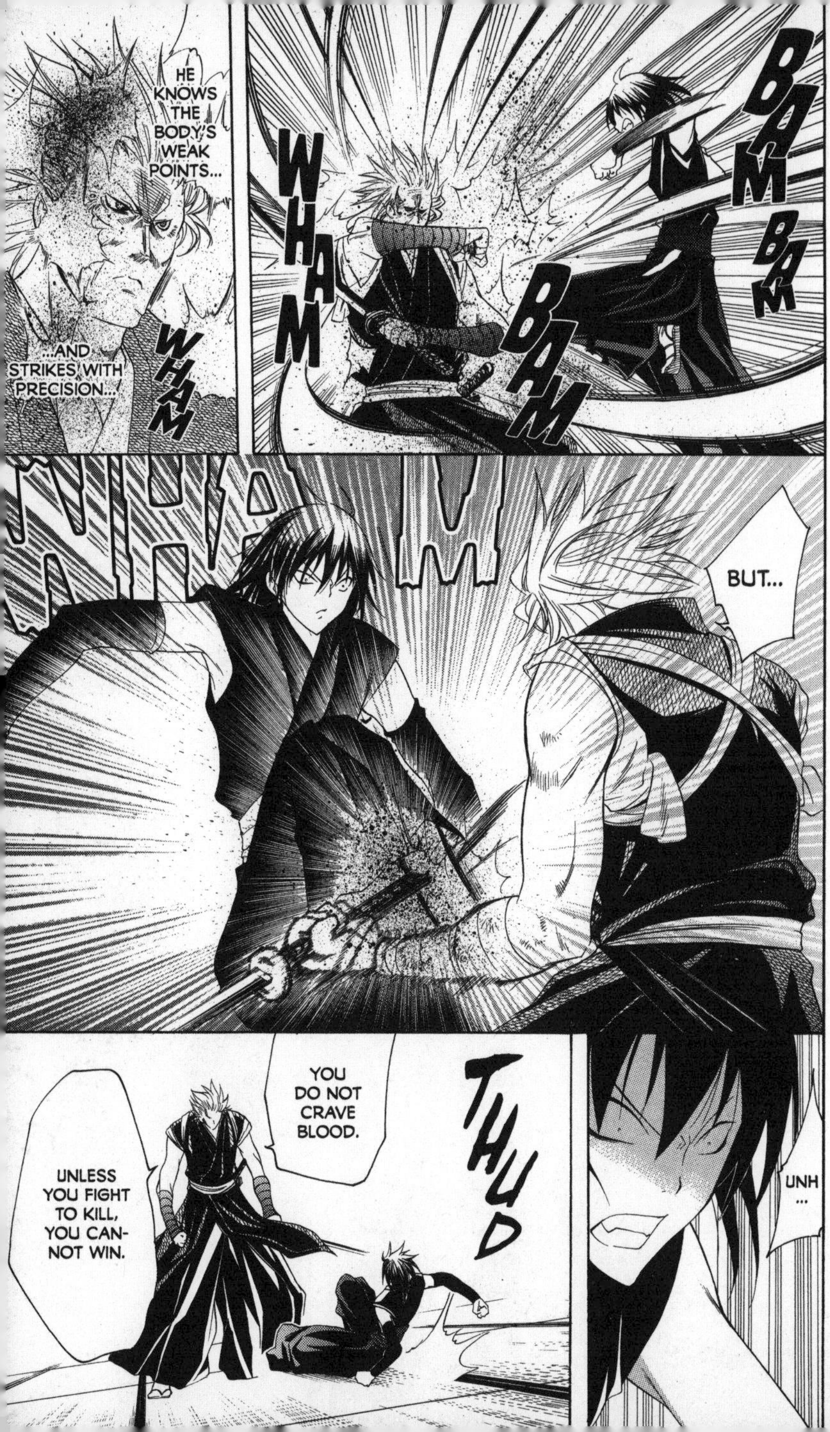
BAM BAM
BAM
WHAM
HE KNOWS THE BODY'S WEAK POINTS...
...AND STRIKES WITH PRECISION...
WHAM
WHAM
BUT...
UNH ...
THUD
YOU DO NOT CRAVE BLOOD.
UNLESS YOU FIGHT TO KILL, YOU CAN-NOT WIN.

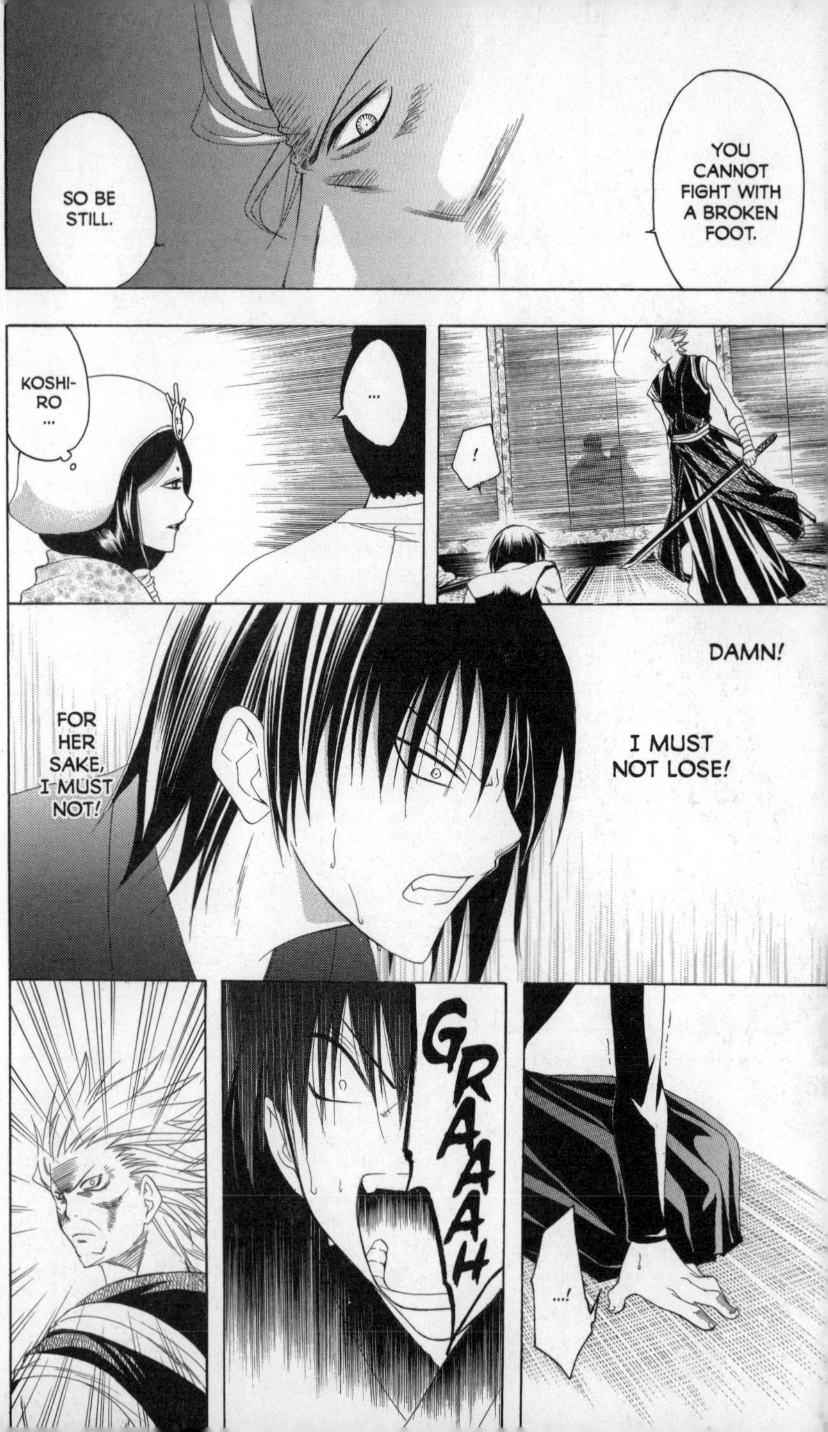
YOU CANNOT FIGHT WITH A BROKEN FOOT.
SO BE STILL.
!
...
KOSHIRO ...
DAMN!
I MUST NOT LOSE!
FOR HER SAKE, I MUST NOT!
...!
GRAAAH

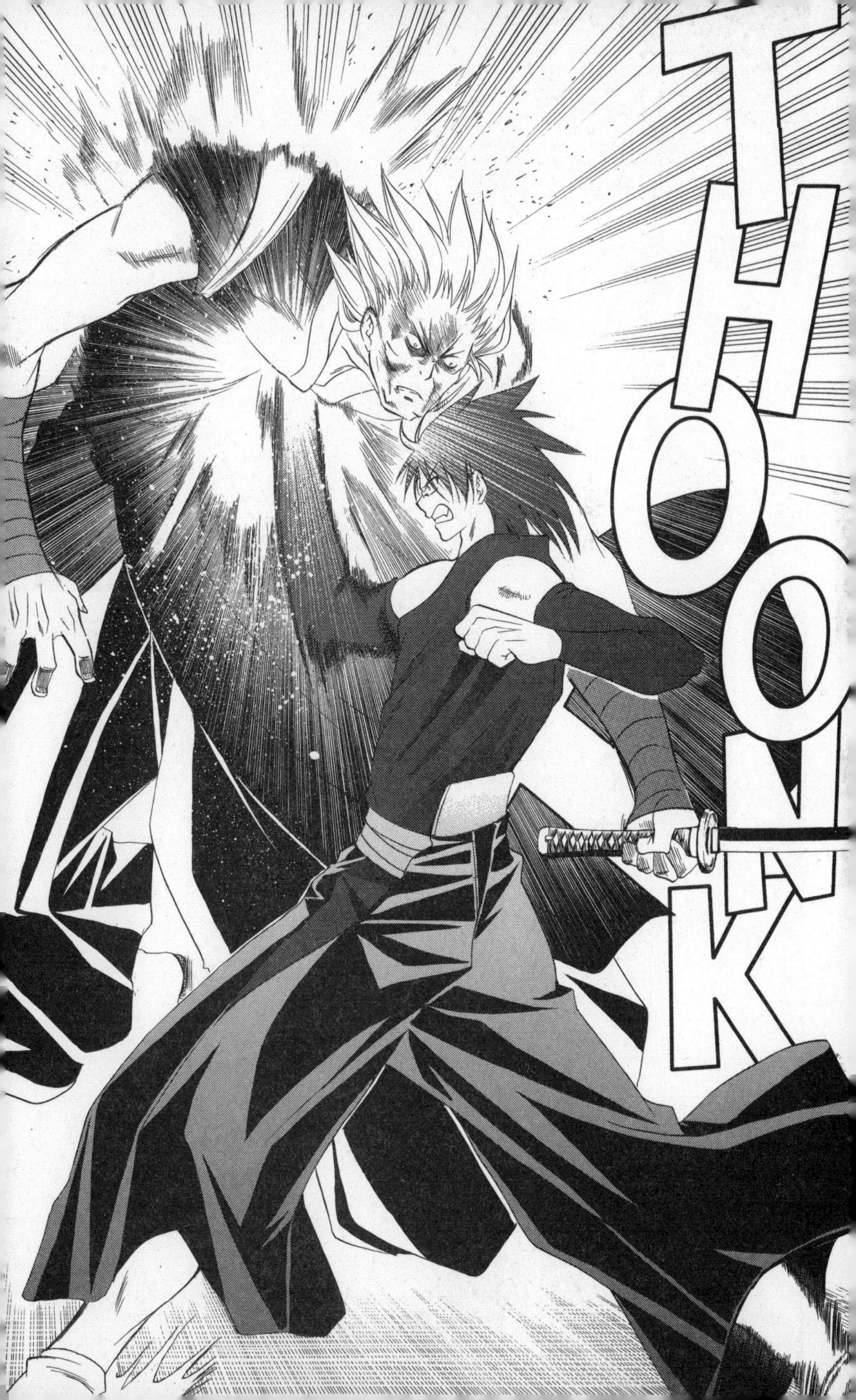
THOONK

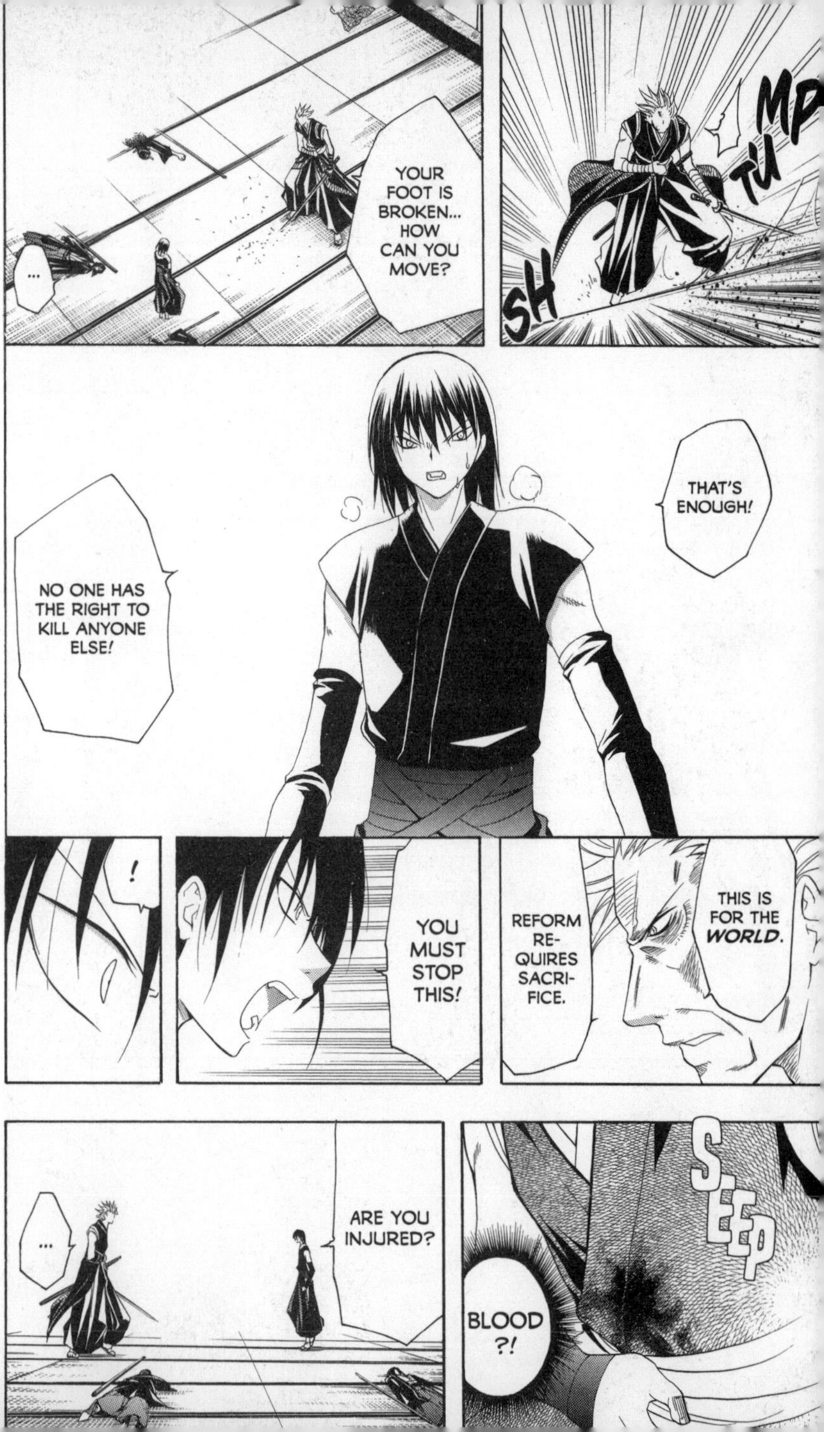
SH
TUMP
YOUR FOOT IS BROKEN... HOW CAN YOU MOVE?
...
THAT'S ENOUGH!
NO ONE HAS THE RIGHT TO KILL ANYONE ELSE!
THIS IS FOR THE *WORLD*.
REFORM RE-QUIRES SACRI-FICE.
YOU MUST STOP THIS!
!
SEEP
BLOOD ?!
ARE YOU INJURED?
...

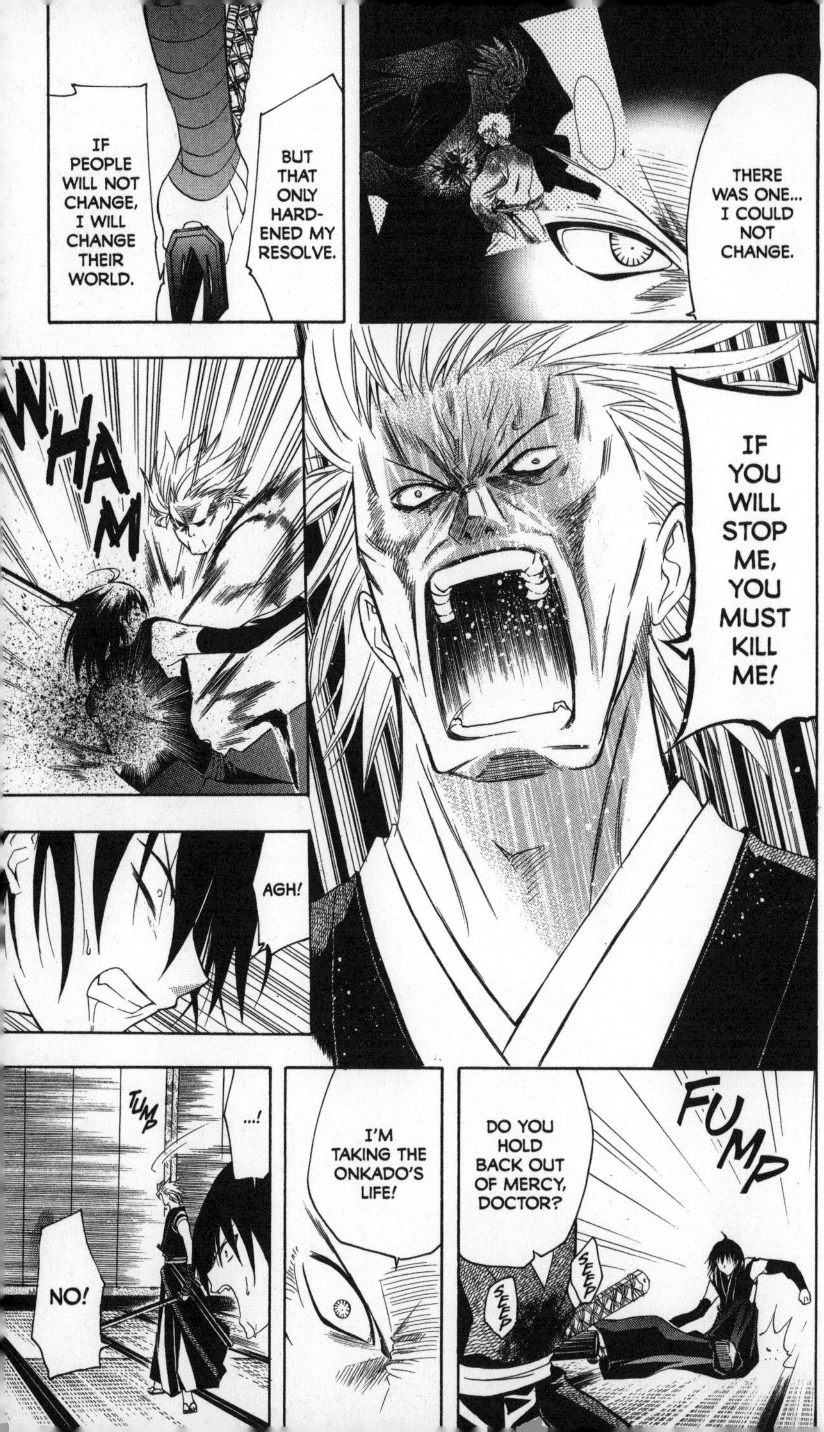

THERE WAS ONE... I COULD NOT CHANGE.
BUT THAT ONLY HARD-ENED MY RESOLVE.
IF PEOPLE WILL NOT CHANGE, I WILL CHANGE THEIR WORLD.
IF YOU WILL STOP ME, YOU MUST KILL ME!
WHAM
AGH!
FUMP
DO YOU HOLD BACK OUT OF MERCY, DOCTOR?
SEEP
SEEP
I'M TAKING THE ONKADO'S LIFE!
...!
TUMP
NO!

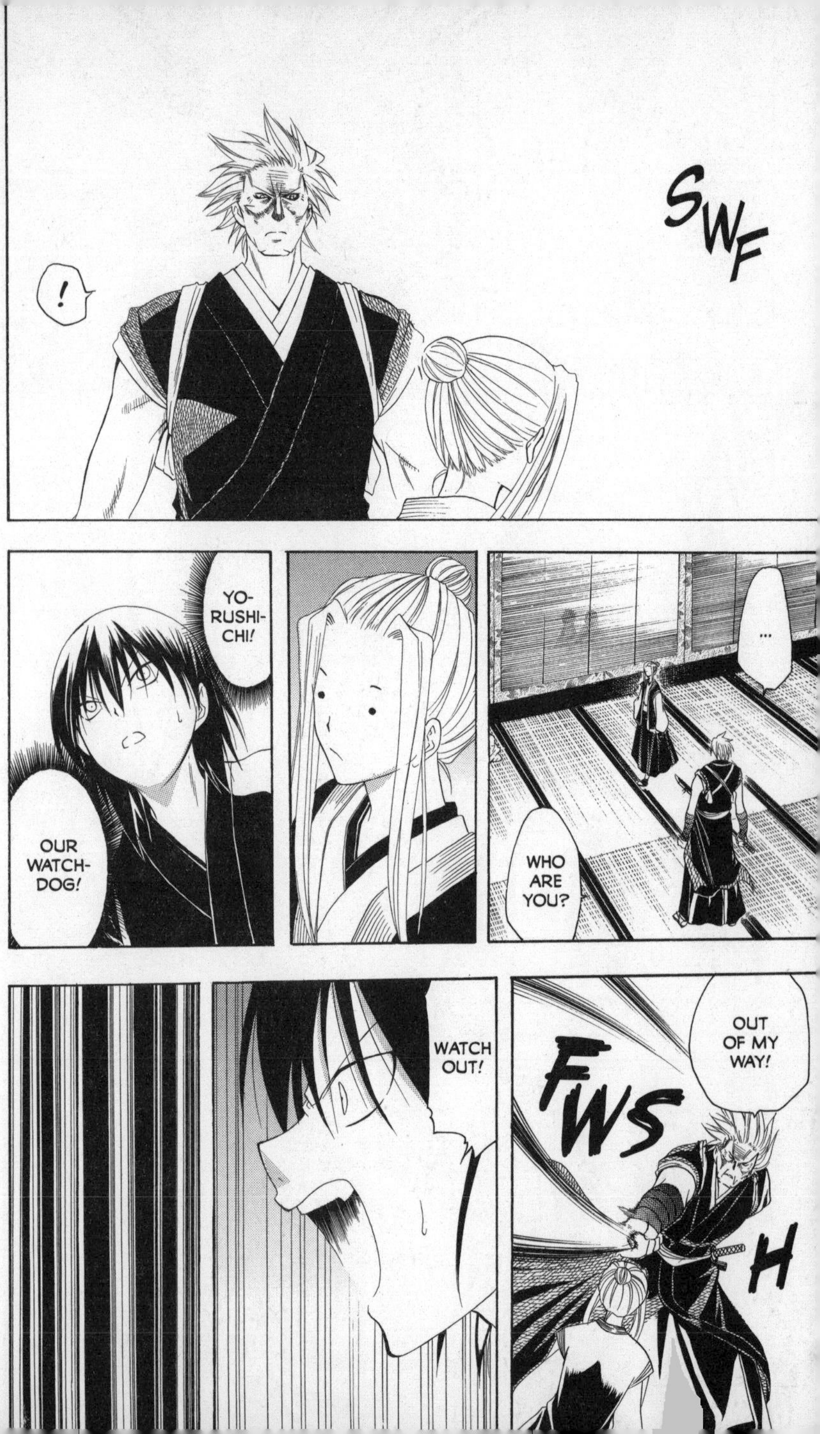
SWF
!
...
WHO ARE YOU?
YO-RUSHI-CHI!
OUR WATCH-DOG!
OUT OF MY WAY!
FWSH
WATCH OUT!

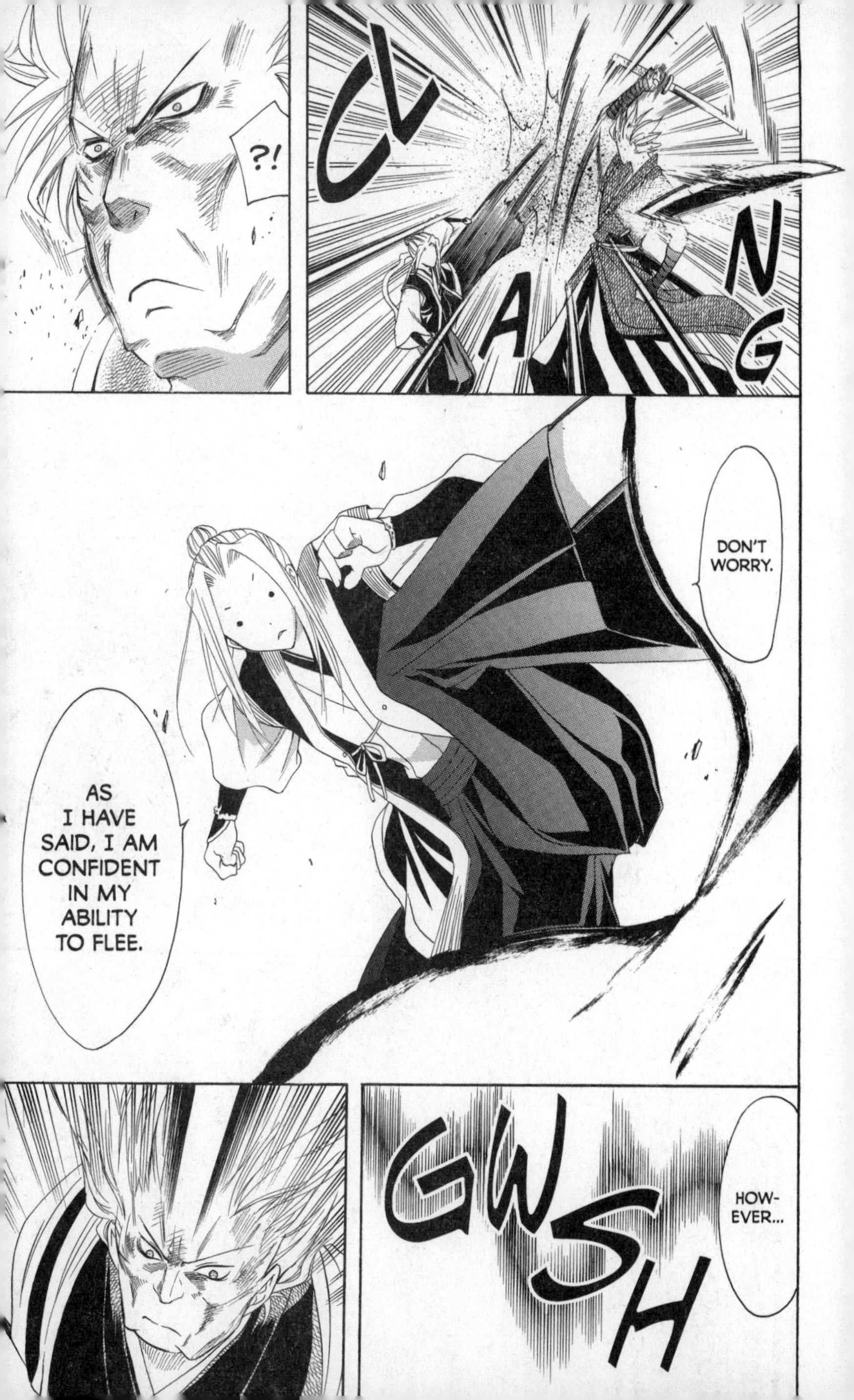
CLANG
?!
DON'T WORRY.
AS I HAVE SAID, I AM CONFIDENT IN MY ABILITY TO FLEE.
HOW-EVER...
GWSH

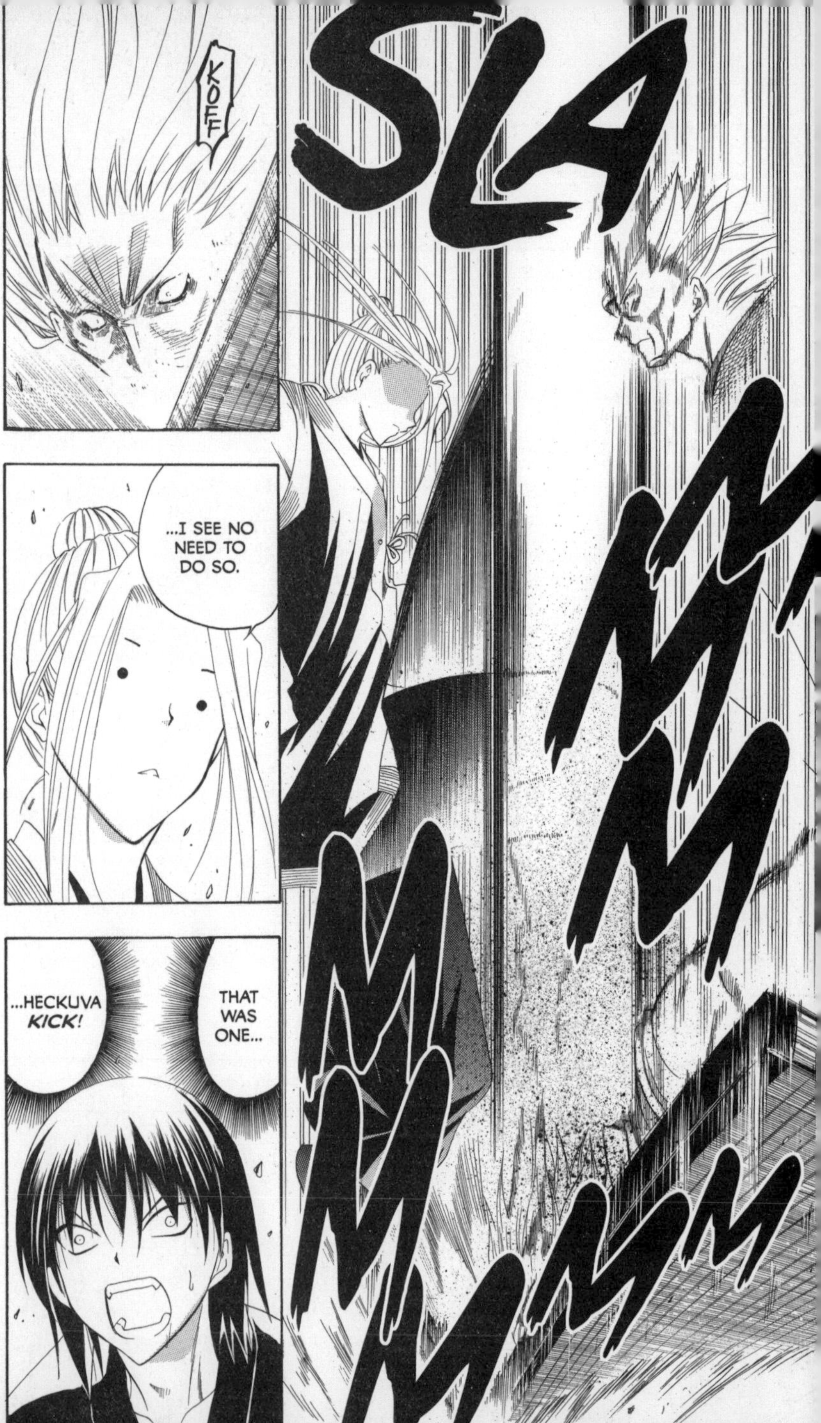
SLAMMM
KOFF
...I SEE NO NEED TO DO SO.
THAT WAS ONE...
...HECKUVA *KICK*!

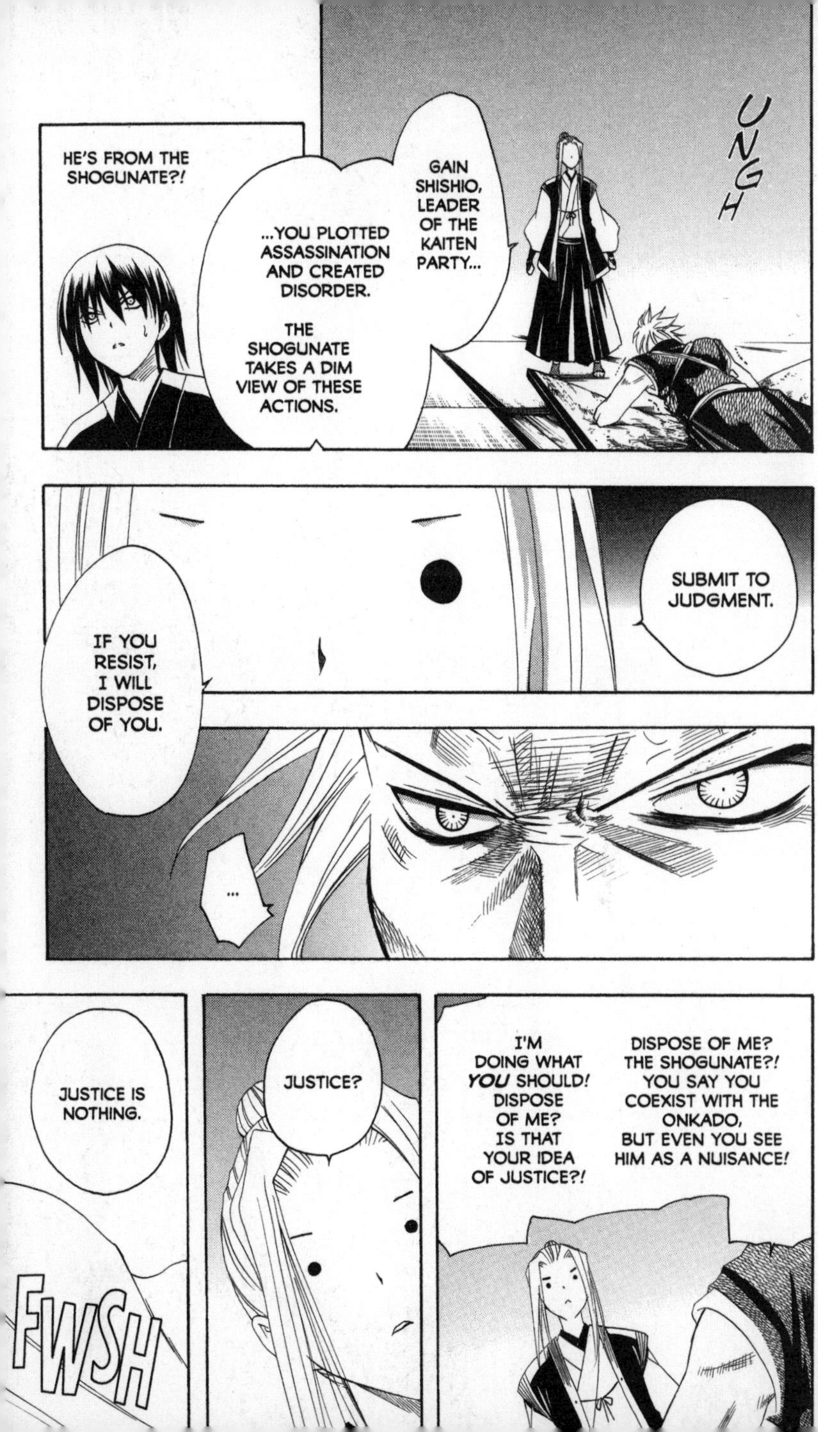
UNGH
GAIN SHISHIO, LEADER OF THE KAITEN PARTY...
...YOU PLOTTED ASSASSINATION AND CREATED DISORDER. THE SHOGUNATE TAKES A DIM VIEW OF THESE ACTIONS.
HE'S FROM THE SHOGUNATE?!
SUBMIT TO JUDGMENT.
IF YOU RESIST, I WILL DISPOSE OF YOU.
...
DISPOSE OF ME? THE SHOGUNATE?! YOU SAY YOU COEXIST WITH THE ONKADO, BUT EVEN YOU SEE HIM AS A NUISANCE!
I'M DOING WHAT *YOU* SHOULD! DISPOSE OF ME? IS THAT YOUR IDEA OF JUSTICE?!
JUSTICE?
JUSTICE IS NOTHING.
FWSH

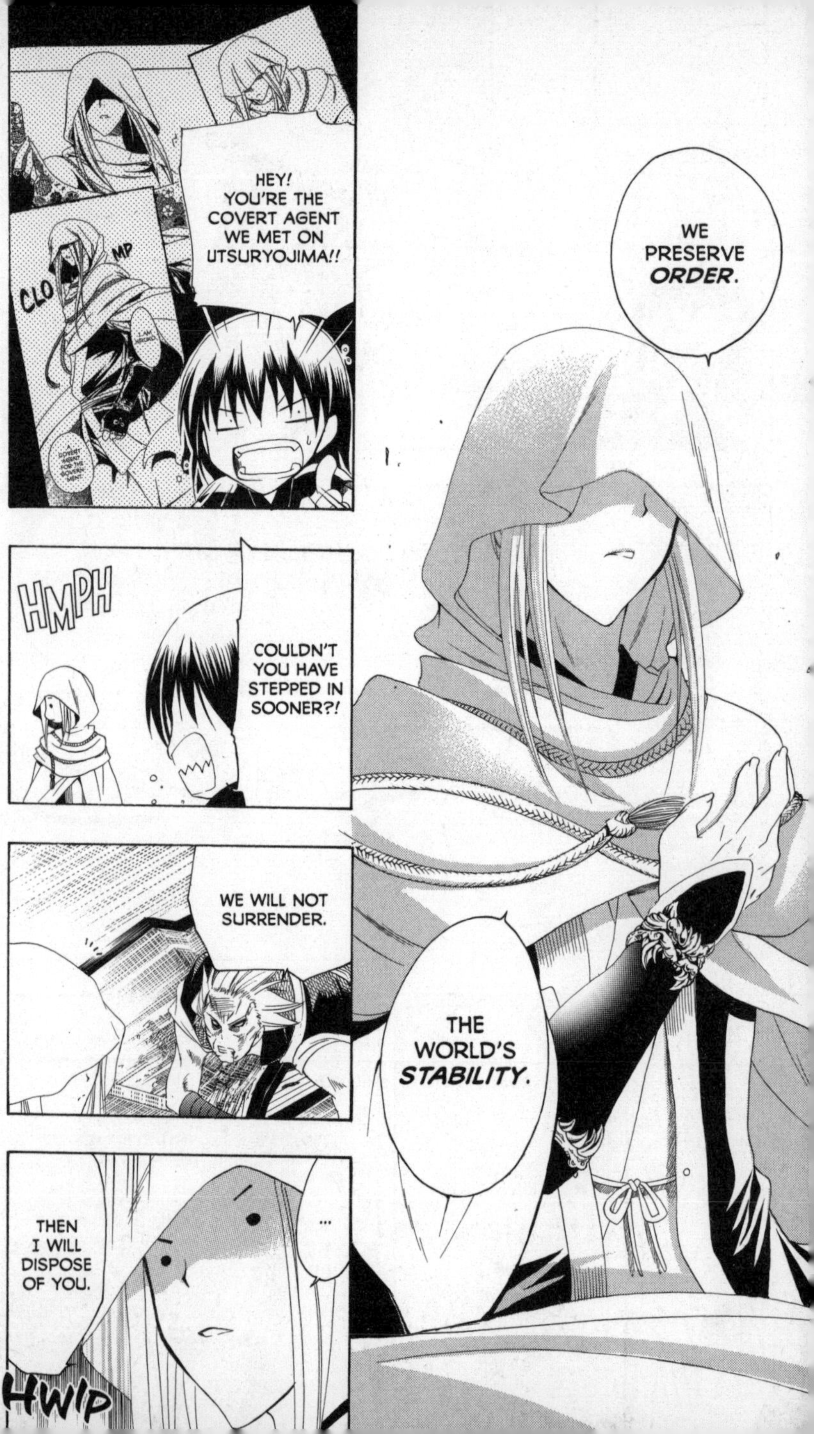
WE PRESERVE ORDER.
THE WORLD'S STABILITY.
HEY! YOU'RE THE COVERT AGENT WE MET ON UTSURYOJIMA!!
CLOMP
I AM HIROKO.
A COVERT AGENT FOR THE GOVERNMENT.
COULDN'T YOU HAVE STEPPED IN SOONER?!
HMPH
WE WILL NOT SURRENDER.
...
THEN I WILL DISPOSE OF YOU.
HWIP

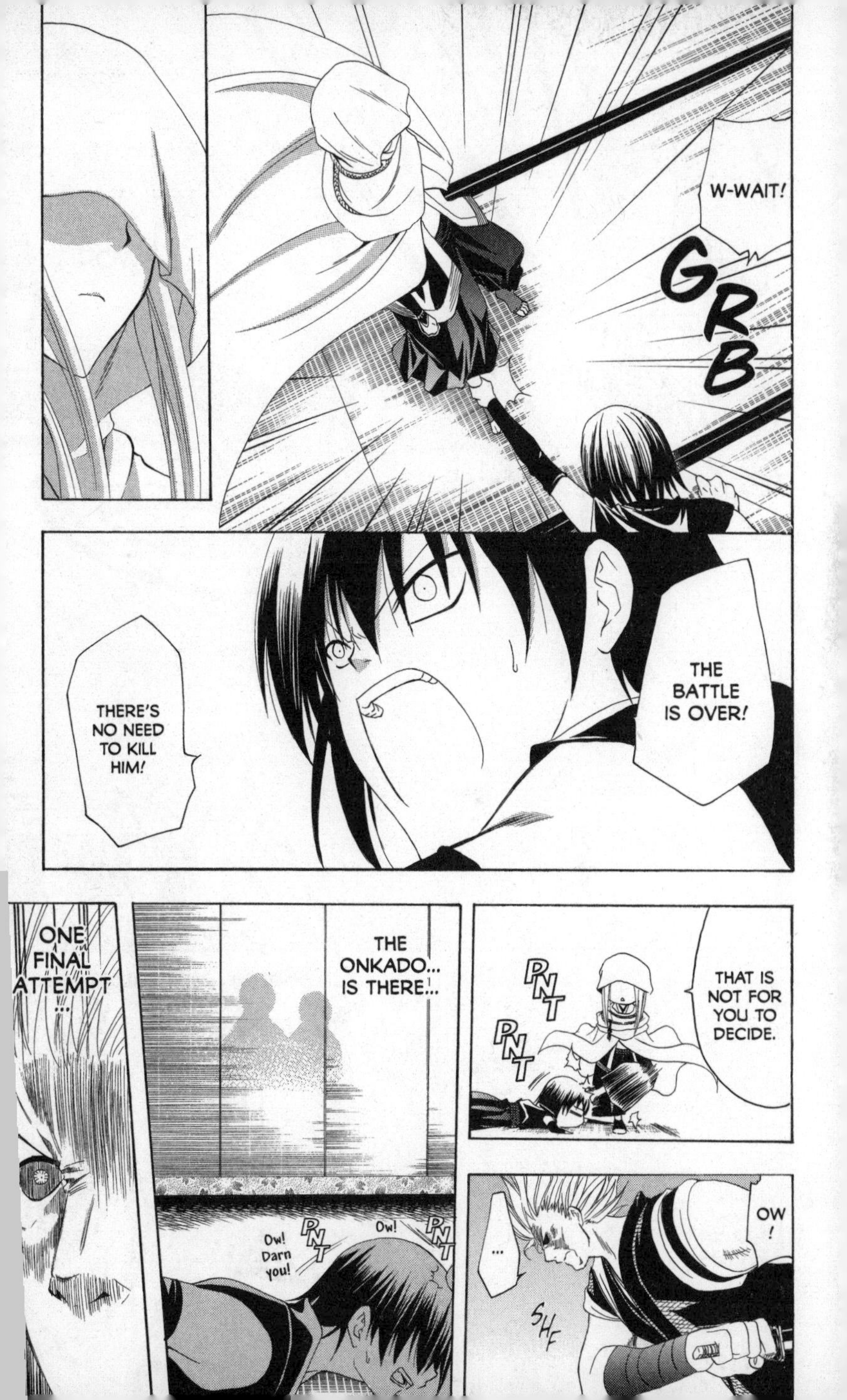
W-WAIT!
GRB
THE BATTLE IS OVER!
THERE'S NO NEED TO KILL HIM!
THAT IS NOT FOR YOU TO DECIDE.
PNT
PNT
OW!
...
SHF
THE ONKADO... IS THERE...
PNT
Ow!
PNT
Ow! Darn you!
ONE FINAL ATTEMPT...

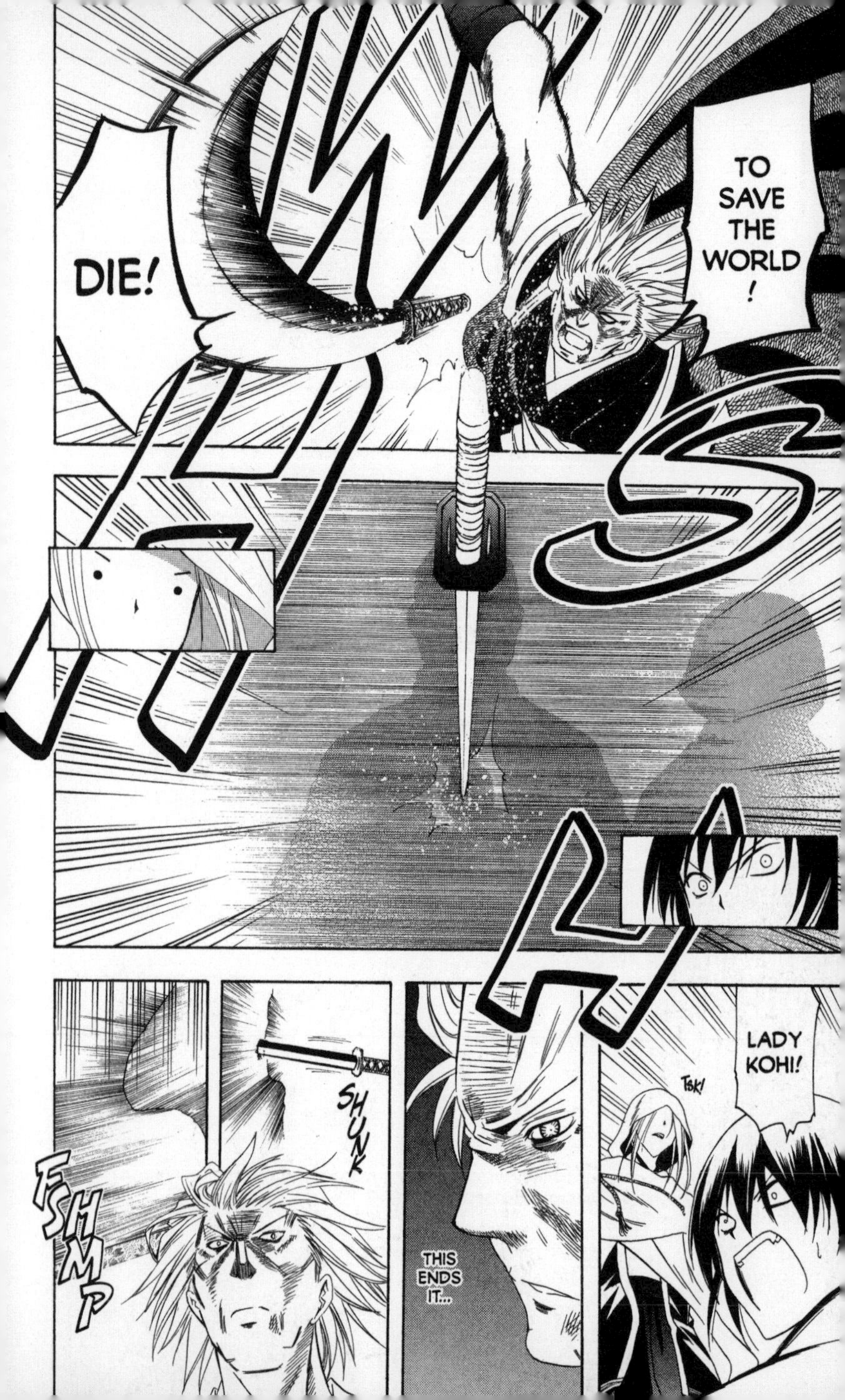
TO SAVE THE WORLD!
DIE!
LADY KOHI!
TSK!
THIS ENDS IT...
SHUNK
FSHMP

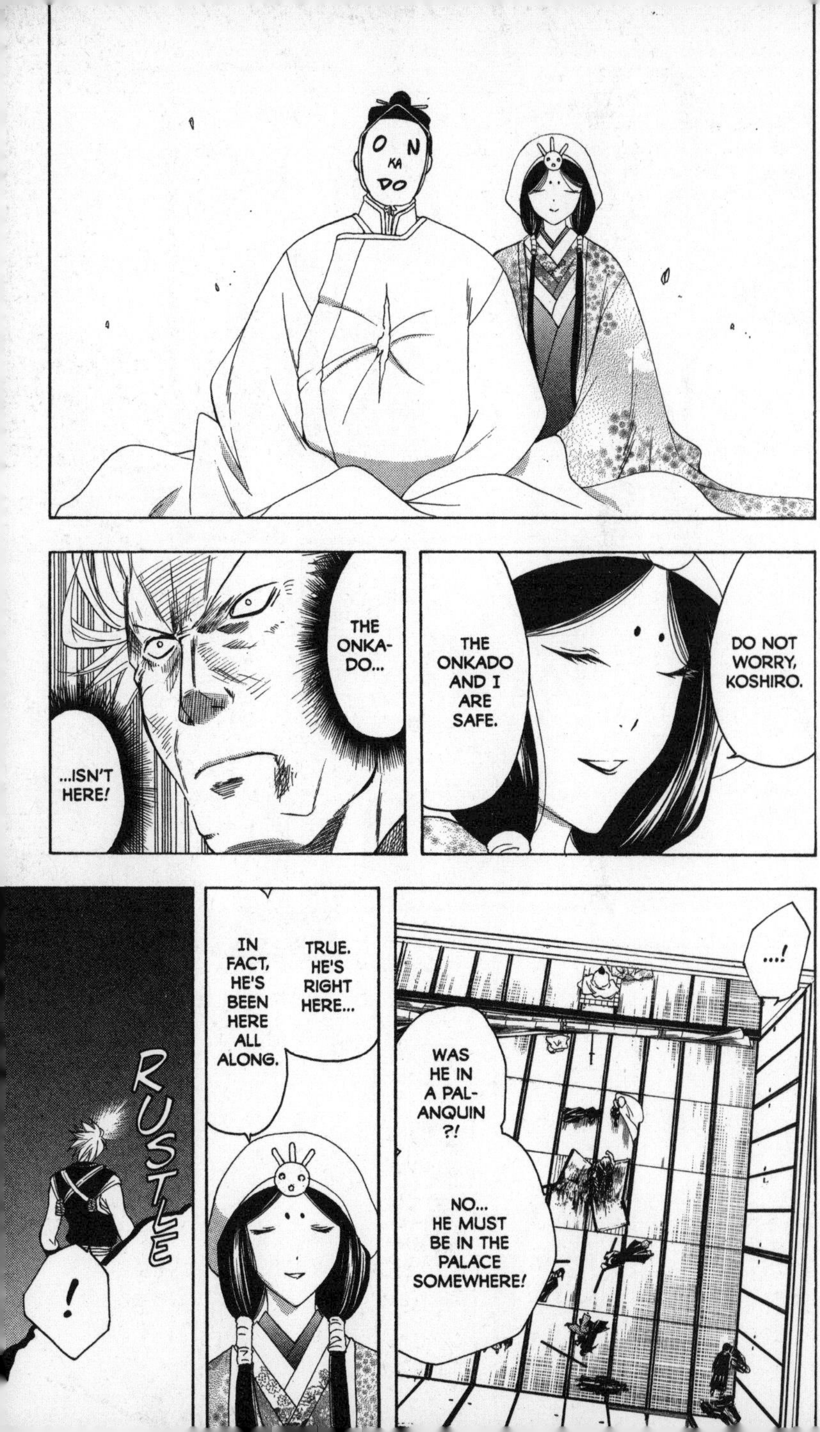
O N KA DO
DO NOT WORRY, KOSHIRO.
THE ONKADO AND I ARE SAFE.
THE ONKA-DO...
...ISN'T HERE!
...!
WAS HE IN A PAL-ANQUIN?!
NO... HE MUST BE IN THE PALACE SOMEWHERE!
TRUE. HE'S RIGHT HERE...
IN FACT, HE'S BEEN HERE ALL ALONG.
RUSTLE
!

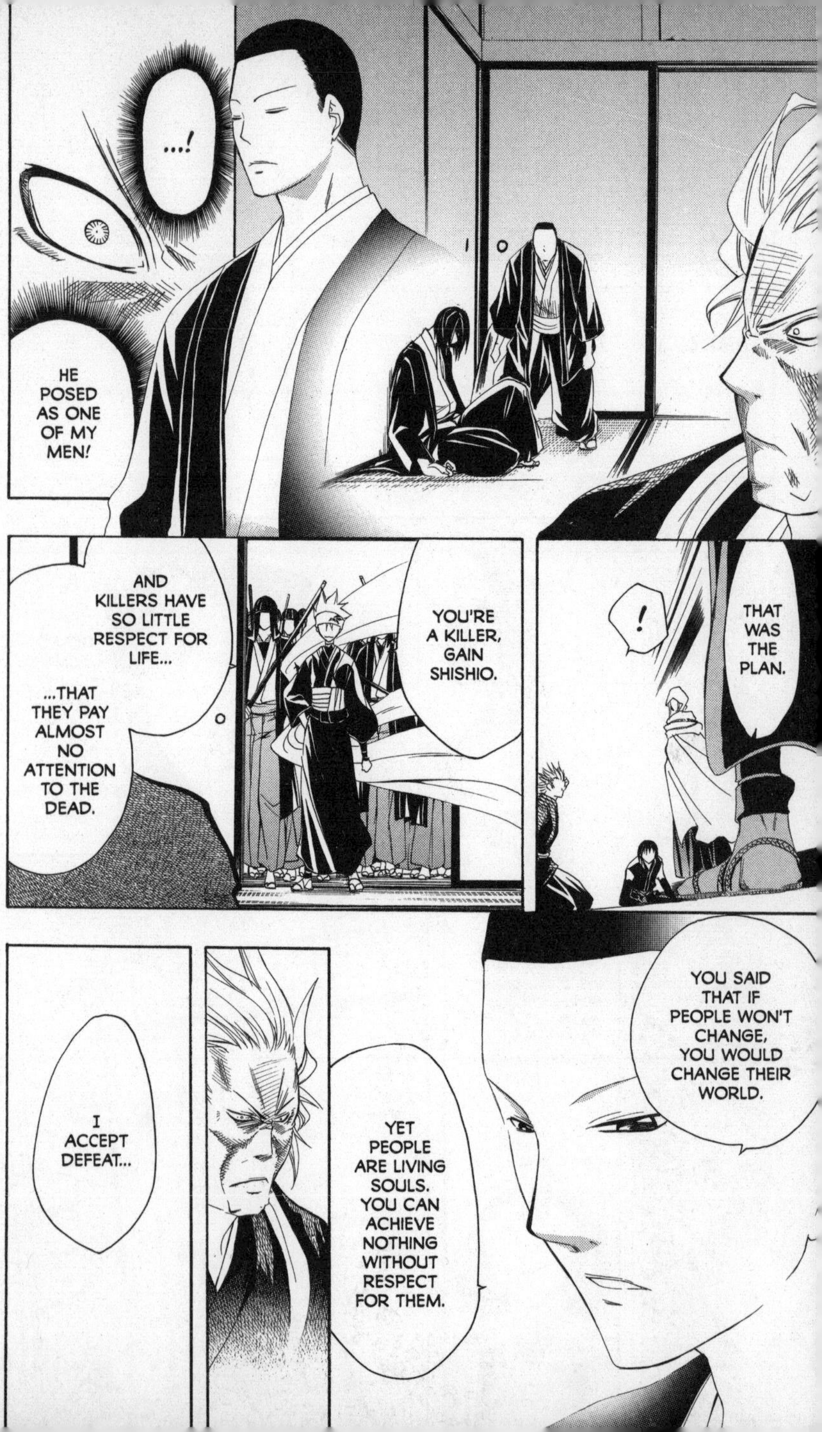

...!
HE POSED AS ONE OF MY MEN!
THAT WAS THE PLAN.
!
YOU'RE A KILLER, GAIN SHISHIO.
AND KILLERS HAVE SO LITTLE RESPECT FOR LIFE...
...THAT THEY PAY ALMOST NO ATTENTION TO THE DEAD.
YOU SAID THAT IF PEOPLE WON'T CHANGE, YOU WOULD CHANGE THEIR WORLD.
YET PEOPLE ARE LIVING SOULS. YOU CAN ACHIEVE NOTHING WITHOUT RESPECT FOR THEM.
I ACCEPT DEFEAT...

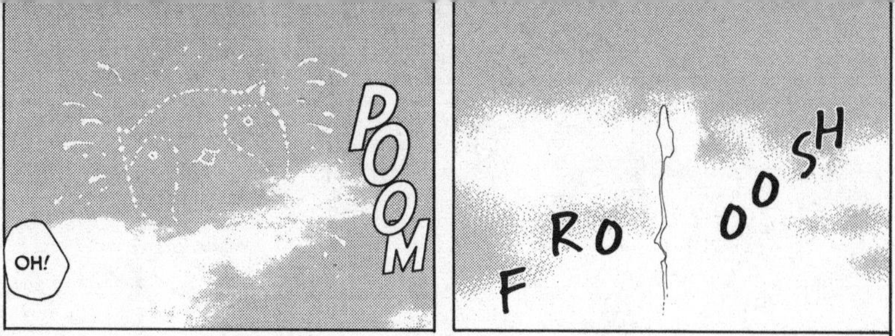
FROOOOSH
POOM
OH!

Chapter 109 Family

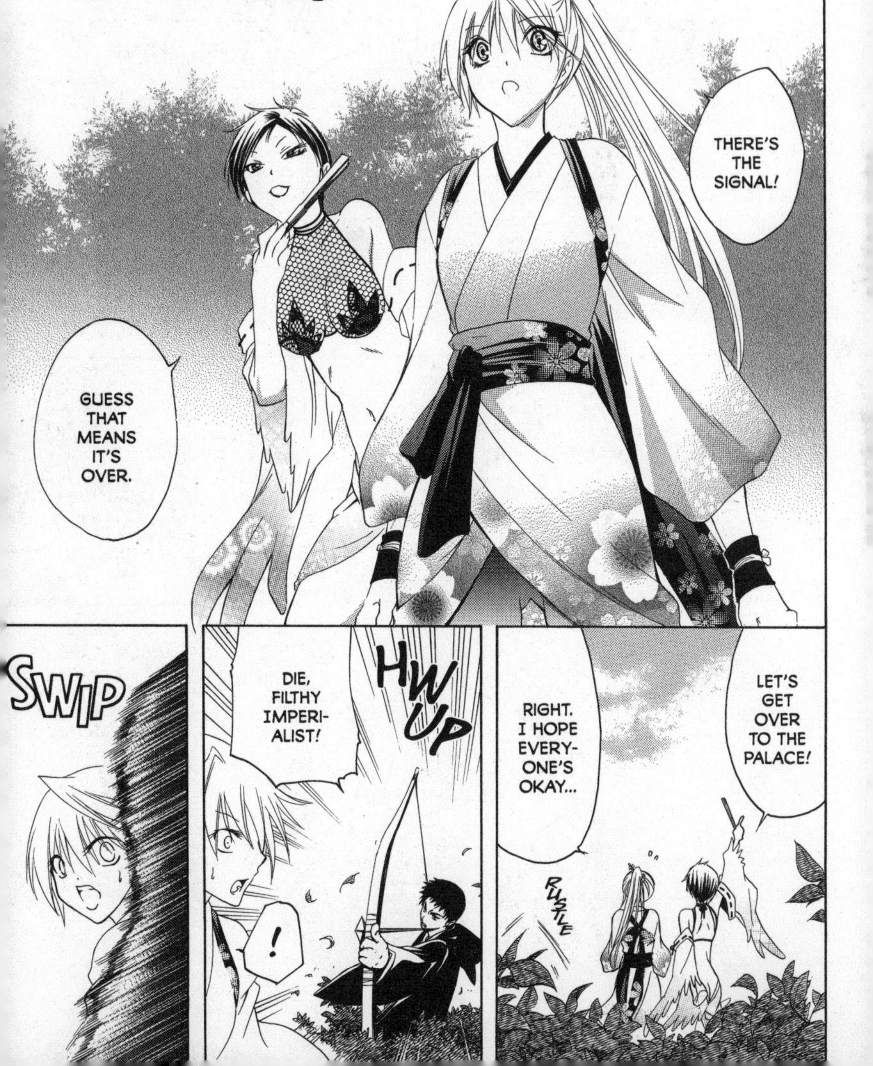
THERE'S THE SIGNAL!
GUESS THAT MEANS IT'S OVER.
LET'S GET OVER TO THE PALACE!
RIGHT. I HOPE EVERY-ONE'S OKAY...
RUSTLE
HWUP
DIE, FILTHY IMPERI-ALIST!
!
SWIP

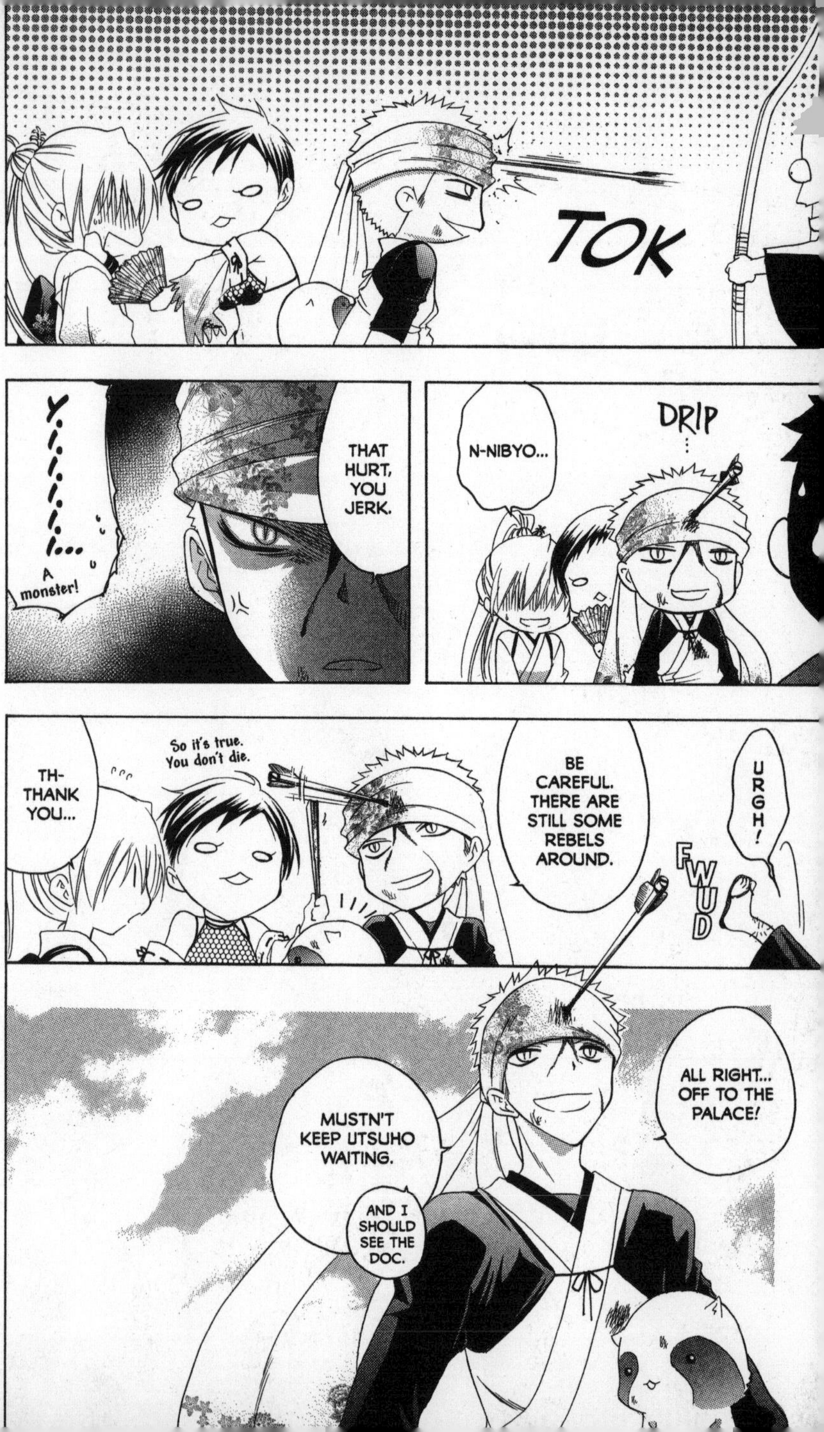
TOK
DRIP
N-NIBYO...
THAT HURT, YOU JERK.
Y...I...I...I...
A monster!
URGH!
FWUD
BE CAREFUL. THERE ARE STILL SOME REBELS AROUND.
So it's true. You don't die.
TH-THANK YOU...
ALL RIGHT... OFF TO THE PALACE!
MUSTN'T KEEP UTSUHO WAITING.
AND I SHOULD SEE THE DOC.

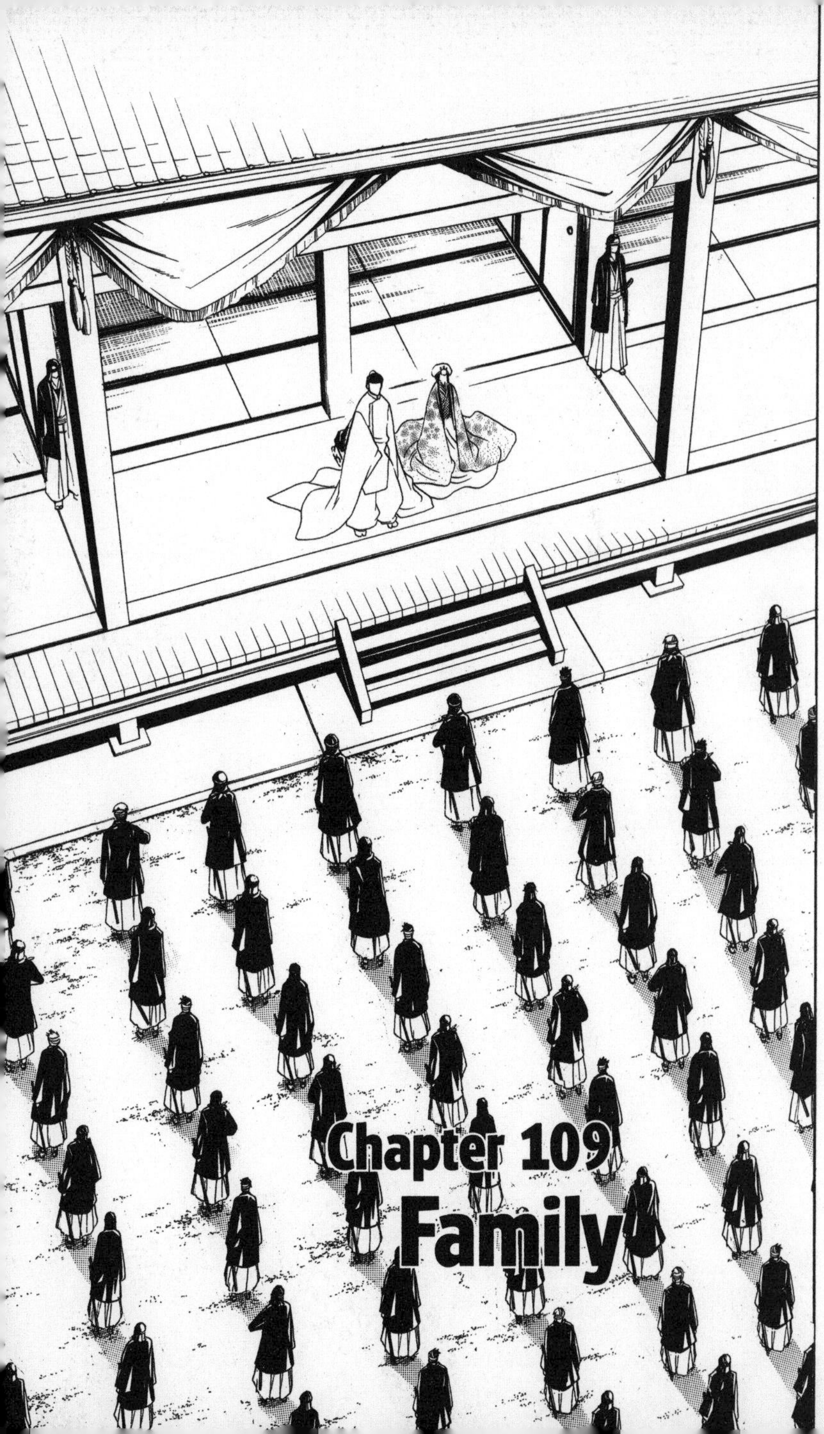
Chapter 109
Family

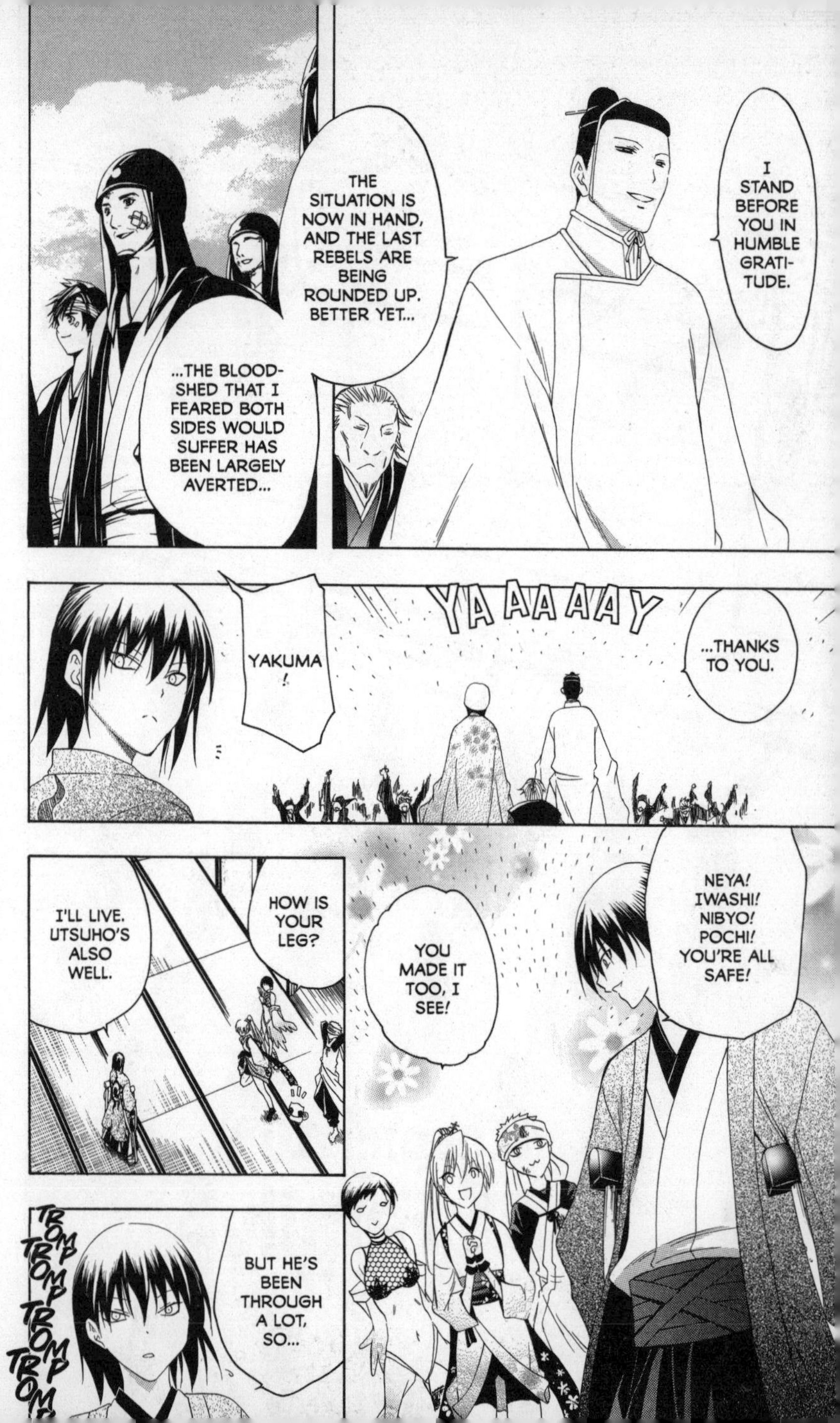
I STAND BEFORE YOU IN HUMBLE GRATITUDE.
THE SITUATION IS NOW IN HAND, AND THE LAST REBELS ARE BEING ROUNDED UP. BETTER YET...
...THE BLOODSHED THAT I FEARED BOTH SIDES WOULD SUFFER HAS BEEN LARGELY AVERTED...
...THANKS TO YOU.
YAAAAAY
YAKUMA!
NEYA! IWASHI! NIBYO! POCHI! YOU'RE ALL SAFE!
YOU MADE IT TOO, I SEE!
HOW IS YOUR LEG?
I'LL LIVE. UTSUHO'S ALSO WELL.
BUT HE'S BEEN THROUGH A LOT, SO...
TROMP TROMP TROMP TROMP

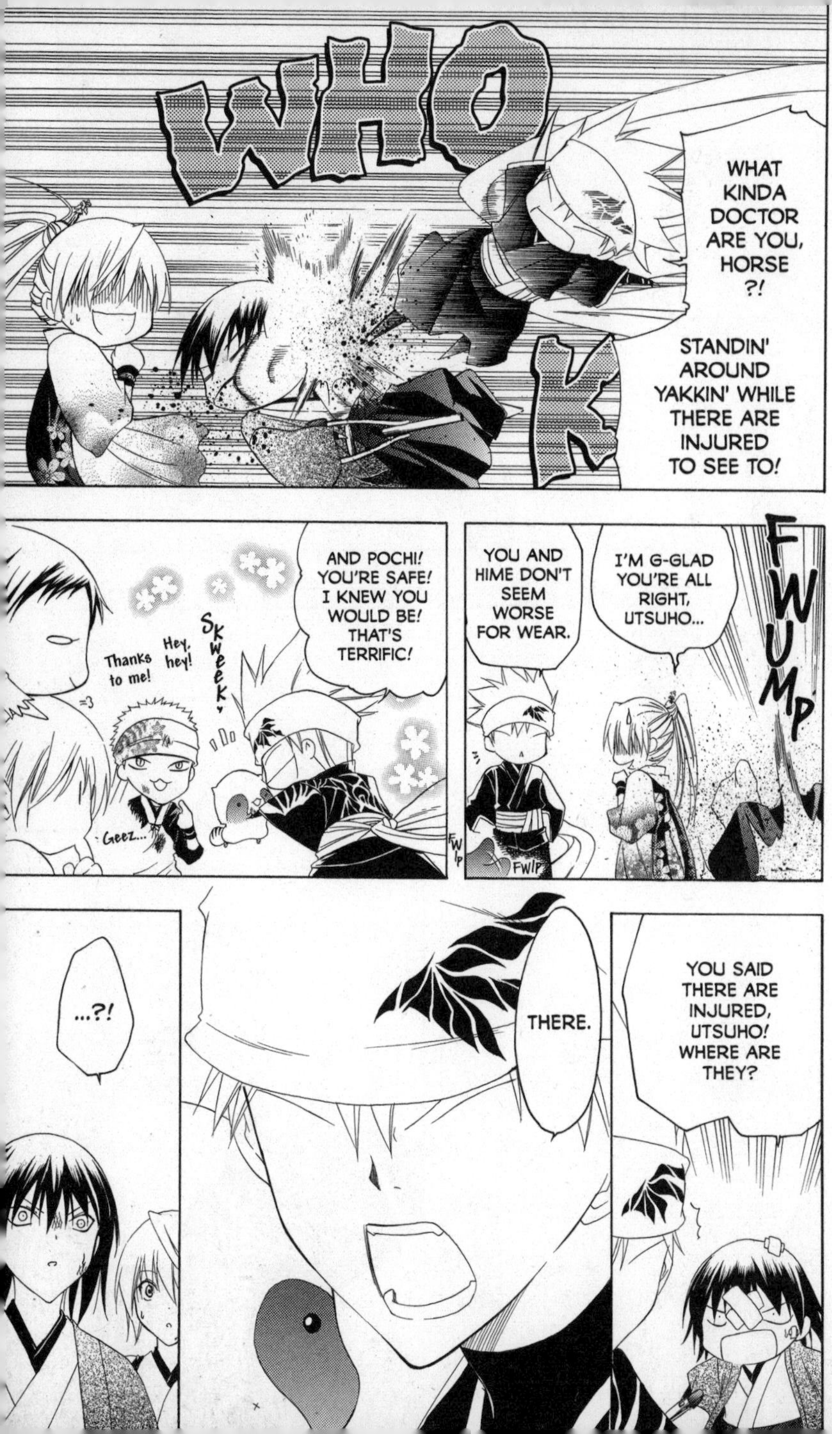
WHOK
WHAT KINDA DOCTOR ARE YOU, HORSE?!
STANDIN' AROUND YAKKIN' WHILE THERE ARE INJURED TO SEE TO!
FWUMP
I'M G-GLAD YOU'RE ALL RIGHT, UTSUHO...
YOU AND HIME DON'T SEEM WORSE FOR WEAR.
FWIP
FWIP
AND POCHI! YOU'RE SAFE! I KNEW YOU WOULD BE! THAT'S TERRIFIC!
SKWEEK
Hey, hey!
Thanks to me!
Geez...
YOU SAID THERE ARE INJURED, UTSUHO! WHERE ARE THEY?
THERE.
...?!

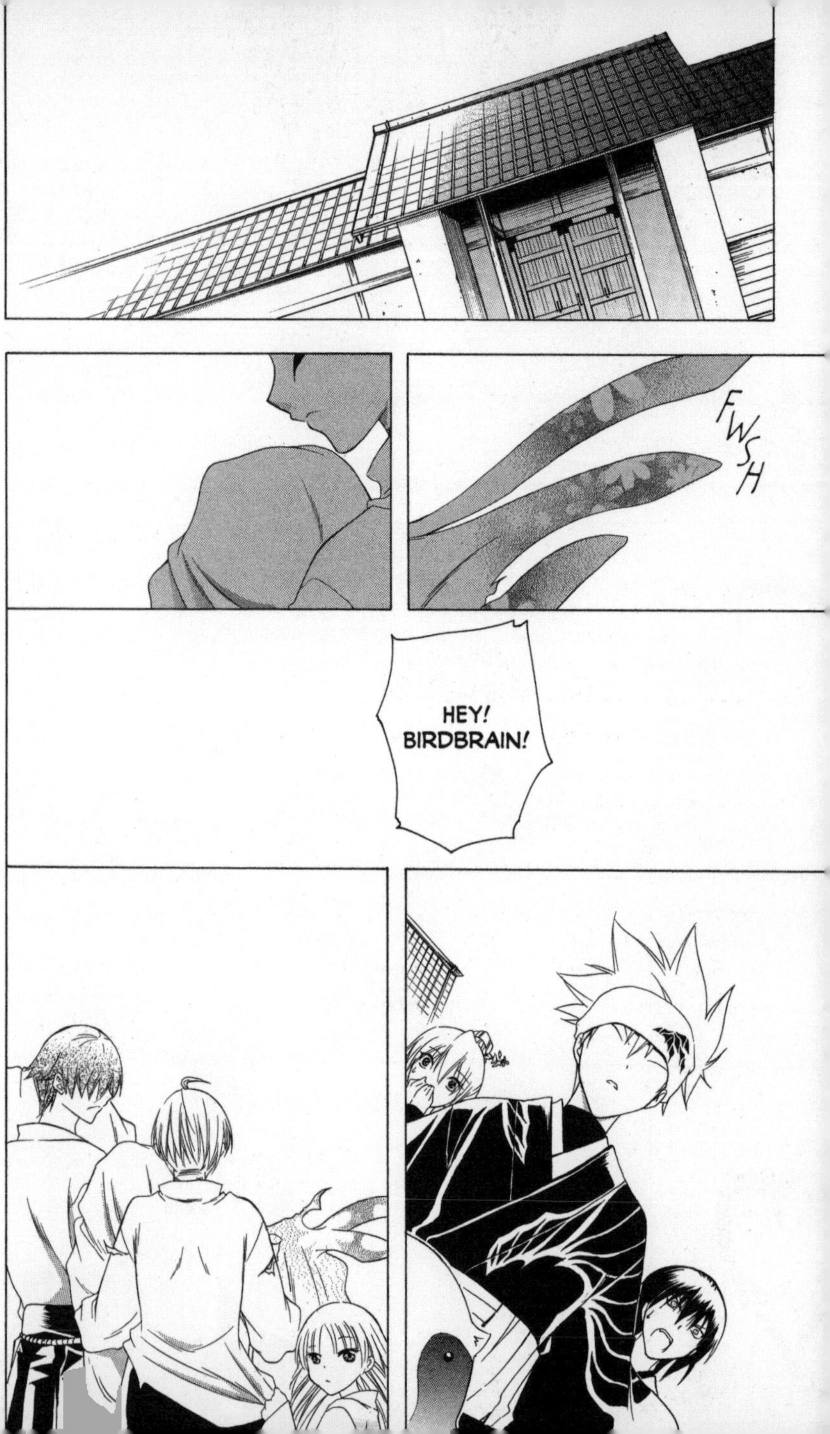
FWSH
HEY! BIRDBRAIN!

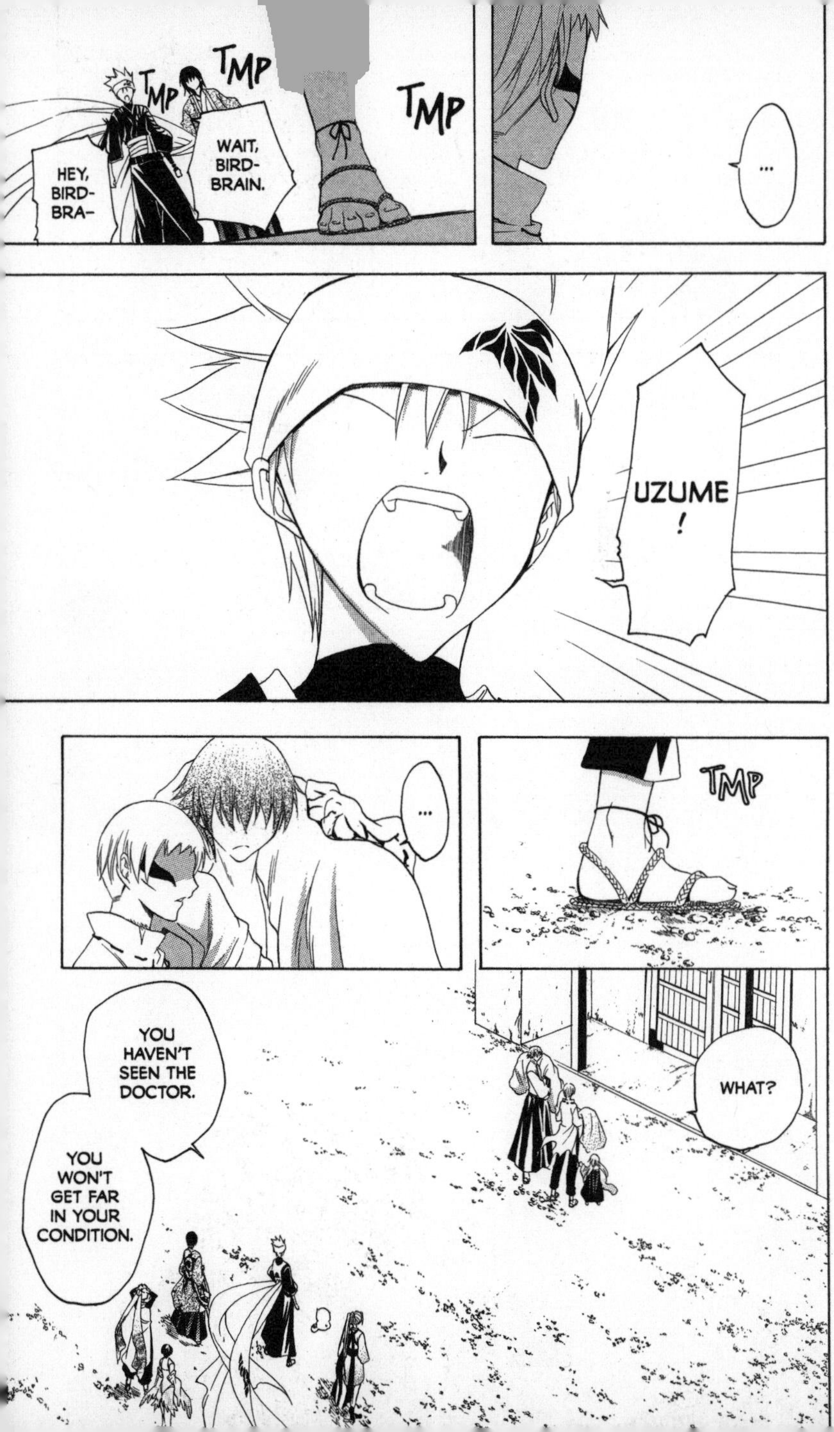
...
TMP
TMP
TMP
WAIT, BIRD-BRAIN.
HEY, BIRD-BRA–
UZUME!
TMP
...
WHAT?
YOU HAVEN'T SEEN THE DOCTOR.
YOU WON'T GET FAR IN YOUR CONDITION.

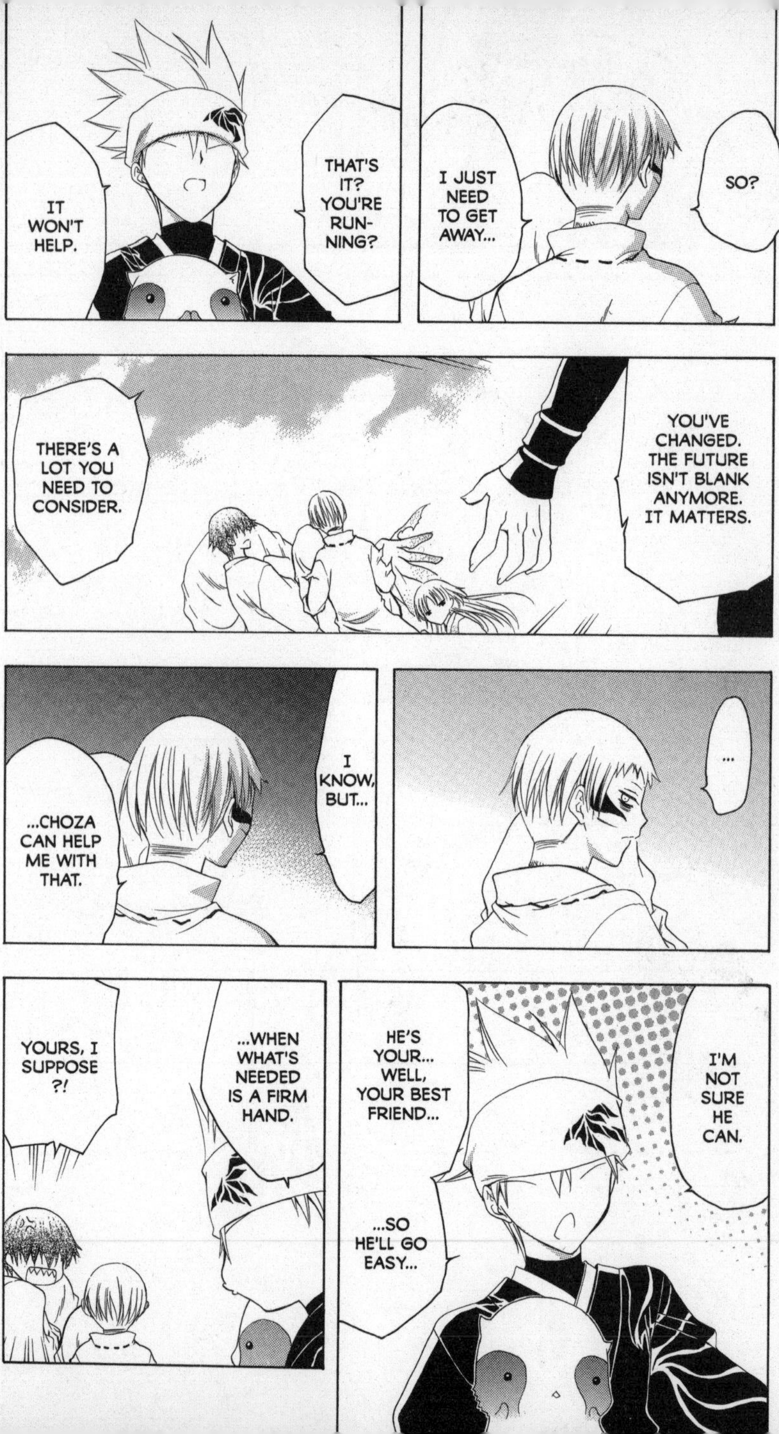
SO?
I JUST NEED TO GET AWAY...
THAT'S IT? YOU'RE RUN-NING?
IT WON'T HELP.
YOU'VE CHANGED. THE FUTURE ISN'T BLANK ANYMORE. IT MATTERS.
THERE'S A LOT YOU NEED TO CONSIDER.
...
I KNOW, BUT...
...CHOZA CAN HELP ME WITH THAT.
I'M NOT SURE HE CAN.
HE'S YOUR... WELL, YOUR BEST FRIEND...
...SO HE'LL GO EASY...
...WHEN WHAT'S NEEDED IS A FIRM HAND.
YOURS, I SUPPOSE ?!

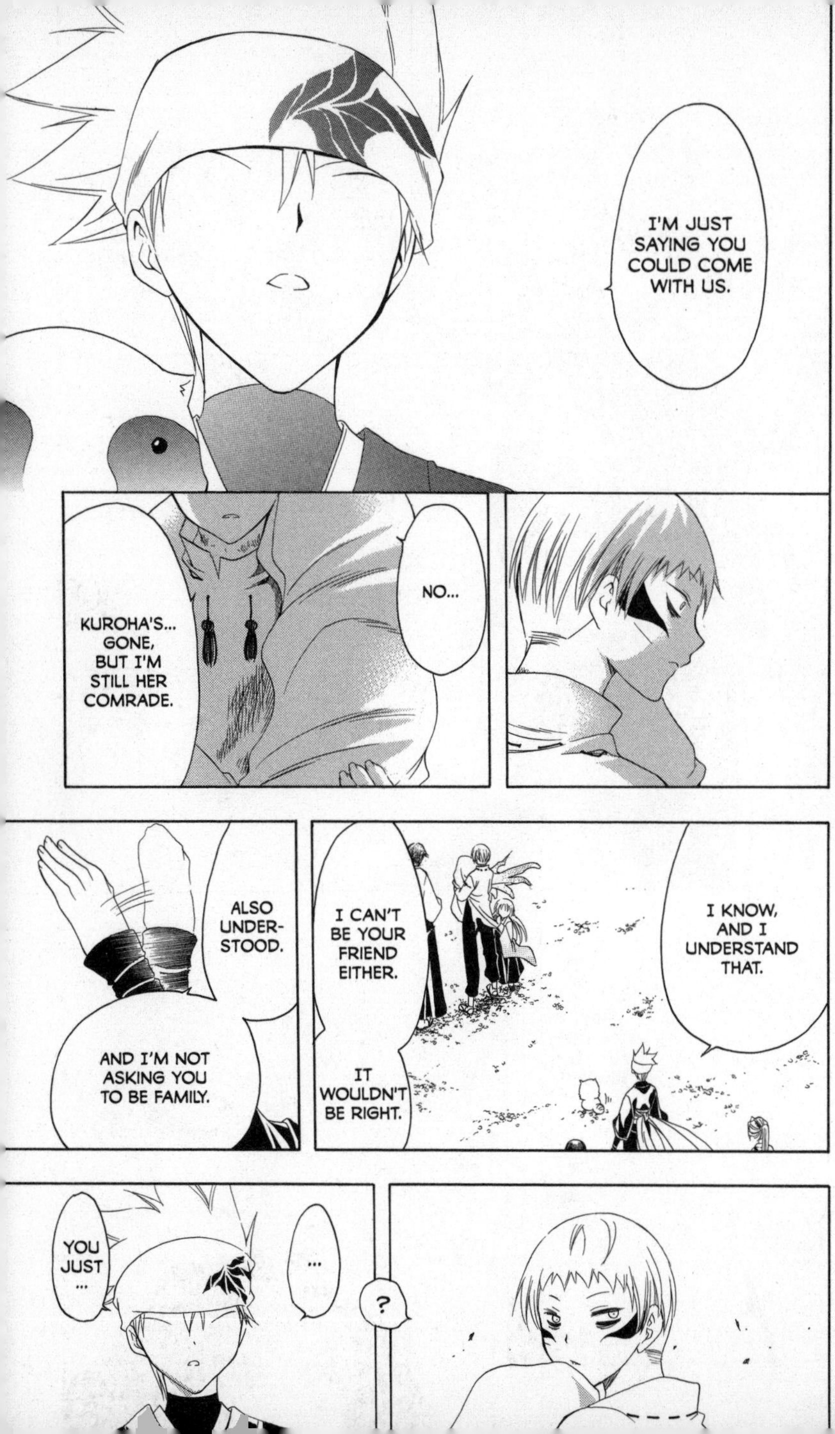
I'M JUST SAYING YOU COULD COME WITH US.
NO...
KUROHA'S... GONE, BUT I'M STILL HER COMRADE.
I KNOW, AND I UNDERSTAND THAT.
I CAN'T BE YOUR FRIEND EITHER.
IT WOULDN'T BE RIGHT.
ALSO UNDER-STOOD.
AND I'M NOT ASKING YOU TO BE FAMILY.
...
?
YOU JUST ...

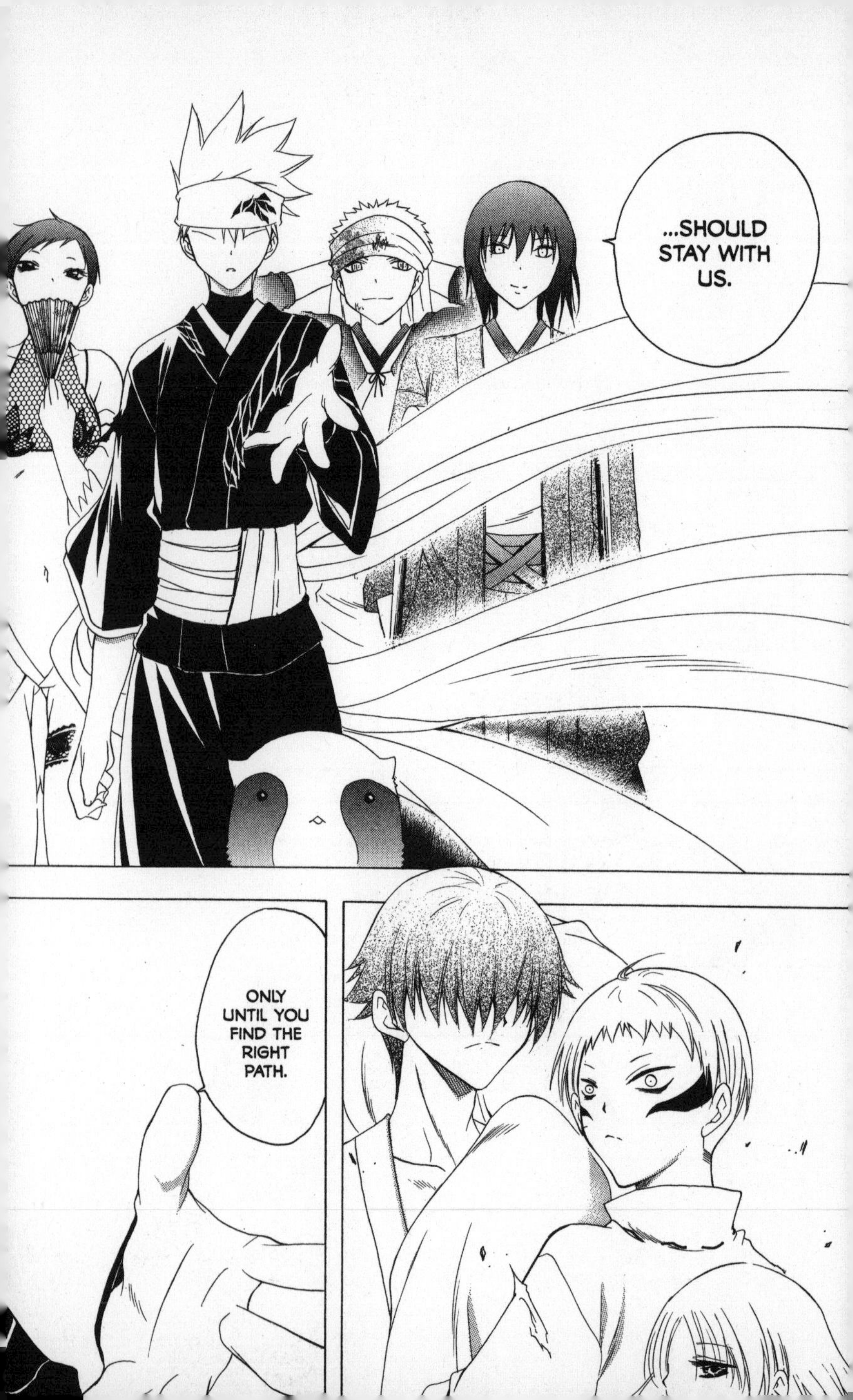
...SHOULD STAY WITH US.
ONLY UNTIL YOU FIND THE RIGHT PATH.

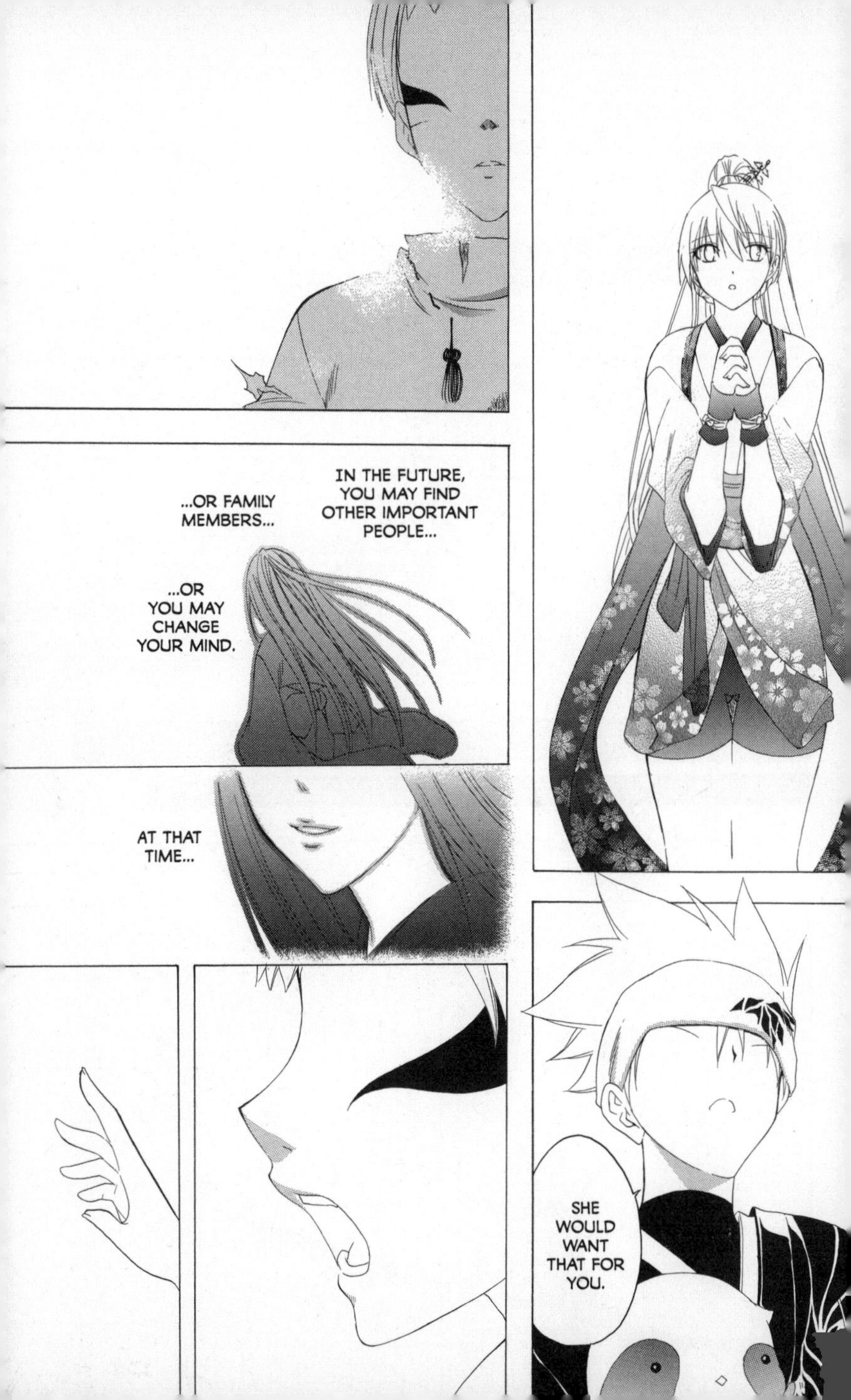
IN THE FUTURE, YOU MAY FIND OTHER IMPORTANT PEOPLE...
...OR FAMILY MEMBERS...
...OR YOU MAY CHANGE YOUR MIND.
AT THAT TIME...
SHE WOULD WANT THAT FOR YOU.

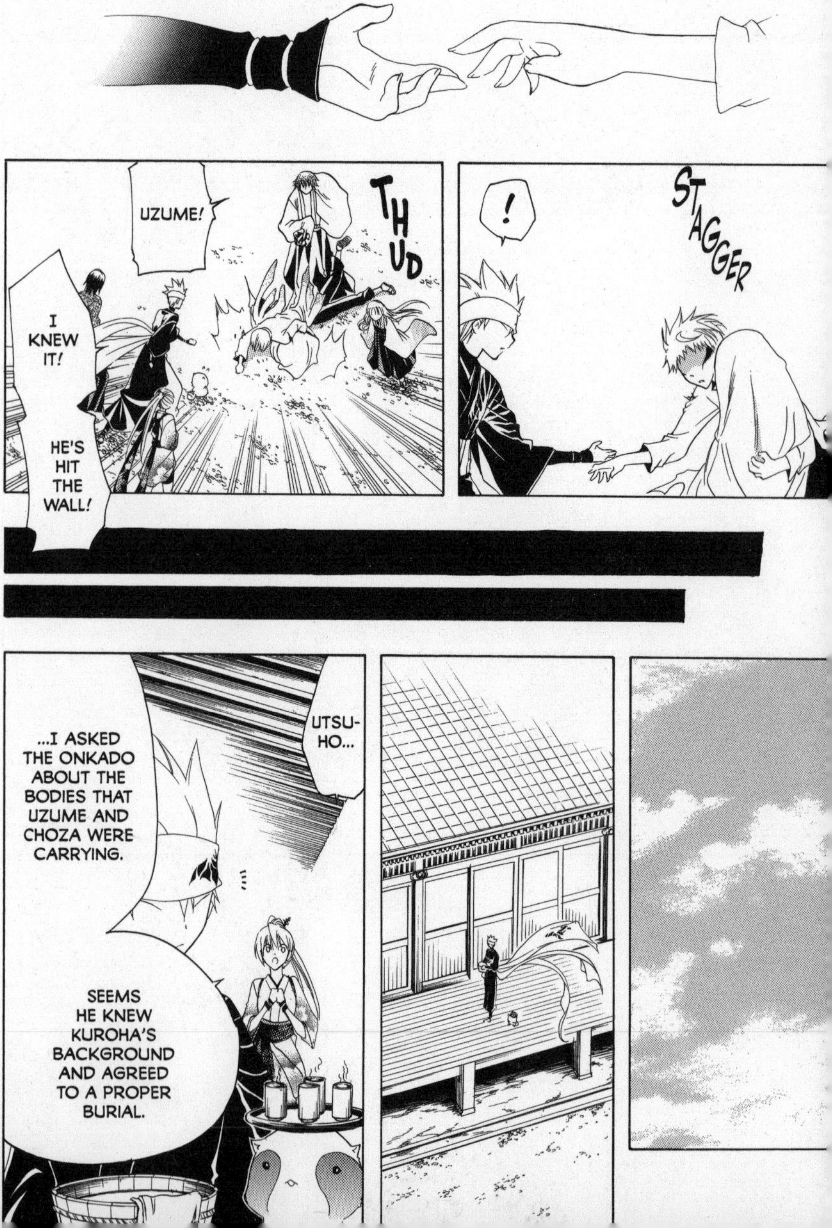
!
STAGGER
UZUME!
THUD
I KNEW IT!
HE'S HIT THE WALL!
UTSU-HO...
...I ASKED THE ONKADO ABOUT THE BODIES THAT UZUME AND CHOZA WERE CARRYING.
SEEMS HE KNEW KUROHA'S BACKGROUND AND AGREED TO A PROPER BURIAL.

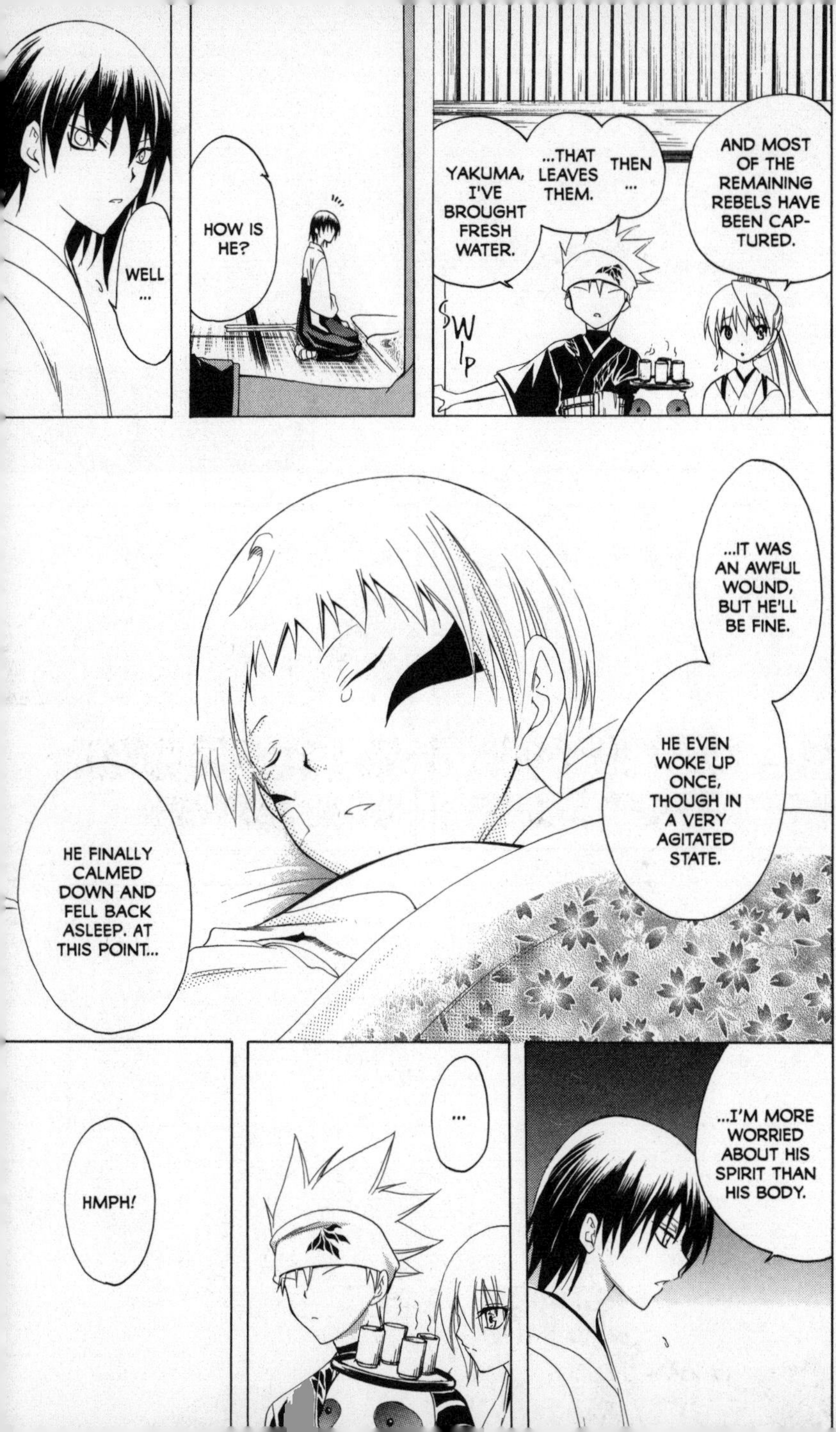
AND MOST OF THE REMAINING REBELS HAVE BEEN CAPTURED.
THEN ...
...THAT LEAVES THEM.
YAKUMA, I'VE BROUGHT FRESH WATER.
SWIP
HOW IS HE?
WELL ...
...IT WAS AN AWFUL WOUND, BUT HE'LL BE FINE.
HE EVEN WOKE UP ONCE, THOUGH IN A VERY AGITATED STATE.
HE FINALLY CALMED DOWN AND FELL BACK ASLEEP. AT THIS POINT...
...I'M MORE WORRIED ABOUT HIS SPIRIT THAN HIS BODY.
...
HMPH!

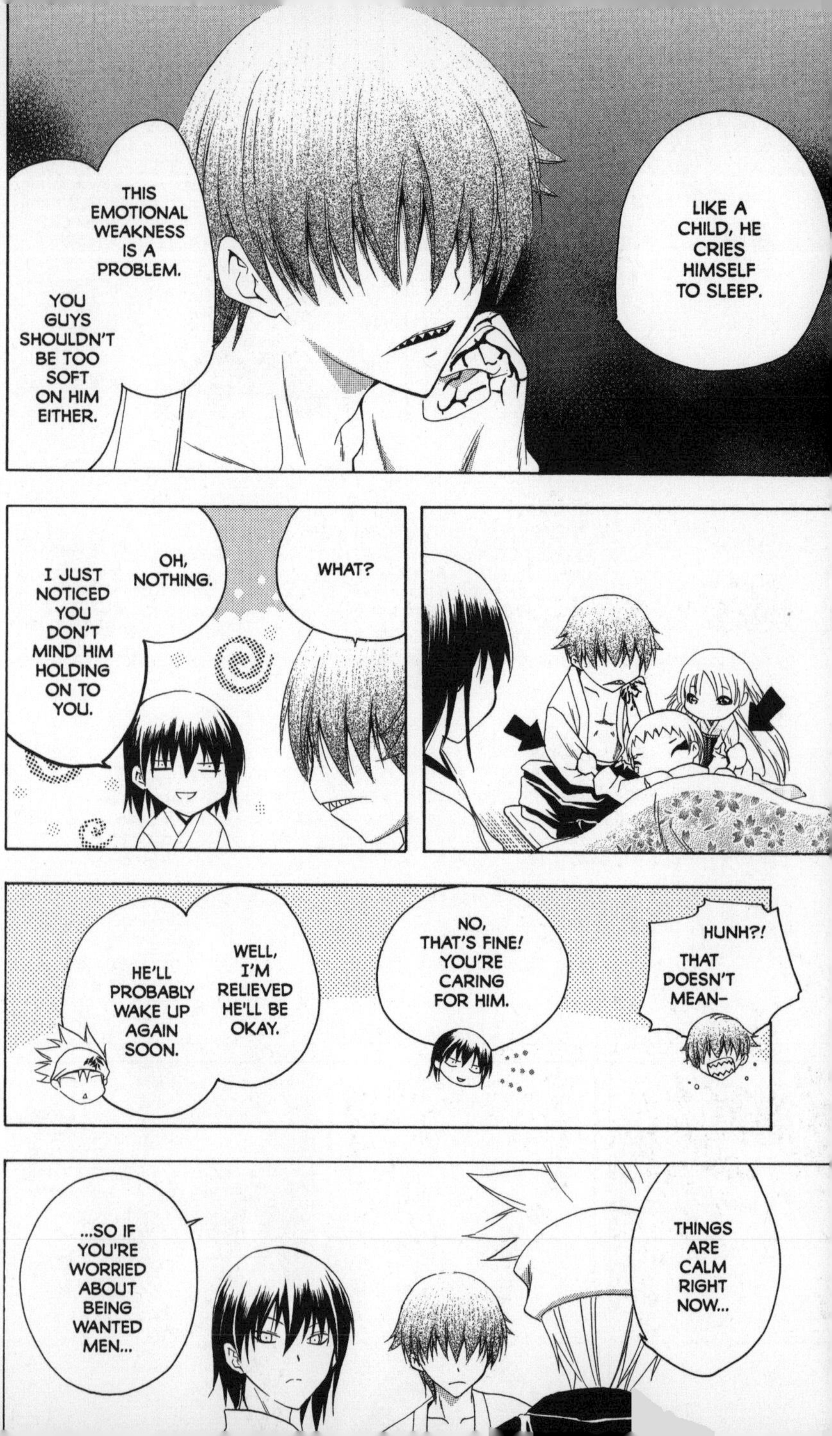
LIKE A CHILD, HE CRIES HIMSELF TO SLEEP.
THIS EMOTIONAL WEAKNESS IS A PROBLEM.
YOU GUYS SHOULDN'T BE TOO SOFT ON HIM EITHER.
WHAT?
OH, NOTHING.
I JUST NOTICED YOU DON'T MIND HIM HOLDING ON TO YOU.
HUNH?!
THAT DOESN'T MEAN–
NO, THAT'S FINE! YOU'RE CARING FOR HIM.
WELL, I'M RELIEVED HE'LL BE OKAY.
HE'LL PROBABLY WAKE UP AGAIN SOON.
THINGS ARE CALM RIGHT NOW...
...SO IF YOU'RE WORRIED ABOUT BEING WANTED MEN...

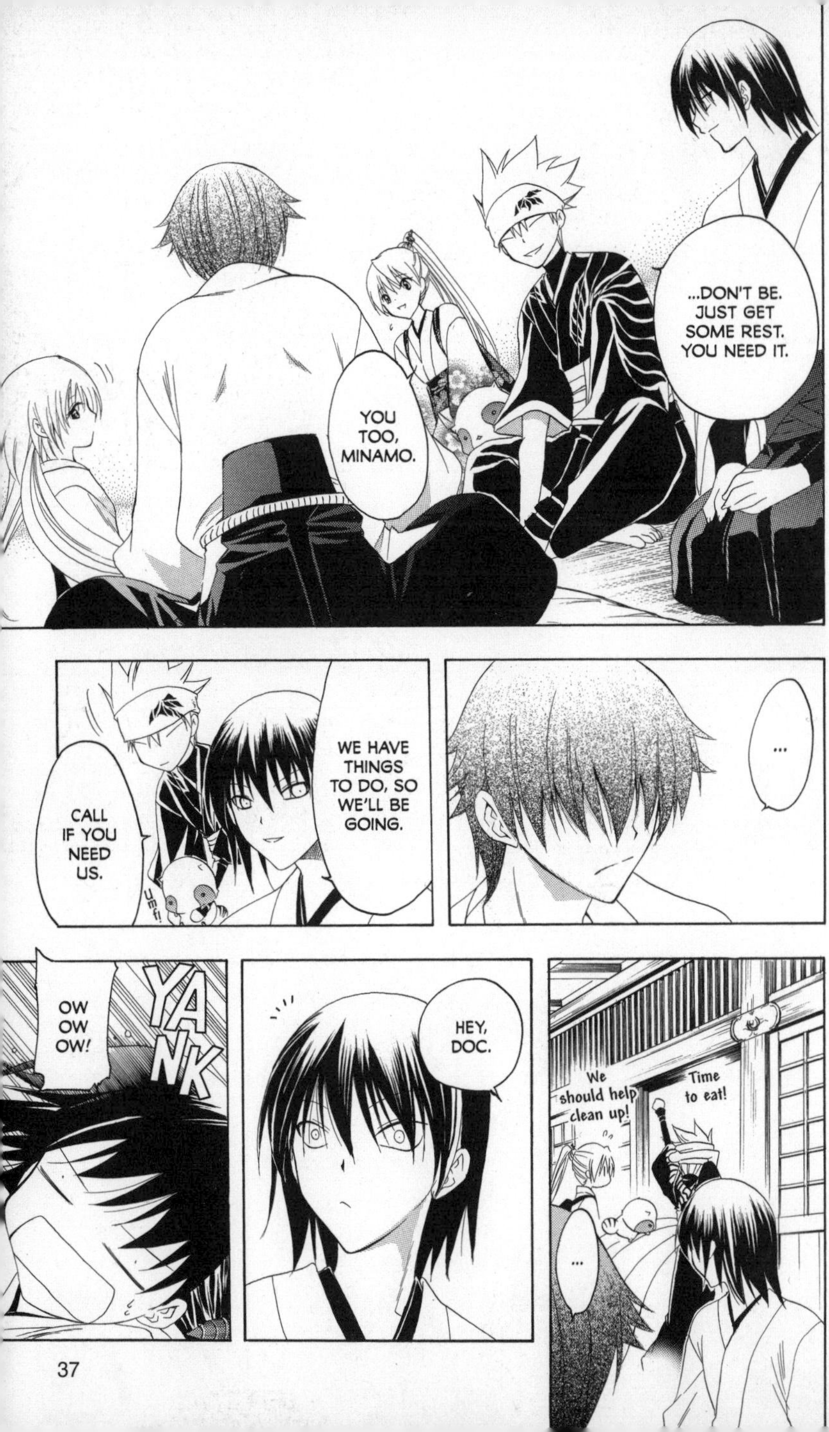
...DON'T BE. JUST GET SOME REST. YOU NEED IT.
YOU TOO, MINAMO.
...
WE HAVE THINGS TO DO, SO WE'LL BE GOING.
CALL IF YOU NEED US.
Umf!
Time to eat!
We should help clean up!
...
HEY, DOC.
YANK
OW OW OW!

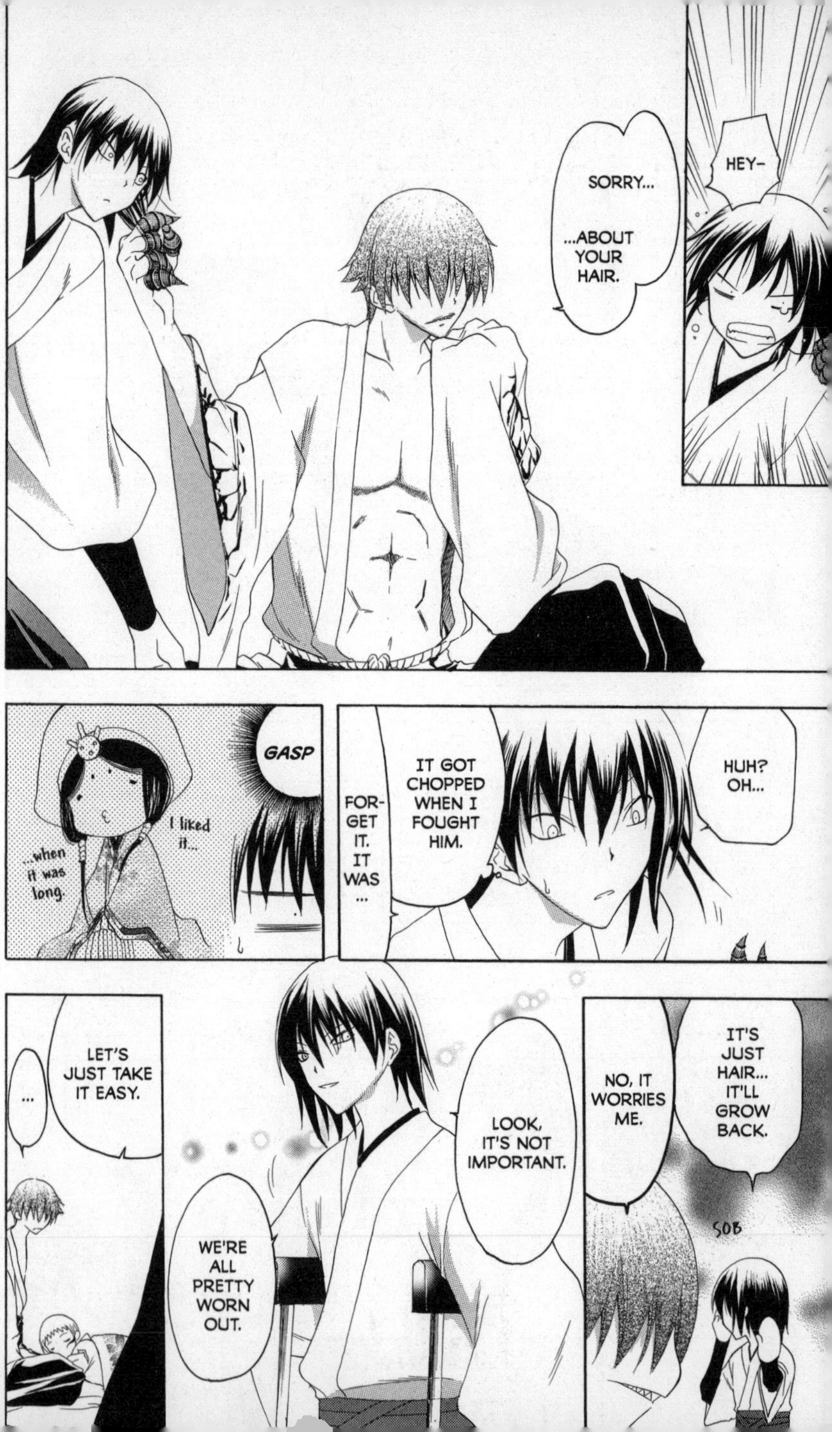
HEY–
SORRY...
...ABOUT YOUR HAIR.
HUH? OH...
IT GOT CHOPPED WHEN I FOUGHT HIM.
FOR-GET IT. IT WAS ...
GASP
I liked it...
...when it was long.
IT'S JUST HAIR... IT'LL GROW BACK.
NO, IT WORRIES ME.
SOB
LOOK, IT'S NOT IMPORTANT.
WE'RE ALL PRETTY WORN OUT.
LET'S JUST TAKE IT EASY.
...

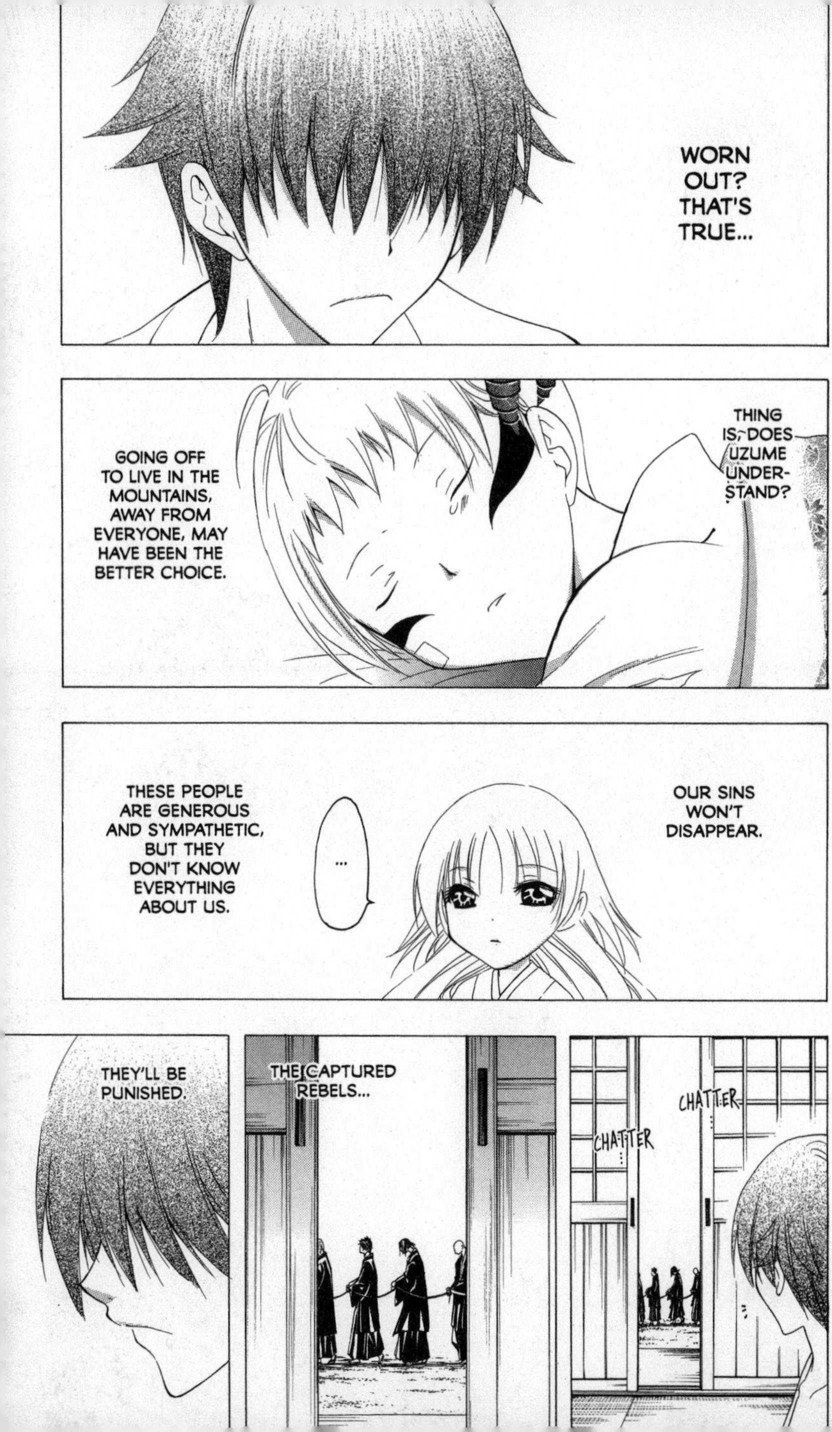
WORN OUT? THAT'S TRUE...
THING IS, DOES UZUME UNDERSTAND?
GOING OFF TO LIVE IN THE MOUNTAINS, AWAY FROM EVERYONE, MAY HAVE BEEN THE BETTER CHOICE.
OUR SINS WON'T DISAPPEAR.
...
THESE PEOPLE ARE GENEROUS AND SYMPATHETIC, BUT THEY DON'T KNOW EVERYTHING ABOUT US.
CHATTER
CHATTER
THE CAPTURED REBELS...
THEY'LL BE PUNISHED.

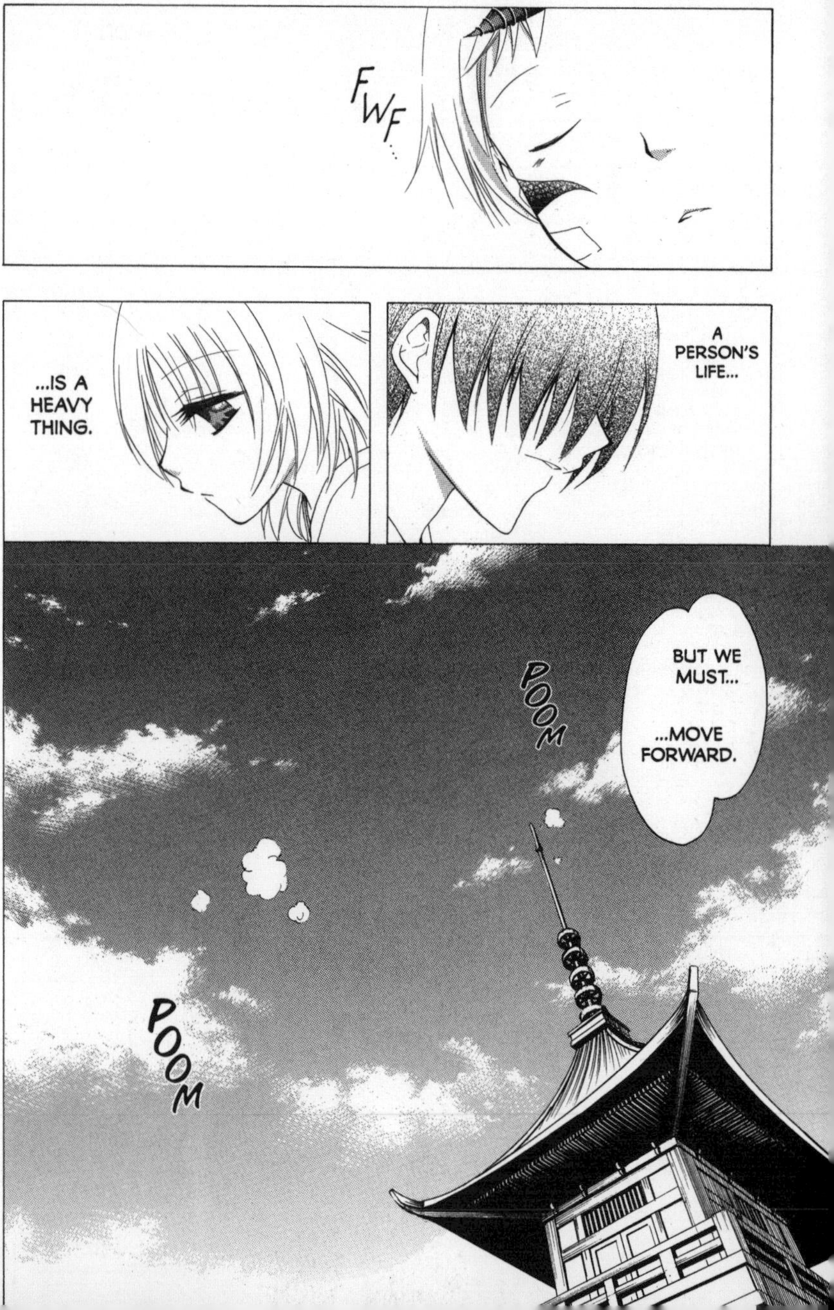
FWF...
A PERSON'S LIFE...
...IS A HEAVY THING.
BUT WE MUST...
...MOVE FORWARD.
POOM
POOM

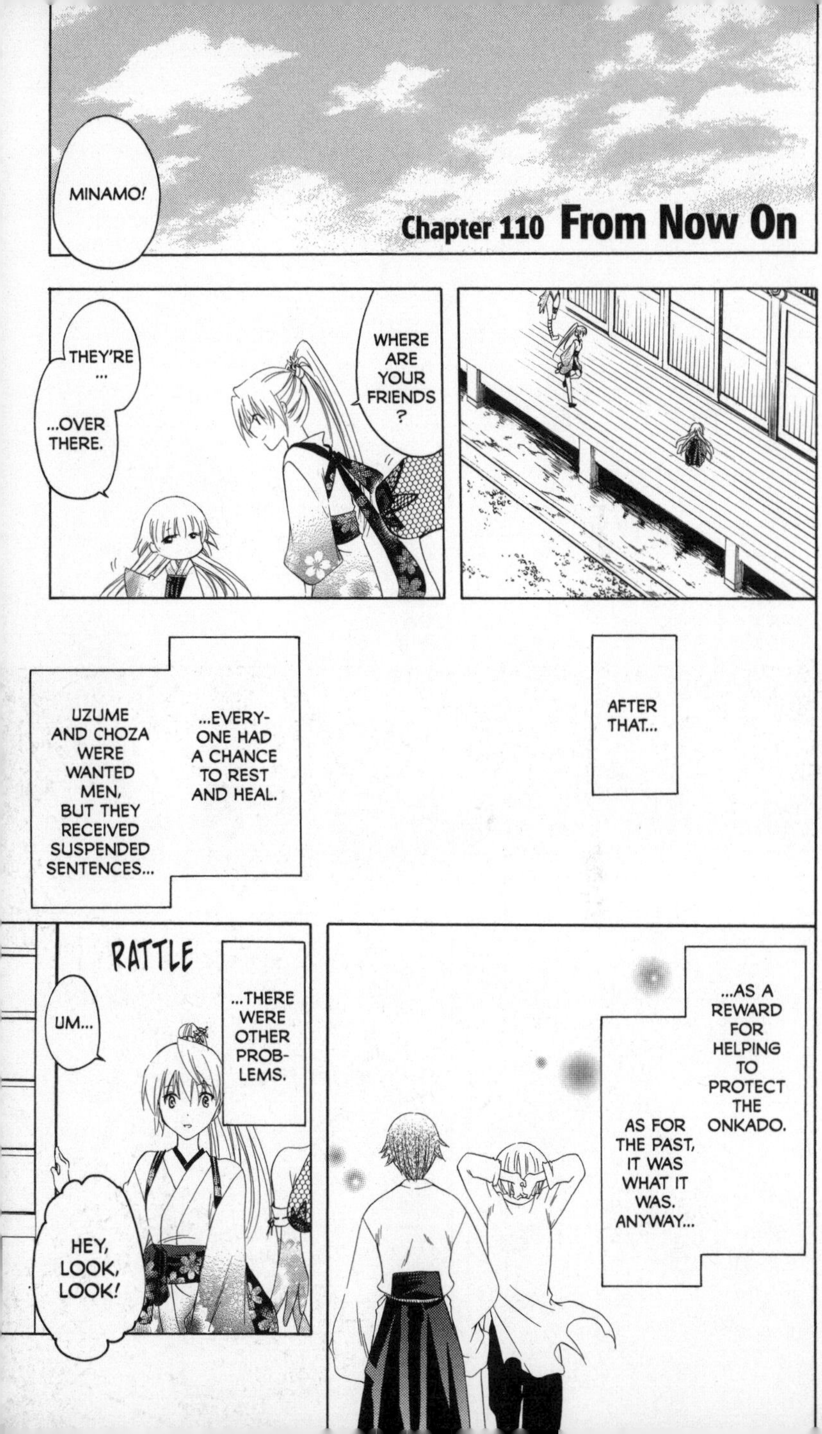
MINAMO!
Chapter 110 From Now On
WHERE ARE YOUR FRIENDS?
THEY'RE...
...OVER THERE.
AFTER THAT...
...EVERY-ONE HAD A CHANCE TO REST AND HEAL.
UZUME AND CHOZA WERE WANTED MEN, BUT THEY RECEIVED SUSPENDED SENTENCES...
...AS A REWARD FOR HELPING TO PROTECT THE ONKADO.
AS FOR THE PAST, IT WAS WHAT IT WAS. ANYWAY...
...THERE WERE OTHER PROB-LEMS.
RATTLE
UM...
HEY, LOOK, LOOK!

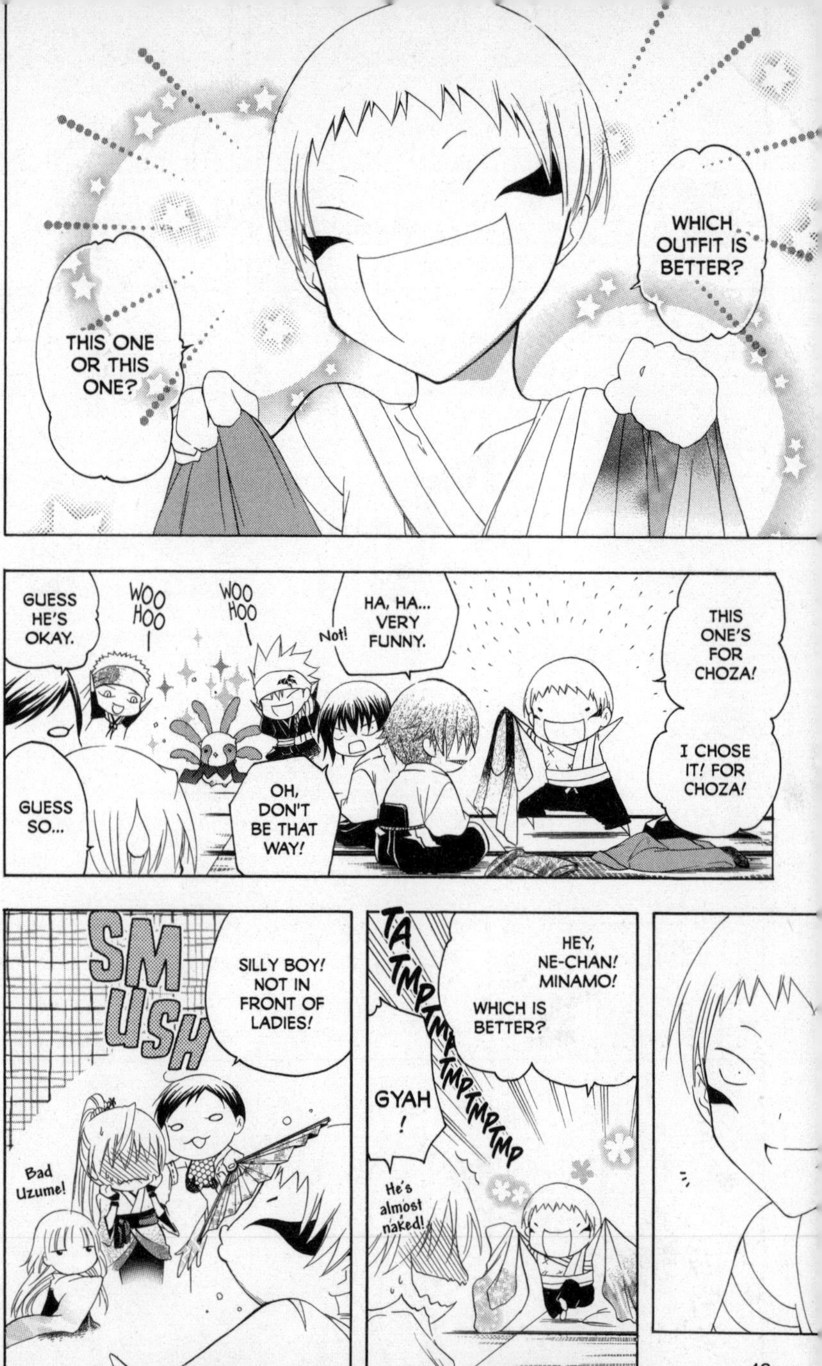
WHICH OUTFIT IS BETTER?
THIS ONE OR THIS ONE?
THIS ONE'S FOR CHOZA!
I CHOSE IT! FOR CHOZA!
HA, HA... VERY FUNNY.
Not!
WOO HOO
WOO HOO
GUESS HE'S OKAY.
OH, DON'T BE THAT WAY!
GUESS SO...
HEY, NE-CHAN! MINAMO!
WHICH IS BETTER?
TATMPATMPATMPATMPATMPATMP
GYAH!
He's almost naked!
SMUSH
SILLY BOY! NOT IN FRONT OF LADIES!
Bad Uzume!

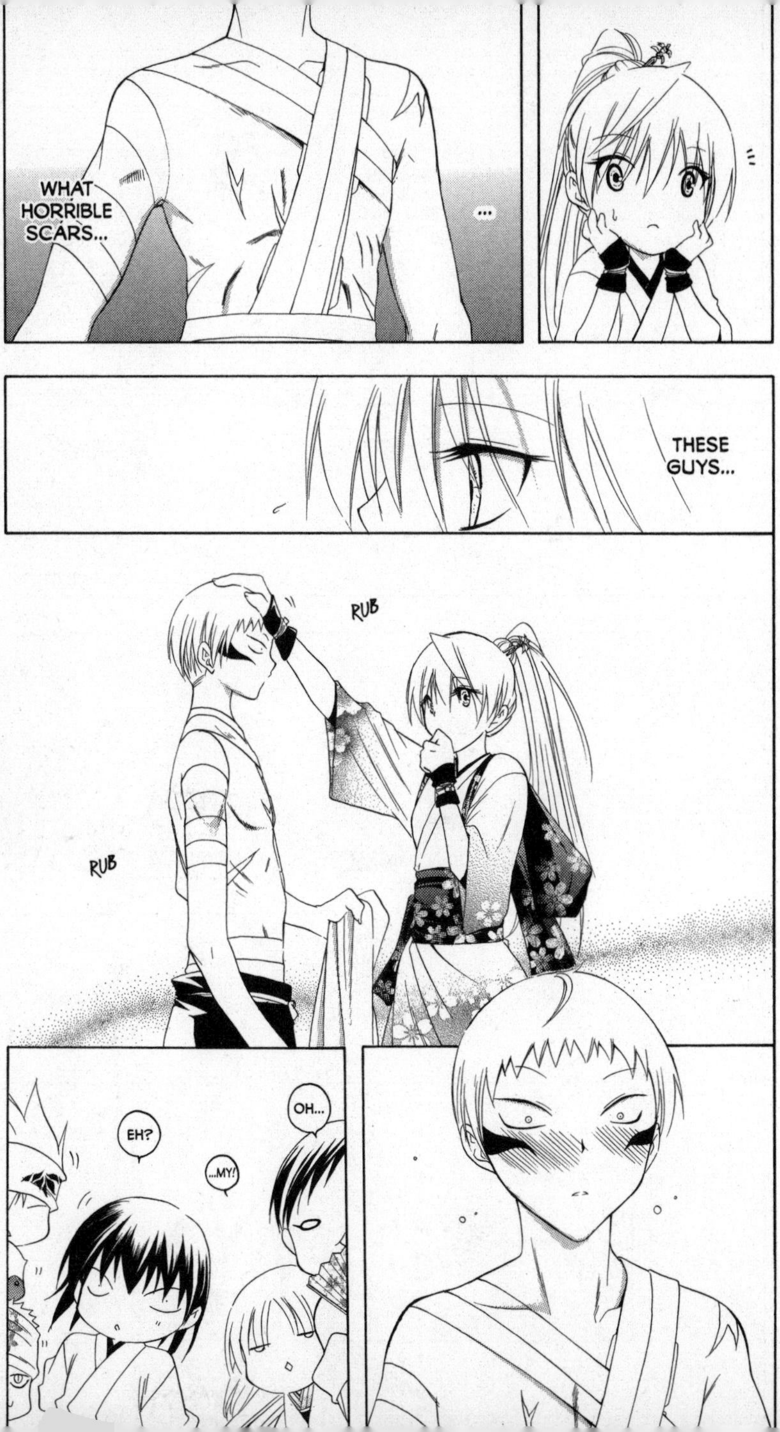
...
WHAT HORRIBLE SCARS...
THESE GUYS...
RUB
RUB
OH...
...MY!
EH?

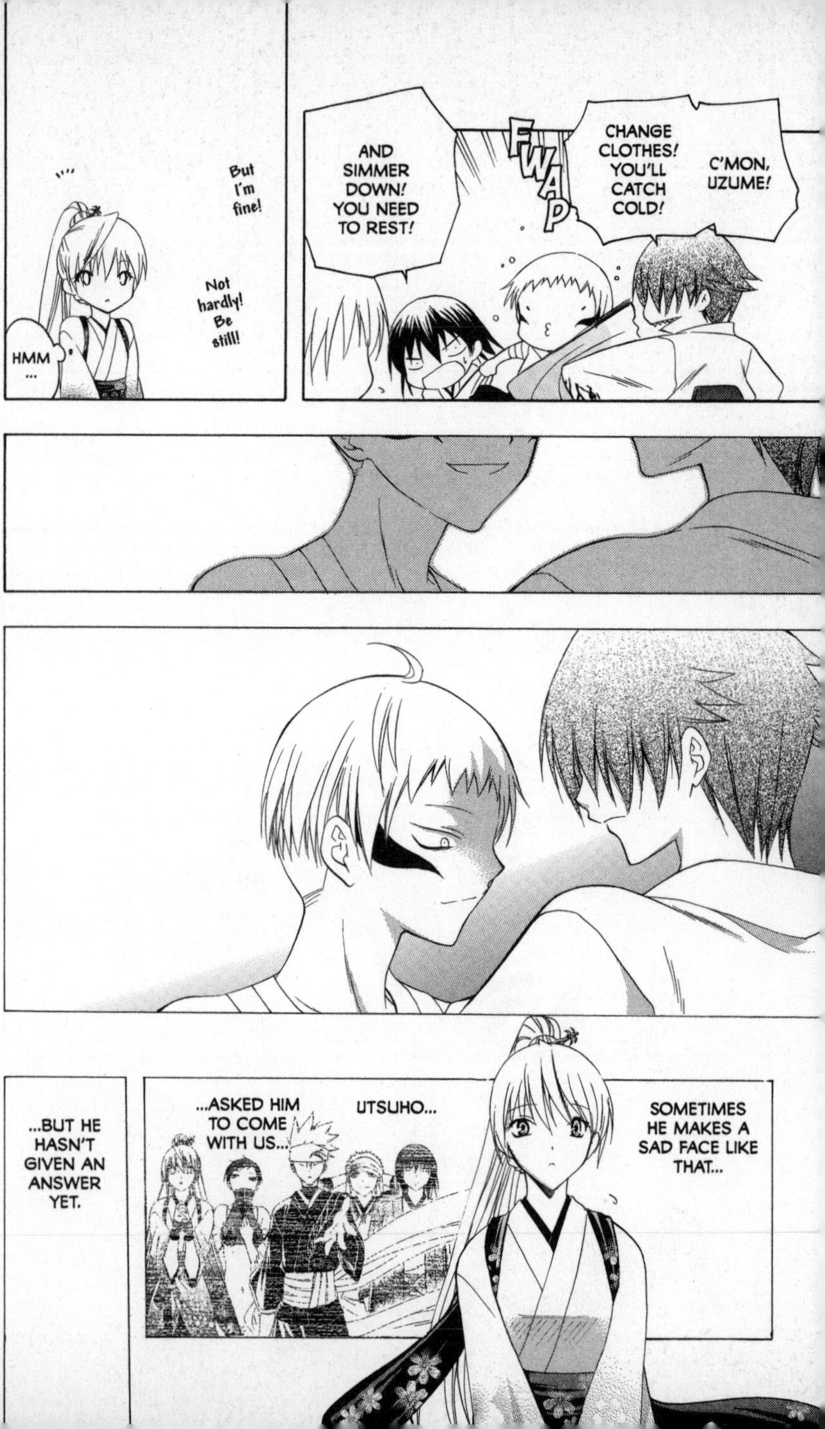
C'MON, UZUME!
CHANGE CLOTHES! YOU'LL CATCH COLD!
FWAP
AND SIMMER DOWN! YOU NEED TO REST!
But I'm fine!
Not hardly! Be still!
HMM ...
SOMETIMES HE MAKES A SAD FACE LIKE THAT...
UTSUHO...
...ASKED HIM TO COME WITH US...
...BUT HE HASN'T GIVEN AN ANSWER YET.

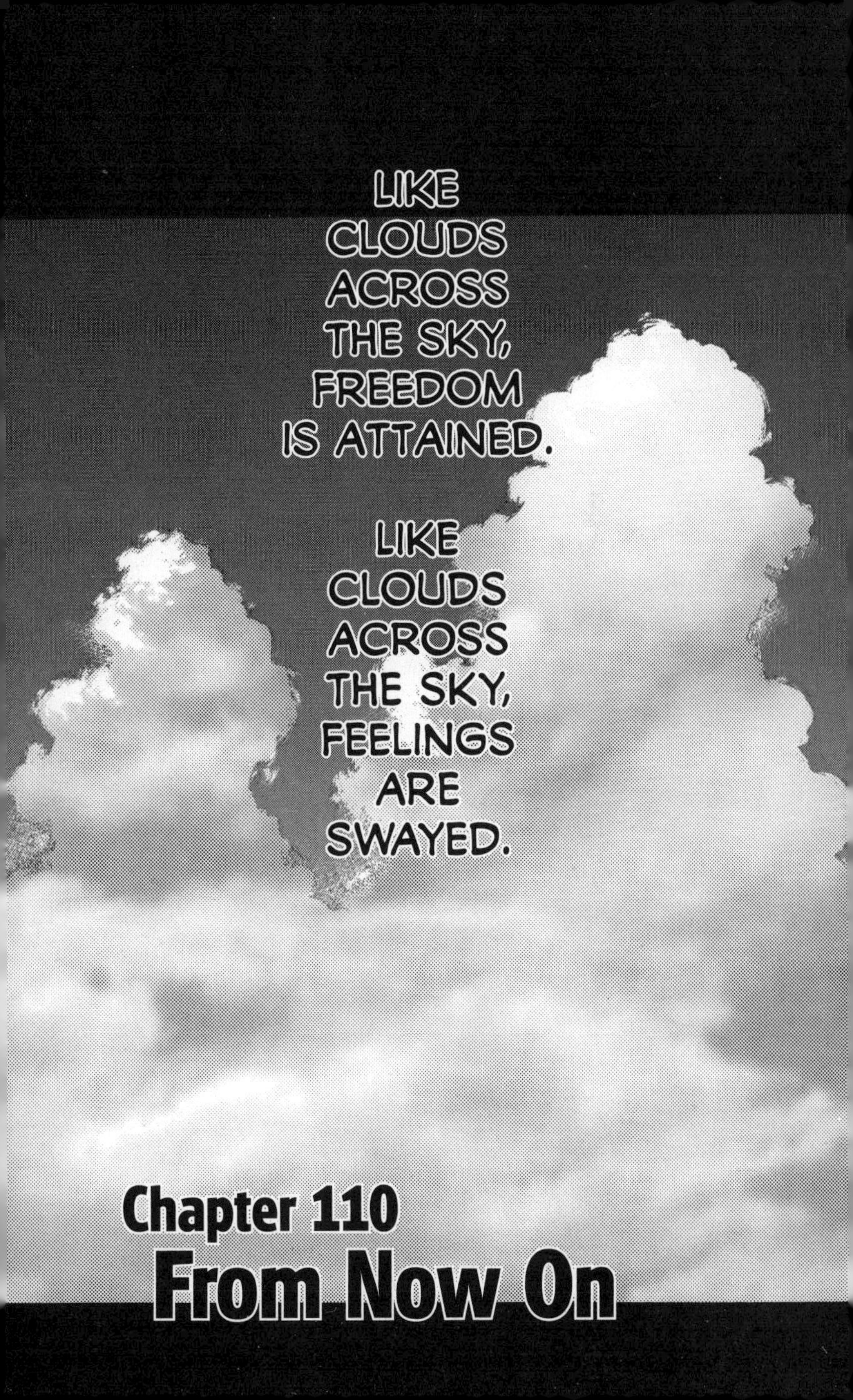
LIKE CLOUDS ACROSS THE SKY, FREEDOM IS ATTAINED.
LIKE CLOUDS ACROSS THE SKY, FEELINGS ARE SWAYED.

Chapter 110
From Now On

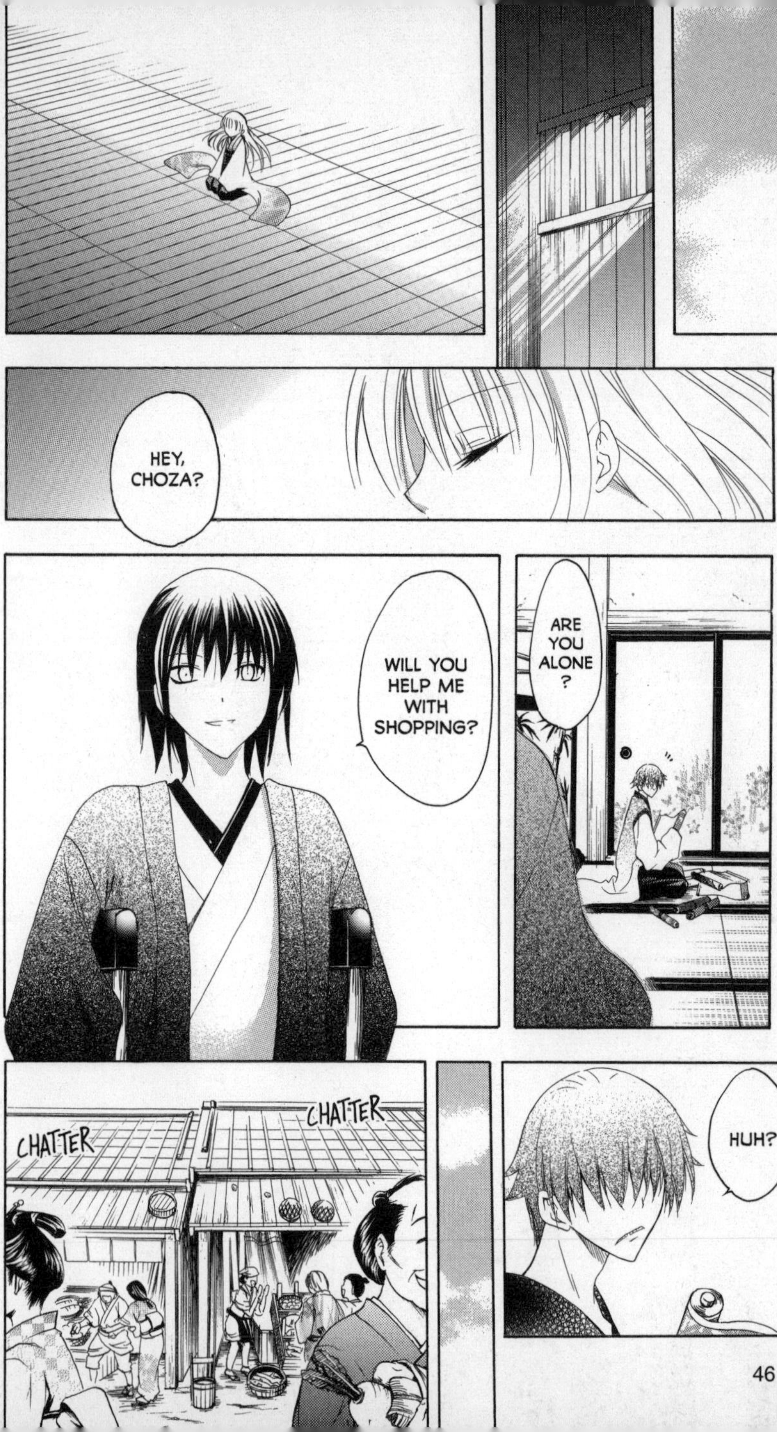
HEY, CHOZA?
ARE YOU ALONE?
WILL YOU HELP ME WITH SHOPPING?
HUH?
CHATTER
CHATTER

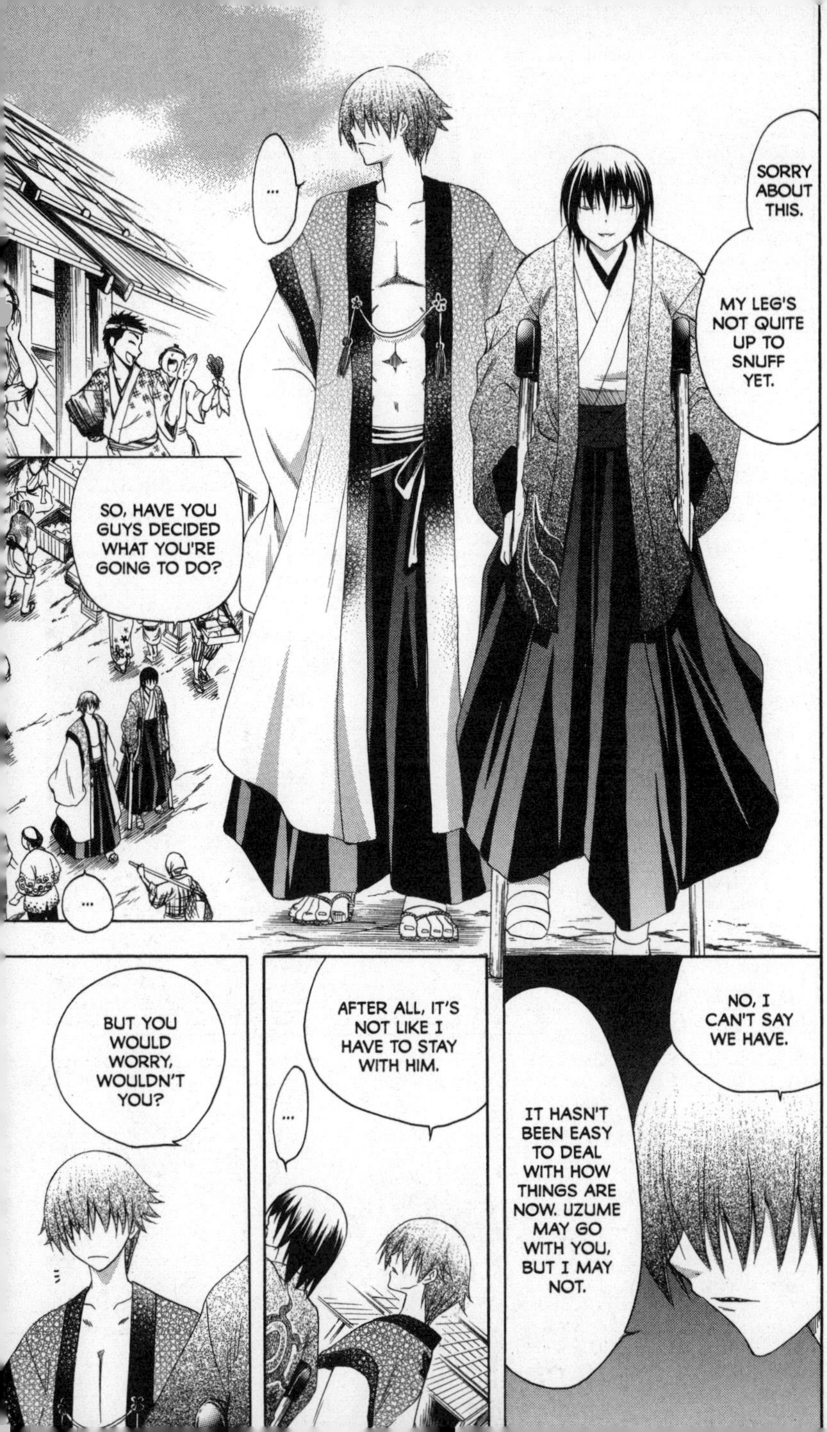
SORRY ABOUT THIS.
MY LEG'S NOT QUITE UP TO SNUFF YET.
...
SO, HAVE YOU GUYS DECIDED WHAT YOU'RE GOING TO DO?
...
NO, I CAN'T SAY WE HAVE.
IT HASN'T BEEN EASY TO DEAL WITH HOW THINGS ARE NOW. UZUME MAY GO WITH YOU, BUT I MAY NOT.
AFTER ALL, IT'S NOT LIKE I HAVE TO STAY WITH HIM.
...
BUT YOU WOULD WORRY, WOULDN'T YOU?

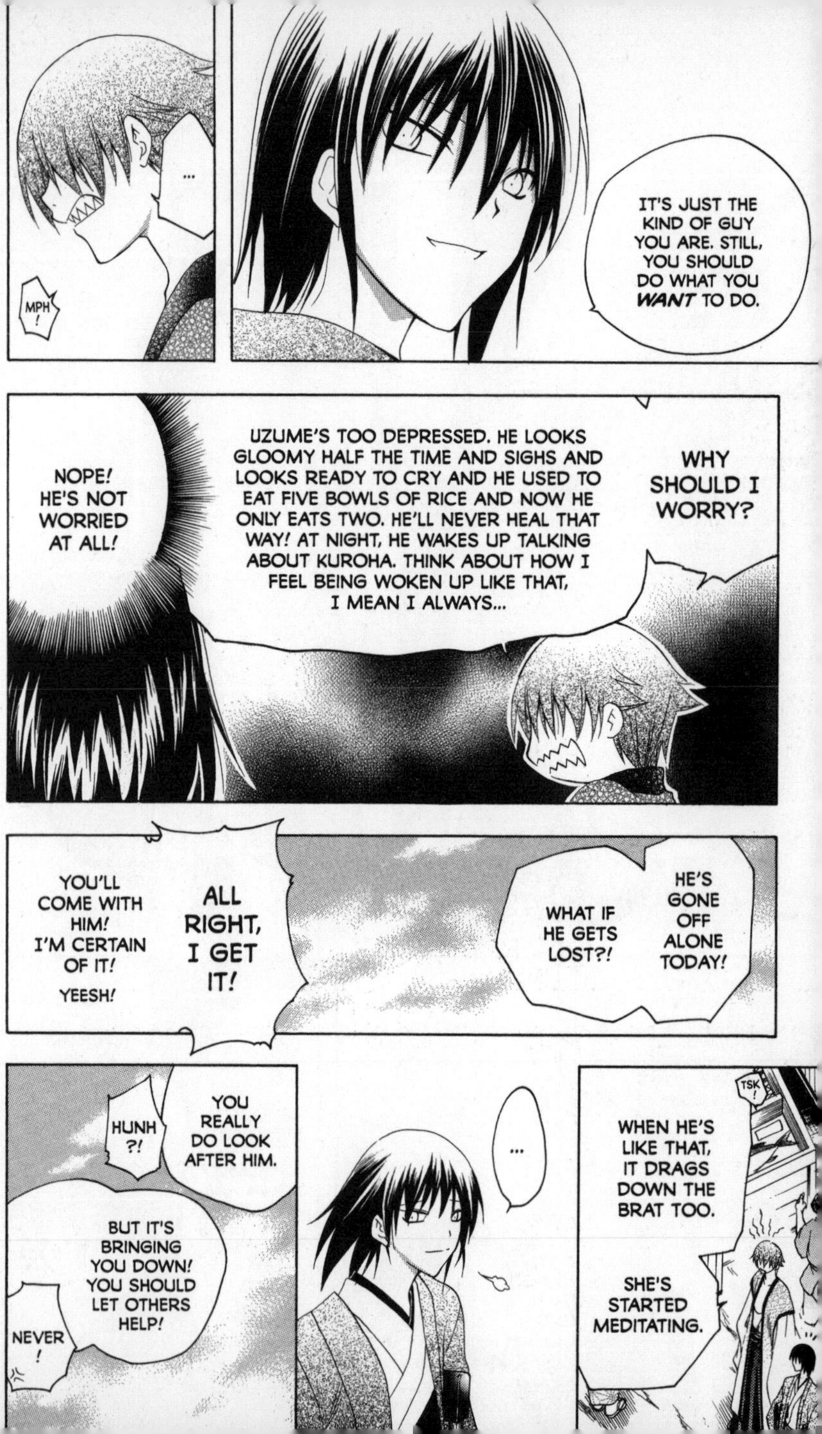
IT'S JUST THE KIND OF GUY YOU ARE. STILL, YOU SHOULD DO WHAT YOU *WANT* TO DO.
...
MPH!
WHY SHOULD I WORRY?
UZUME'S TOO DEPRESSED. HE LOOKS GLOOMY HALF THE TIME AND SIGHS AND LOOKS READY TO CRY AND HE USED TO EAT FIVE BOWLS OF RICE AND NOW HE ONLY EATS TWO. HE'LL NEVER HEAL THAT WAY! AT NIGHT, HE WAKES UP TALKING ABOUT KUROHA. THINK ABOUT HOW I FEEL BEING WOKEN UP LIKE THAT, I MEAN I ALWAYS...
NOPE! HE'S NOT WORRIED AT ALL!
HE'S GONE OFF ALONE TODAY!
WHAT IF HE GETS LOST?!
ALL RIGHT, I GET IT!
YOU'LL COME WITH HIM! I'M CERTAIN OF IT!
YEESH!
TSK!
WHEN HE'S LIKE THAT, IT DRAGS DOWN THE BRAT TOO.
SHE'S STARTED MEDITATING.
...
YOU REALLY DO LOOK AFTER HIM.
HUNH?!
BUT IT'S BRINGING YOU DOWN! YOU SHOULD LET OTHERS HELP!
NEVER!

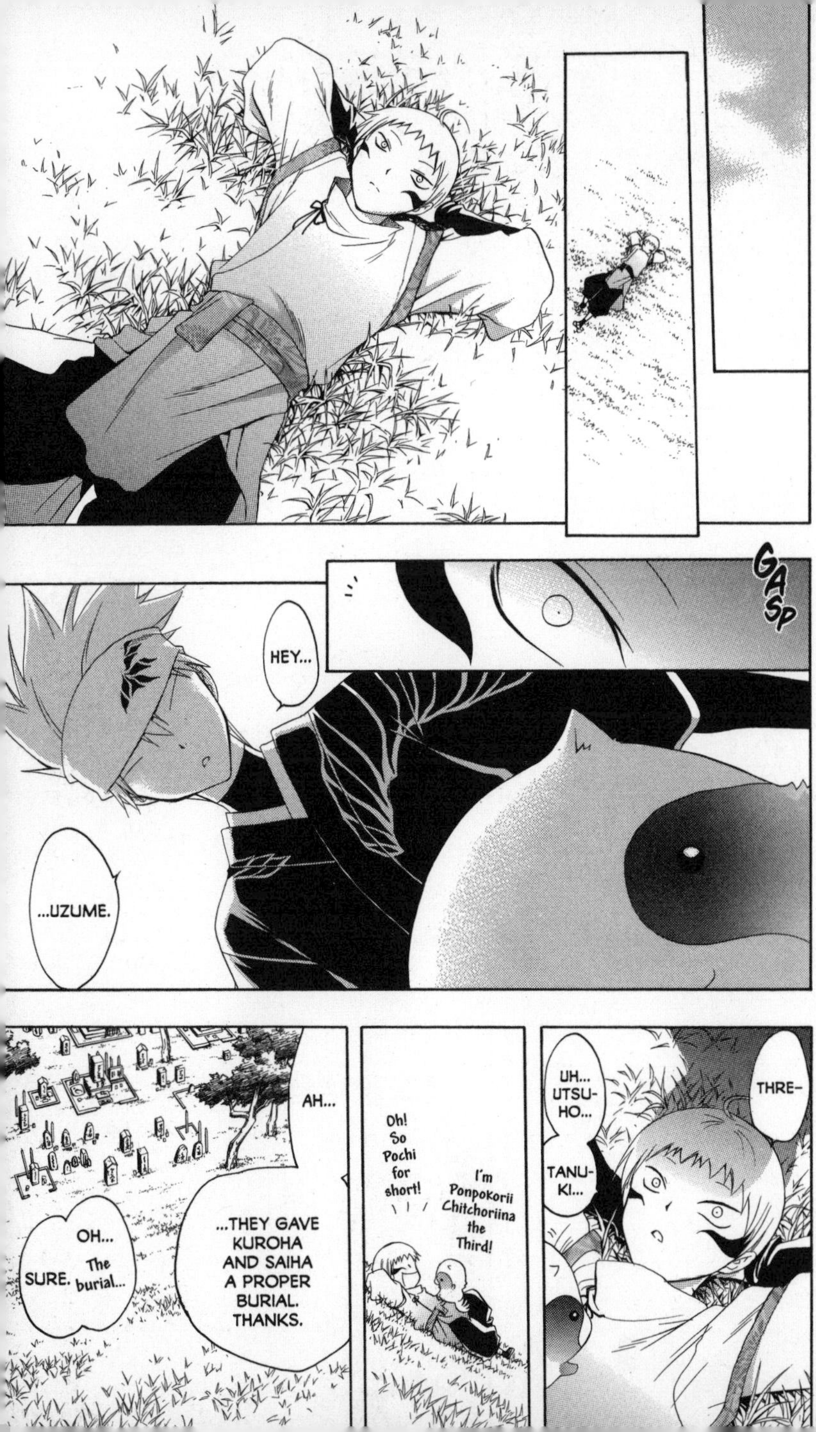
GASP
HEY...
...UZUME.
THRE-
UH... UTSU-HO...
TANU-KI...
I'm Ponpokorii Chitchoriina the Third!
Oh! So Pochi for short!
AH...
...THEY GAVE KUROHA AND SAIHA A PROPER BURIAL. THANKS.
OH... SURE.
The burial...

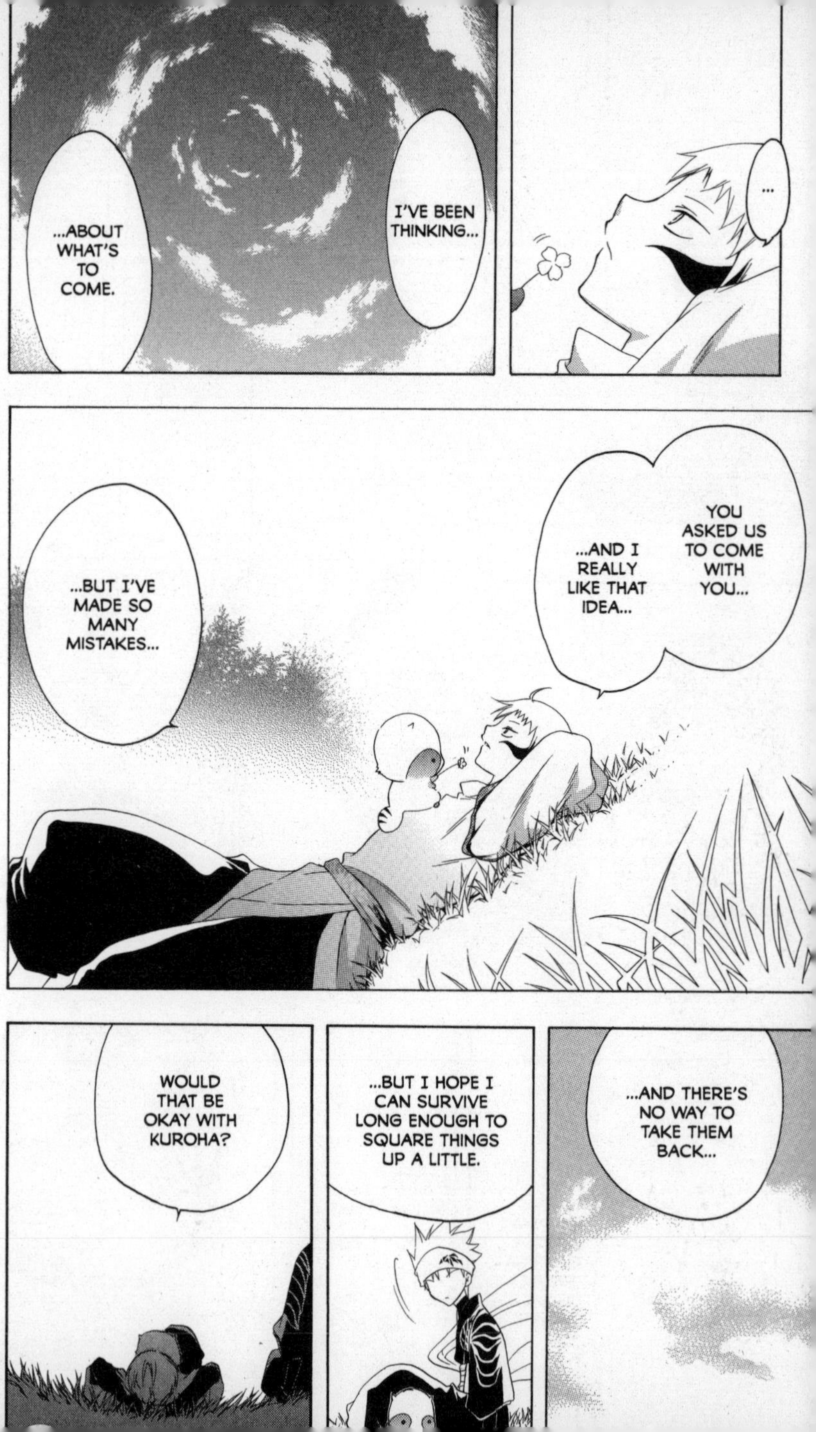
...
I'VE BEEN THINKING...
...ABOUT WHAT'S TO COME.
YOU ASKED US TO COME WITH YOU...
...AND I REALLY LIKE THAT IDEA...
...BUT I'VE MADE SO MANY MISTAKES...
...AND THERE'S NO WAY TO TAKE THEM BACK...
...BUT I HOPE I CAN SURVIVE LONG ENOUGH TO SQUARE THINGS UP A LITTLE.
WOULD THAT BE OKAY WITH KUROHA?

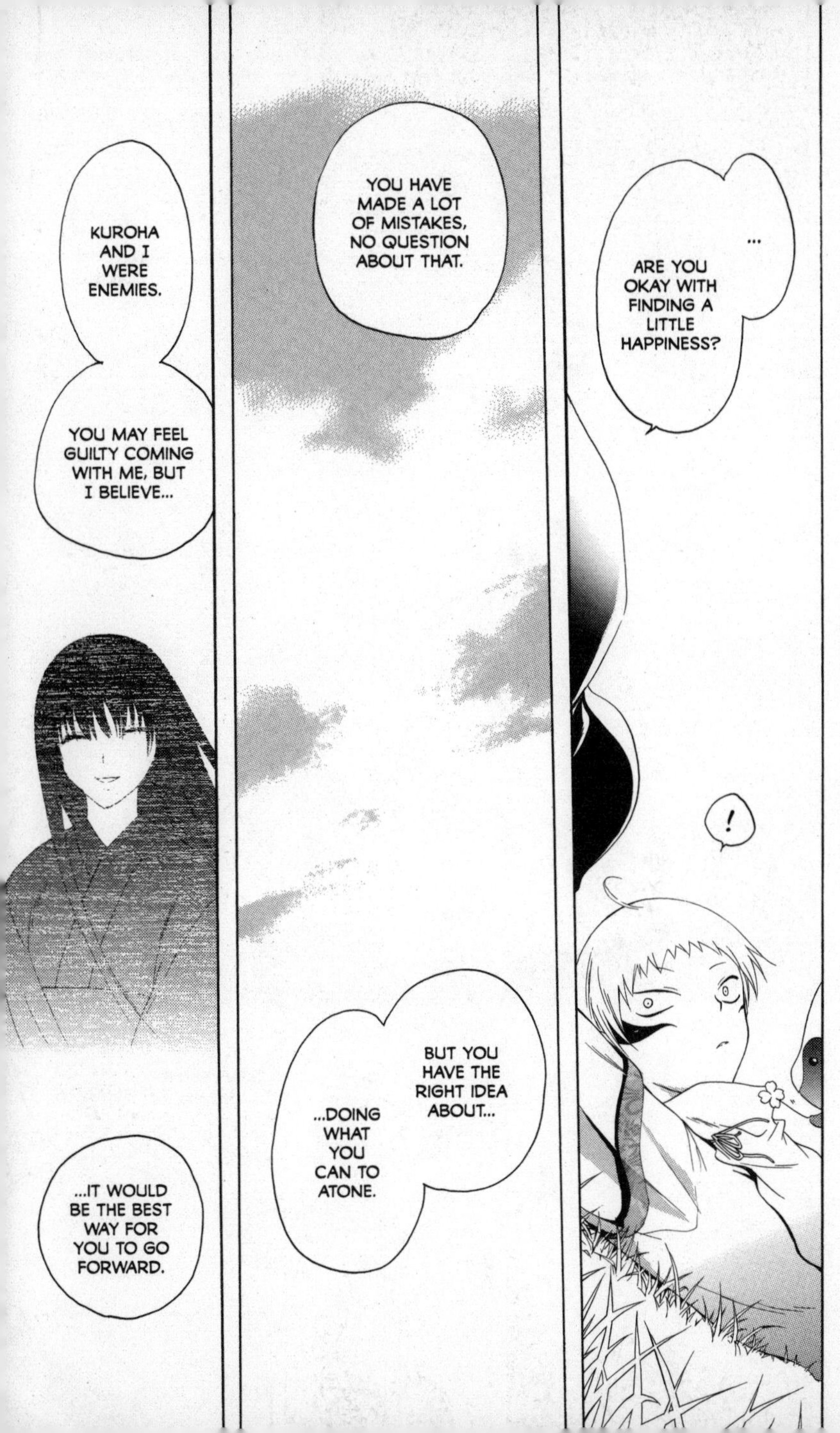
...
ARE YOU OKAY WITH FINDING A LITTLE HAPPINESS?
!
YOU HAVE MADE A LOT OF MISTAKES, NO QUESTION ABOUT THAT.
BUT YOU HAVE THE RIGHT IDEA ABOUT...
...DOING WHAT YOU CAN TO ATONE.
KUROHA AND I WERE ENEMIES.
YOU MAY FEEL GUILTY COMING WITH ME, BUT I BELIEVE...
...IT WOULD BE THE BEST WAY FOR YOU TO GO FORWARD.

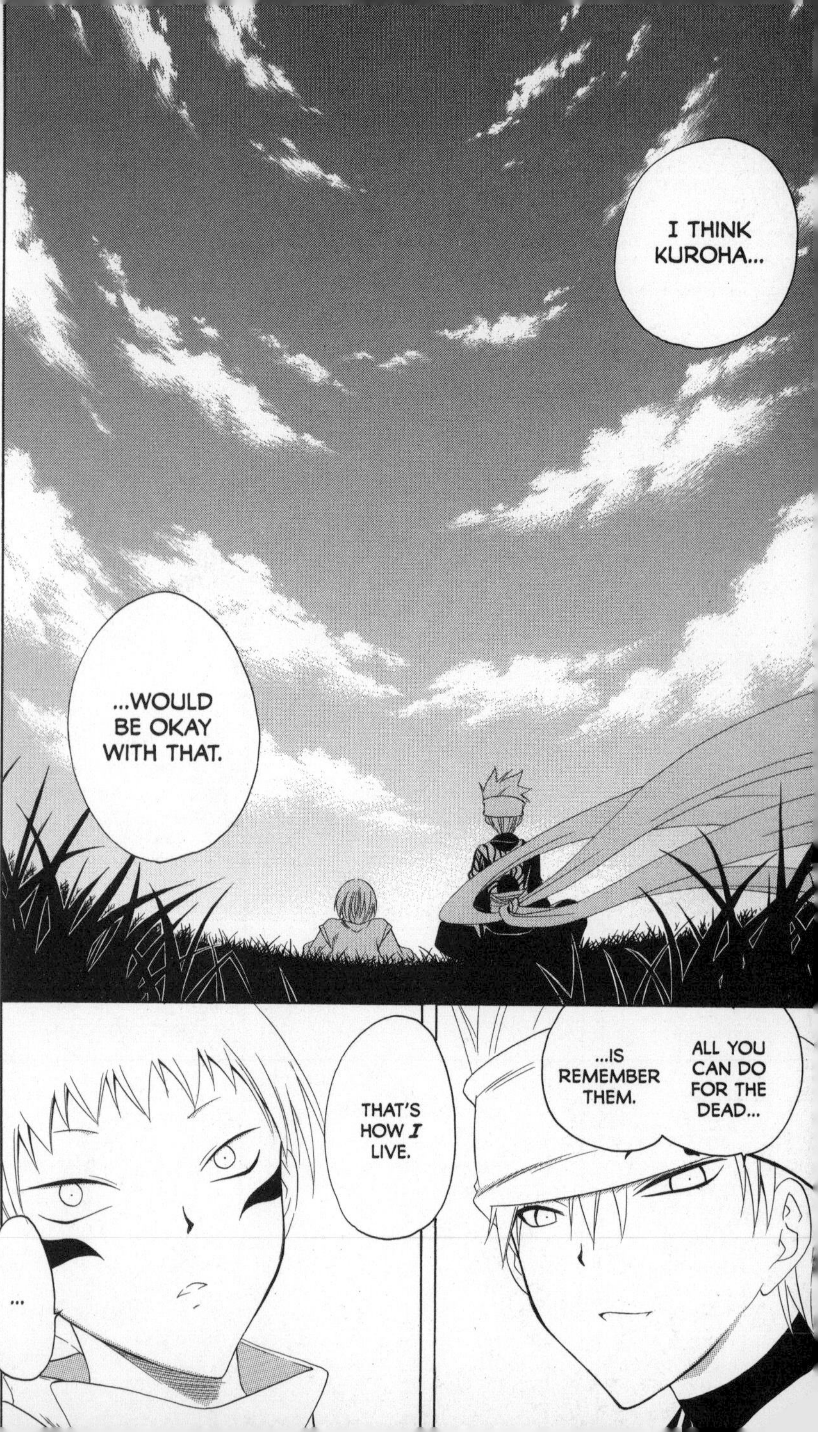
I THINK KUROHA...
...WOULD BE OKAY WITH THAT.
ALL YOU CAN DO FOR THE DEAD...
...IS REMEMBER THEM.
THAT'S HOW *I* LIVE.
...

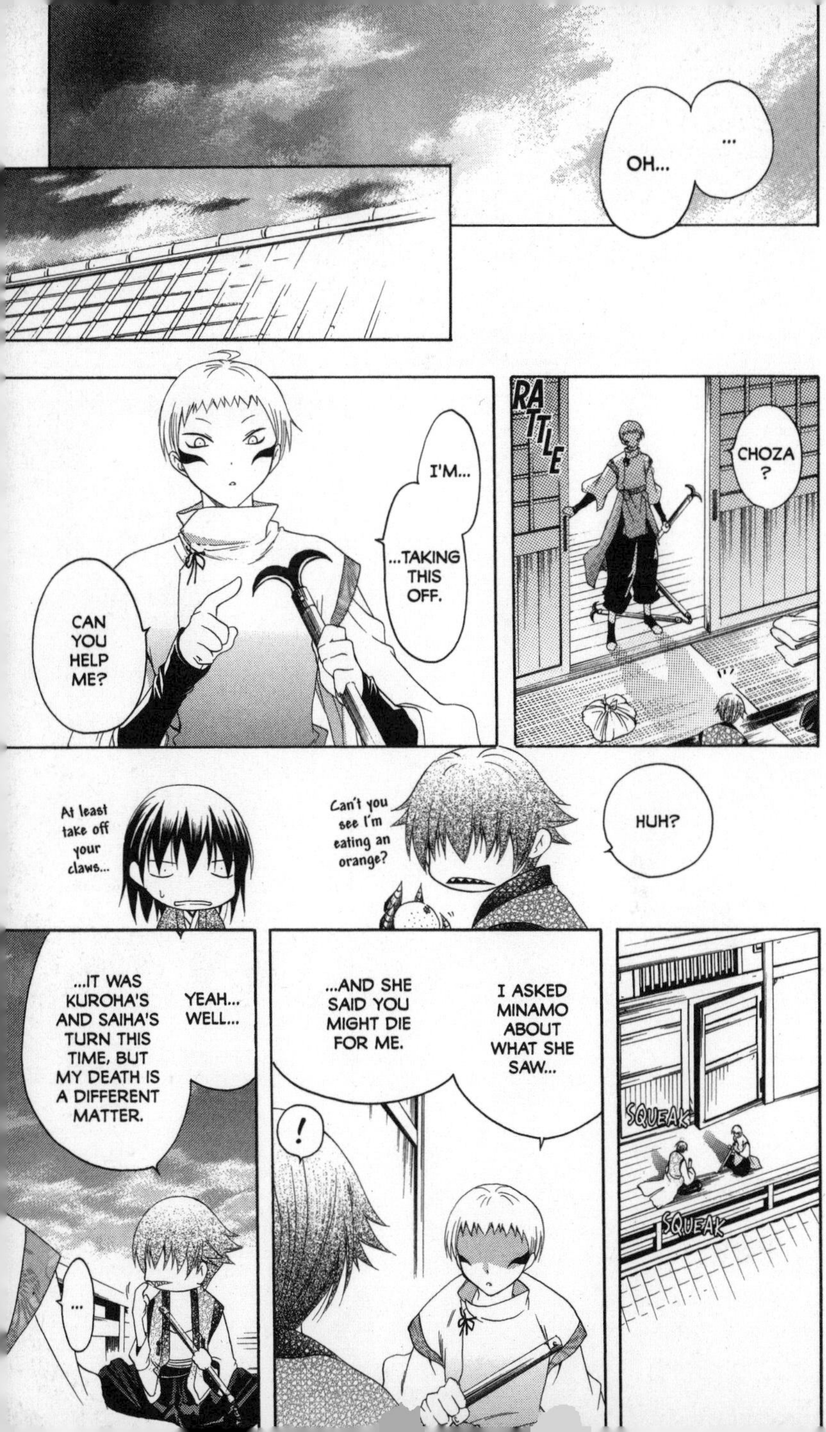
...
OH...
RATTLE
CHOZA?
I'M...
...TAKING THIS OFF.
CAN YOU HELP ME?
HUH?
Can't you see I'm eating an orange?
At least take off your claws...
SQUEAK
SQUEAK
I ASKED MINAMO ABOUT WHAT SHE SAW...
...AND SHE SAID YOU MIGHT DIE FOR ME.
!
YEAH... WELL...
...IT WAS KUROHA'S AND SAIHA'S TURN THIS TIME, BUT MY DEATH IS A DIFFERENT MATTER.
...

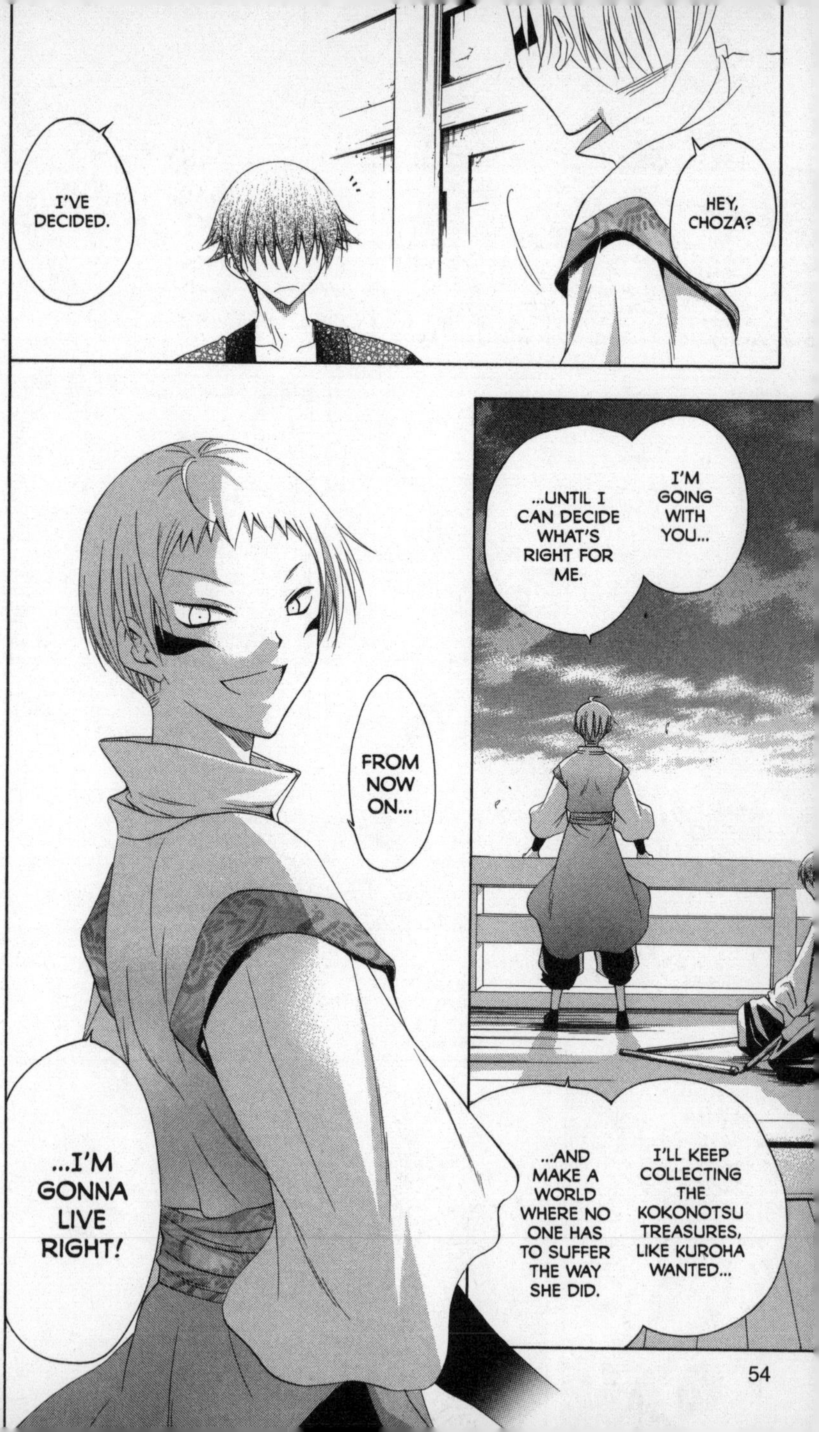
HEY, CHOZA?
I'VE DECIDED.
I'M GOING WITH YOU...
...UNTIL I CAN DECIDE WHAT'S RIGHT FOR ME.
I'LL KEEP COLLECTING THE KOKONOTSU TREASURES, LIKE KUROHA WANTED...
...AND MAKE A WORLD WHERE NO ONE HAS TO SUFFER THE WAY SHE DID.
FROM NOW ON...
...I'M GONNA LIVE RIGHT!

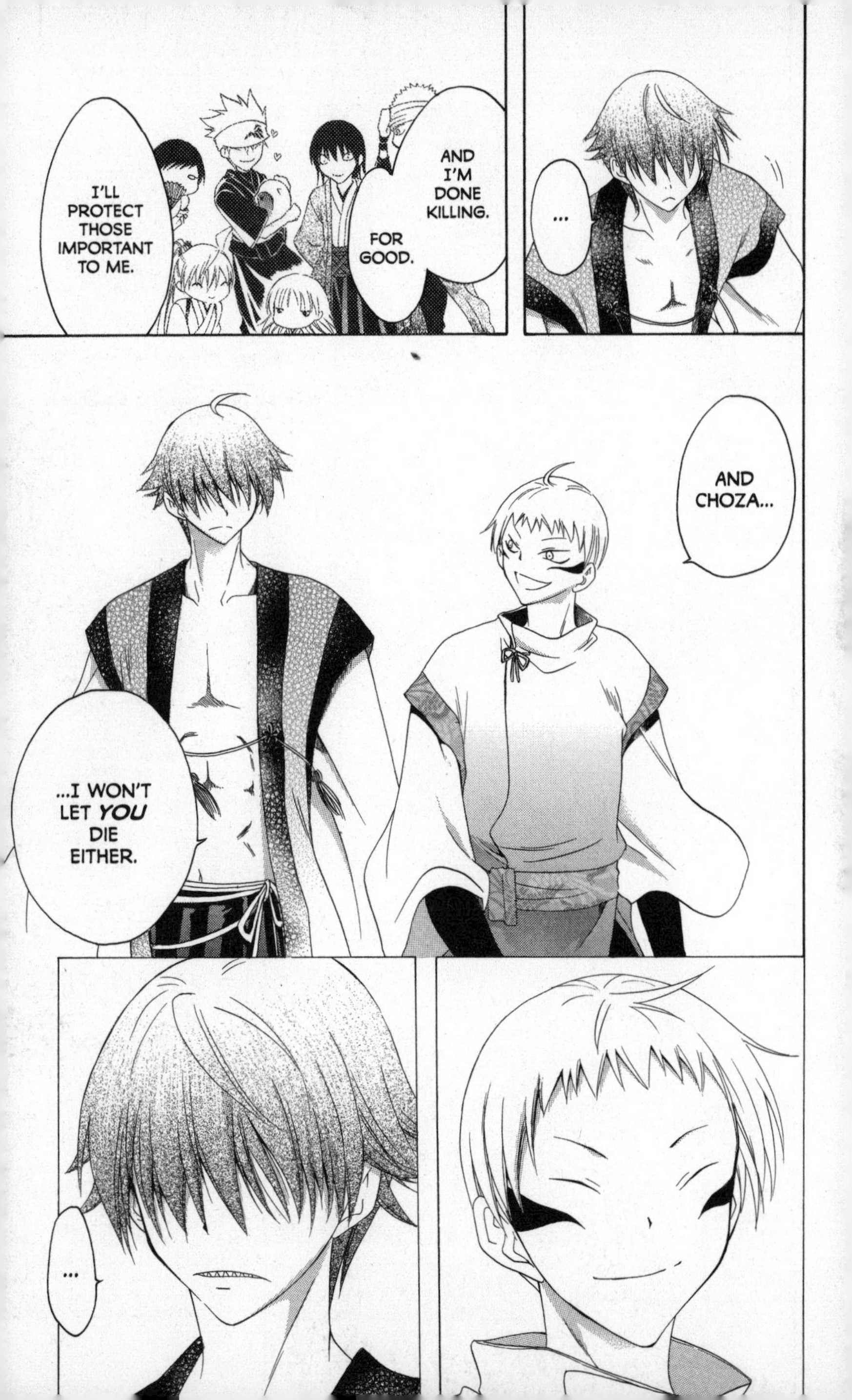
...
AND I'M DONE KILLING.
FOR GOOD.
I'LL PROTECT THOSE IMPORTANT TO ME.
AND CHOZA...
...I WON'T LET *YOU* DIE EITHER.
...

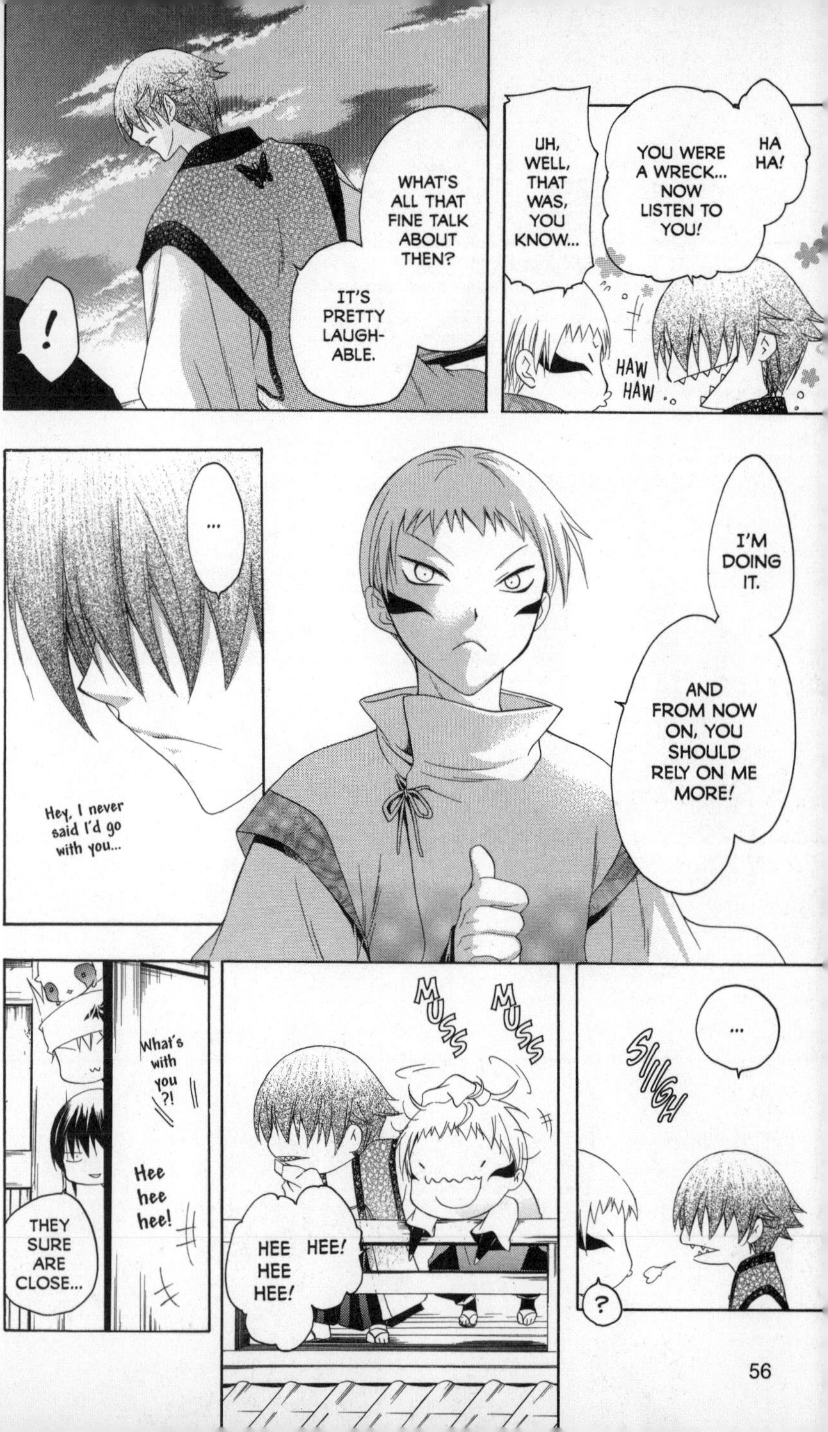

HA HA!
YOU WERE A WRECK... NOW LISTEN TO YOU!
UH, WELL, THAT WAS, YOU KNOW...
HAW HAW
WHAT'S ALL THAT FINE TALK ABOUT THEN?
IT'S PRETTY LAUGH-ABLE.
!
I'M DOING IT.
AND FROM NOW ON, YOU SHOULD RELY ON ME MORE!
...
Hey, I never said I'd go with you...
...
SIIGH
?
MUSS MUSS
HEE HEE! HEE HEE!
What's with you?!
Hee hee hee!
THEY SURE ARE CLOSE...

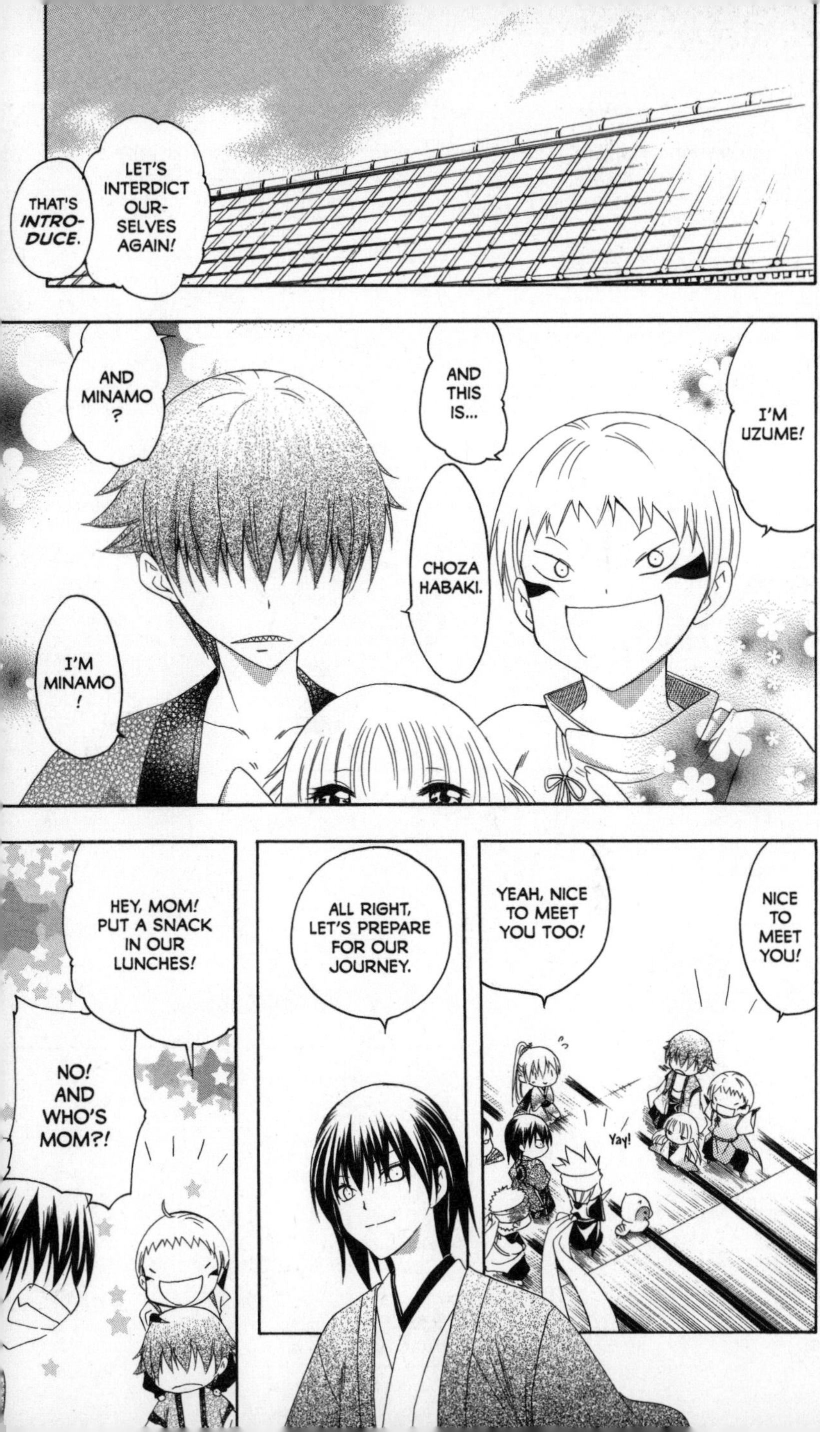
LET'S INTERDICT OUR-SELVES AGAIN!
THAT'S *INTRO-DUCE*.
I'M UZUME!
AND THIS IS...
CHOZA HABAKI.
AND MINAMO?
I'M MINAMO!
NICE TO MEET YOU!
YEAH, NICE TO MEET YOU TOO!
Yay!
ALL RIGHT, LET'S PREPARE FOR OUR JOURNEY.
HEY, MOM! PUT A SNACK IN OUR LUNCHES!
NO! AND WHO'S MOM?!

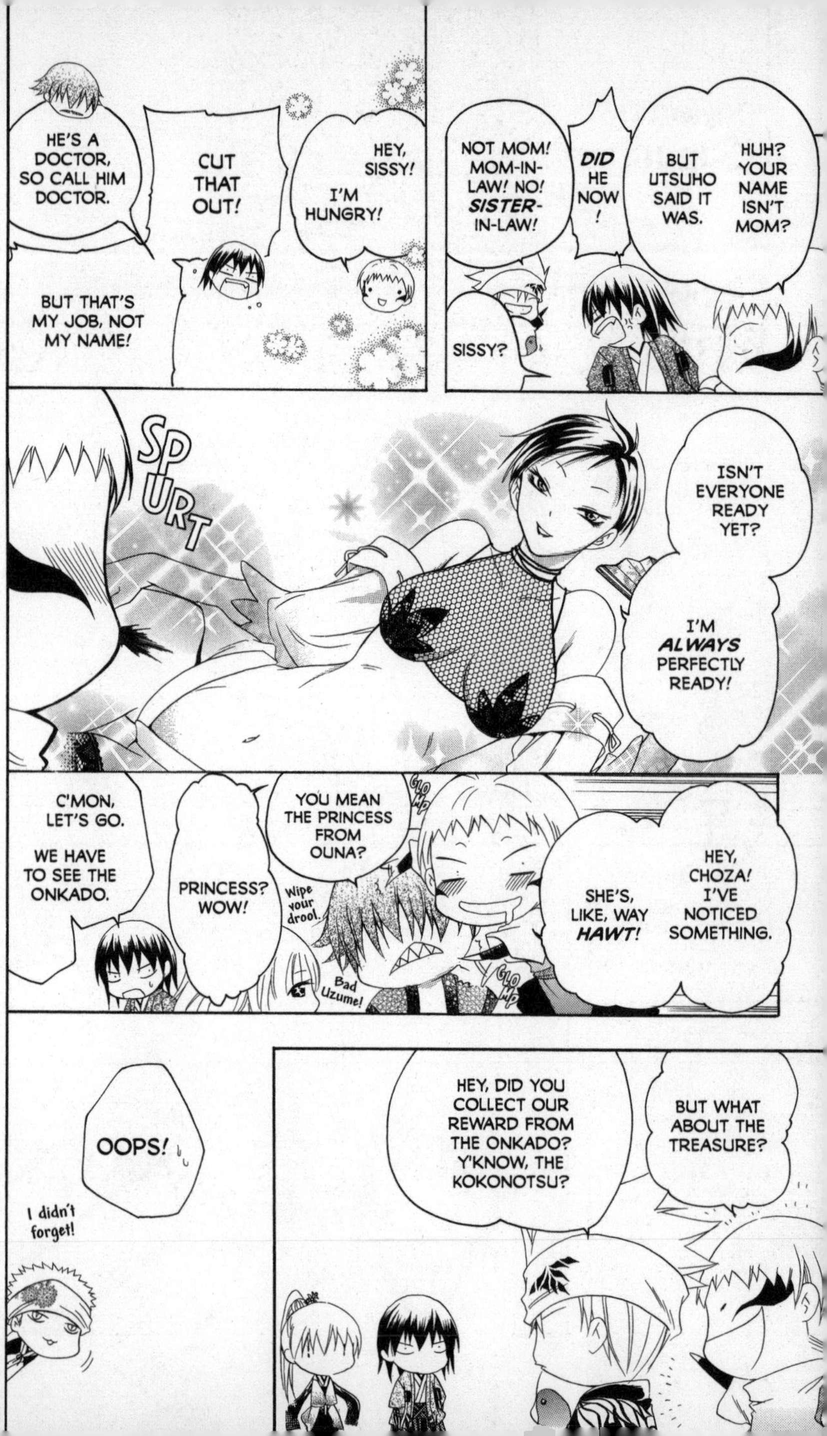
HUH? YOUR NAME ISN'T MOM?
BUT UTSUHO SAID IT WAS.
DID HE NOW!
NOT MOM! MOM-IN-LAW! NO! SISTER-IN-LAW!
SISSY?
HEY, SISSY! I'M HUNGRY!
CUT THAT OUT!
HE'S A DOCTOR, SO CALL HIM DOCTOR.
BUT THAT'S MY JOB, NOT MY NAME!
ISN'T EVERYONE READY YET?
SPURT
I'M ALWAYS PERFECTLY READY!
HEY, CHOZA! I'VE NOTICED SOMETHING.
SHE'S, LIKE, WAY HAWT!
GLOMP
GLOMP
YOU MEAN THE PRINCESS FROM OUNA?
Wipe your drool.
Bad Uzume!
PRINCESS? WOW!
C'MON, LET'S GO.
WE HAVE TO SEE THE ONKADO.
BUT WHAT ABOUT THE TREASURE?
HEY, DID YOU COLLECT OUR REWARD FROM THE ONKADO? Y'KNOW, THE KOKONOTSU?
OOPS!
I didn't forget!

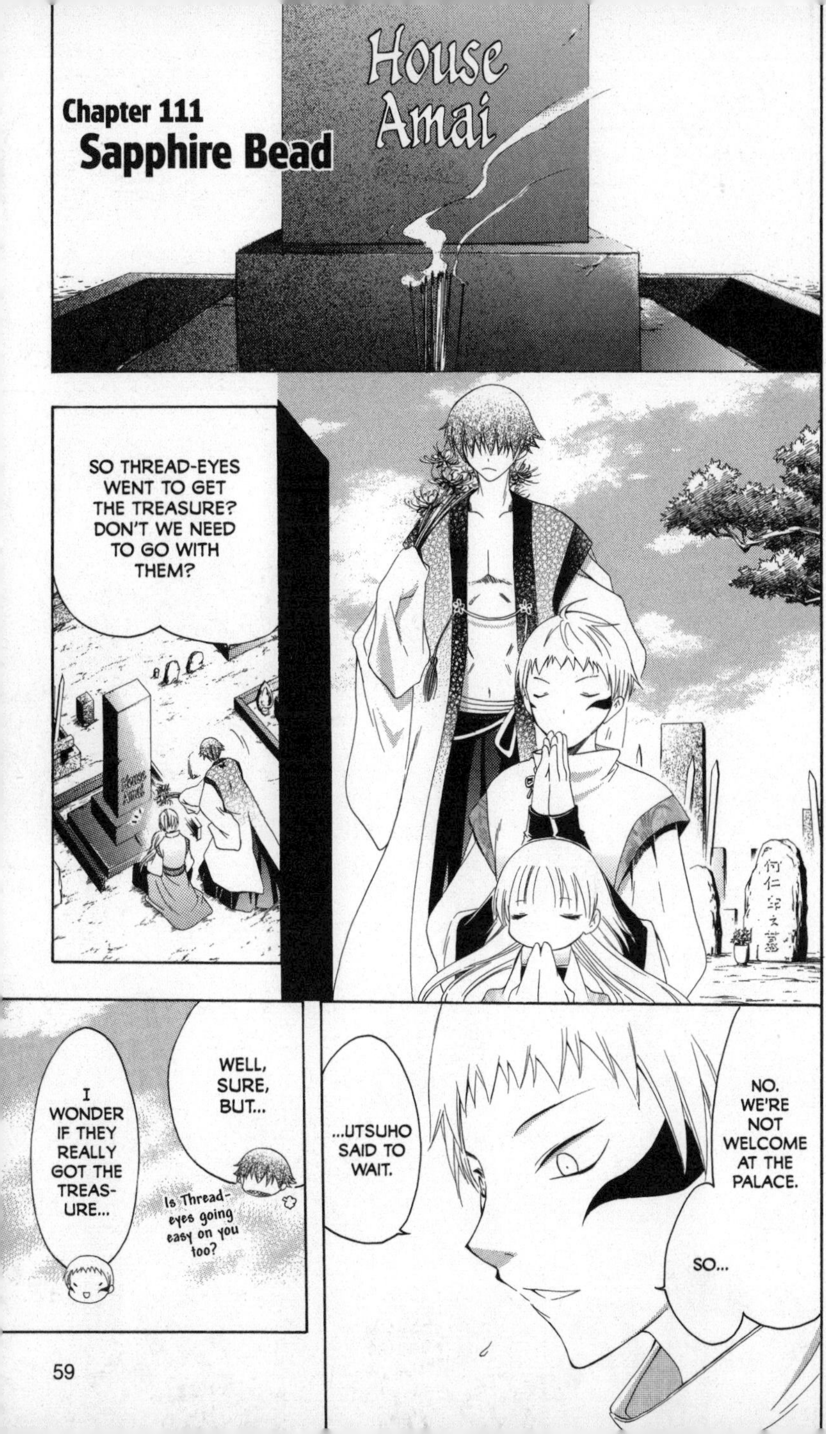
Chapter 111
Sapphire Bead
House Amai
SO THREAD-EYES WENT TO GET THE TREASURE? DON'T WE NEED TO GO WITH THEM?
NO. WE'RE NOT WELCOME AT THE PALACE.
SO...
...UTSUHO SAID TO WAIT.
WELL, SURE, BUT...
Is Thread-eyes going easy on you too?
I WONDER IF THEY REALLY GOT THE TREAS-URE...

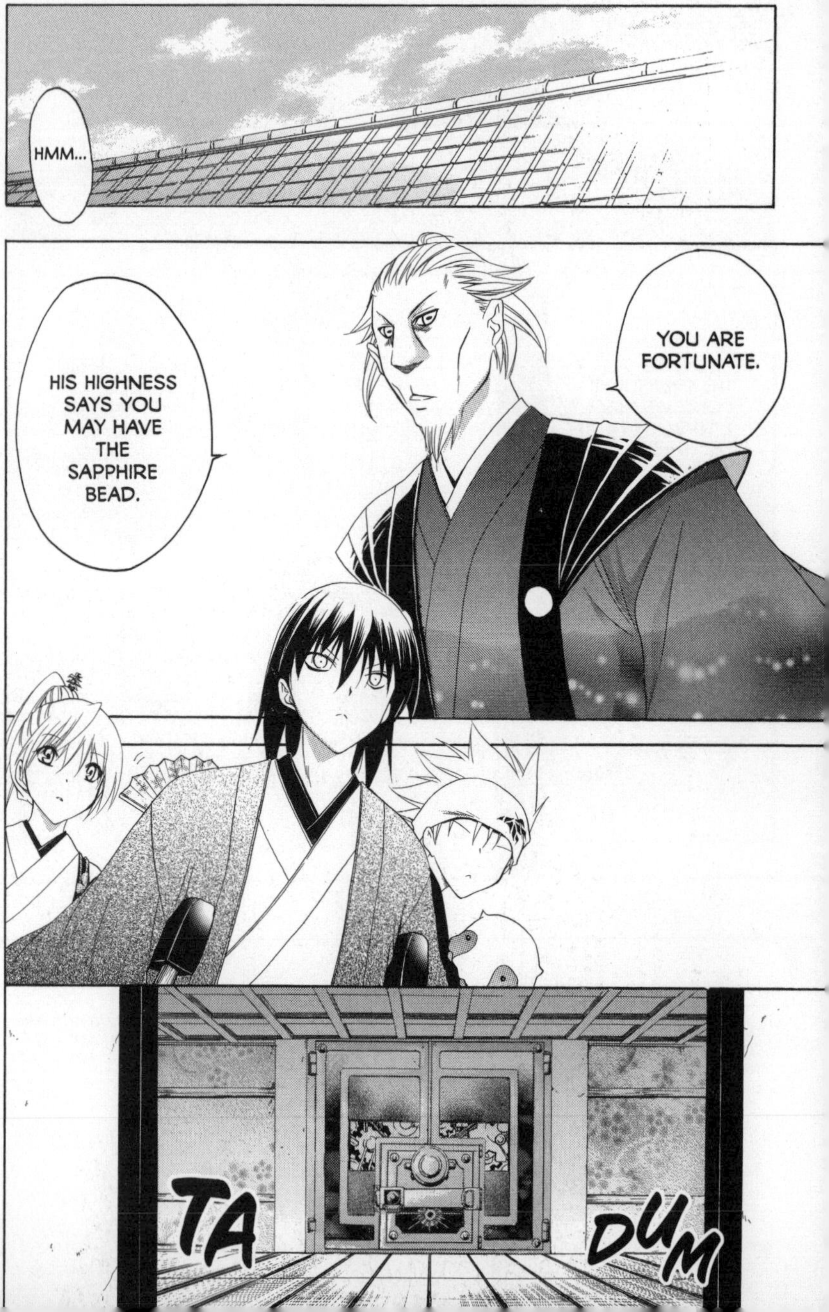
HMM...
YOU ARE FORTUNATE.
HIS HIGHNESS SAYS YOU MAY HAVE THE SAPPHIRE BEAD.
TA
DUM

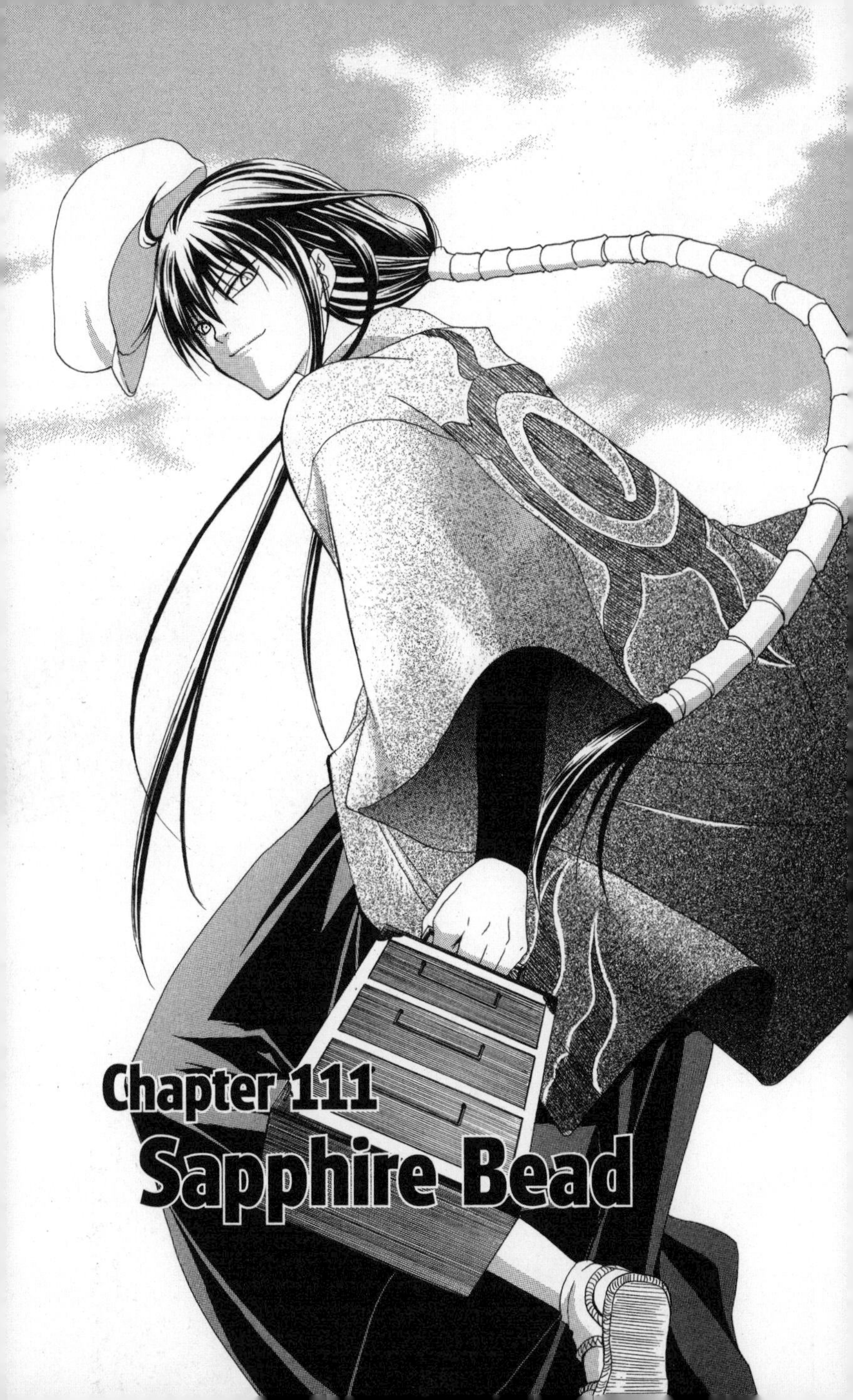
Chapter 111
Sapphire Bead

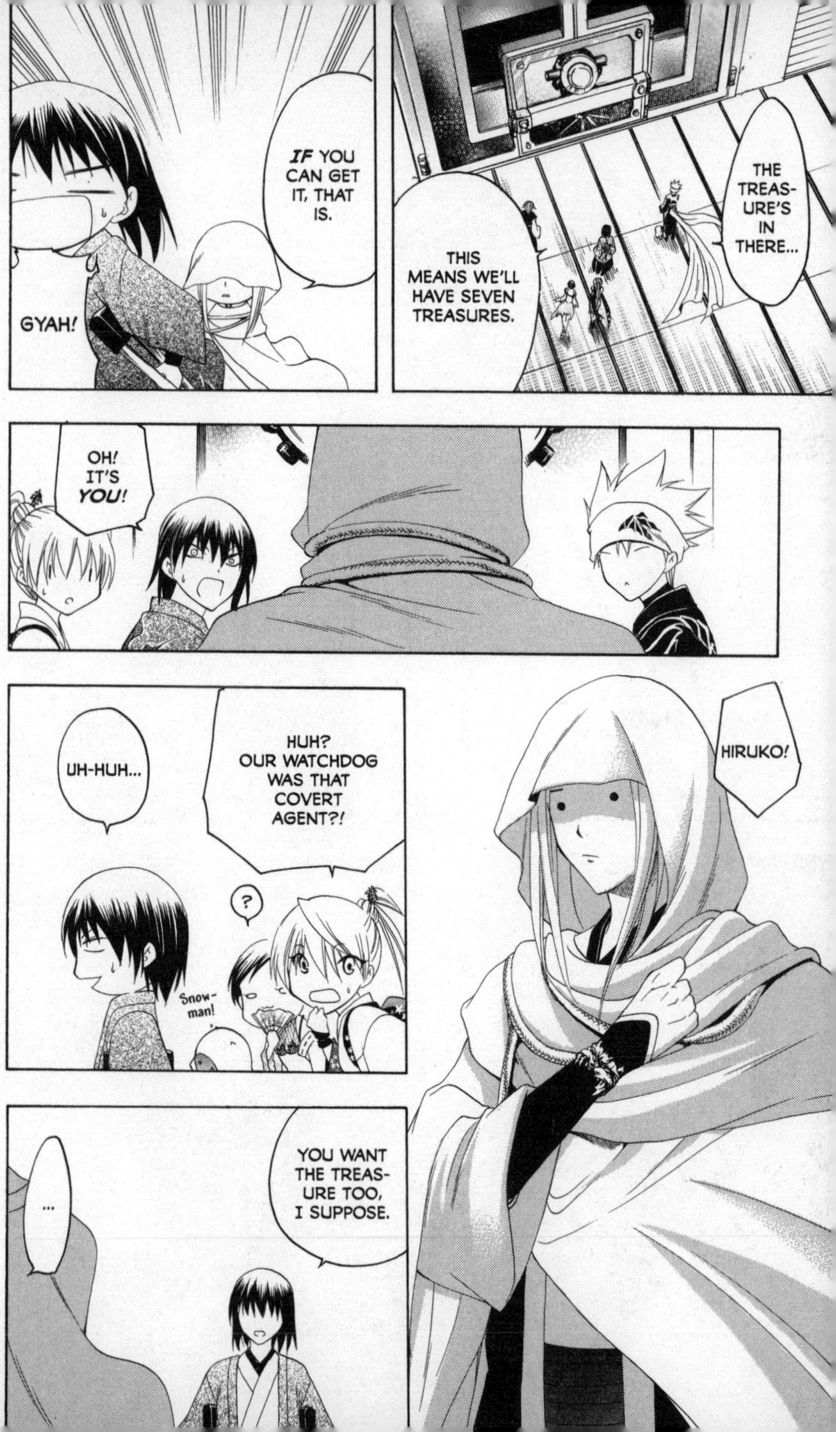
THE TREAS-URE'S IN THERE...
THIS MEANS WE'LL HAVE SEVEN TREASURES.
IF YOU CAN GET IT, THAT IS.
GYAH!
OH! IT'S YOU!
HIRUKO!
HUH? OUR WATCHDOG WAS THAT COVERT AGENT?!
UH-HUH...
?
Snow-man!
YOU WANT THE TREAS-URE TOO, I SUPPOSE.
...

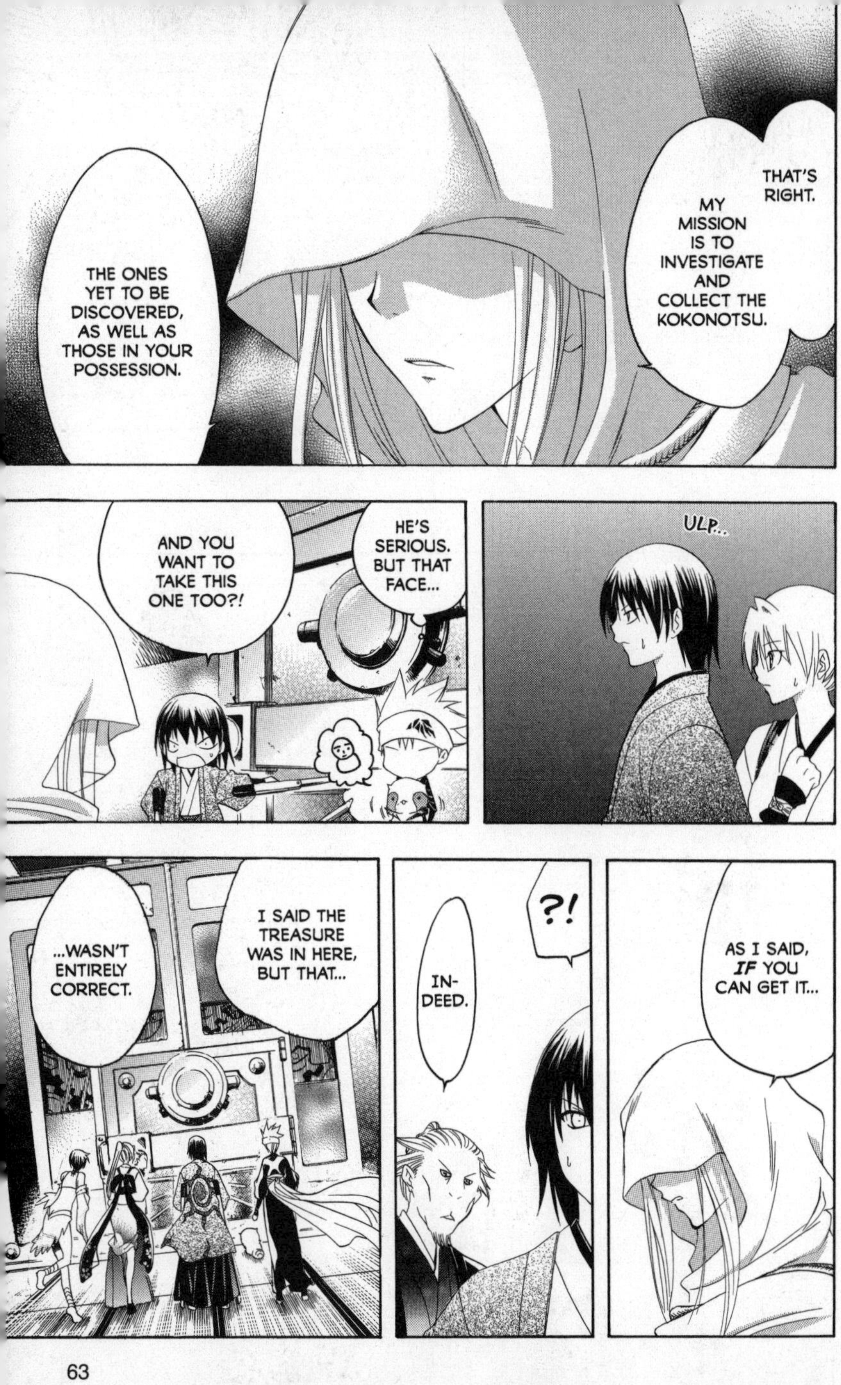
THAT'S RIGHT.
MY MISSION IS TO INVESTIGATE AND COLLECT THE KOKONOTSU.
THE ONES YET TO BE DISCOVERED, AS WELL AS THOSE IN YOUR POSSESSION.
ULP...
HE'S SERIOUS. BUT THAT FACE...
AND YOU WANT TO TAKE THIS ONE TOO?!
AS I SAID, *IF* YOU CAN GET IT...
?!
IN-DEED.
I SAID THE TREASURE WAS IN HERE, BUT THAT...
...WASN'T ENTIRELY CORRECT.

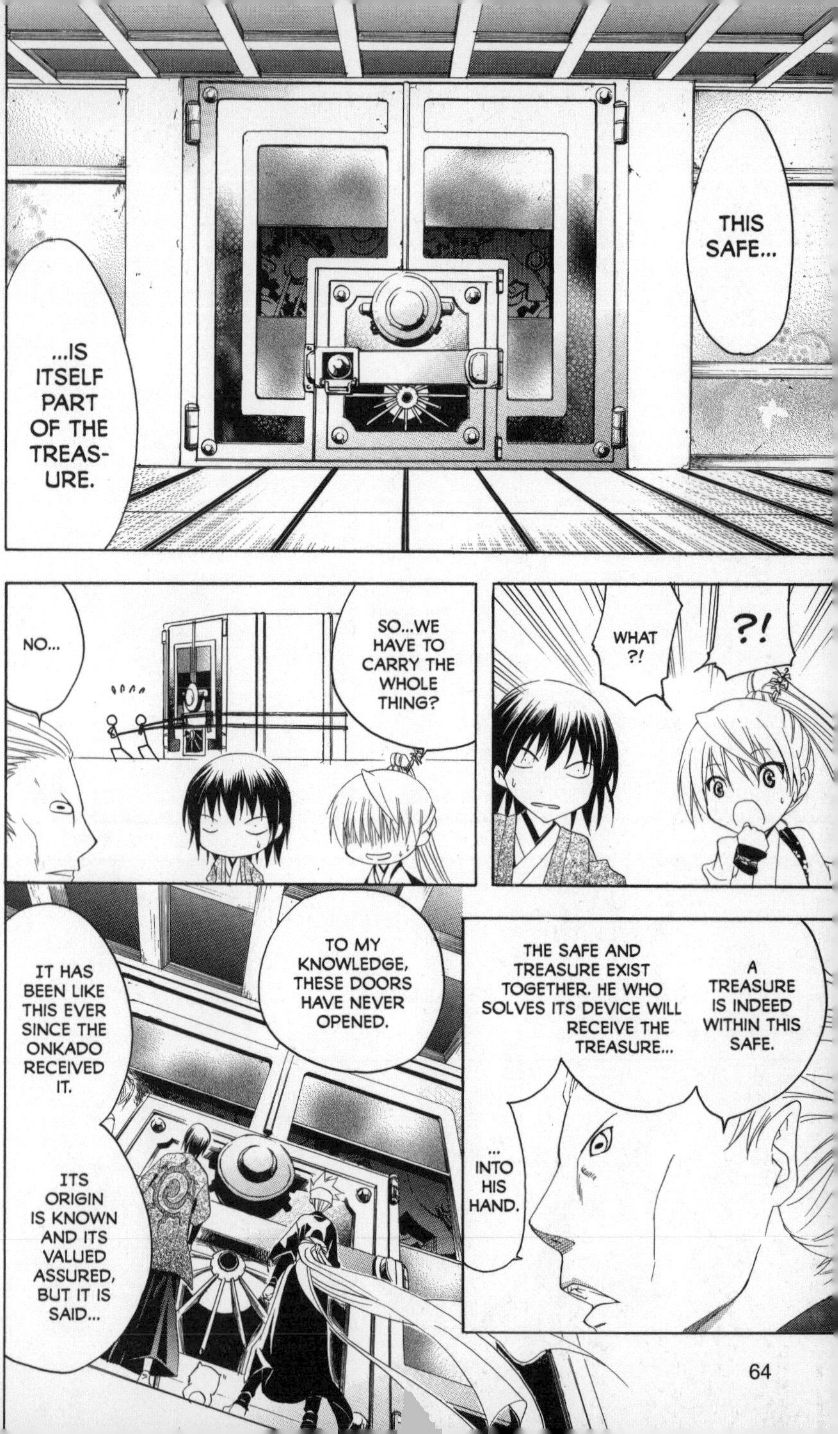
THIS SAFE...
...IS ITSELF PART OF THE TREASURE.
?!
WHAT ?!
SO...WE HAVE TO CARRY THE WHOLE THING?
NO...
A TREASURE IS INDEED WITHIN THIS SAFE.
THE SAFE AND TREASURE EXIST TOGETHER. HE WHO SOLVES ITS DEVICE WILL RECEIVE THE TREASURE...
...INTO HIS HAND.
TO MY KNOWLEDGE, THESE DOORS HAVE NEVER OPENED.
IT HAS BEEN LIKE THIS EVER SINCE THE ONKADO RECEIVED IT.
ITS ORIGIN IS KNOWN AND ITS VALUED ASSURED, BUT IT IS SAID...

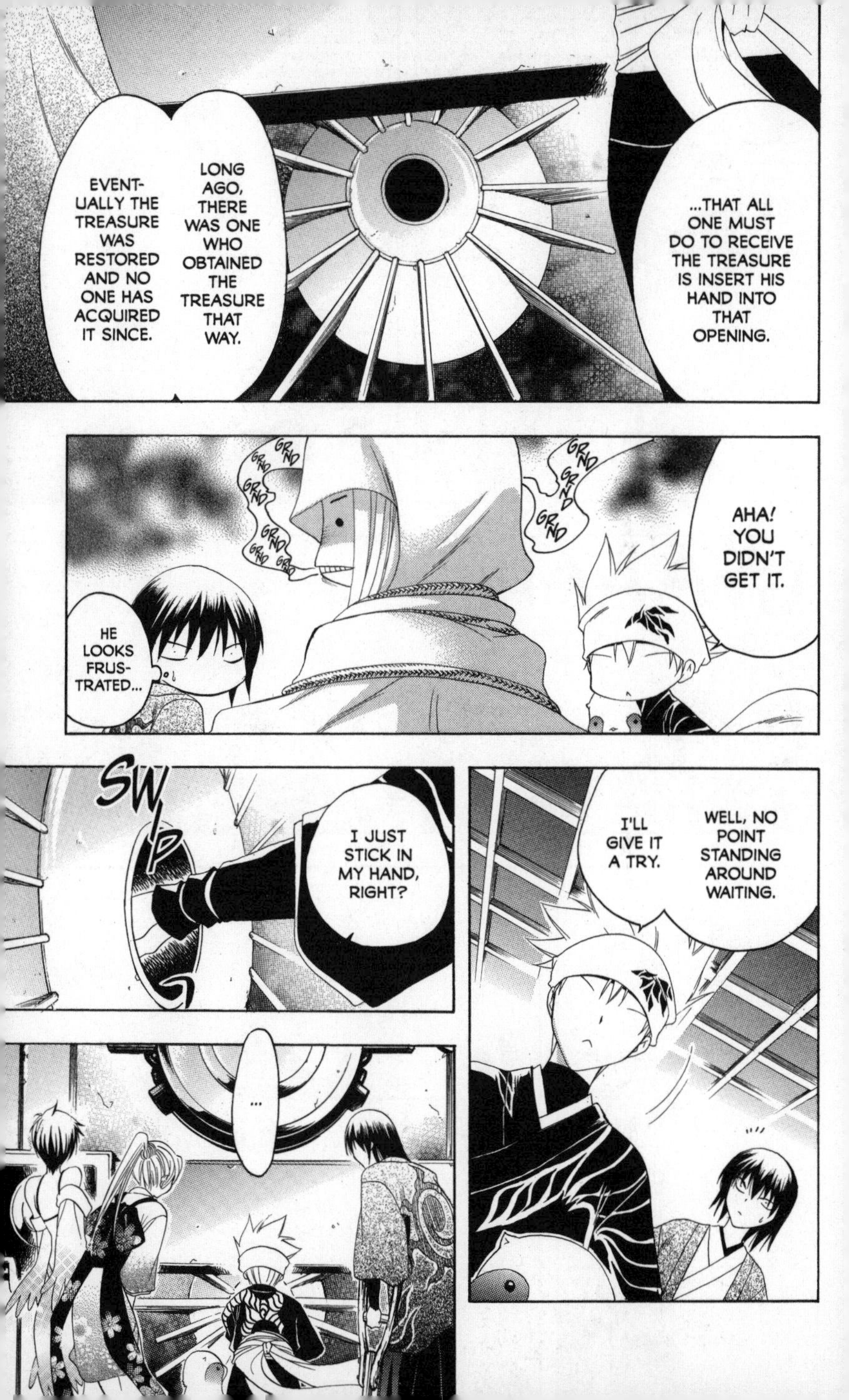
...THAT ALL ONE MUST DO TO RECEIVE THE TREASURE IS INSERT HIS HAND INTO THAT OPENING.
LONG AGO, THERE WAS ONE WHO OBTAINED THE TREASURE THAT WAY.
EVENT-UALLY THE TREASURE WAS RESTORED AND NO ONE HAS ACQUIRED IT SINCE.
AHA! YOU DIDN'T GET IT.
GRND GRND GRND
GRND GRND GRND GRND GRND
HE LOOKS FRUS-TRATED...
WELL, NO POINT STANDING AROUND WAITING.
I'LL GIVE IT A TRY.
I JUST STICK IN MY HAND, RIGHT?
SWIP
...

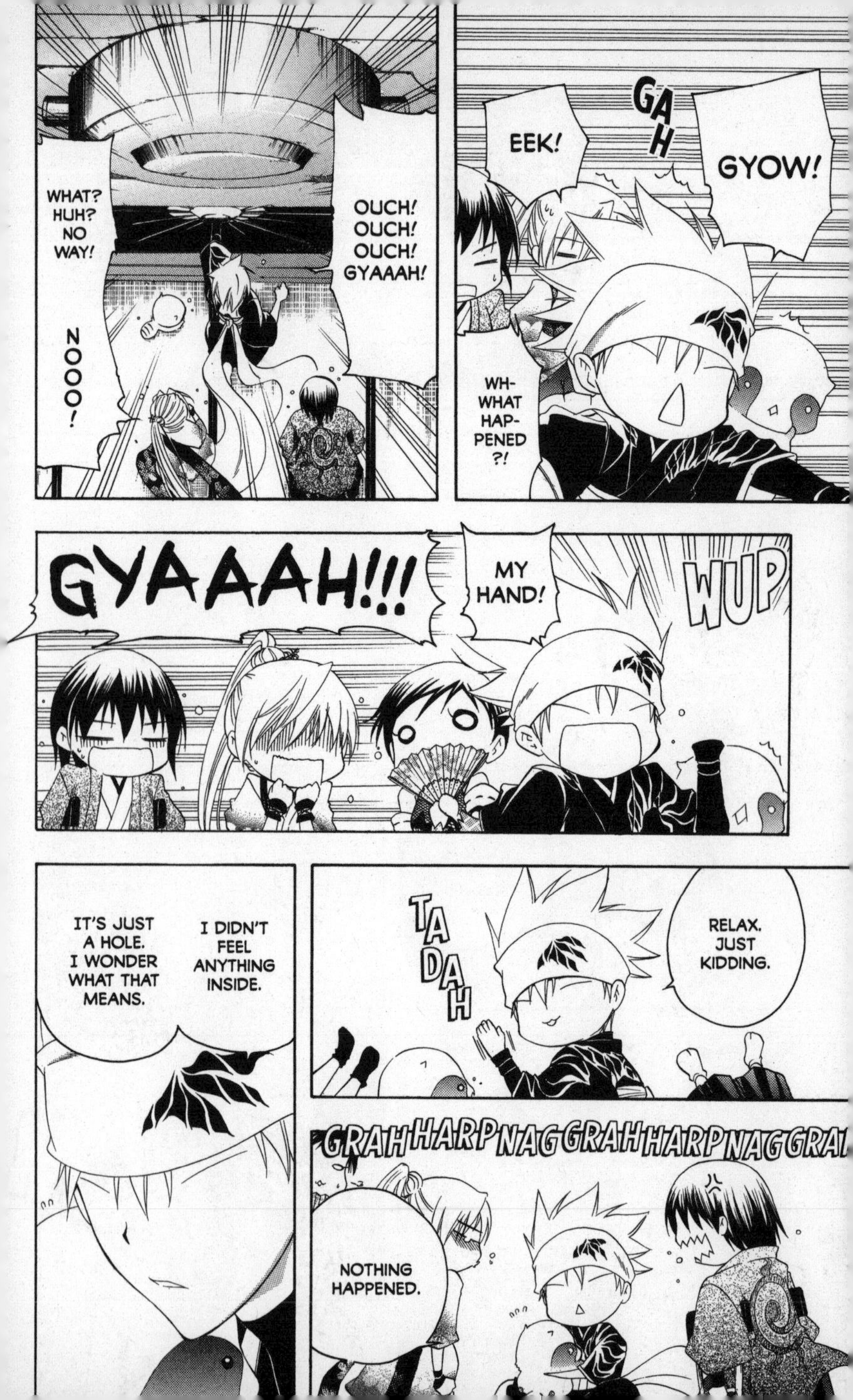
GYOW!
GAH
EEK!
WH-WHAT HAP-PENED?!
OUCH! OUCH! OUCH! GYAAAH!
WHAT? HUH? NO WAY!
NOOOO!
WUP
MY HAND!
GYAAAH!!!
RELAX. JUST KIDDING.
TADAH
GRAHHARPNAGGRAHHARPNAGGRAI
NOTHING HAPPENED.
I DIDN'T FEEL ANYTHING INSIDE.
IT'S JUST A HOLE. I WONDER WHAT THAT MEANS.

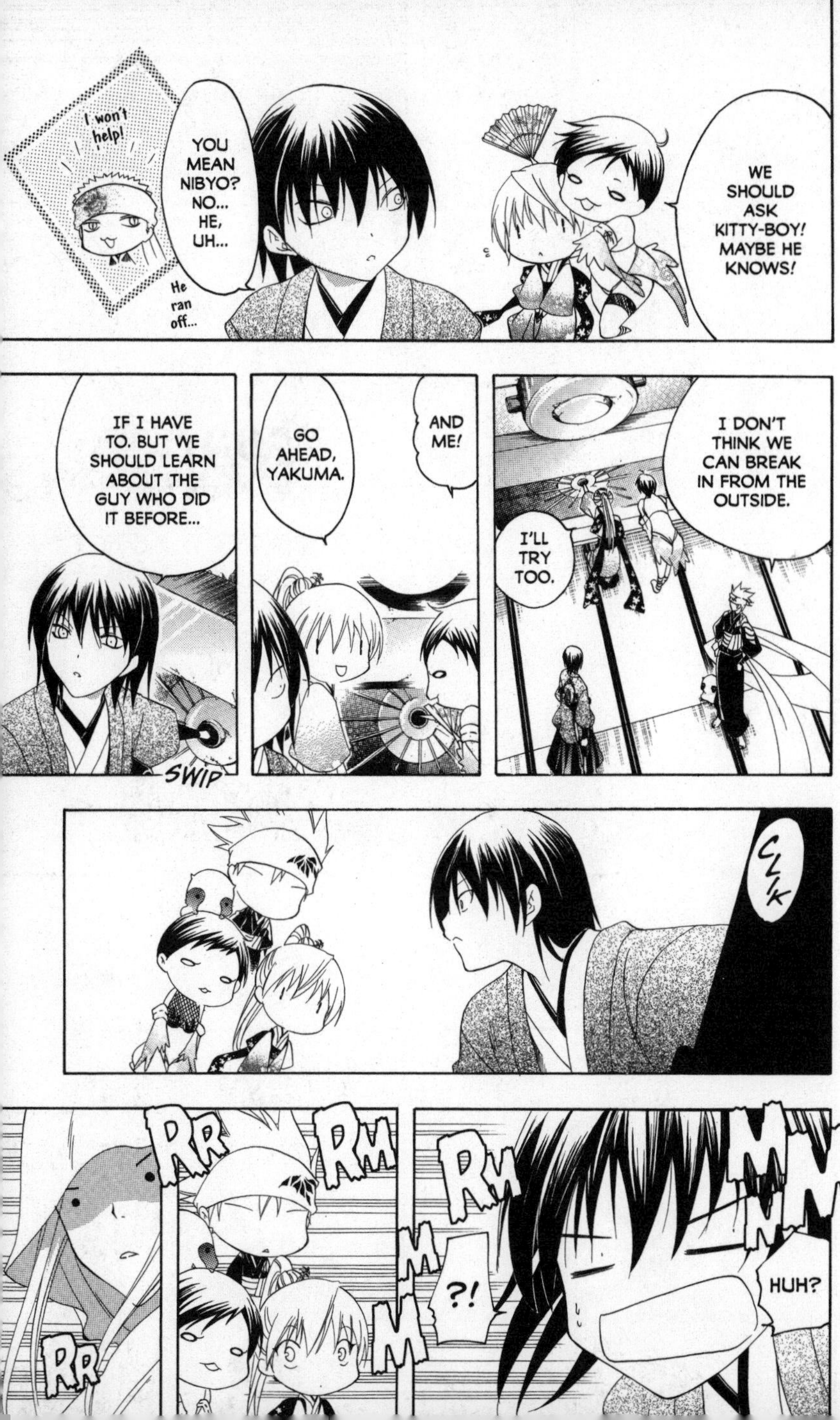
WE SHOULD ASK KITTY-BOY! MAYBE HE KNOWS!
YOU MEAN NIBYO? NO... HE, UH...
He ran off...
I won't help!
I DON'T THINK WE CAN BREAK IN FROM THE OUTSIDE.
I'LL TRY TOO.
AND ME!
GO AHEAD, YAKUMA.
IF I HAVE TO. BUT WE SHOULD LEARN ABOUT THE GUY WHO DID IT BEFORE...
SWIP
CLIK
MM
NM
HUH?
RM
?!
M
M
RR
RM
RR

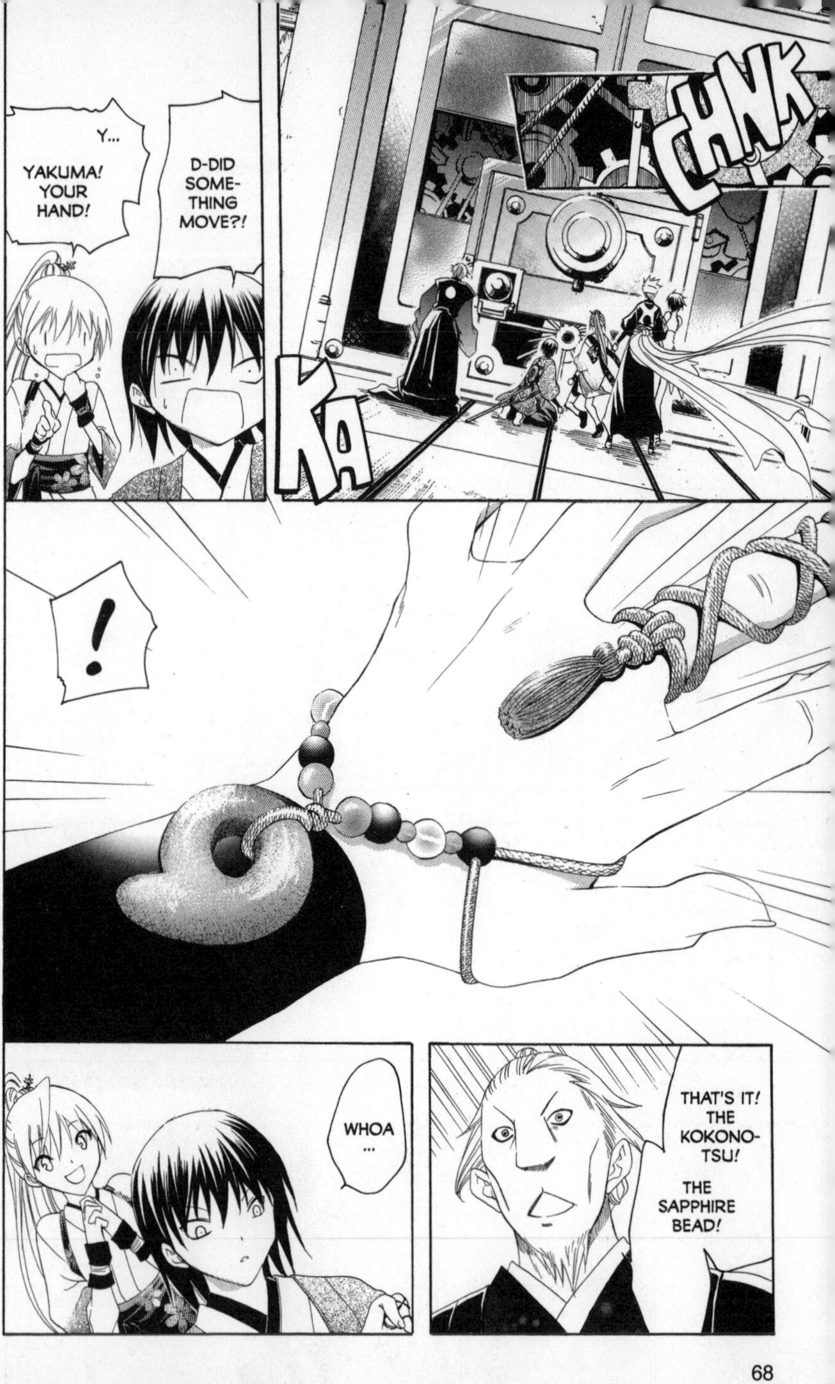
CHNK
KA
D-DID SOMETHING MOVE?!
Y... YAKUMA! YOUR HAND!
!
THAT'S IT! THE KOKONOTSU!
THE SAPPHIRE BEAD!
WHOA ...

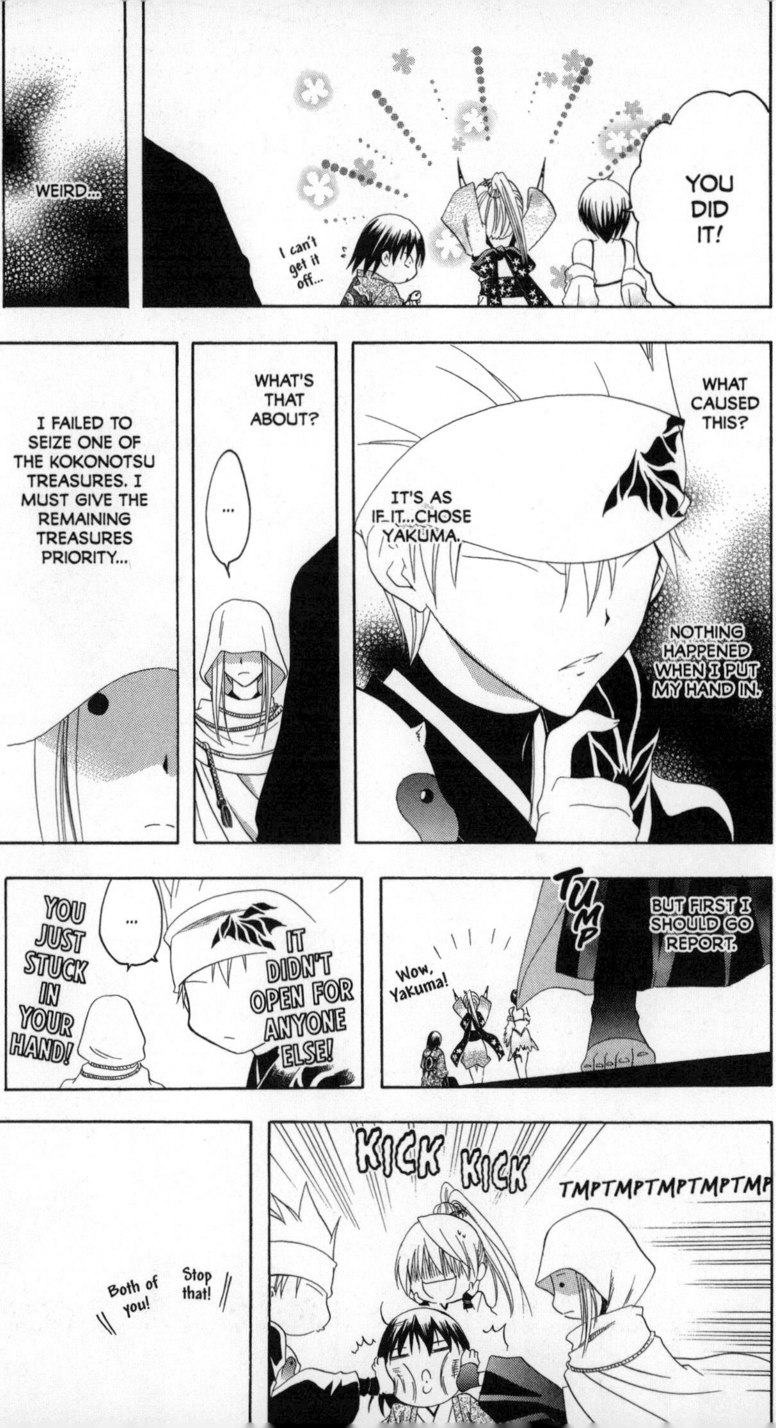
YOU DID IT!
I can't get it off...
WEIRD...
WHAT CAUSED THIS?
IT'S AS IF IT...CHOSE YAKUMA.
NOTHING HAPPENED WHEN I PUT MY HAND IN.
WHAT'S THAT ABOUT?
...
I FAILED TO SEIZE ONE OF THE KOKONOTSU TREASURES. I MUST GIVE THE REMAINING TREASURES PRIORITY...
TUMP
BUT FIRST I SHOULD GO REPORT.
Wow, Yakuma!
IT DIDN'T OPEN FOR ANYONE ELSE!
...
YOU JUST STUCK IN YOUR HAND!
KICK KICK
TMPTMPTMPTMPTMP
Stop that!
Both of you!

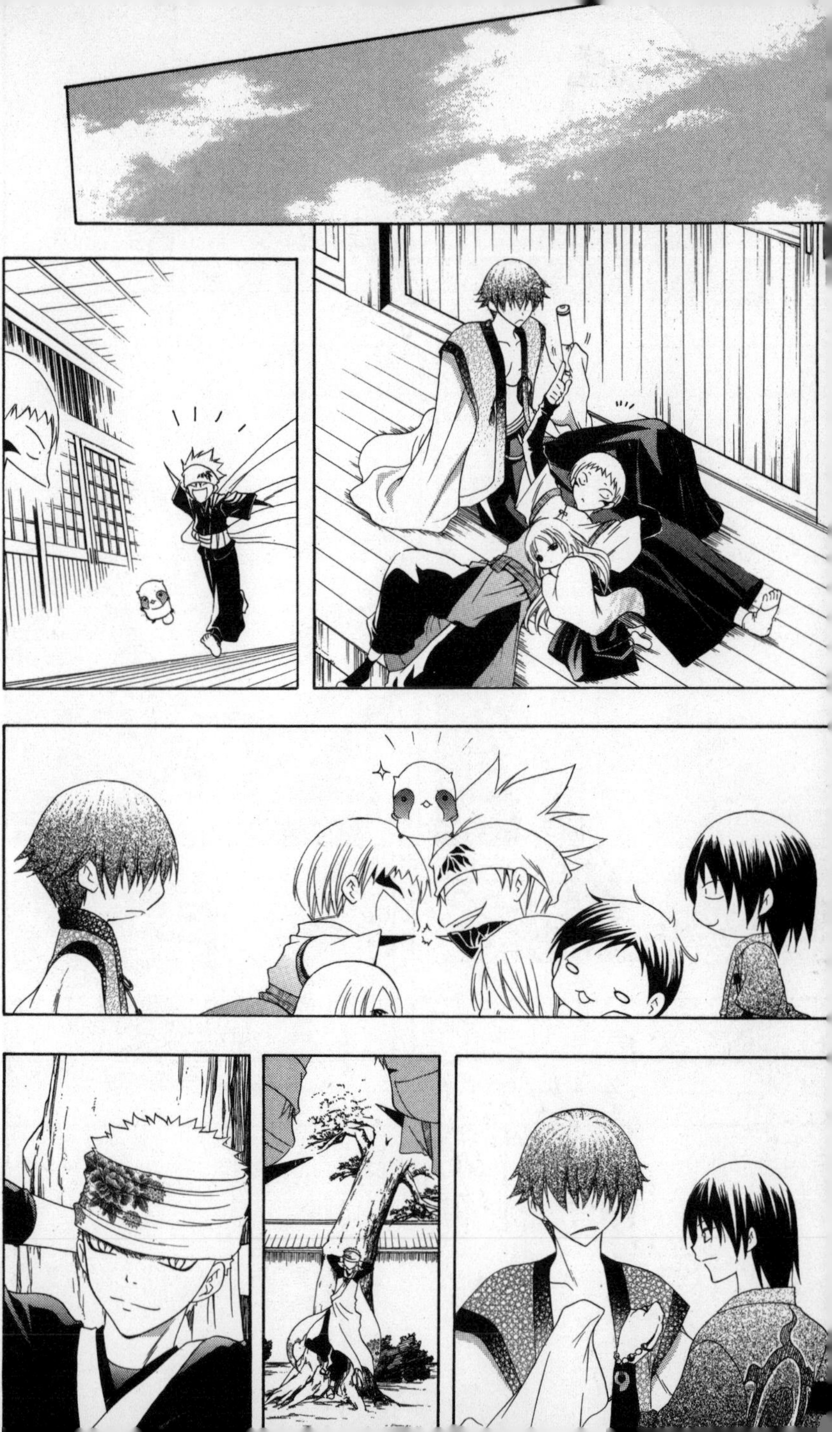

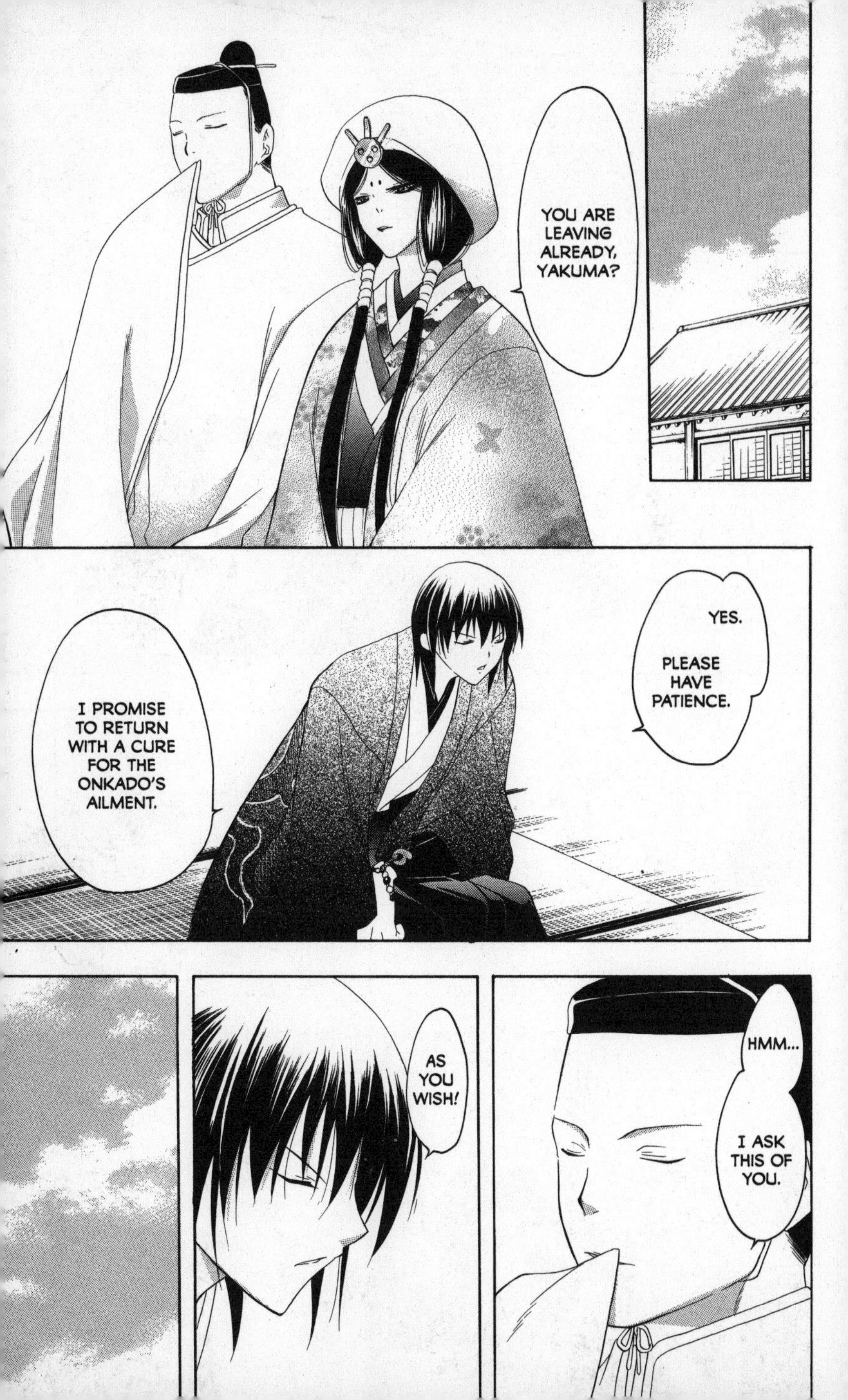
YOU ARE LEAVING ALREADY, YAKUMA?
YES.
PLEASE HAVE PATIENCE.
I PROMISE TO RETURN WITH A CURE FOR THE ONKADO'S AILMENT.
HMM...
I ASK THIS OF YOU.
AS YOU WISH!

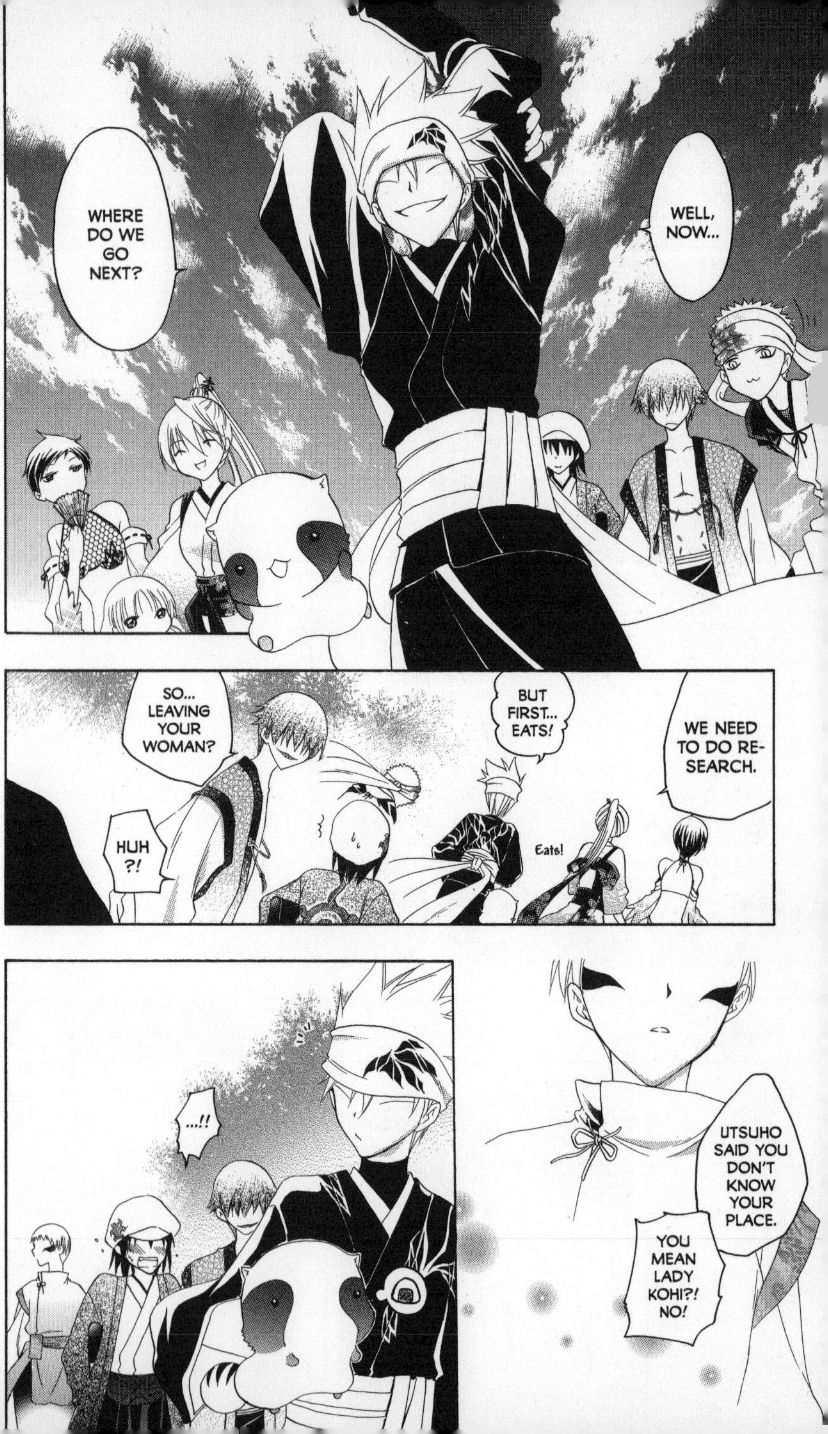
WELL, NOW...
WHERE DO WE GO NEXT?
WE NEED TO DO RE-SEARCH.
BUT FIRST... EATS!
SO... LEAVING YOUR WOMAN?
Eats!
HUH?!
UTSUHO SAID YOU DON'T KNOW YOUR PLACE.
YOU MEAN LADY KOHI?! NO!
...!!

...LET'S GO.

UZUME...

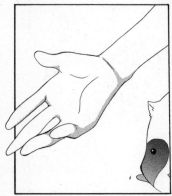

YEAH...

...OKAY!

HEY, KUROHA. CAN I DO THIS?

I'M GOING TO WORK HARD TO MAKE...

...A HAPPY WORLD.

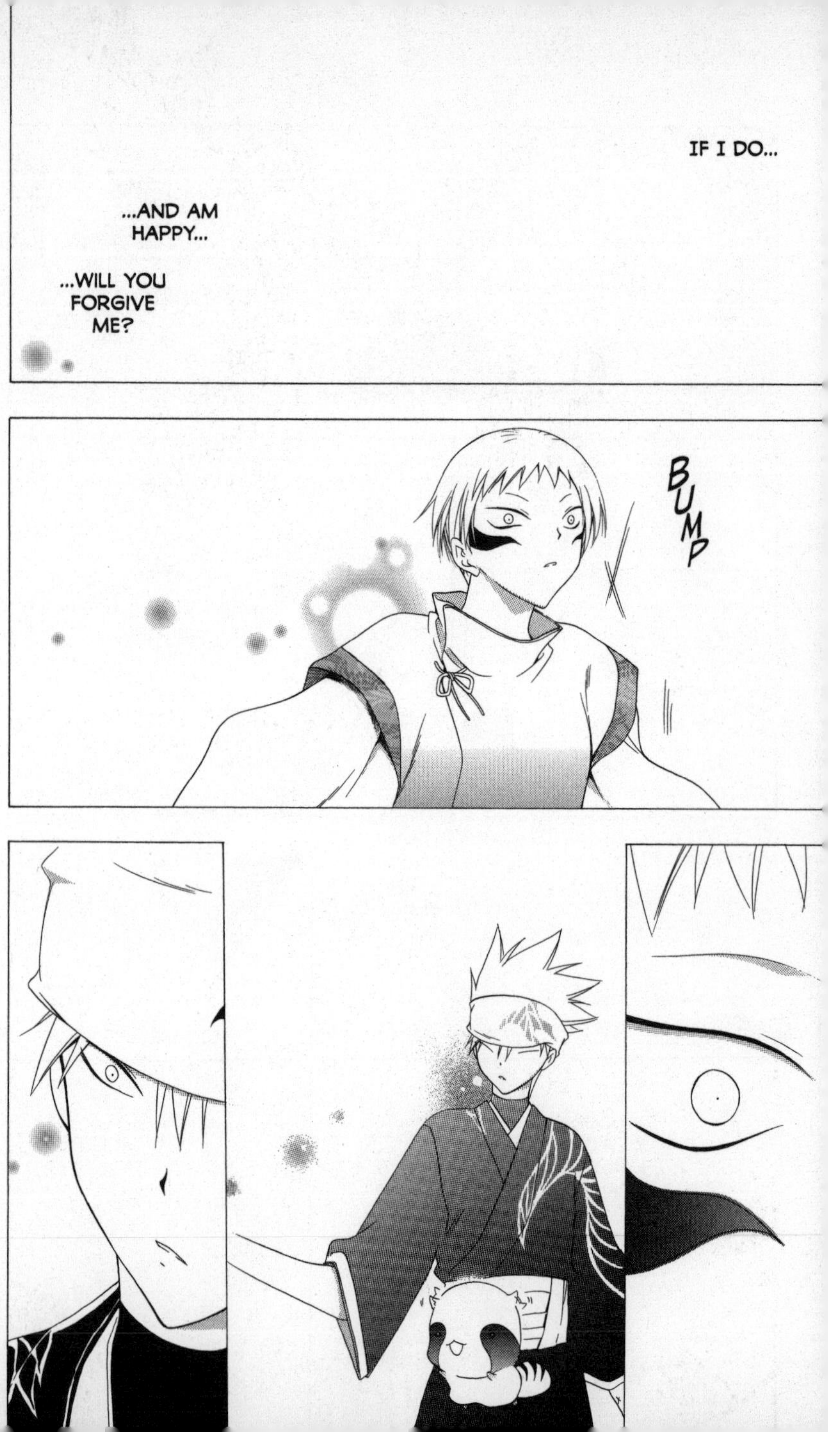
IF I DO...
...AND AM HAPPY...
...WILL YOU FORGIVE ME?
BUMP

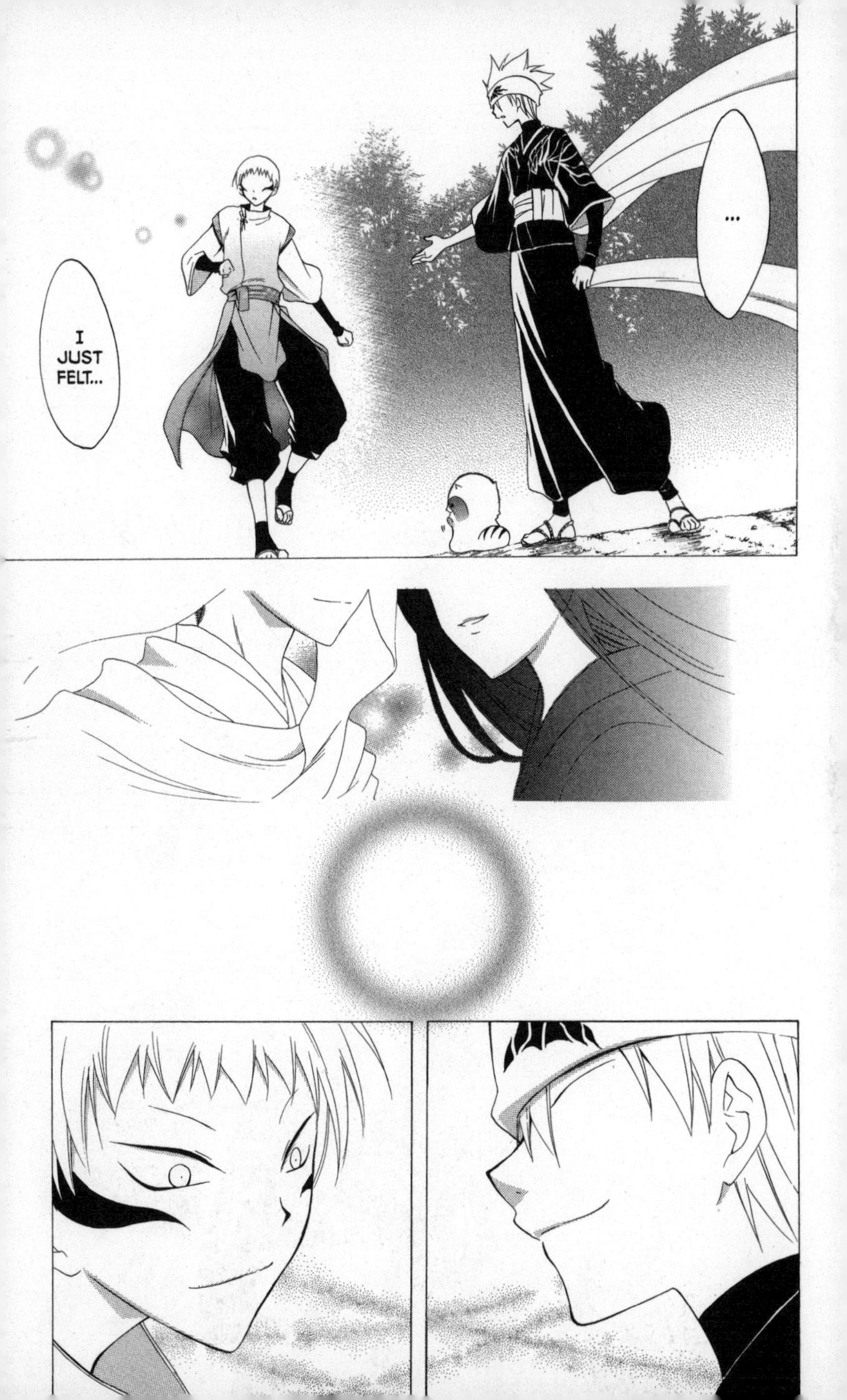
...
I JUST FELT...

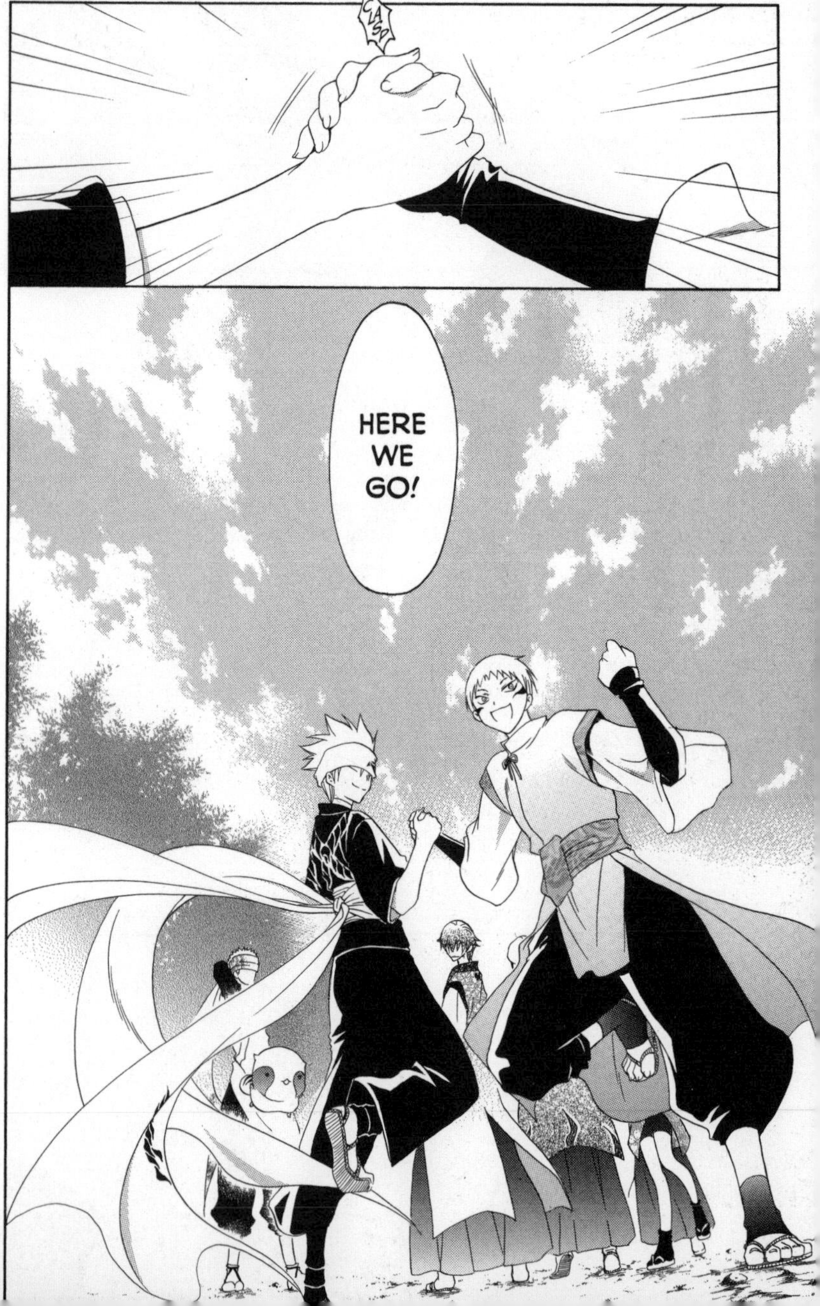
CLASP
HERE WE GO!

Chapter 112 Comrades

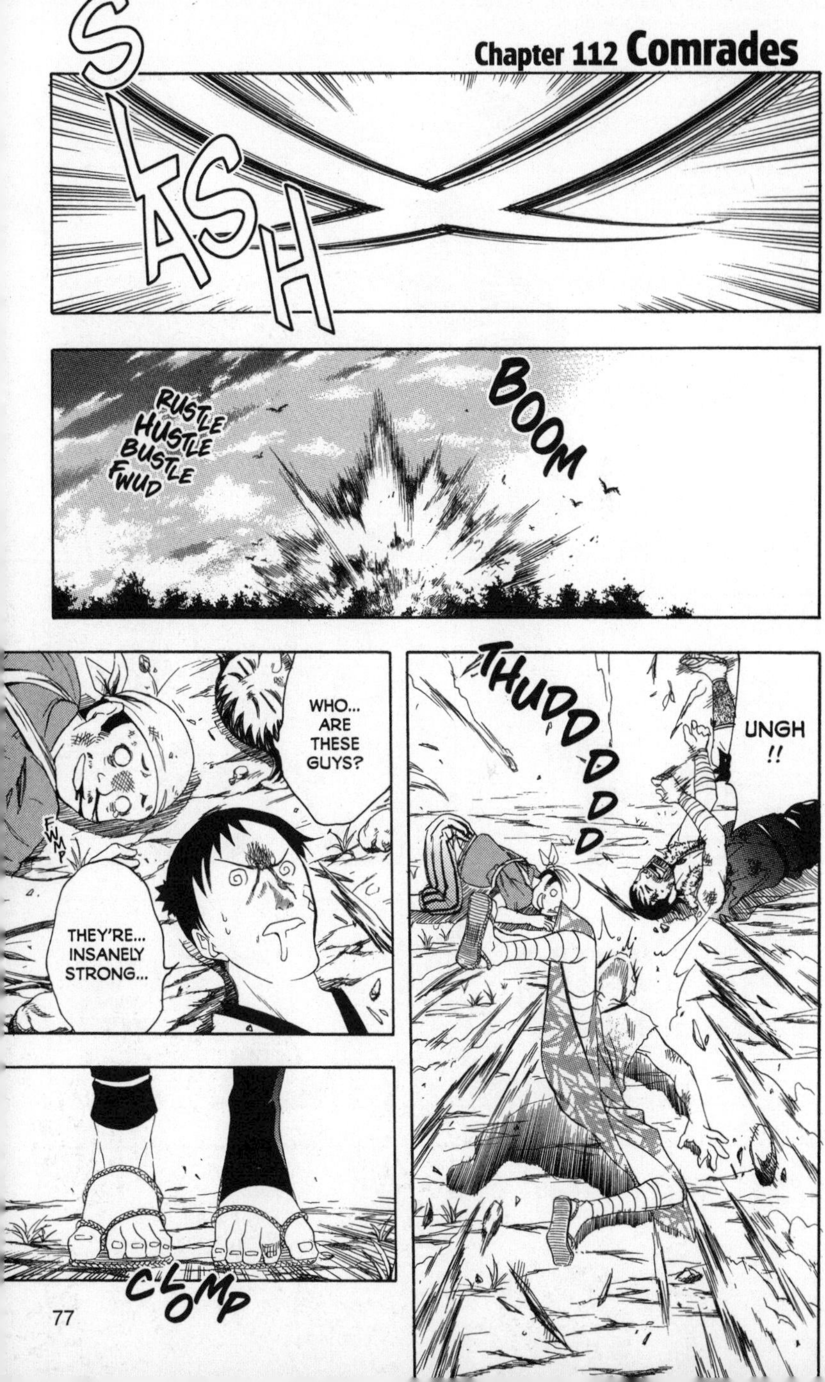
SLASH
BOOM
RUSTLE
HUSTLE
BUSTLE
FWUD
THUDDDDD
UNGH !!
WHO... ARE THESE GUYS?
FWMP
THEY'RE... INSANELY STRONG...
CLOMP

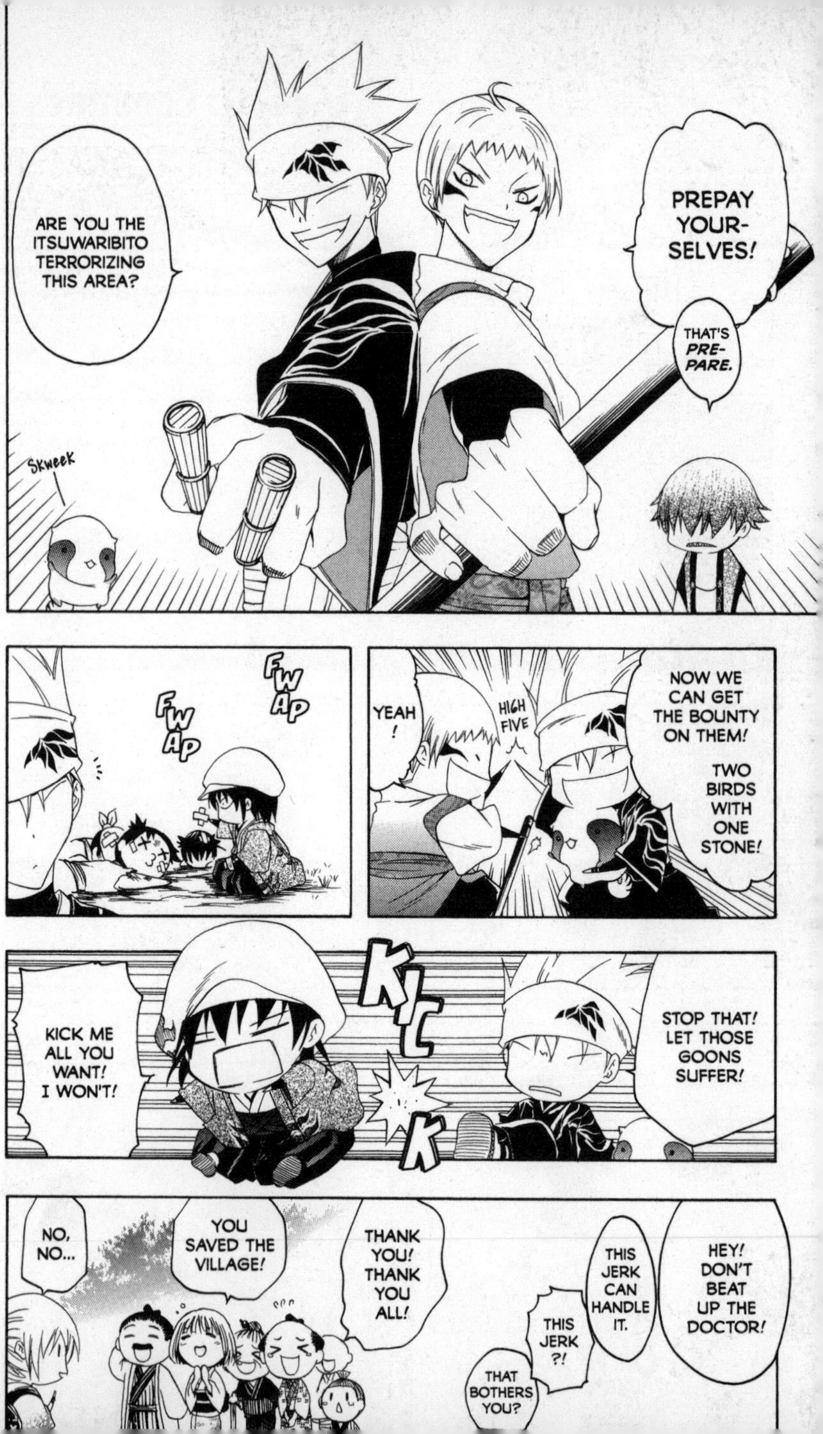
PREPAY YOUR-SELVES!
THAT'S PRE-PARE.
ARE YOU THE ITSUWARIBITO TERRORIZING THIS AREA?
Skweek
NOW WE CAN GET THE BOUNTY ON THEM!
TWO BIRDS WITH ONE STONE!
HIGH FIVE
YEAH!
FWAP
FWAP
STOP THAT! LET THOSE GOONS SUFFER!
KICK
KICK ME ALL YOU WANT! I WON'T!
HEY! DON'T BEAT UP THE DOCTOR!
THIS JERK CAN HANDLE IT.
THIS JERK?!
THAT BOTHERS YOU?
THANK YOU! THANK YOU ALL!
YOU SAVED THE VILLAGE!
NO, NO...

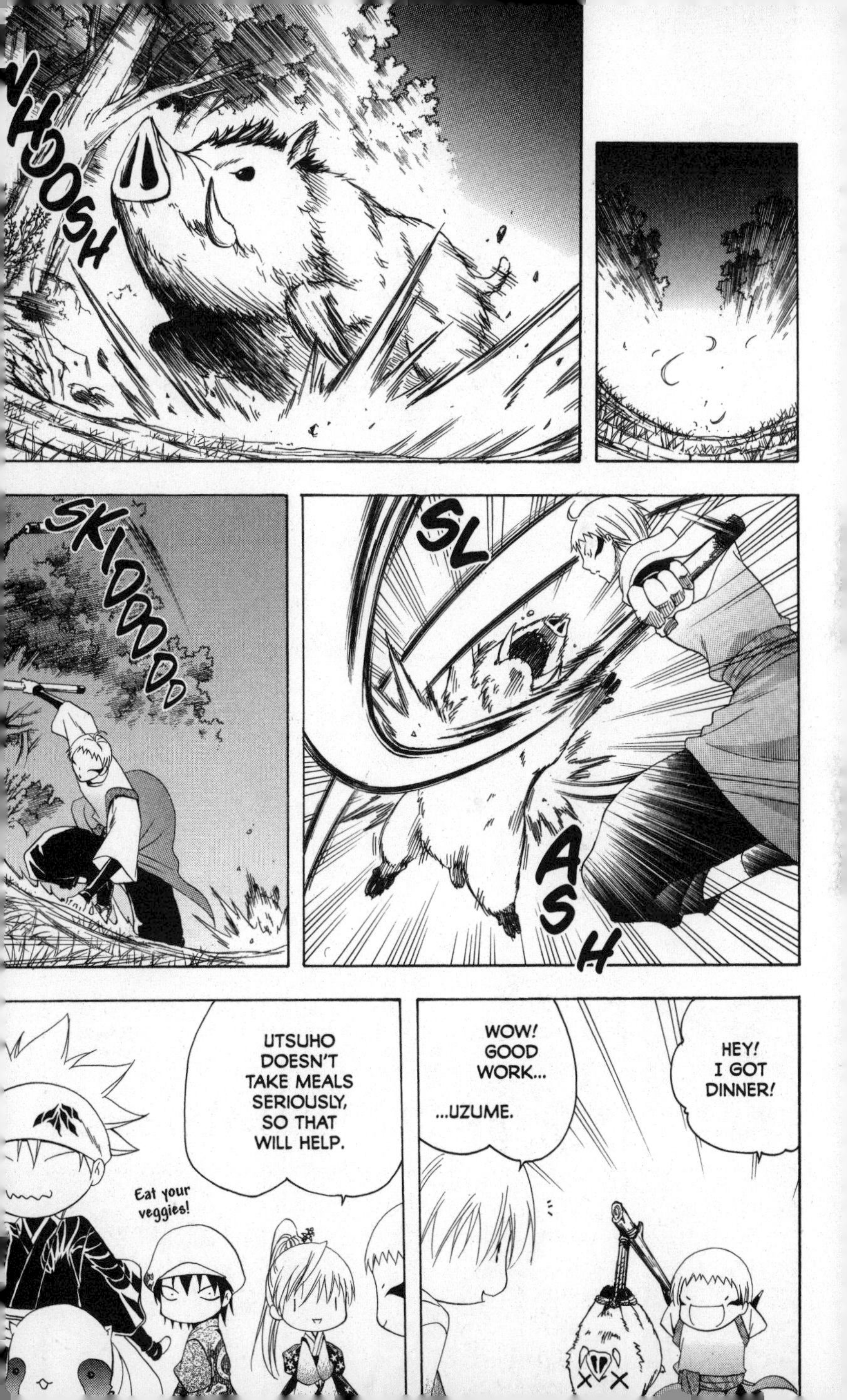
WHOOSH
SLASH
SKIDOOOOO
HEY! I GOT DINNER!
WOW! GOOD WORK...
...UZUME.
UTSUHO DOESN'T TAKE MEALS SERIOUSLY, SO THAT WILL HELP.
Eat your veggies!

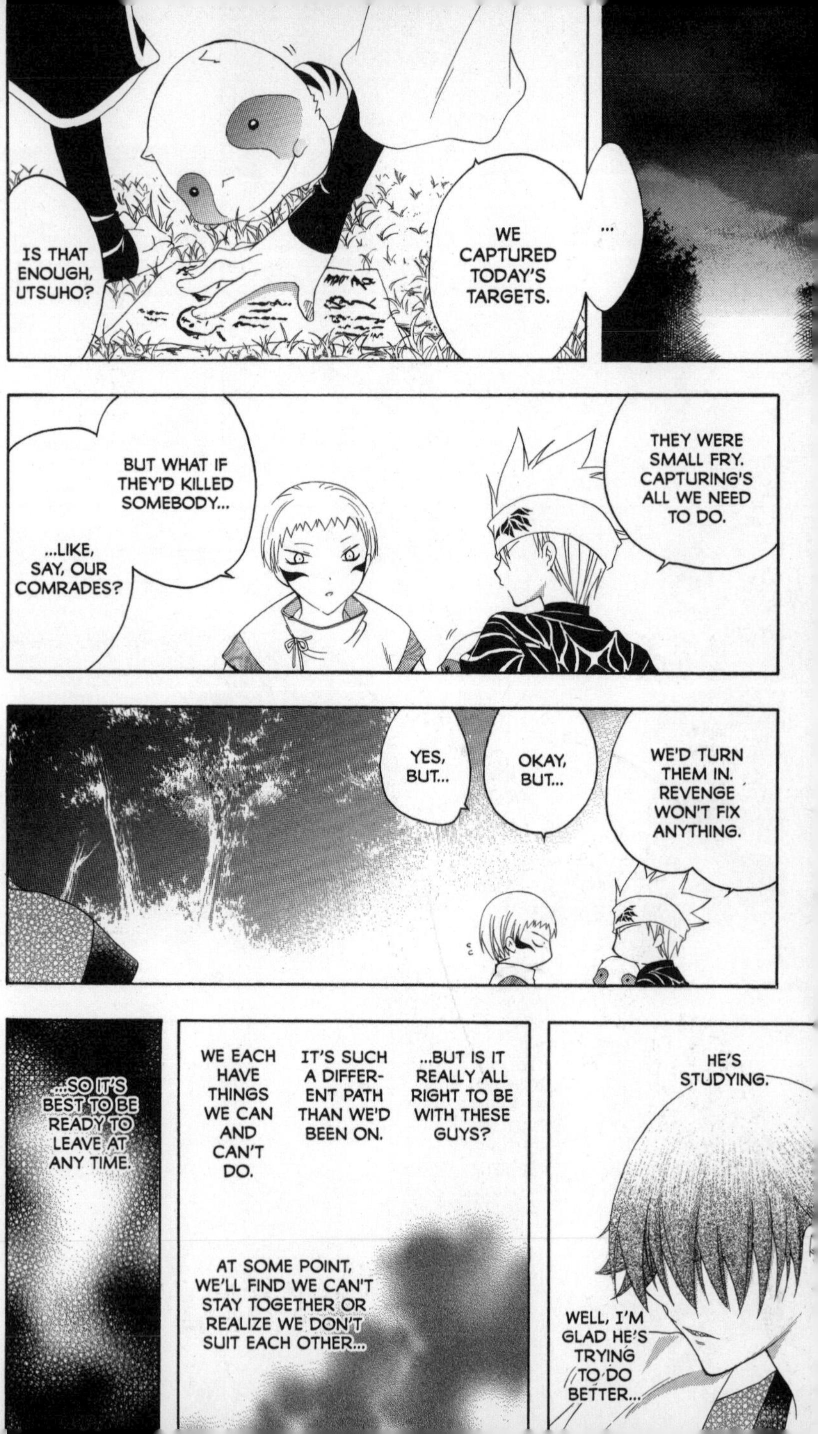
...
WE CAPTURED TODAY'S TARGETS.
IS THAT ENOUGH, UTSUHO?
THEY WERE SMALL FRY. CAPTURING'S ALL WE NEED TO DO.
BUT WHAT IF THEY'D KILLED SOMEBODY...
...LIKE, SAY, OUR COMRADES?
WE'D TURN THEM IN. REVENGE WON'T FIX ANYTHING.
OKAY, BUT...
YES, BUT...
HE'S STUDYING.
WELL, I'M GLAD HE'S TRYING TO DO BETTER...
...BUT IS IT REALLY ALL RIGHT TO BE WITH THESE GUYS?
IT'S SUCH A DIFFERENT PATH THAN WE'D BEEN ON.
WE EACH HAVE THINGS WE CAN AND CAN'T DO.
AT SOME POINT, WE'LL FIND WE CAN'T STAY TOGETHER OR REALIZE WE DON'T SUIT EACH OTHER...
...SO IT'S BEST TO BE READY TO LEAVE AT ANY TIME.

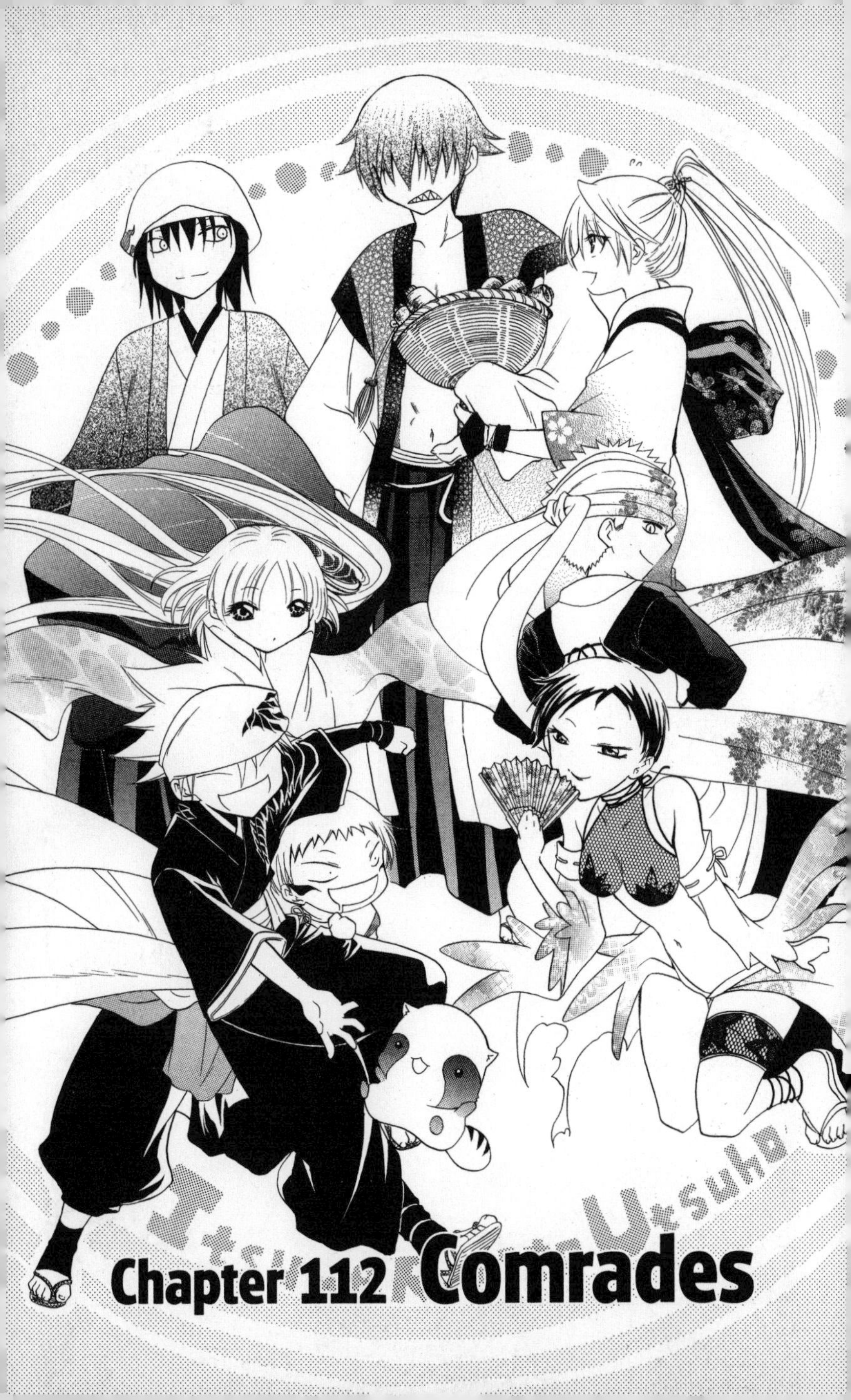

Chapter 112 Comrades

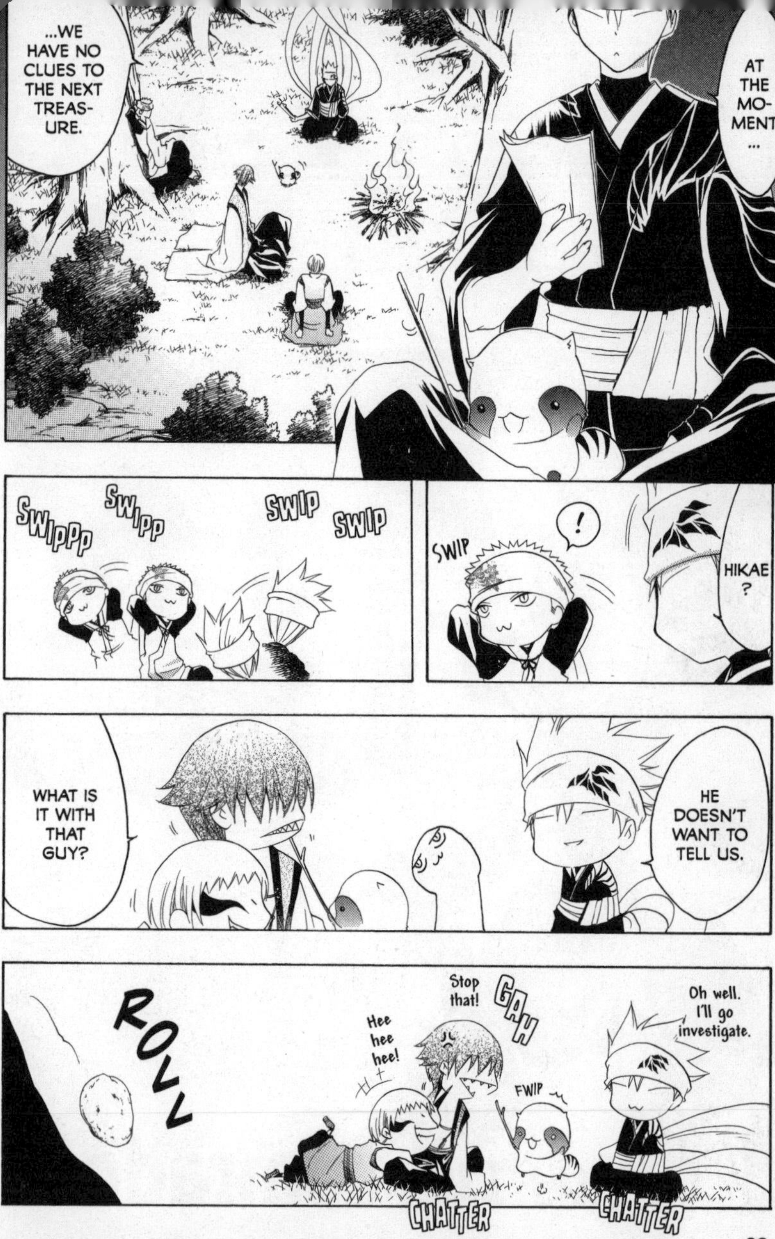
AT THE MO-MENT ...
...WE HAVE NO CLUES TO THE NEXT TREAS-URE.
HIKAE ?
!
SWIP
SWIP
SWIP
SWIPP
SWIPPP
HE DOESN'T WANT TO TELL US.
WHAT IS IT WITH THAT GUY?
Oh well. I'll go investigate.
CHATTER
GAH
Stop that!
FWIP
Hee hee hee!
CHATTER
ROLL

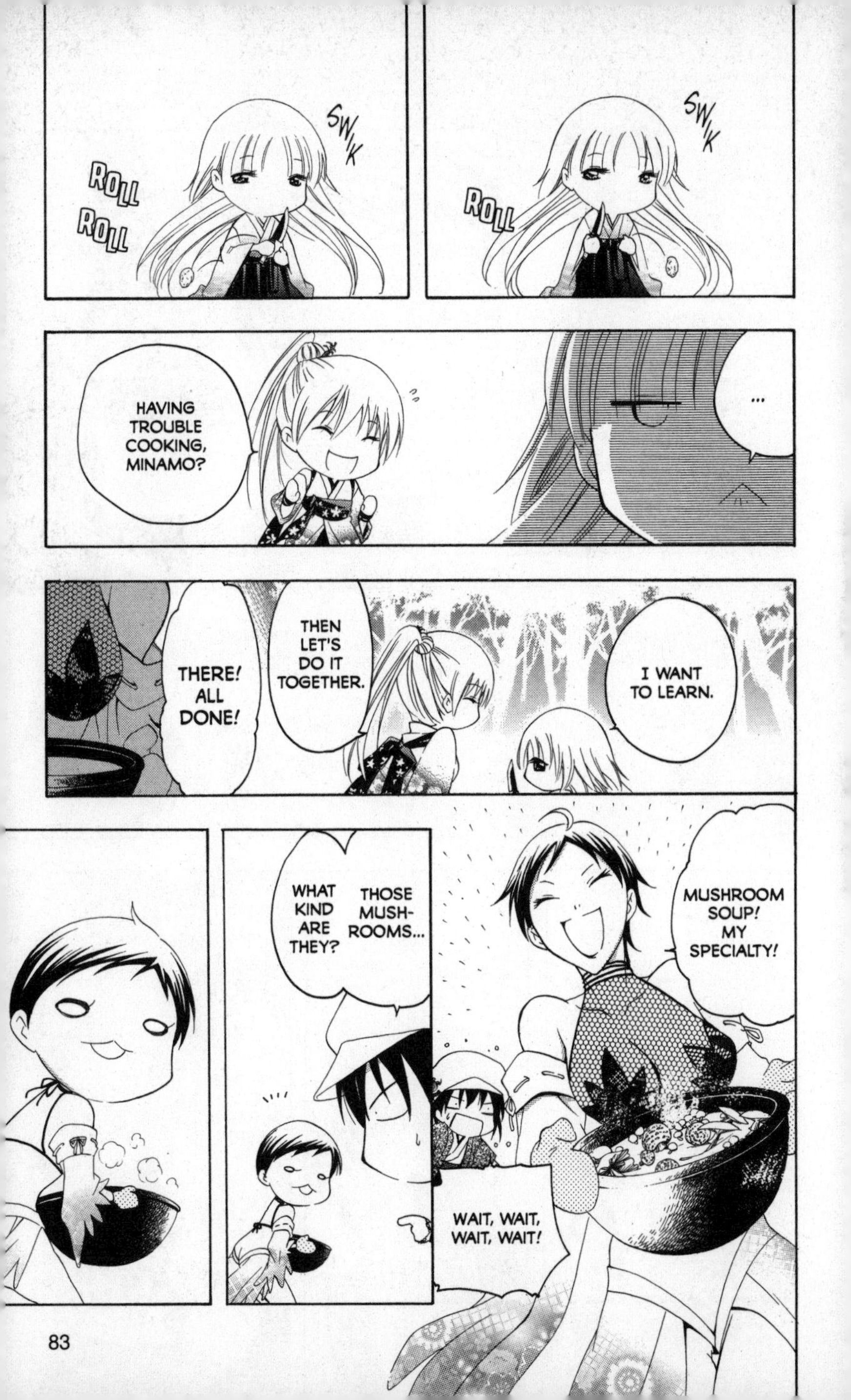
SWIK
ROLL
SWIK
ROLL ROLL
...
HAVING TROUBLE COOKING, MINAMO?
I WANT TO LEARN.
THEN LET'S DO IT TOGETHER.
THERE! ALL DONE!
MUSHROOM SOUP! MY SPECIALTY!
THOSE MUSH-ROOMS...
WHAT KIND ARE THEY?
WAIT, WAIT, WAIT, WAIT!

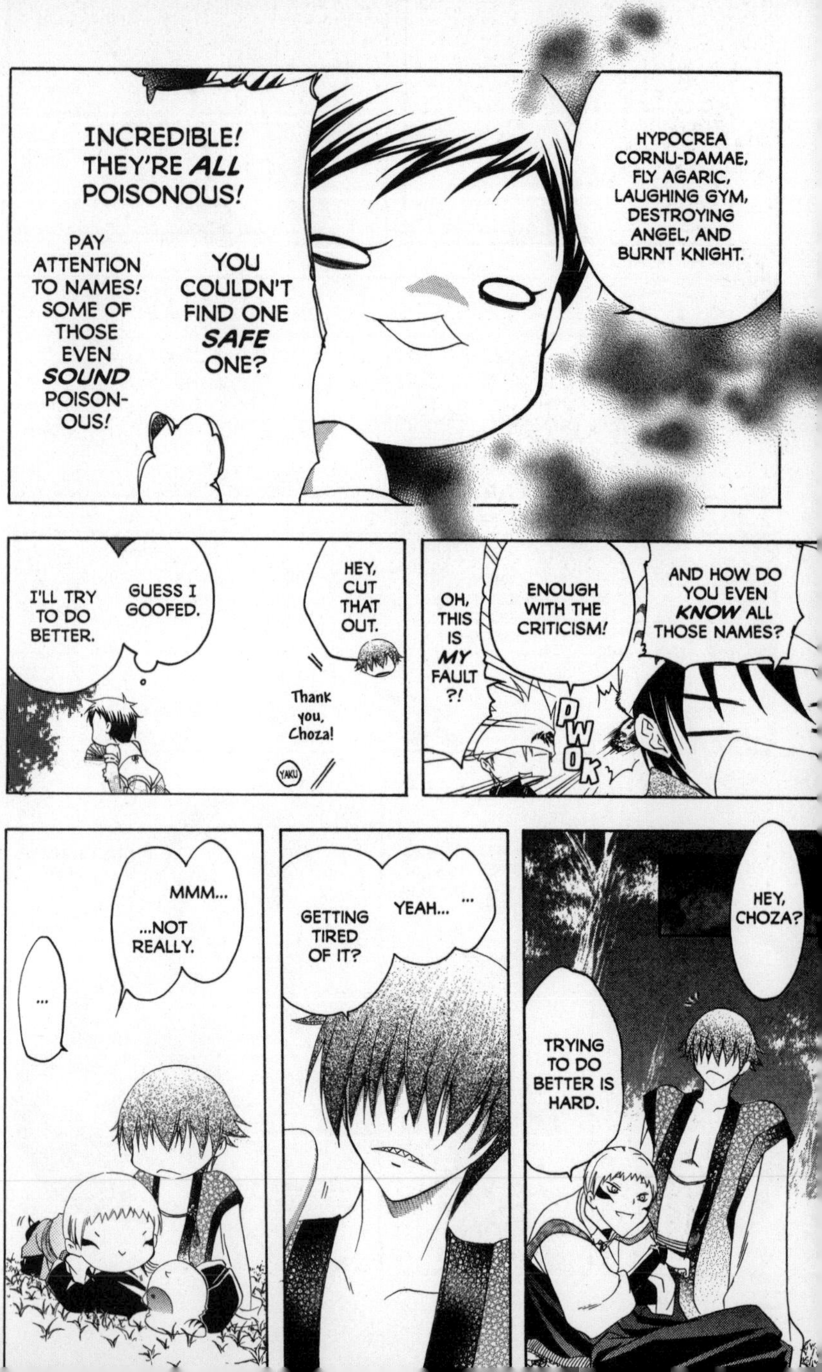
HYPOCREA CORNU-DAMAE, FLY AGARIC, LAUGHING GYM, DESTROYING ANGEL, AND BURNT KNIGHT.
INCREDIBLE! THEY'RE *ALL* POISONOUS!
YOU COULDN'T FIND ONE *SAFE* ONE?
PAY ATTENTION TO NAMES! SOME OF THOSE EVEN *SOUND* POISON-OUS!
AND HOW DO YOU EVEN *KNOW* ALL THOSE NAMES?
PWOK
ENOUGH WITH THE CRITICISM!
OH, THIS IS *MY* FAULT?!
HEY, CUT THAT OUT.
Thank you, Choza!
YAKU
GUESS I GOOFED.
I'LL TRY TO DO BETTER.
HEY, CHOZA?
TRYING TO DO BETTER IS HARD.
...
YEAH...
GETTING TIRED OF IT?
MMM...
...NOT REALLY.
...

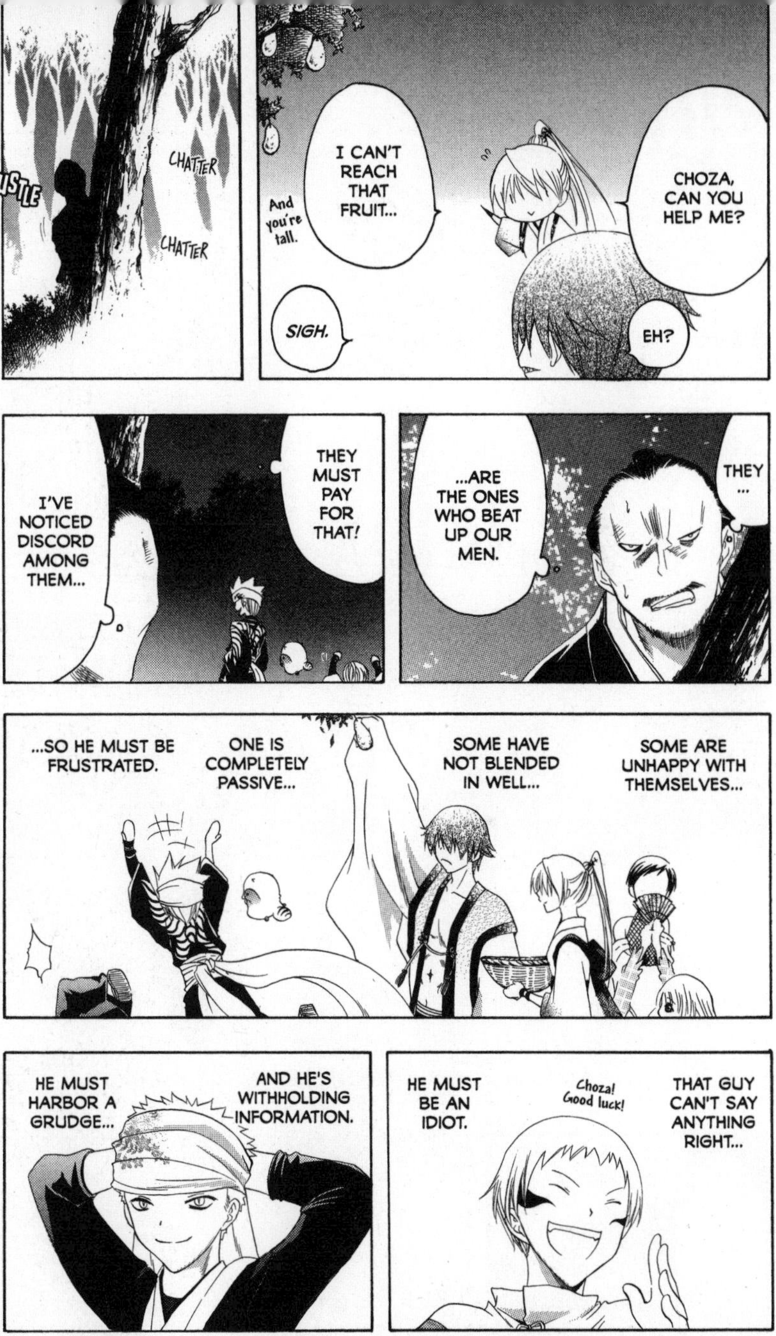
CHOZA, CAN YOU HELP ME?
I CAN'T REACH THAT FRUIT...
And you're tall.
EH?
SIGH.
RUSTLE
CHATTER
CHATTER
THEY ...
...ARE THE ONES WHO BEAT UP OUR MEN.
THEY MUST PAY FOR THAT!
I'VE NOTICED DISCORD AMONG THEM...
SOME ARE UNHAPPY WITH THEMSELVES...
SOME HAVE NOT BLENDED IN WELL...
ONE IS COMPLETELY PASSIVE...
...SO HE MUST BE FRUSTRATED.
THAT GUY CAN'T SAY ANYTHING RIGHT...
Choza! Good luck!
HE MUST BE AN IDIOT.
AND HE'S WITHHOLDING INFORMATION.
HE MUST HARBOR A GRUDGE...

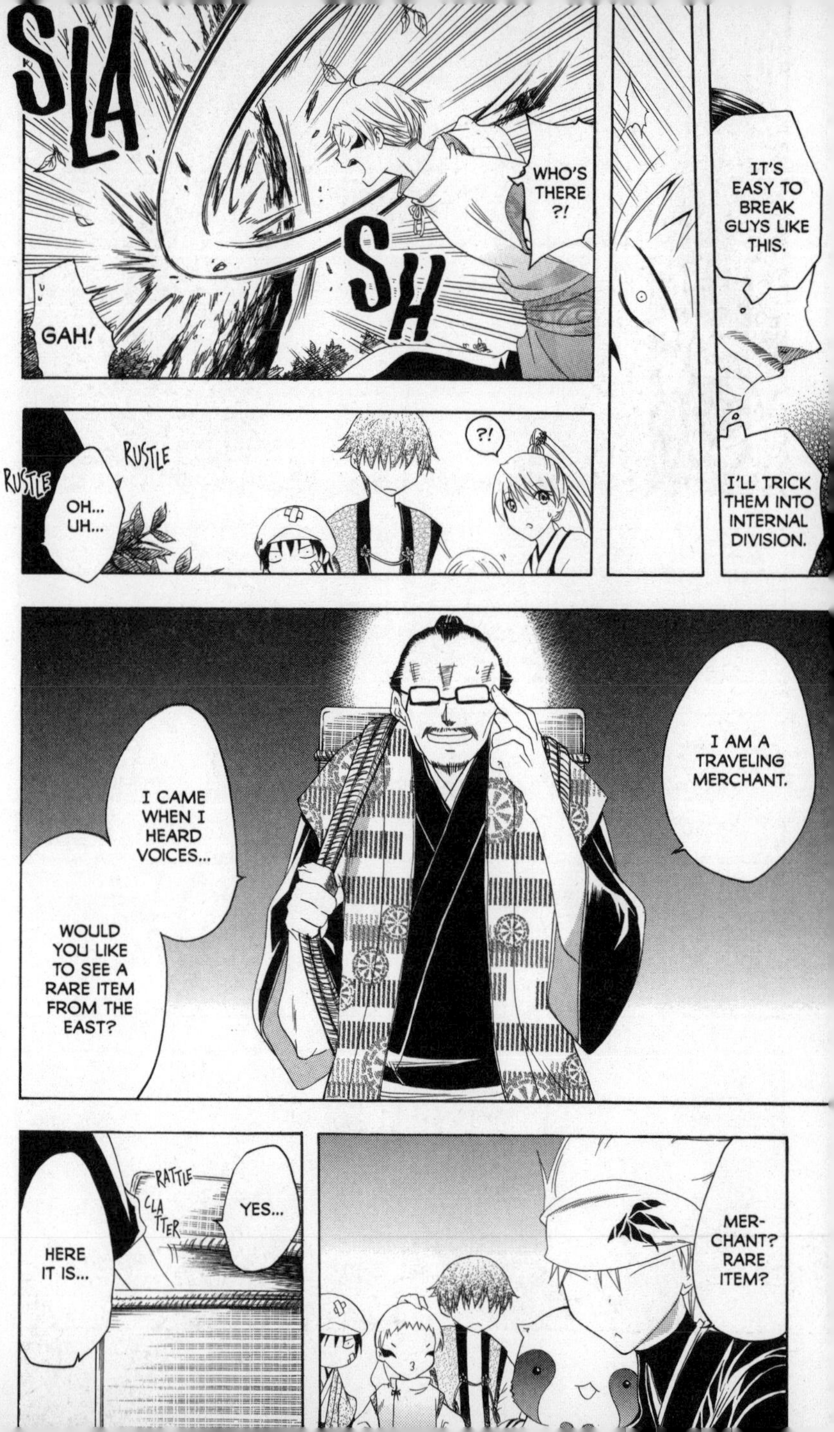
IT'S EASY TO BREAK GUYS LIKE THIS.
I'LL TRICK THEM INTO INTERNAL DIVISION.
SLA
SH
WHO'S THERE?!
GAH!
?!
RUSTLE
RUSTLE
OH... UH...
I AM A TRAVELING MERCHANT.
I CAME WHEN I HEARD VOICES...
WOULD YOU LIKE TO SEE A RARE ITEM FROM THE EAST?
MER-CHANT? RARE ITEM?
YES...
RATTLE
CLATTER
HERE IT IS...

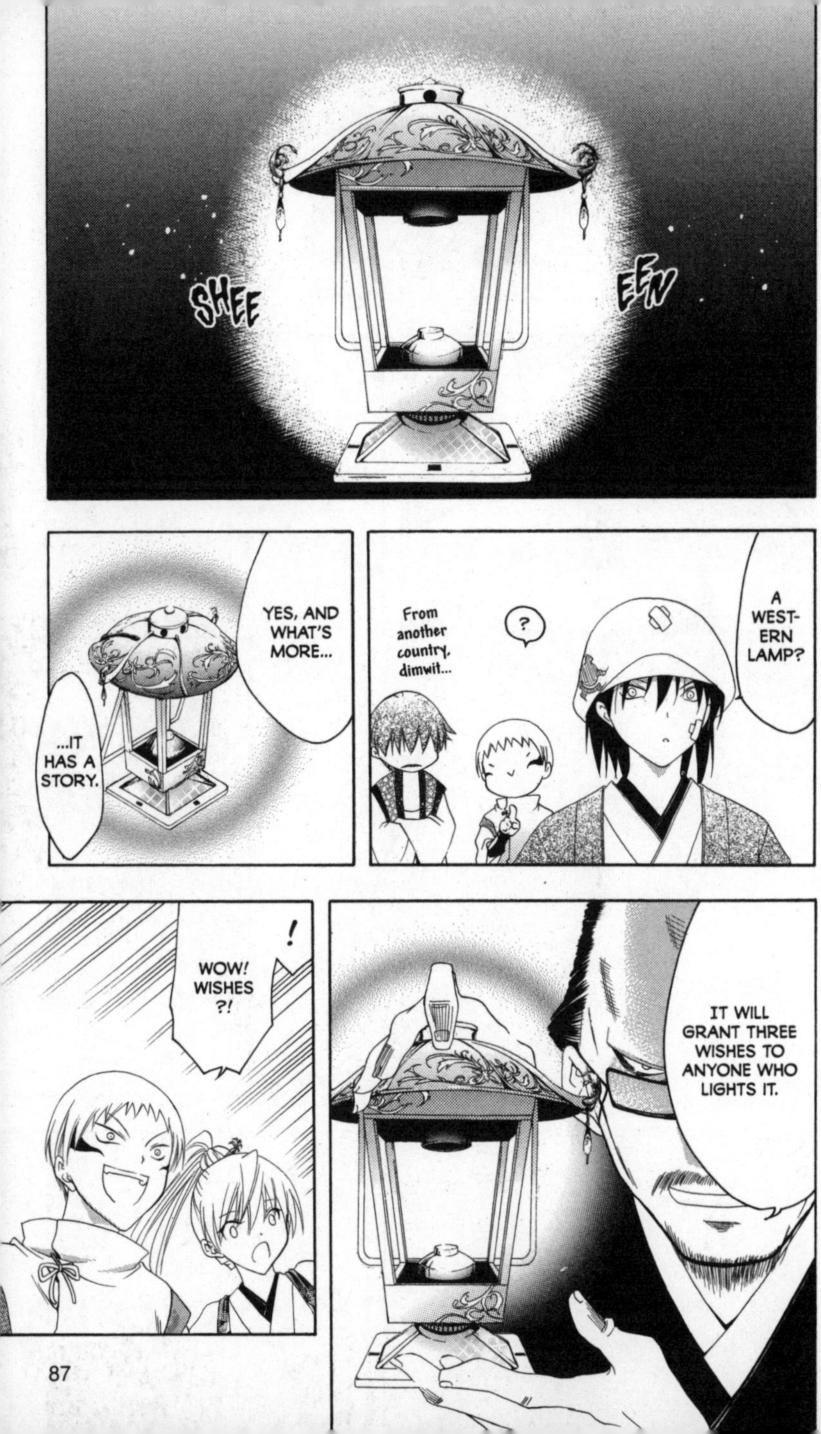
SHEE
EEN
A WEST-ERN LAMP?
?
From another country, dimwit...
YES, AND WHAT'S MORE...
...IT HAS A STORY.
IT WILL GRANT THREE WISHES TO ANYONE WHO LIGHTS IT.
!
WOW! WISHES?!

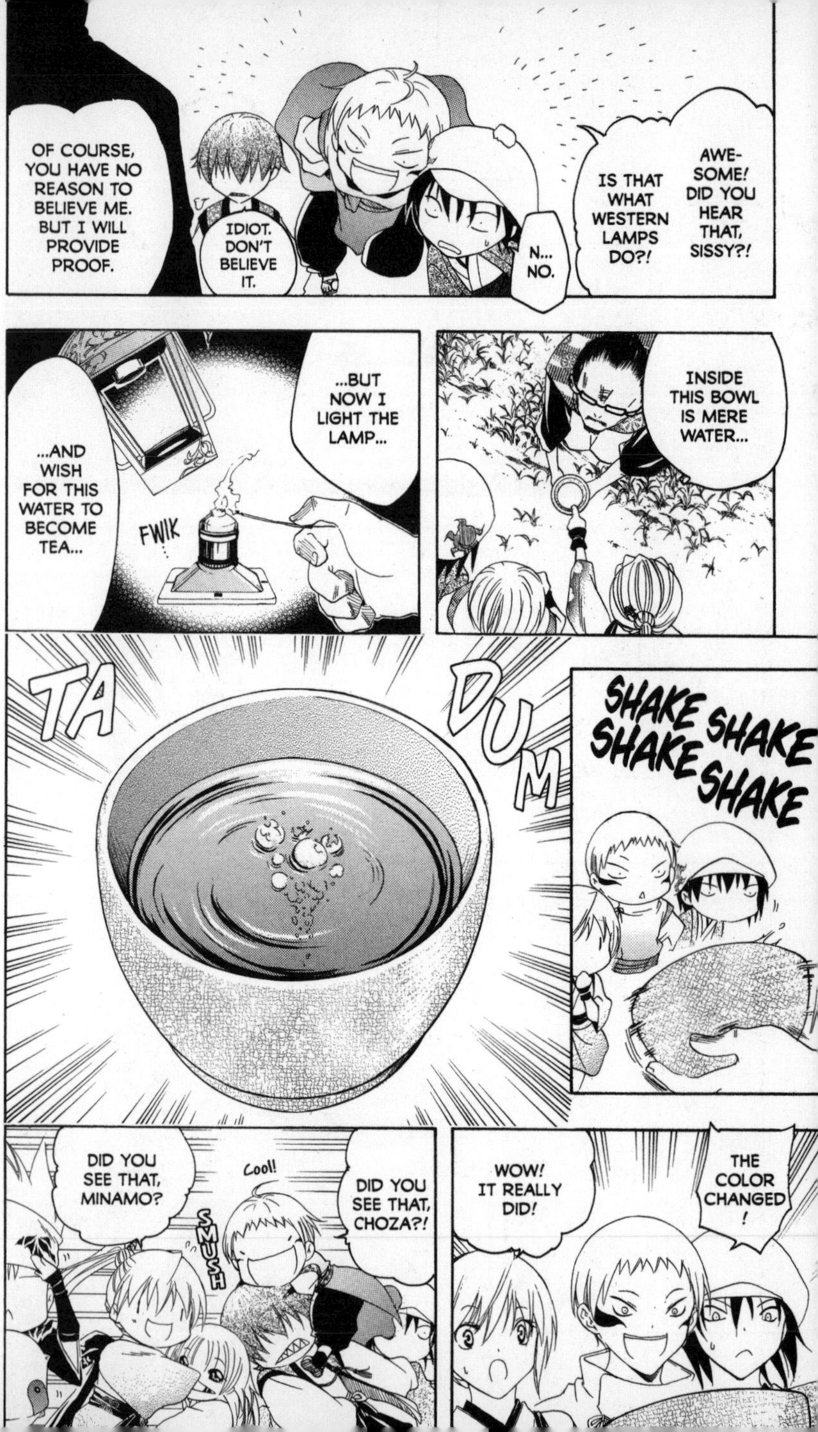
AWE-SOME! DID YOU HEAR THAT, SISSY?!
IS THAT WHAT WESTERN LAMPS DO?!
N... NO.
IDIOT. DON'T BELIEVE IT.
OF COURSE, YOU HAVE NO REASON TO BELIEVE ME. BUT I WILL PROVIDE PROOF.
INSIDE THIS BOWL IS MERE WATER...
...BUT NOW I LIGHT THE LAMP...
FWIK
...AND WISH FOR THIS WATER TO BECOME TEA...
SHAKE SHAKE SHAKE SHAKE
TA DUM
THE COLOR CHANGED!
WOW! IT REALLY DID!
DID YOU SEE THAT, CHOZA?!
Cool!
SMUSH
DID YOU SEE THAT, MINAMO?

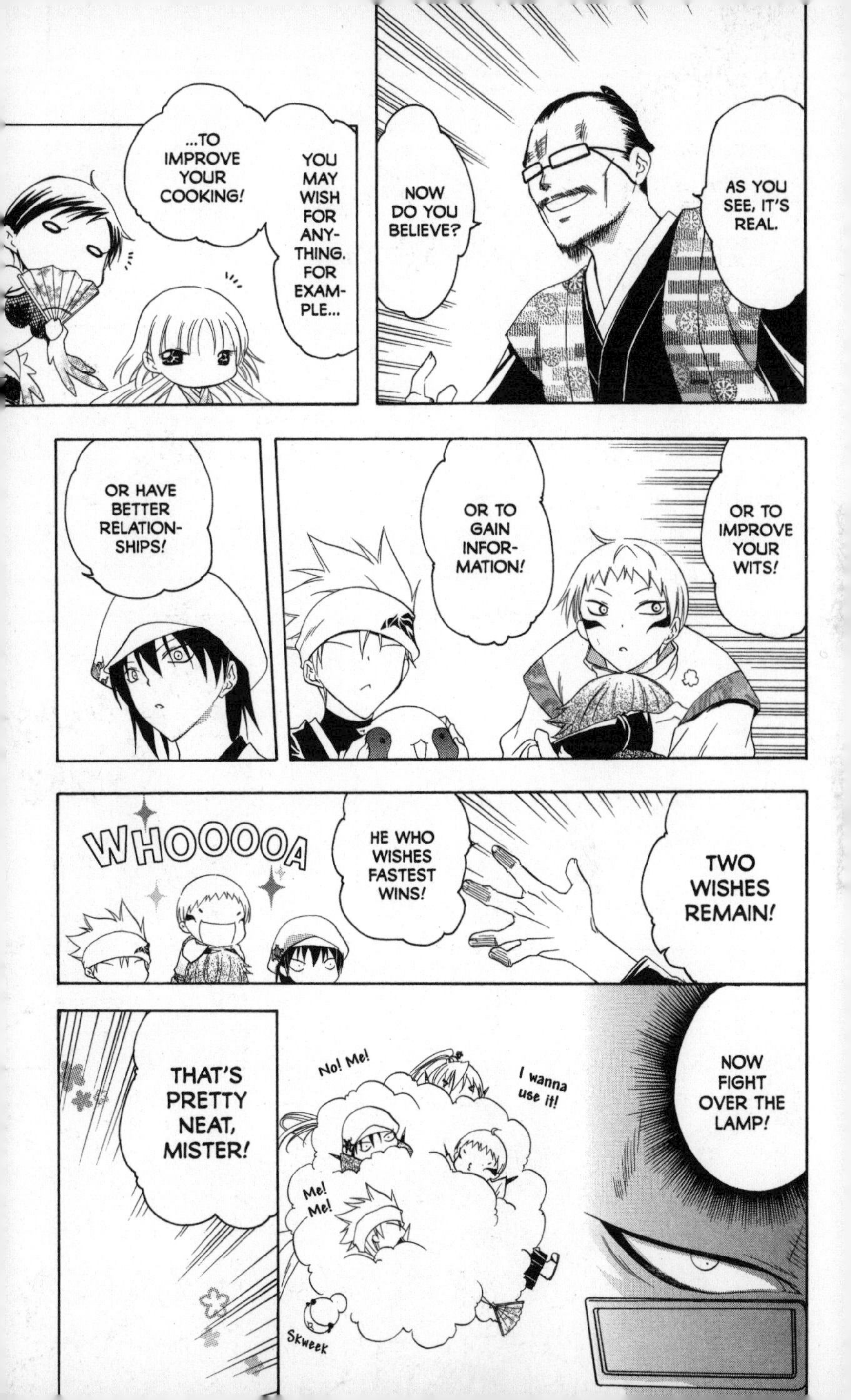
AS YOU SEE, IT'S REAL.
NOW DO YOU BELIEVE?
YOU MAY WISH FOR ANY-THING. FOR EXAM-PLE...
...TO IMPROVE YOUR COOKING!
OR TO IMPROVE YOUR WITS!
OR TO GAIN INFOR-MATION!
OR HAVE BETTER RELATION-SHIPS!
TWO WISHES REMAIN!
HE WHO WISHES FASTEST WINS!
WHOOOOA
NOW FIGHT OVER THE LAMP!
I wanna use it!
No! Me!
THAT'S PRETTY NEAT, MISTER!
Me! Me!
Skweek

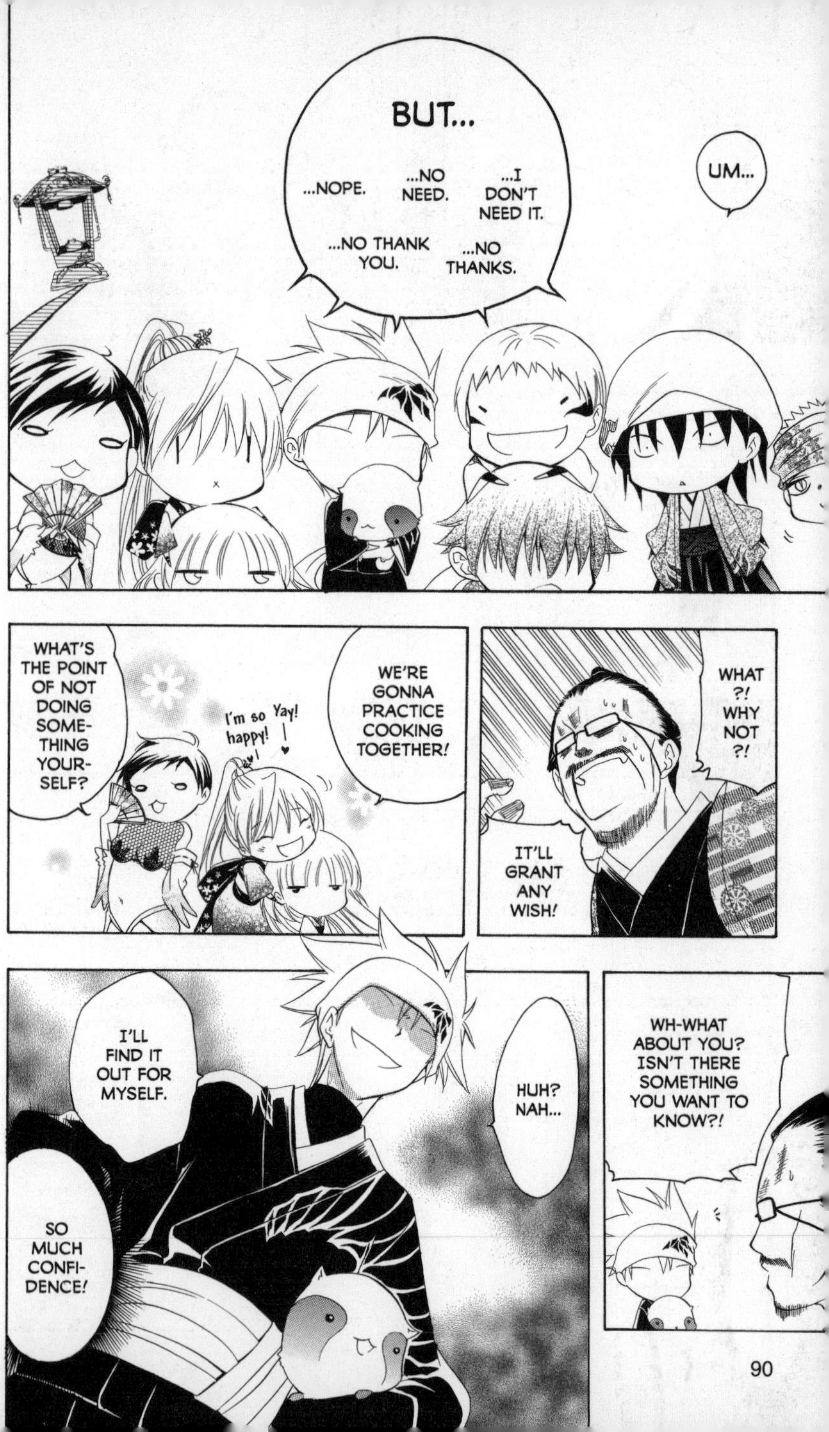
UM...
BUT...
...I DON'T NEED IT.
...NO NEED.
...NOPE.
...NO THANKS.
...NO THANK YOU.
WHAT?! WHY NOT?!
IT'LL GRANT ANY WISH!
WE'RE GONNA PRACTICE COOKING TOGETHER!
Yay!
I'm so happy!
WHAT'S THE POINT OF NOT DOING SOMETHING YOURSELF?
WH-WHAT ABOUT YOU? ISN'T THERE SOMETHING YOU WANT TO KNOW?!
HUH? NAH...
I'LL FIND IT OUT FOR MYSELF.
SO MUCH CONFIDENCE!

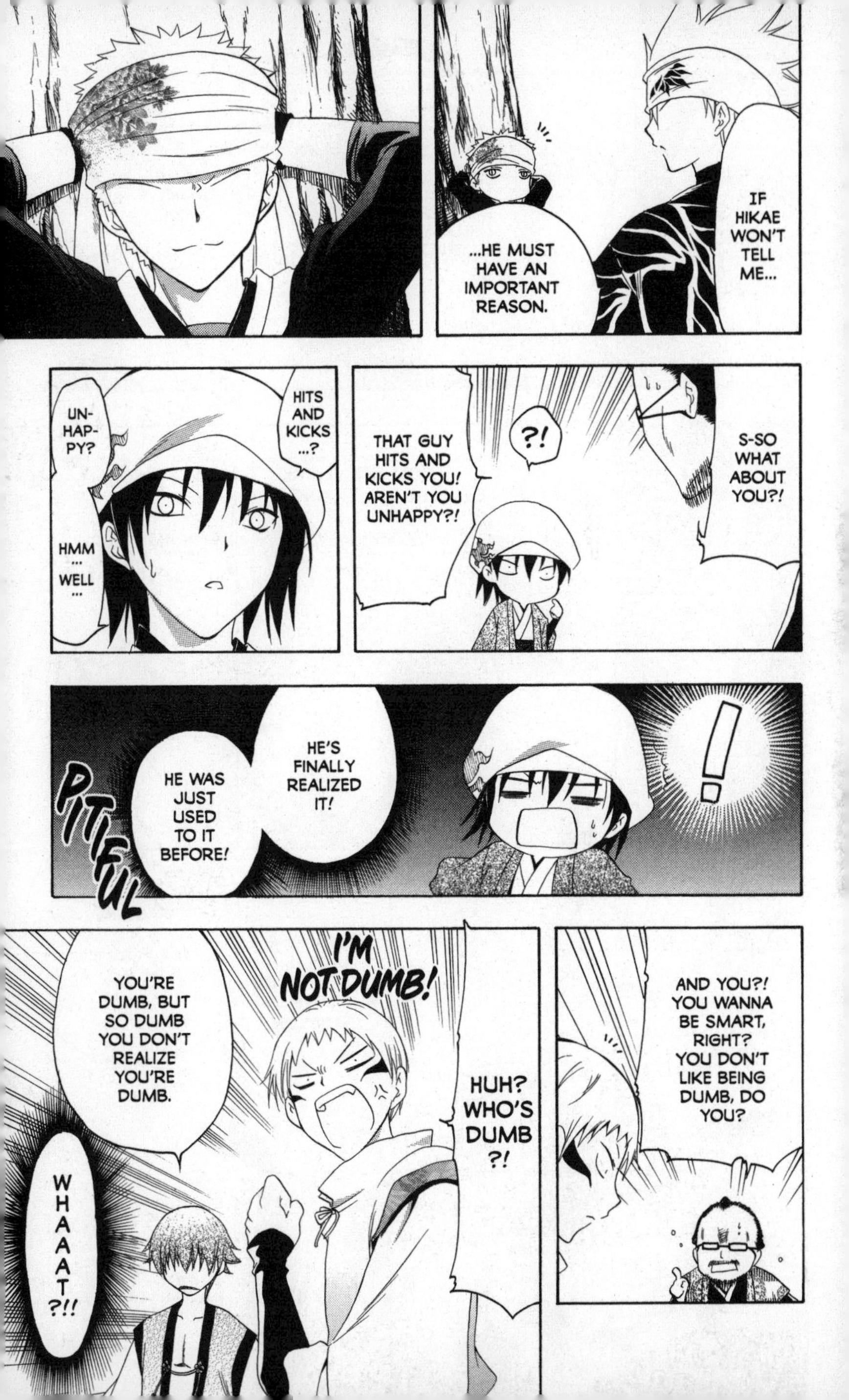
IF HIKAE WON'T TELL ME...
...HE MUST HAVE AN IMPORTANT REASON.
S-SO WHAT ABOUT YOU?!
?!
THAT GUY HITS AND KICKS YOU! AREN'T YOU UNHAPPY?!
HITS AND KICKS...?
UN-HAPPY?
HMM... WELL...
!
HE'S FINALLY REALIZED IT!
HE WAS JUST USED TO IT BEFORE!
PITIFUL
AND YOU?! YOU WANNA BE SMART, RIGHT? YOU DON'T LIKE BEING DUMB, DO YOU?
HUH? WHO'S DUMB?!
I'M NOT DUMB!
YOU'RE DUMB, BUT SO DUMB YOU DON'T REALIZE YOU'RE DUMB.
WHAAAAT?!!

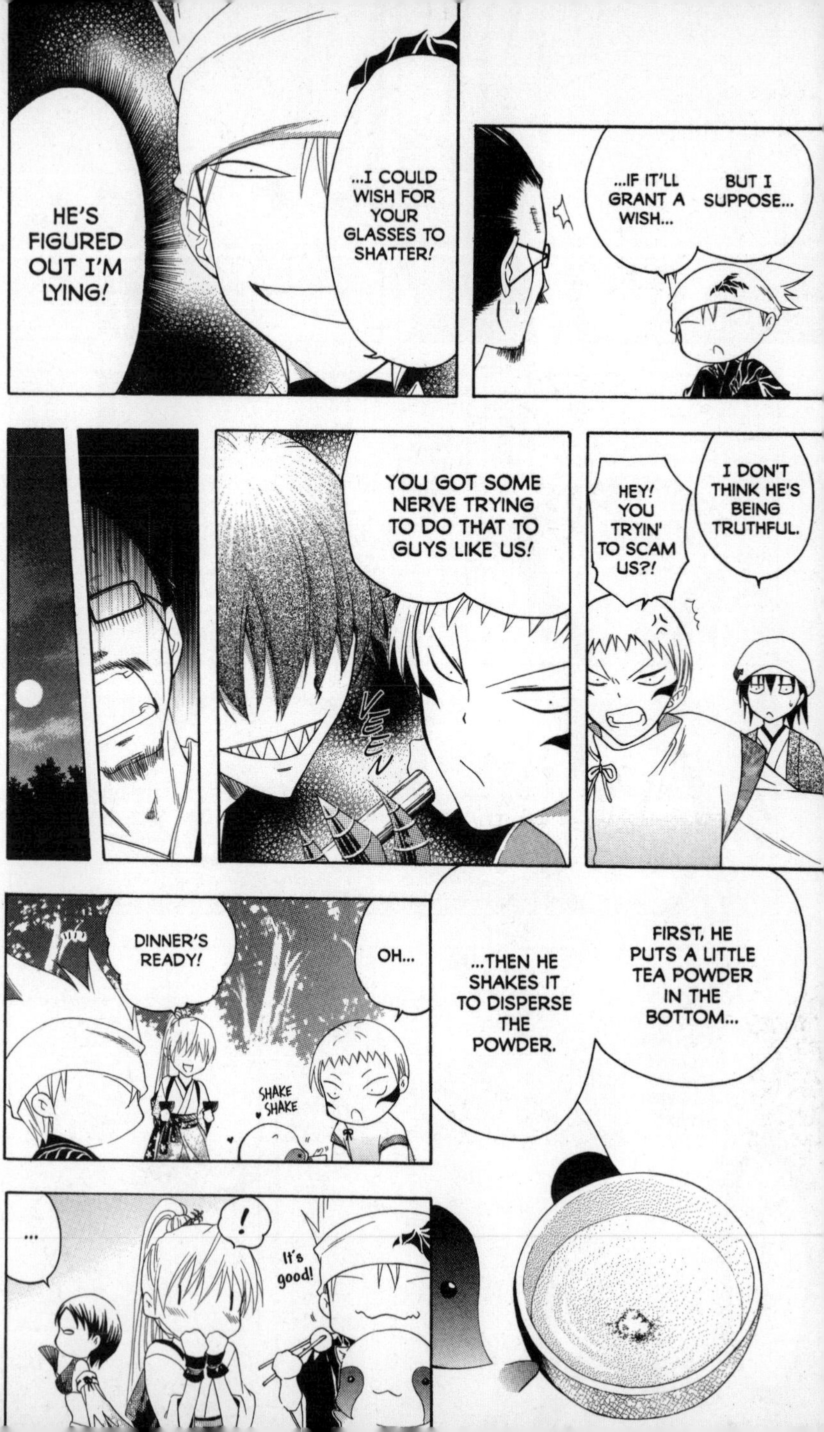
BUT I SUPPOSE...
...IF IT'LL GRANT A WISH...
...I COULD WISH FOR YOUR GLASSES TO SHATTER!
HE'S FIGURED OUT I'M LYING!
I DON'T THINK HE'S BEING TRUTHFUL.
HEY! YOU TRYIN' TO SCAM US?!
YOU GOT SOME NERVE TRYING TO DO THAT TO GUYS LIKE US!
VEEN
FIRST, HE PUTS A LITTLE TEA POWDER IN THE BOTTOM...
...THEN HE SHAKES IT TO DISPERSE THE POWDER.
OH...
DINNER'S READY!
SHAKE SHAKE
!
It's good!
...

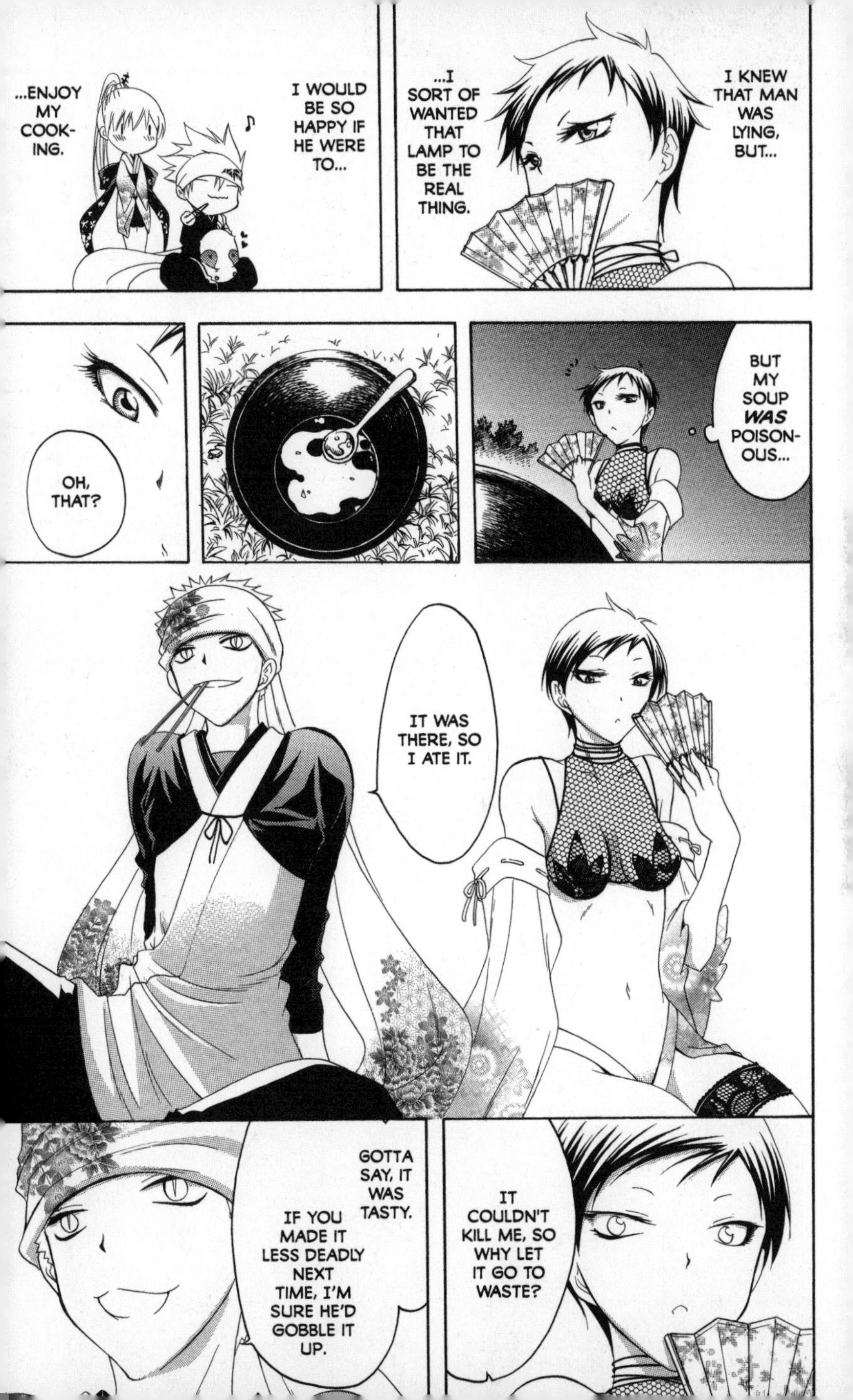
I KNEW THAT MAN WAS LYING, BUT...
...I SORT OF WANTED THAT LAMP TO BE THE REAL THING.
I WOULD BE SO HAPPY IF HE WERE TO...
...ENJOY MY COOKING.
BUT MY SOUP *WAS* POISONOUS...
OH, THAT?
IT WAS THERE, SO I ATE IT.
IT COULDN'T KILL ME, SO WHY LET IT GO TO WASTE?
GOTTA SAY, IT WAS TASTY.
IF YOU MADE IT LESS DEADLY NEXT TIME, I'M SURE HE'D GOBBLE IT UP.

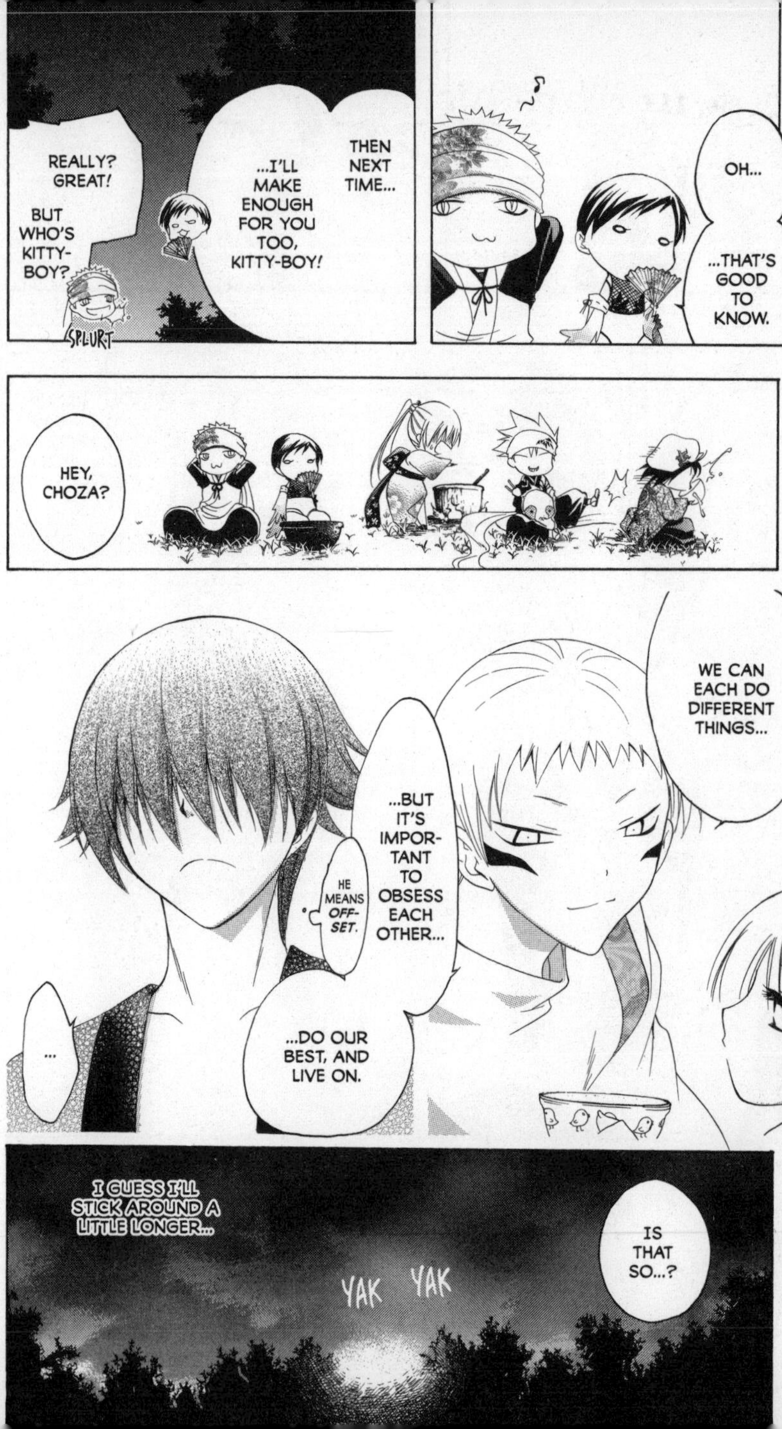
OH...
...THAT'S GOOD TO KNOW.
THEN NEXT TIME...
...I'LL MAKE ENOUGH FOR YOU TOO, KITTY-BOY!
REALLY? GREAT!
BUT WHO'S KITTY-BOY?
SPLURT
HEY, CHOZA?
WE CAN EACH DO DIFFERENT THINGS...
...BUT IT'S IMPORTANT TO OBSESS EACH OTHER...
HE MEANS *OFF-SET*.
...DO OUR BEST, AND LIVE ON.
...
IS THAT SO...?
YAK YAK
I GUESS I'LL STICK AROUND A LITTLE LONGER...

Chapter 113 Hihiba's Tale

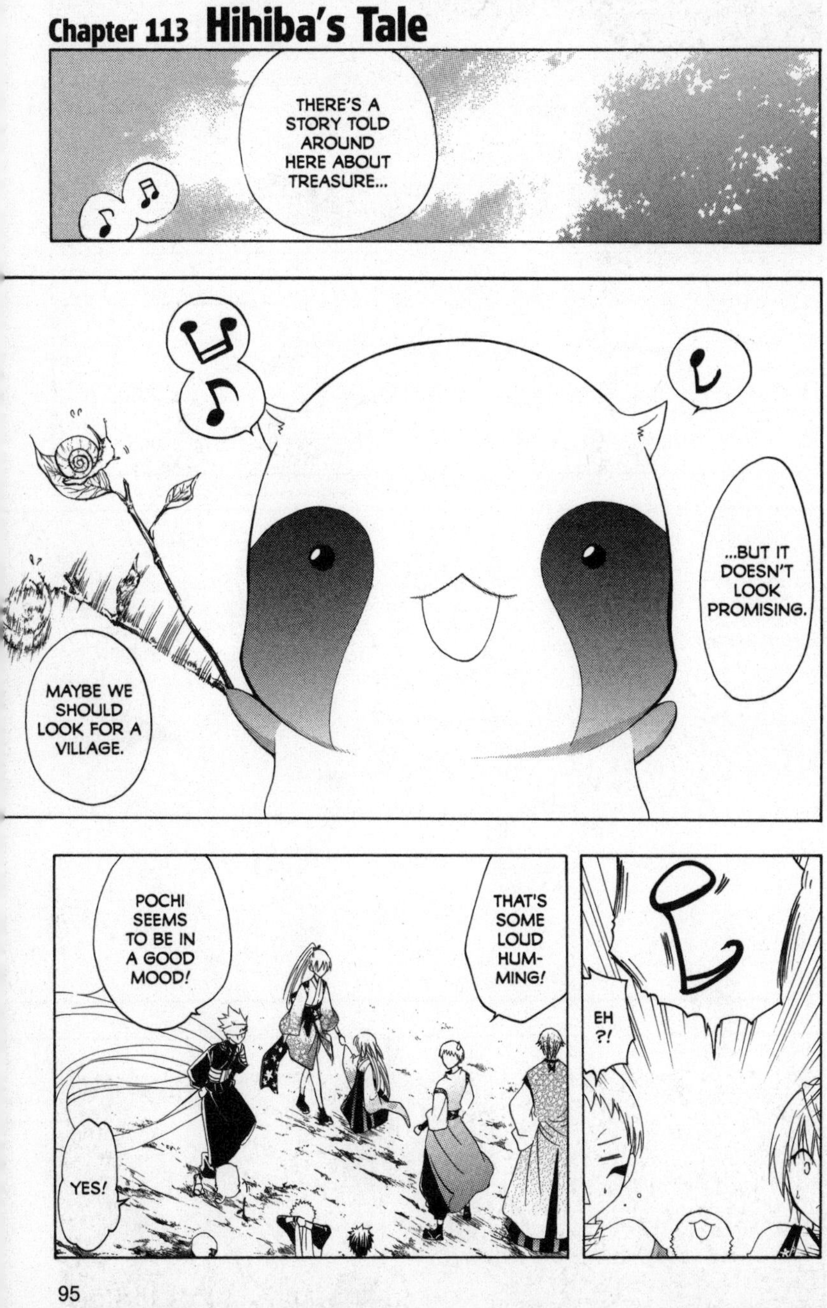

THERE'S A STORY TOLD AROUND HERE ABOUT TREASURE...
...BUT IT DOESN'T LOOK PROMISING.
MAYBE WE SHOULD LOOK FOR A VILLAGE.
EH ?!
THAT'S SOME LOUD HUMMING!
POCHI SEEMS TO BE IN A GOOD MOOD!
YES!

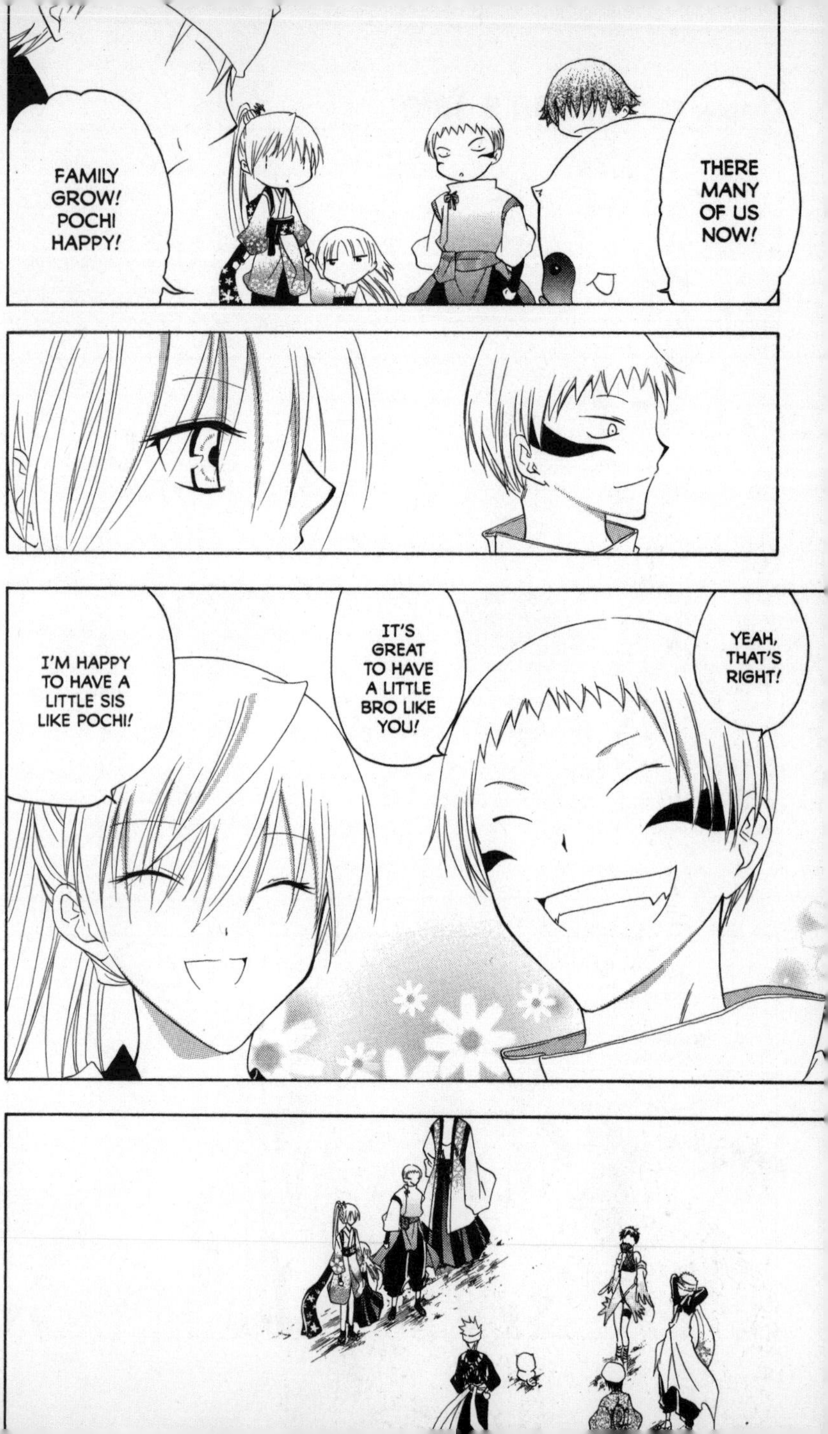
THERE MANY OF US NOW!
FAMILY GROW! POCHI HAPPY!
YEAH, THAT'S RIGHT!
IT'S GREAT TO HAVE A LITTLE BRO LIKE YOU!
I'M HAPPY TO HAVE A LITTLE SIS LIKE POCHI!

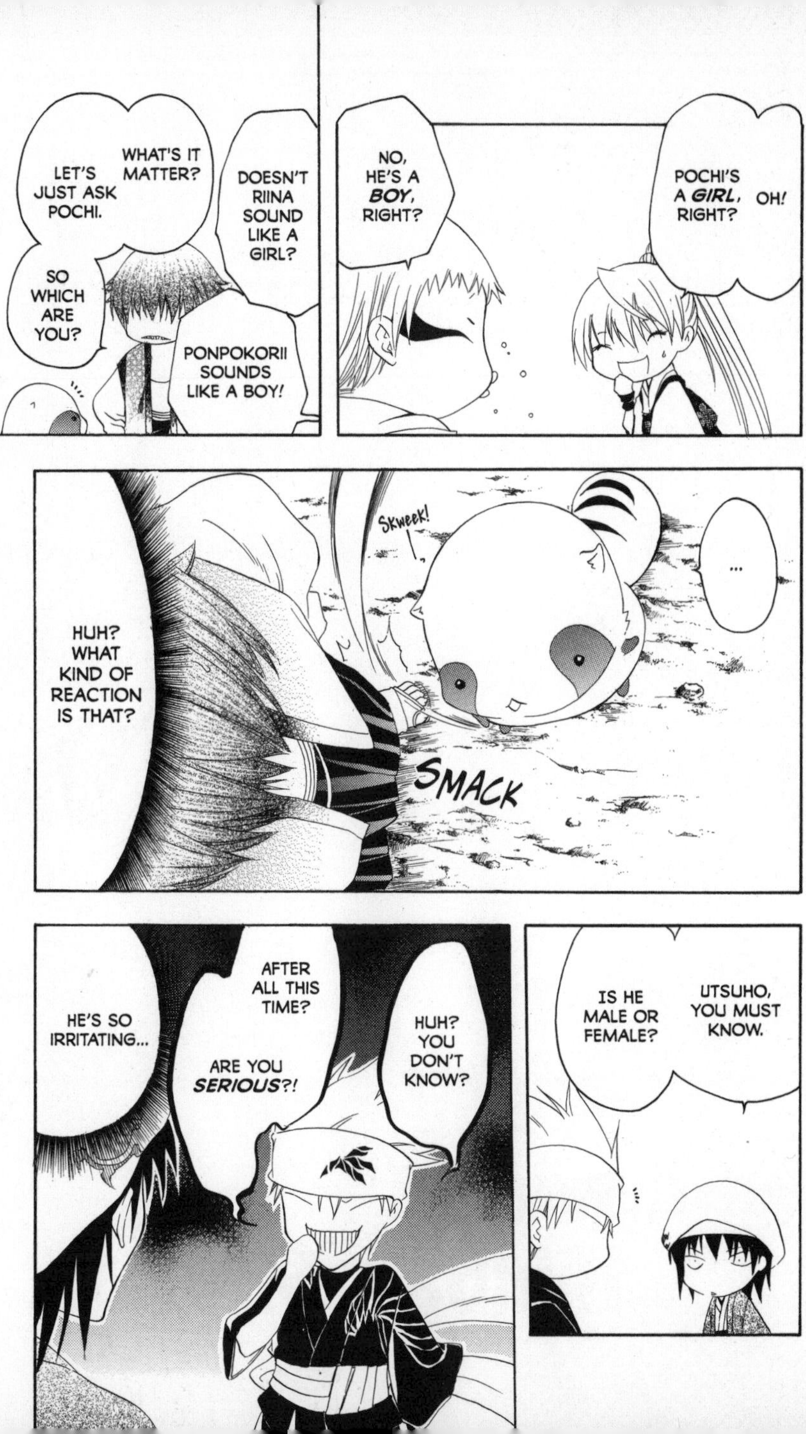
OH!
POCHI'S A GIRL, RIGHT?
NO, HE'S A BOY, RIGHT?
DOESN'T RIINA SOUND LIKE A GIRL?
PONPOKORII SOUNDS LIKE A BOY!
WHAT'S IT MATTER?
LET'S JUST ASK POCHI.
SO WHICH ARE YOU?
...
Skweek!
SMACK
HUH? WHAT KIND OF REACTION IS THAT?
UTSUHO, YOU MUST KNOW.
IS HE MALE OR FEMALE?
HUH? YOU DON'T KNOW?
AFTER ALL THIS TIME?
ARE YOU SERIOUS?!
HE'S SO IRRITATING...

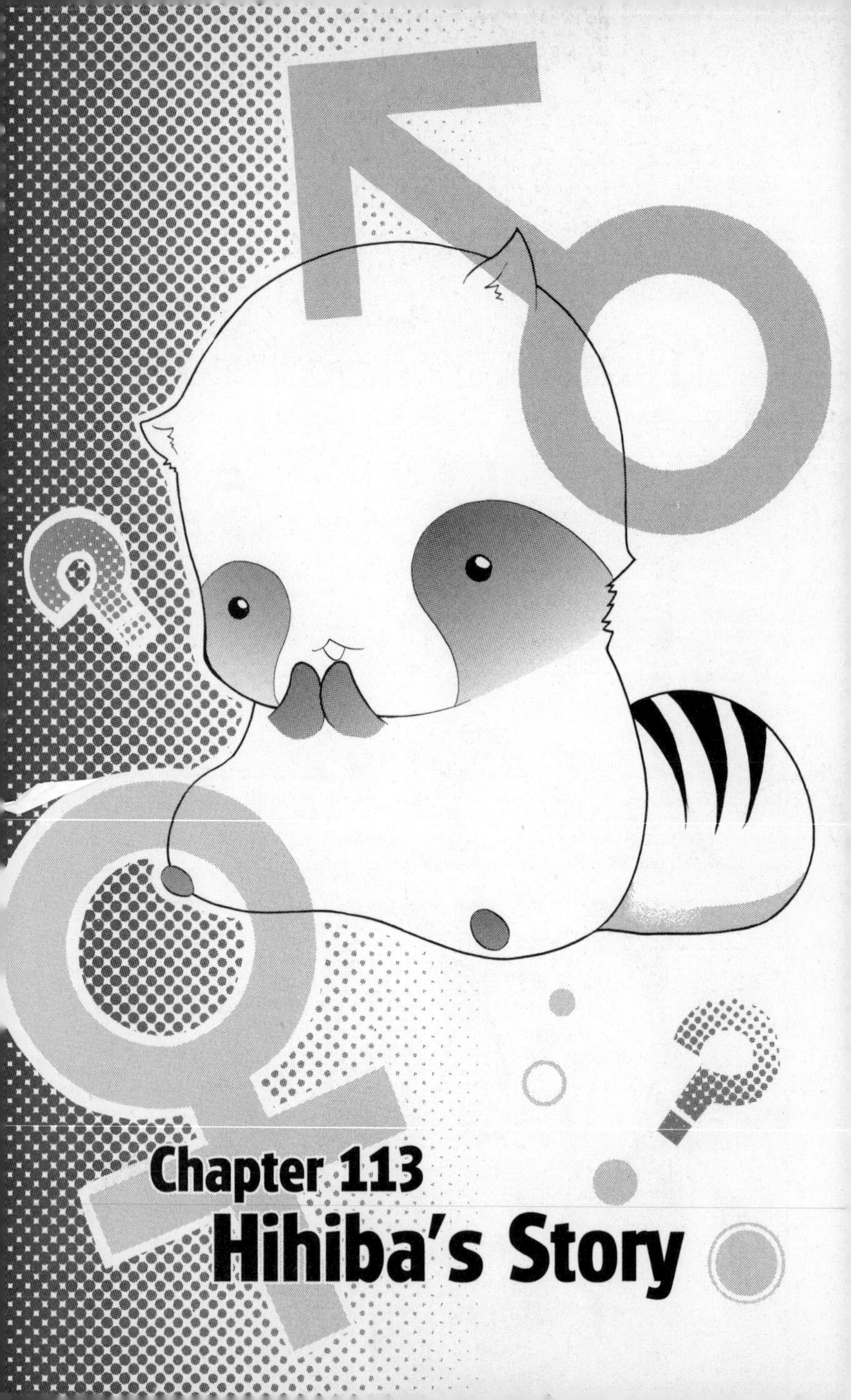

Chapter 113
Hihiba's Story

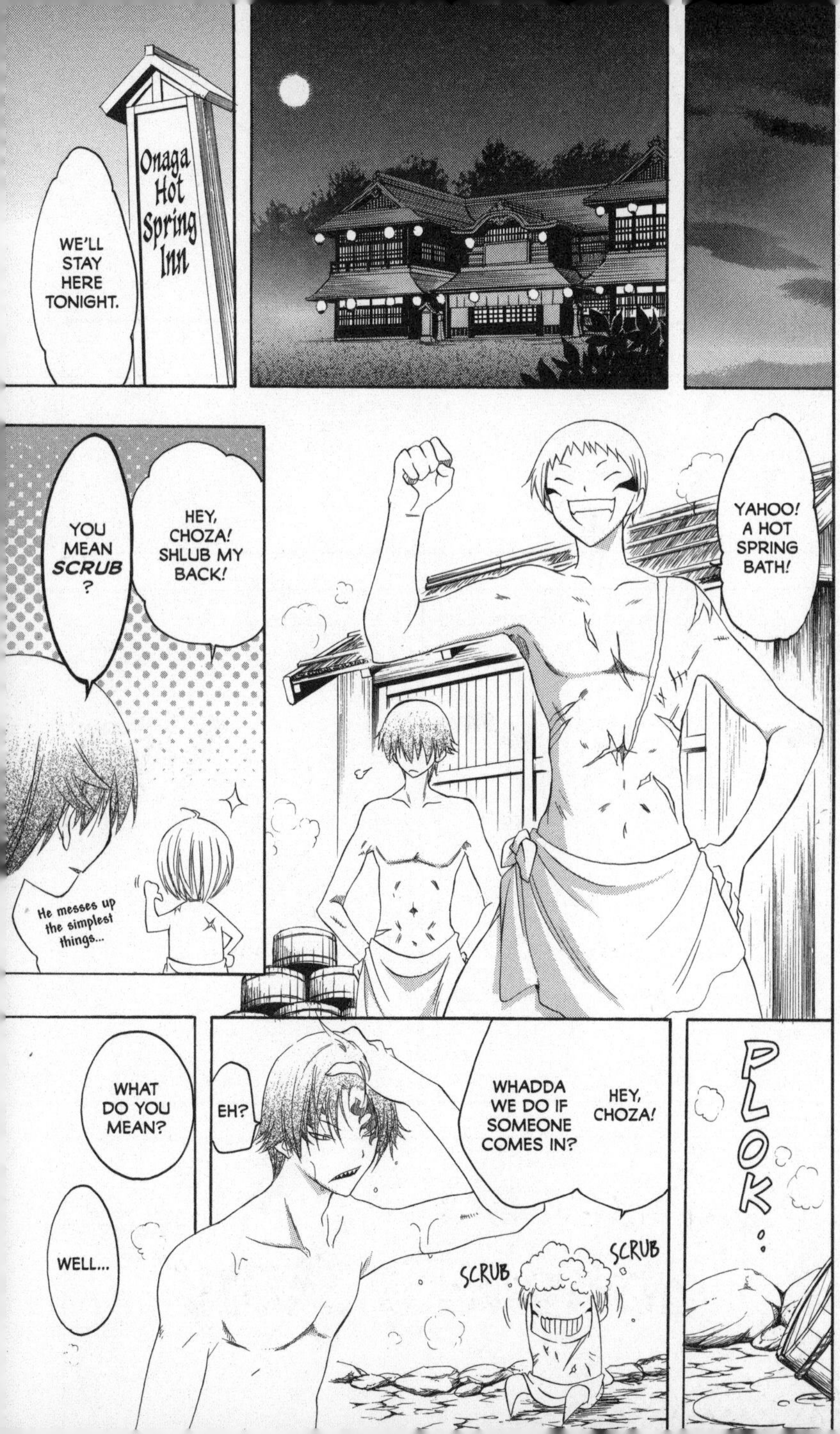
Onaga Hot Spring Inn
WE'LL STAY HERE TONIGHT.
YAHOO! A HOT SPRING BATH!
HEY, CHOZA! SHLUB MY BACK!
YOU MEAN SCRUB?
He messes up the simplest things...
PLOK
HEY, CHOZA!
WHADDA WE DO IF SOMEONE COMES IN?
EH?
SCRUB
SCRUB
WHAT DO YOU MEAN?
WELL...

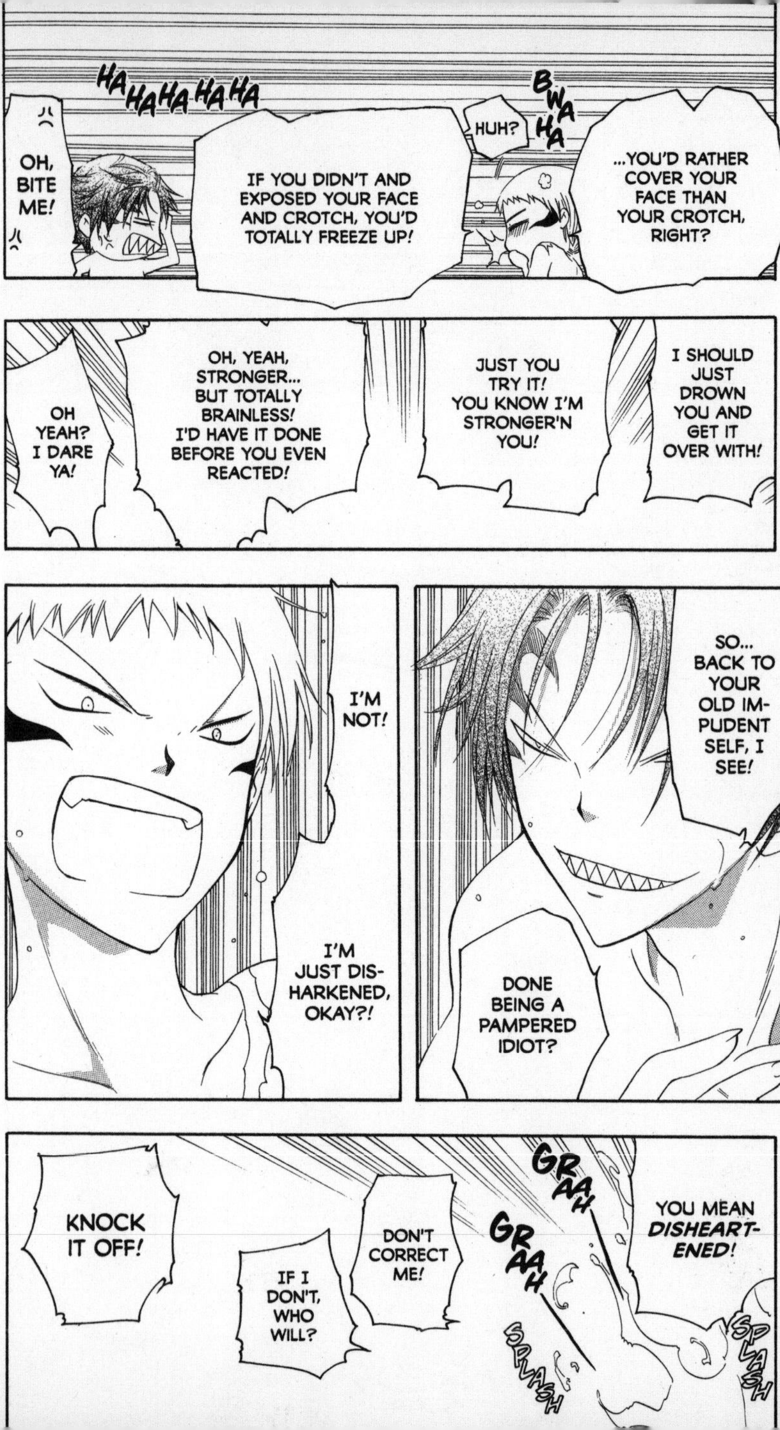
...YOU'D RATHER COVER YOUR FACE THAN YOUR CROTCH, RIGHT?
BWAHA
HUH?
IF YOU DIDN'T AND EXPOSED YOUR FACE AND CROTCH, YOU'D TOTALLY FREEZE UP!
HAHAHAHAHA
OH, BITE ME!
I SHOULD JUST DROWN YOU AND GET IT OVER WITH!
JUST YOU TRY IT! YOU KNOW I'M STRONGER'N YOU!
OH, YEAH, STRONGER... BUT TOTALLY BRAINLESS! I'D HAVE IT DONE BEFORE YOU EVEN REACTED!
OH YEAH? I DARE YA!
SO... BACK TO YOUR OLD IM-PUDENT SELF, I SEE!
DONE BEING A PAMPERED IDIOT?
I'M NOT!
I'M JUST DIS-HARKENED, OKAY?!
YOU MEAN *DISHEARTENED!*
GRAAH
GRAAH
SPLASH
SPLASH
DON'T CORRECT ME!
IF I DON'T, WHO WILL?
KNOCK IT OFF!

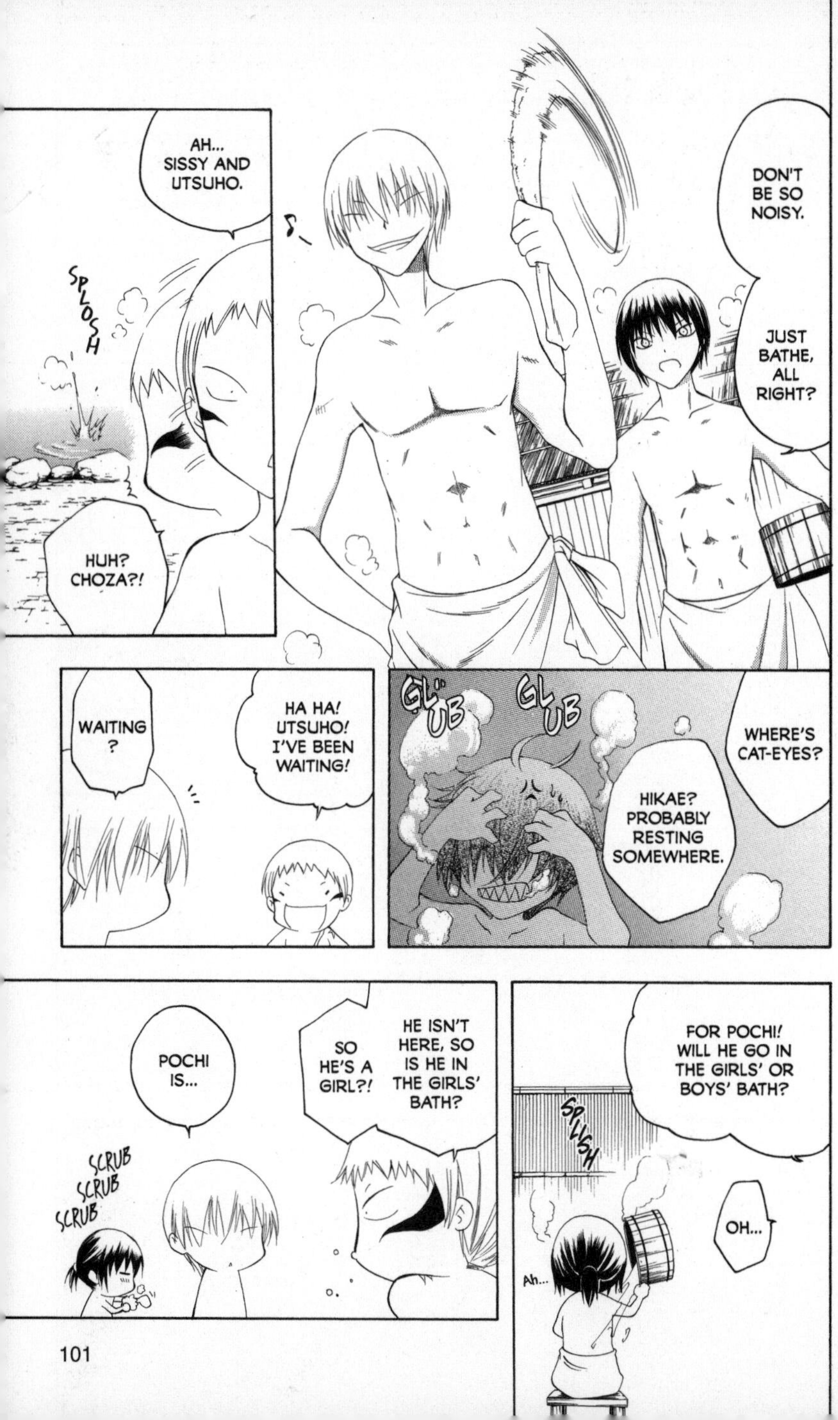
DON'T BE SO NOISY.
JUST BATHE, ALL RIGHT?
AH... SISSY AND UTSUHO.
SPLOSH
HUH? CHOZA?!
WHERE'S CAT-EYES?
HIKAE? PROBABLY RESTING SOMEWHERE.
GLUB GLUB
HA HA! UTSUHO! I'VE BEEN WAITING!
WAITING?
FOR POCHI! WILL HE GO IN THE GIRLS' OR BOYS' BATH?
SPLISH
OH...
Ah...
HE ISN'T HERE, SO IS HE IN THE GIRLS' BATH?
SO HE'S A GIRL?!
POCHI IS...
SCRUB SCRUB SCRUB

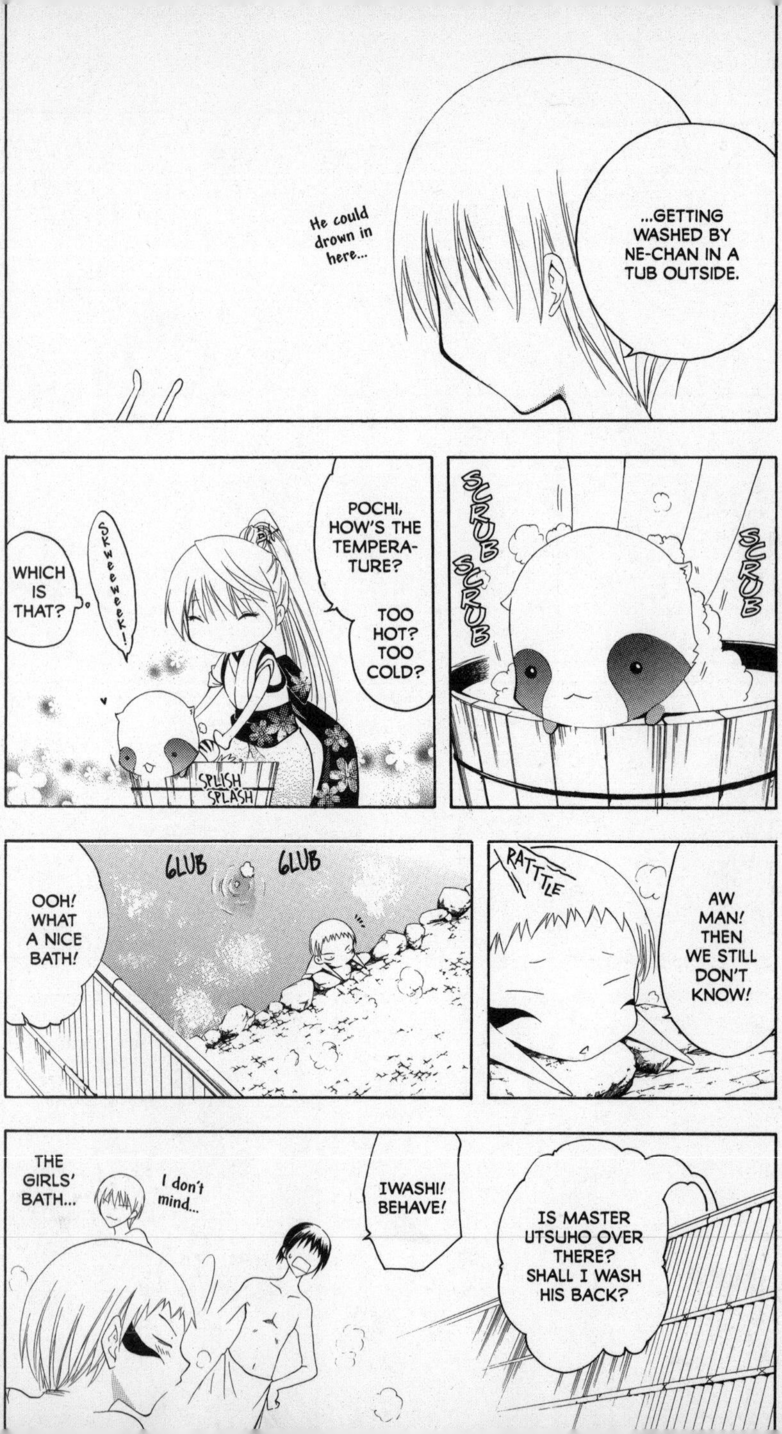
...GETTING WASHED BY NE-CHAN IN A TUB OUTSIDE.
He could drown in here...
SCRUB SCRUB
SCRUB SCRUB
POCHI, HOW'S THE TEMPERA-TURE?
TOO HOT? TOO COLD?
Skweeweek!
WHICH IS THAT?
SPLISH SPLASH
RATTTLE
AW MAN! THEN WE STILL DON'T KNOW!
GLUB GLUB
OOH! WHAT A NICE BATH!
IS MASTER UTSUHO OVER THERE? SHALL I WASH HIS BACK?
IWASHI! BEHAVE!
I don't mind...
THE GIRLS' BATH...

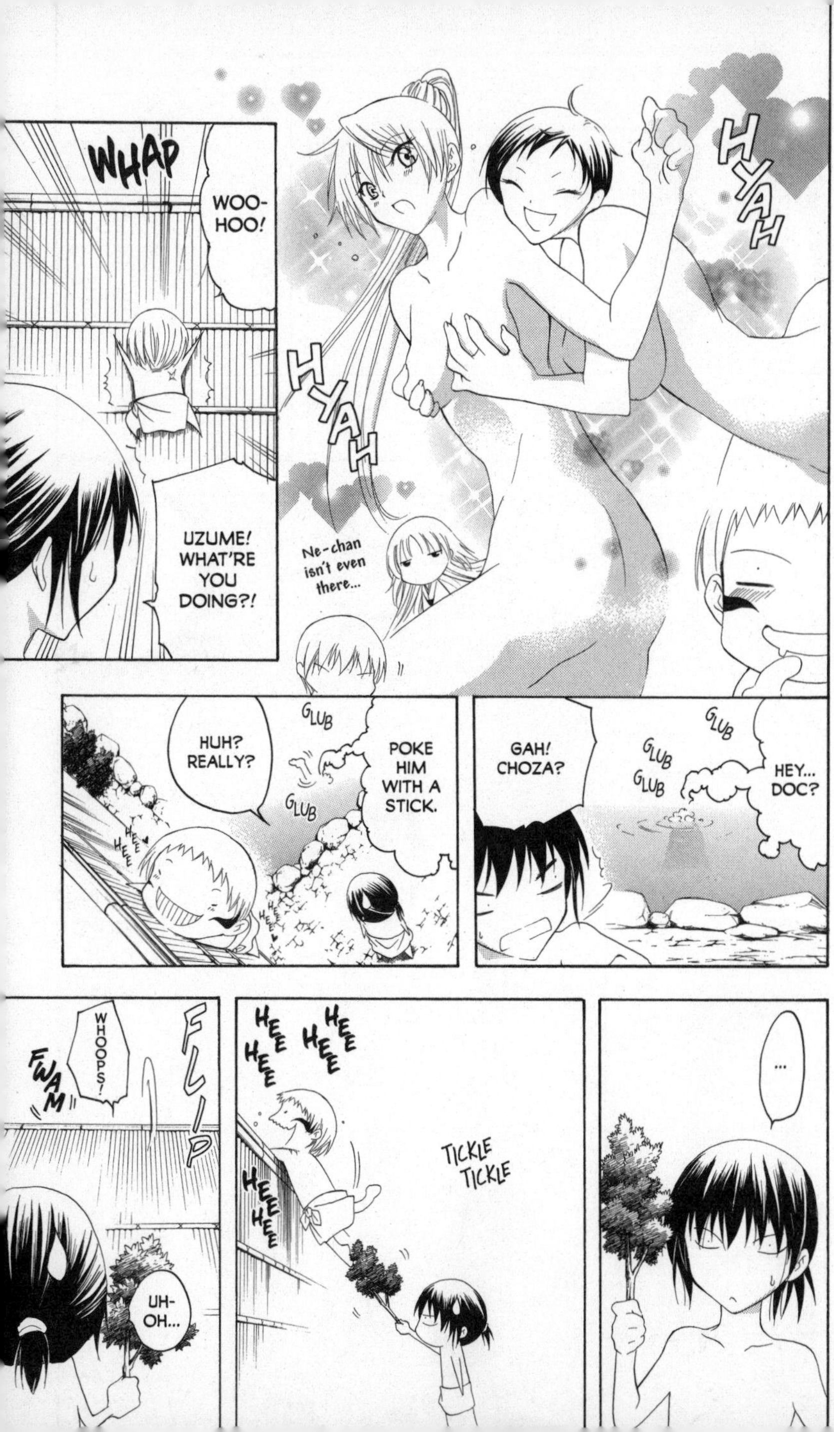
HYAH
HYAH
Ne-chan isn't even there...
WHAP
WOO-HOO!
UZUME! WHAT'RE YOU DOING?!
GLUB
GLUB
GLUB
HEY... DOC?
GAH! CHOZA?
GLUB
POKE HIM WITH A STICK.
HUH? REALLY?
GLUB
HEE HEE
HEE HEE
...
HEE HEE HEE HEE
TICKLE TICKLE
HEE HEE
FLIP
WHOOPS!
FWAM
UH-OH...

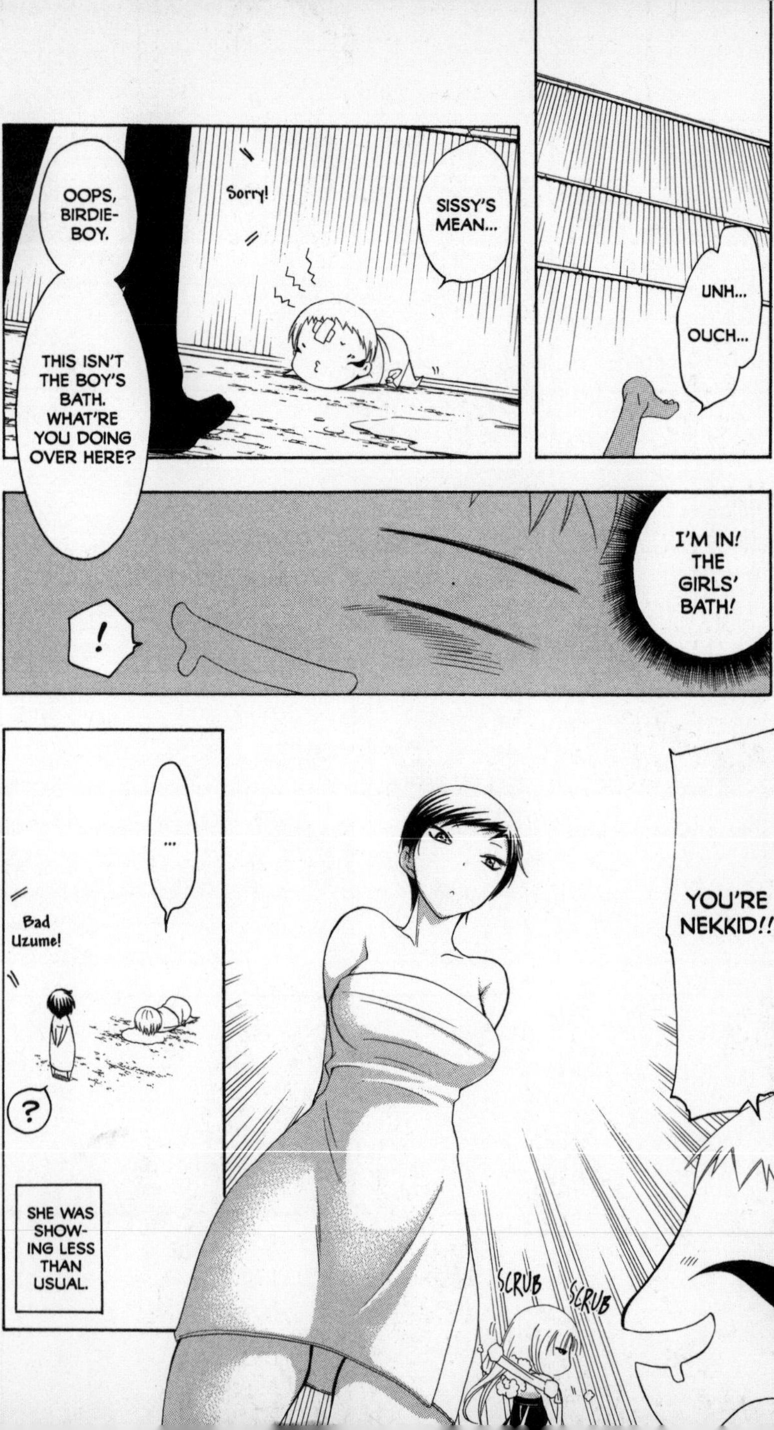
UNH...
OUCH...
SISSY'S MEAN...
Sorry!
OOPS, BIRDIE-BOY.
THIS ISN'T THE BOY'S BATH. WHAT'RE YOU DOING OVER HERE?
I'M IN! THE GIRLS' BATH!
!
YOU'RE NEKKID!!
SCRUB
SCRUB
...
Bad Uzume!
?
SHE WAS SHOWING LESS THAN USUAL.

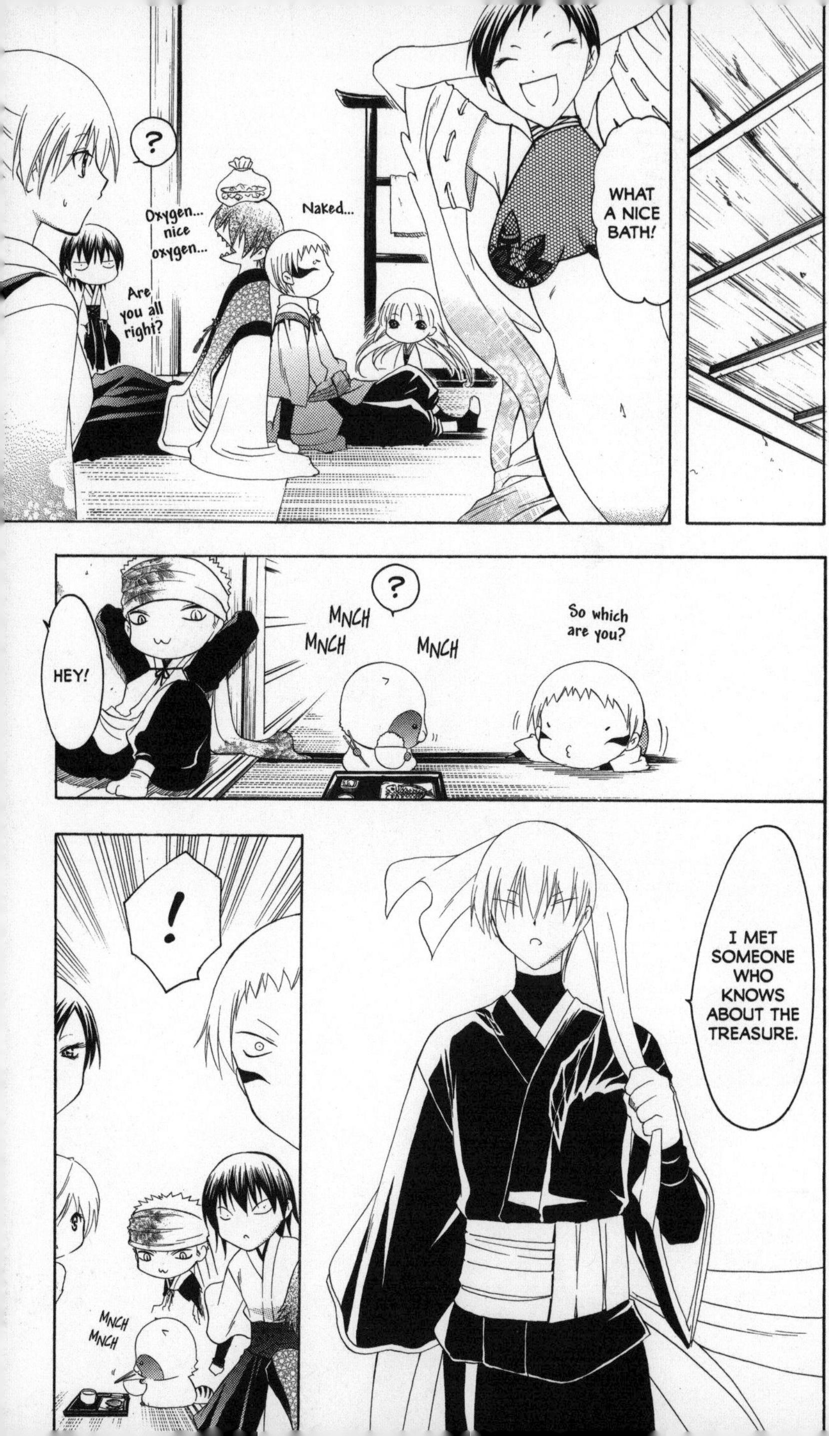
WHAT A NICE BATH!
Naked...
Oxygen... nice oxygen...
?
Are you all right?
So which are you?
MNCH
?
MNCH
MNCH
HEY!
I MET SOMEONE WHO KNOWS ABOUT THE TREASURE.
!
MNCH MNCH

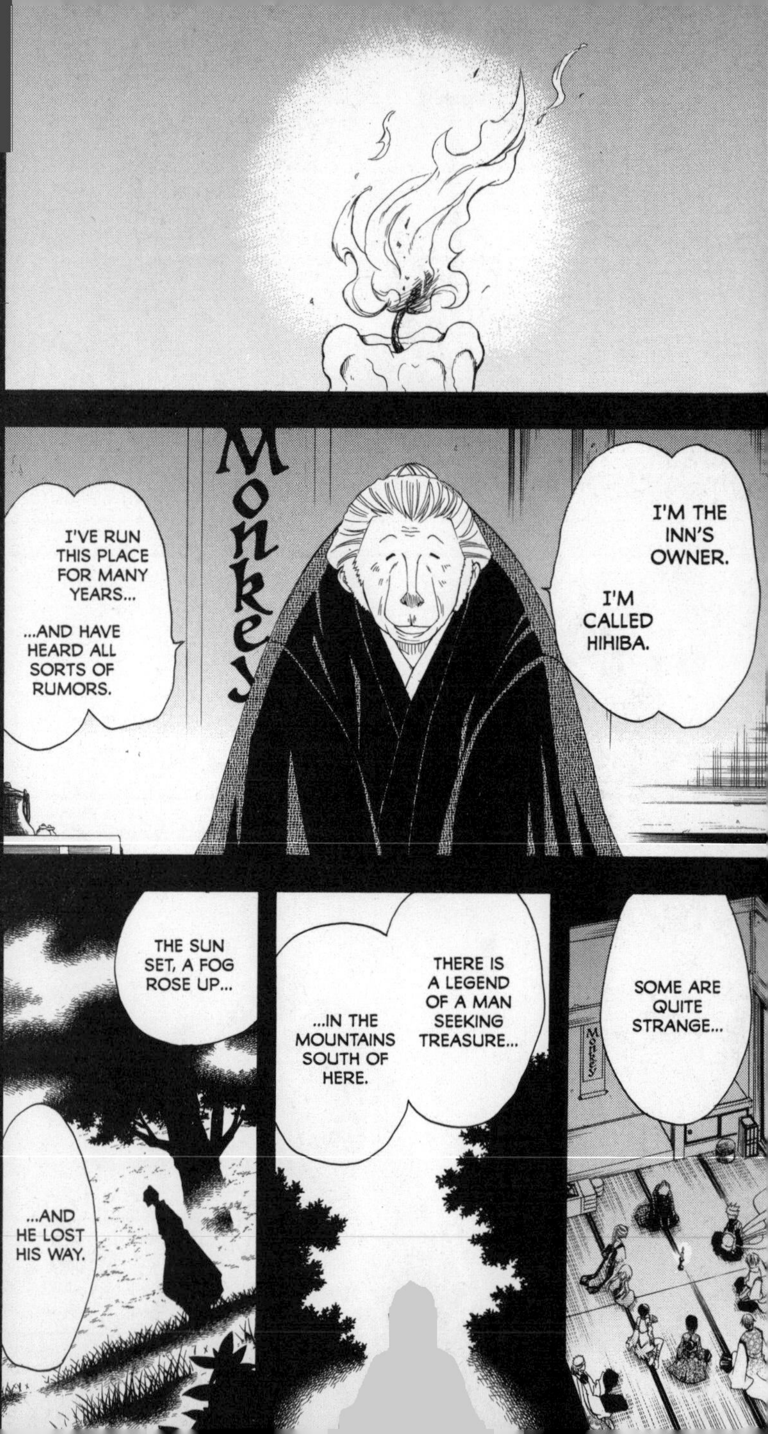
Monkey
I'M THE INN'S OWNER.
I'M CALLED HIHIBA.
I'VE RUN THIS PLACE FOR MANY YEARS...
...AND HAVE HEARD ALL SORTS OF RUMORS.
Monkey
SOME ARE QUITE STRANGE...
THERE IS A LEGEND OF A MAN SEEKING TREASURE...
...IN THE MOUNTAINS SOUTH OF HERE.
THE SUN SET, A FOG ROSE UP...
...AND HE LOST HIS WAY.

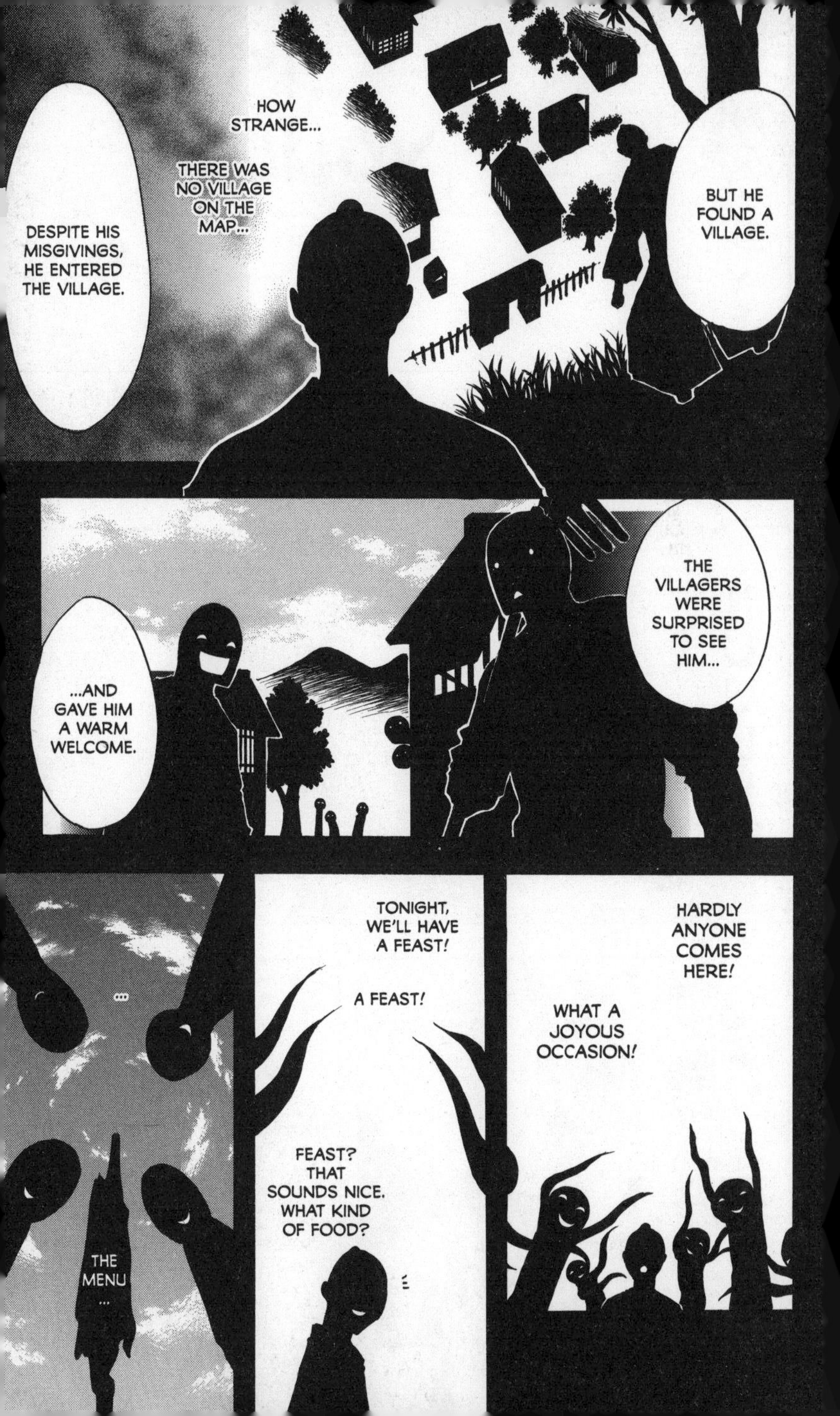
BUT HE FOUND A VILLAGE.
HOW STRANGE...
THERE WAS NO VILLAGE ON THE MAP...
DESPITE HIS MISGIVINGS, HE ENTERED THE VILLAGE.
THE VILLAGERS WERE SURPRISED TO SEE HIM...
...AND GAVE HIM A WARM WELCOME.
HARDLY ANYONE COMES HERE!
WHAT A JOYOUS OCCASION!
TONIGHT, WE'LL HAVE A FEAST!
A FEAST!
FEAST? THAT SOUNDS NICE. WHAT KIND OF FOOD?
...
THE MENU ...

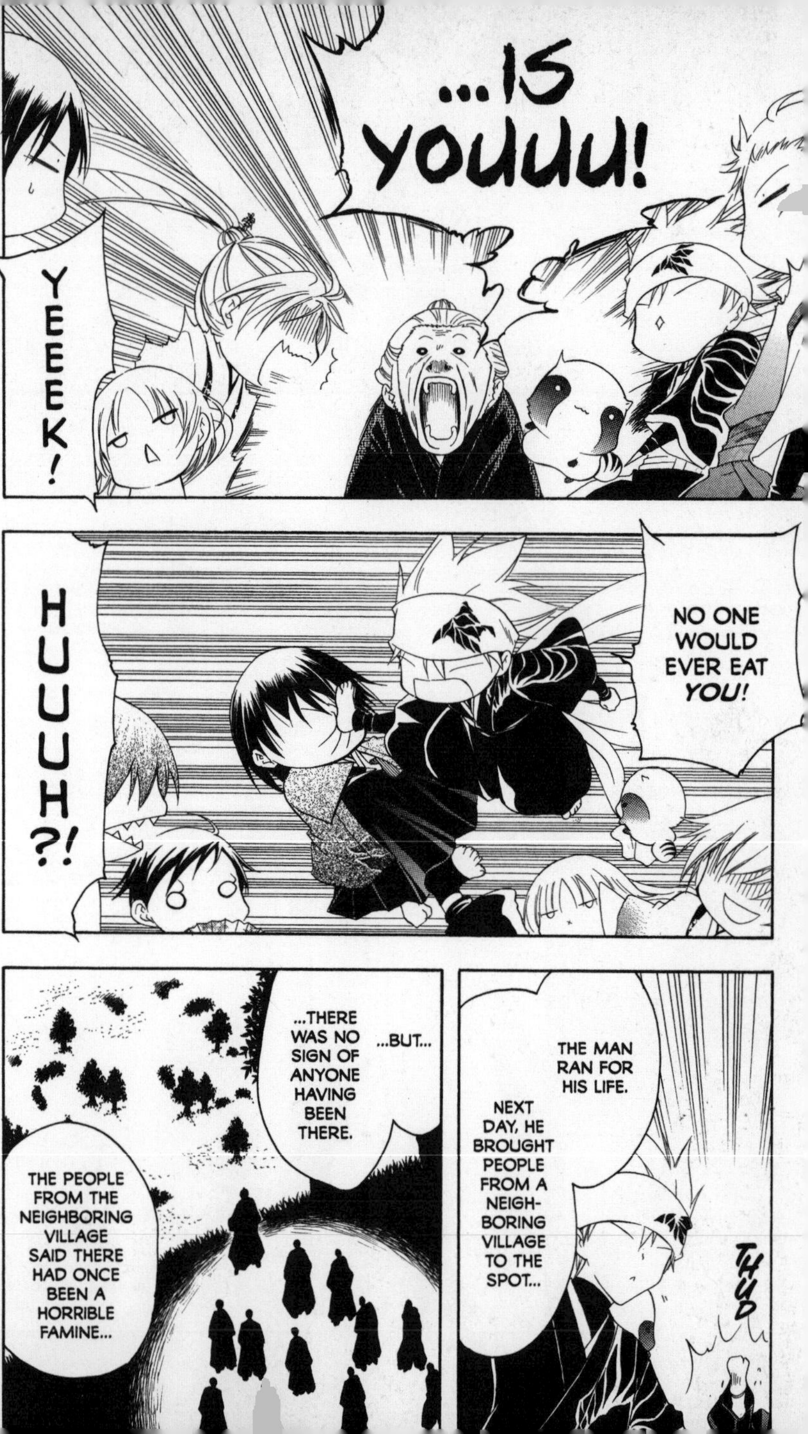
...IS YOUUU!
YEEEK!
NO ONE WOULD EVER EAT *YOU*!
HUUUH?!
THE MAN RAN FOR HIS LIFE.
NEXT DAY, HE BROUGHT PEOPLE FROM A NEIGH-BORING VILLAGE TO THE SPOT...
THUD
...BUT...
...THERE WAS NO SIGN OF ANYONE HAVING BEEN THERE.
THE PEOPLE FROM THE NEIGHBORING VILLAGE SAID THERE HAD ONCE BEEN A HORRIBLE FAMINE...

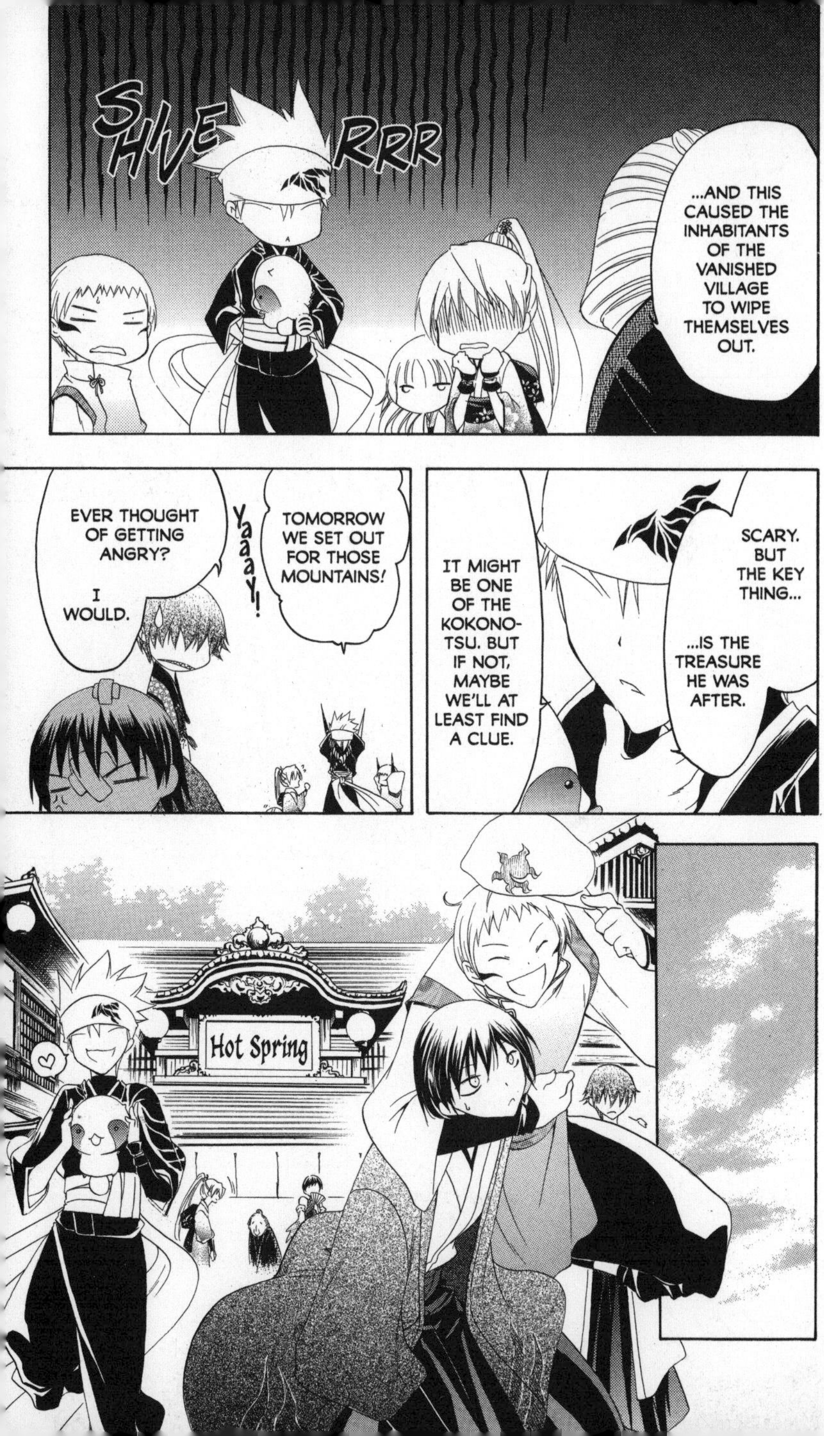
...AND THIS CAUSED THE INHABITANTS OF THE VANISHED VILLAGE TO WIPE THEMSELVES OUT.
SHIVERRR
SCARY. BUT THE KEY THING...
...IS THE TREASURE HE WAS AFTER.
IT MIGHT BE ONE OF THE KOKONOTSU. BUT IF NOT, MAYBE WE'LL AT LEAST FIND A CLUE.
TOMORROW WE SET OUT FOR THOSE MOUNTAINS!
Yaaay!
EVER THOUGHT OF GETTING ANGRY?
I WOULD.
Hot Spring

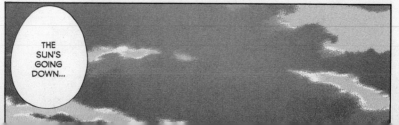

THE SUN'S GOING DOWN...

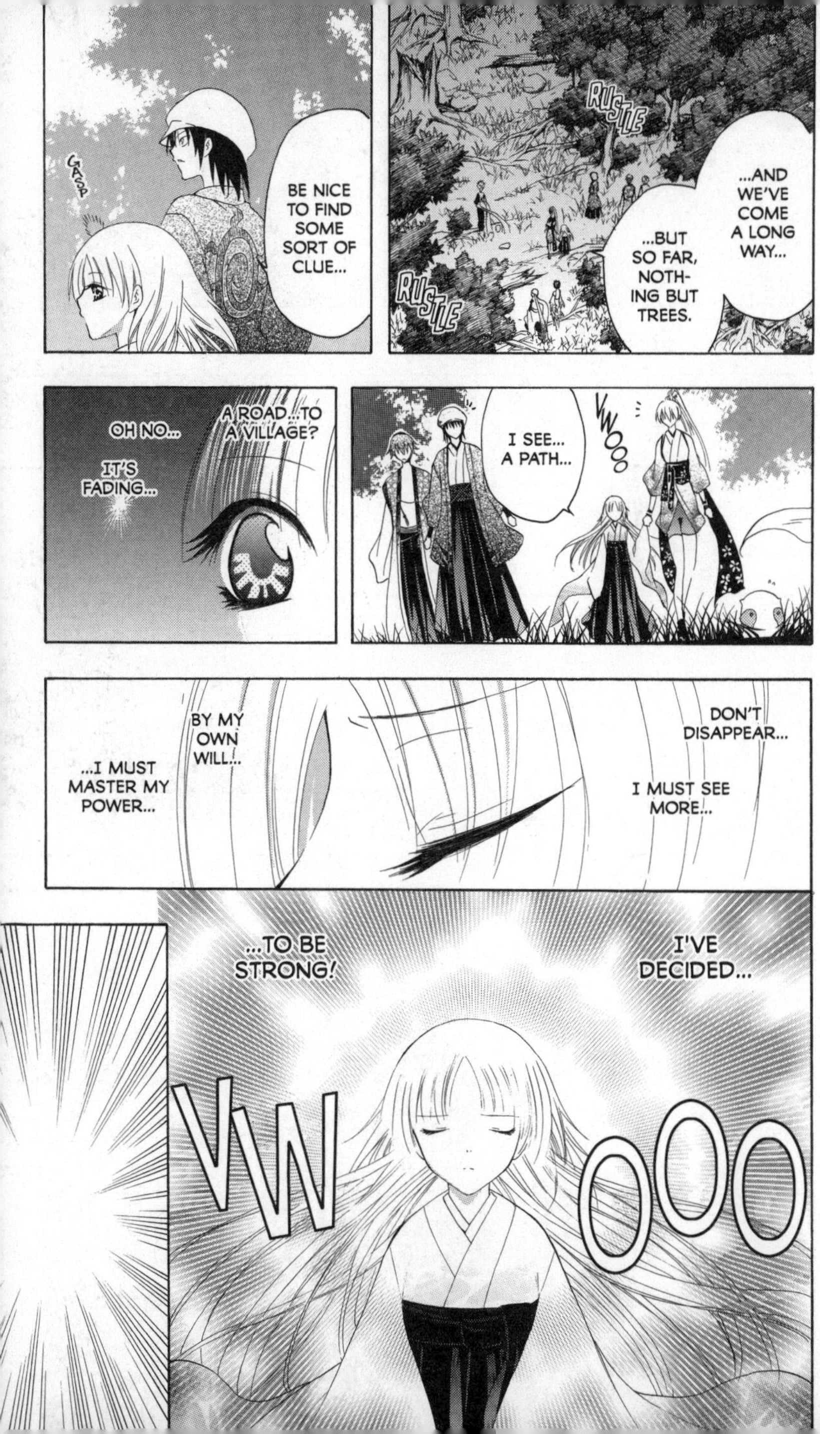
RUSTLE
...AND WE'VE COME A LONG WAY...
...BUT SO FAR, NOTHING BUT TREES.
RUSTLE
BE NICE TO FIND SOME SORT OF CLUE...
GASP
VWOOO
I SEE... A PATH...
A ROAD...TO A VILLAGE?
OH NO...
IT'S FADING...
DON'T DISAPPEAR...
I MUST SEE MORE...
BY MY OWN WILL...
...I MUST MASTER MY POWER...
I'VE DECIDED...
...TO BE STRONG!
VWOOO

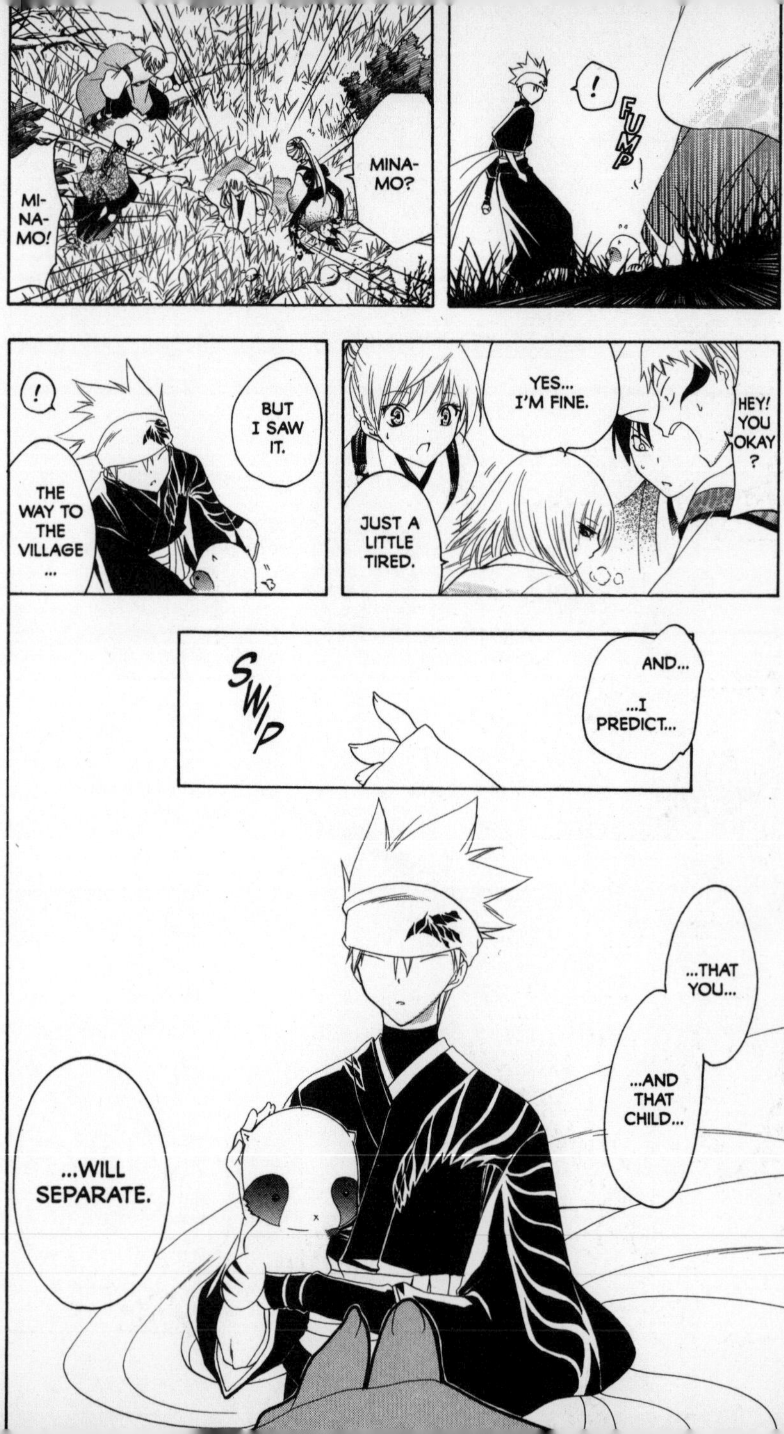
!
FUMP
MINA-MO?
MI-NA-MO!
HEY! YOU OKAY?
YES... I'M FINE.
JUST A LITTLE TIRED.
!
BUT I SAW IT.
THE WAY TO THE VILLAGE...
AND...
...I PREDICT...
SWIP
...THAT YOU...
...AND THAT CHILD...
...WILL SEPARATE.

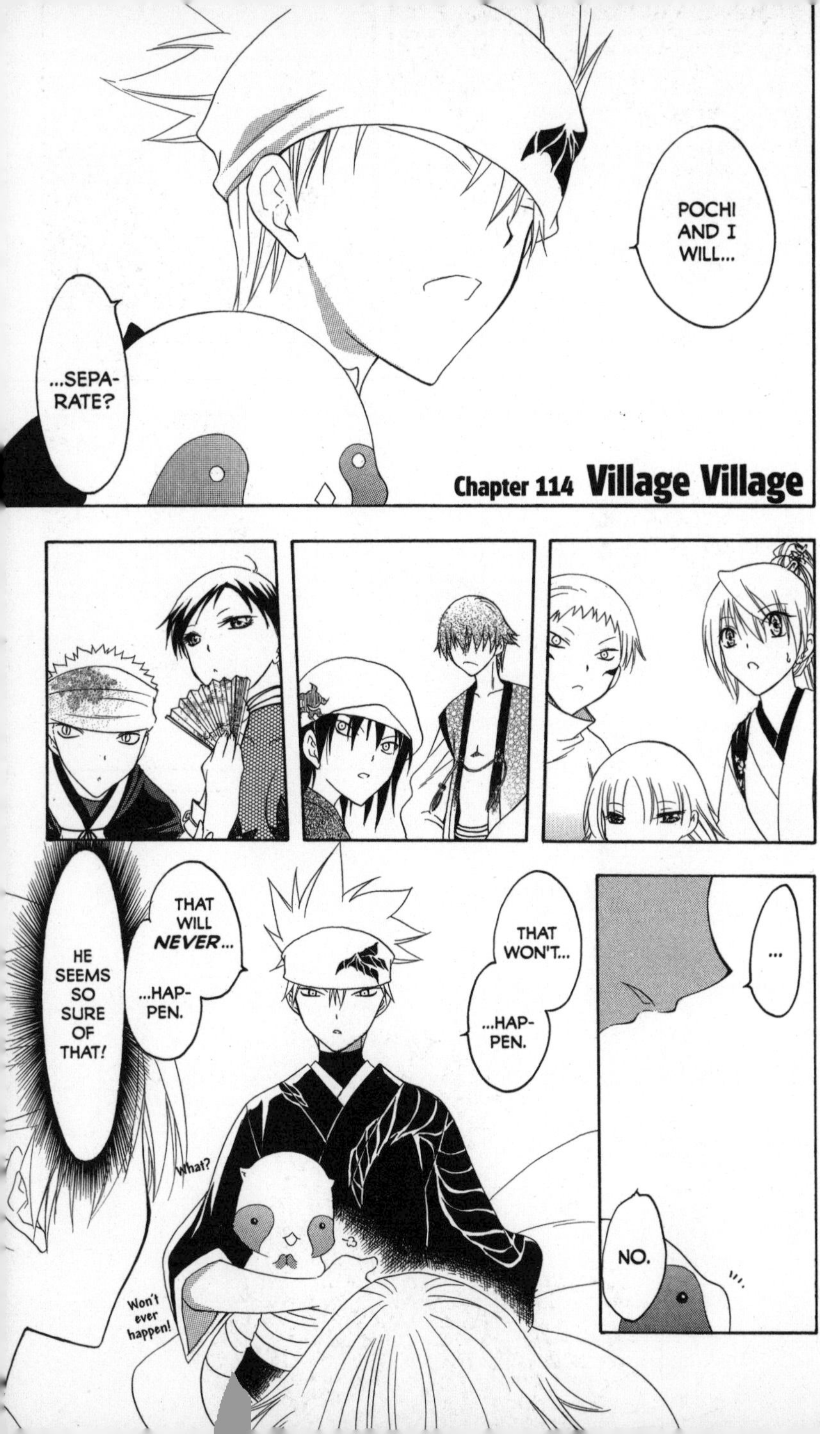
POCHI AND I WILL...
...SEPARATE?
Chapter 114 Village Village
...
NO.
THAT WON'T...
...HAPPEN.
THAT WILL NEVER...
...HAPPEN.
HE SEEMS SO SURE OF THAT!
What?
Won't ever happen!

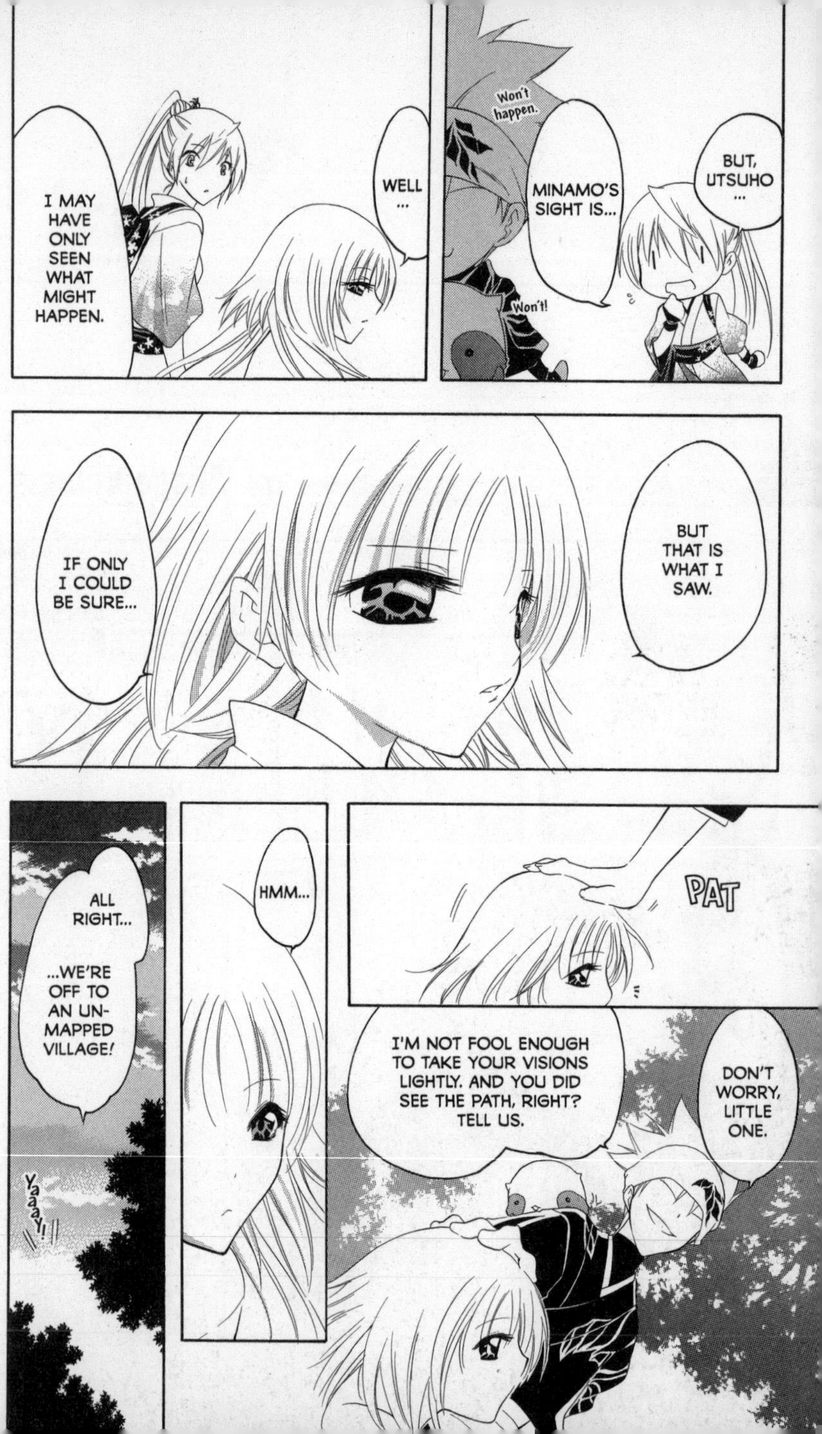
BUT, UTSUHO ...
Won't happen.
MINAMO'S SIGHT IS...
Won't!
WELL ...
I MAY HAVE ONLY SEEN WHAT MIGHT HAPPEN.
BUT THAT IS WHAT I SAW.
IF ONLY I COULD BE SURE...
PAT
DON'T WORRY, LITTLE ONE.
I'M NOT FOOL ENOUGH TO TAKE YOUR VISIONS LIGHTLY. AND YOU DID SEE THE PATH, RIGHT? TELL US.
HMM...
ALL RIGHT...
...WE'RE OFF TO AN UN-MAPPED VILLAGE!
Yaaay!!

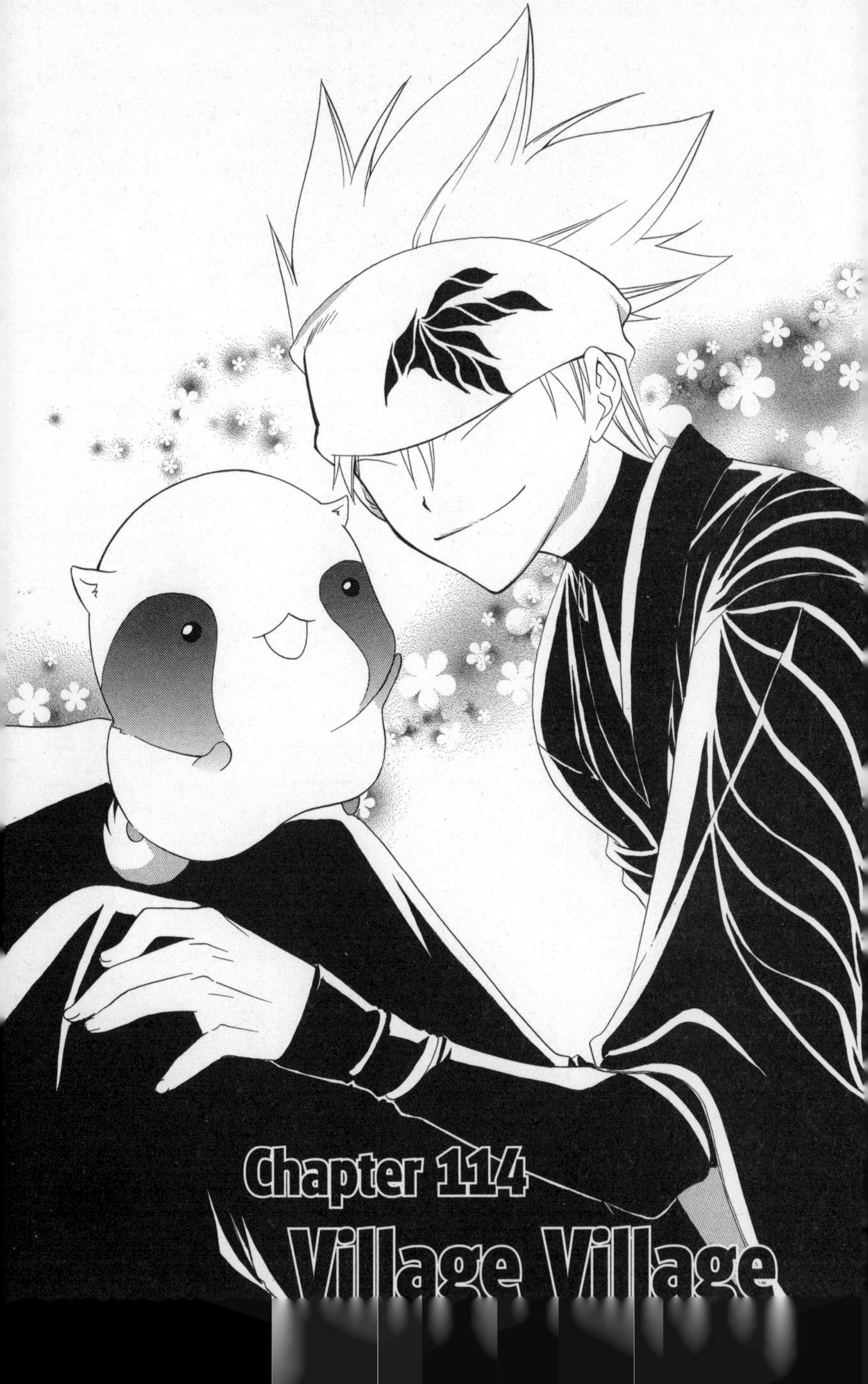
Chapter 114
Village Village

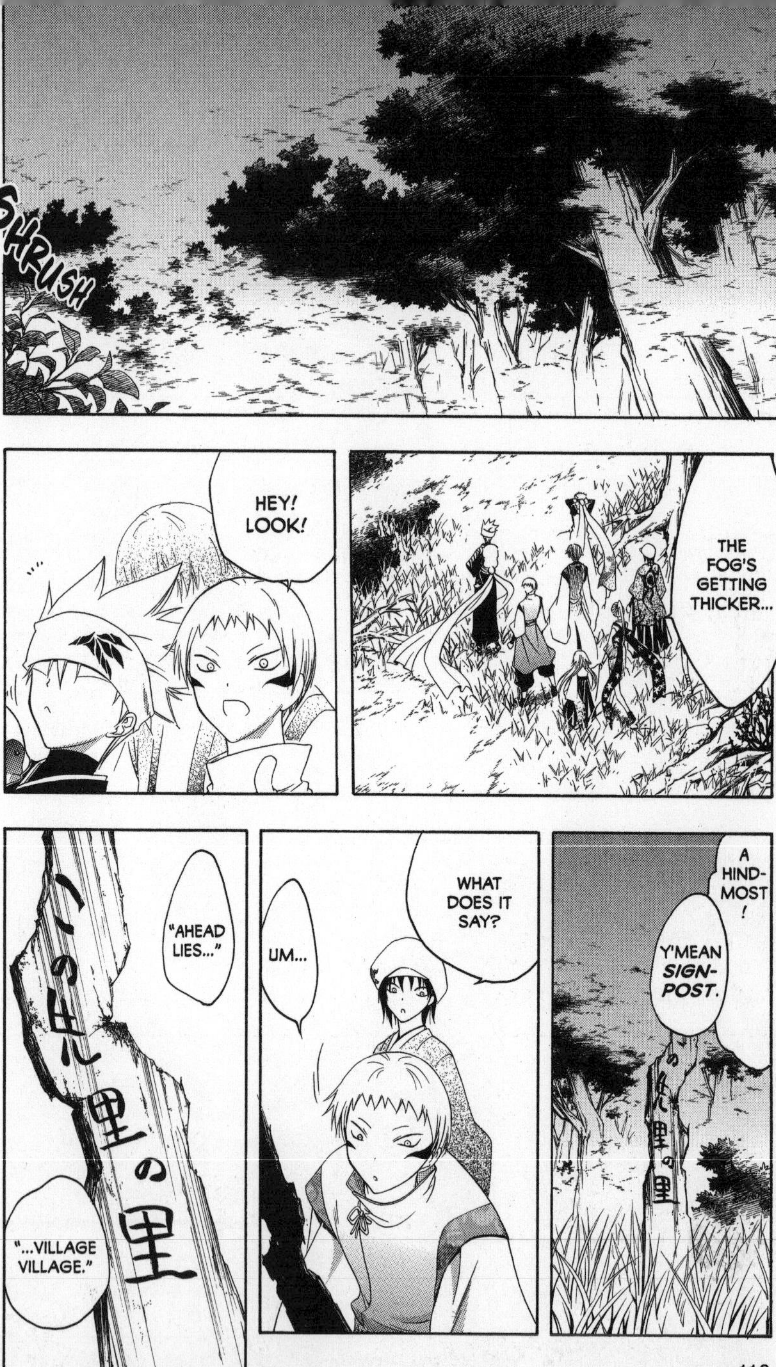
SHRUSH
THE FOG'S GETTING THICKER...
HEY! LOOK!
...
A HIND-MOST!
Y'MEAN *SIGN-POST*.
WHAT DOES IT SAY?
UM...
“AHEAD LIES...”
この先里の里
“...VILLAGE VILLAGE.”

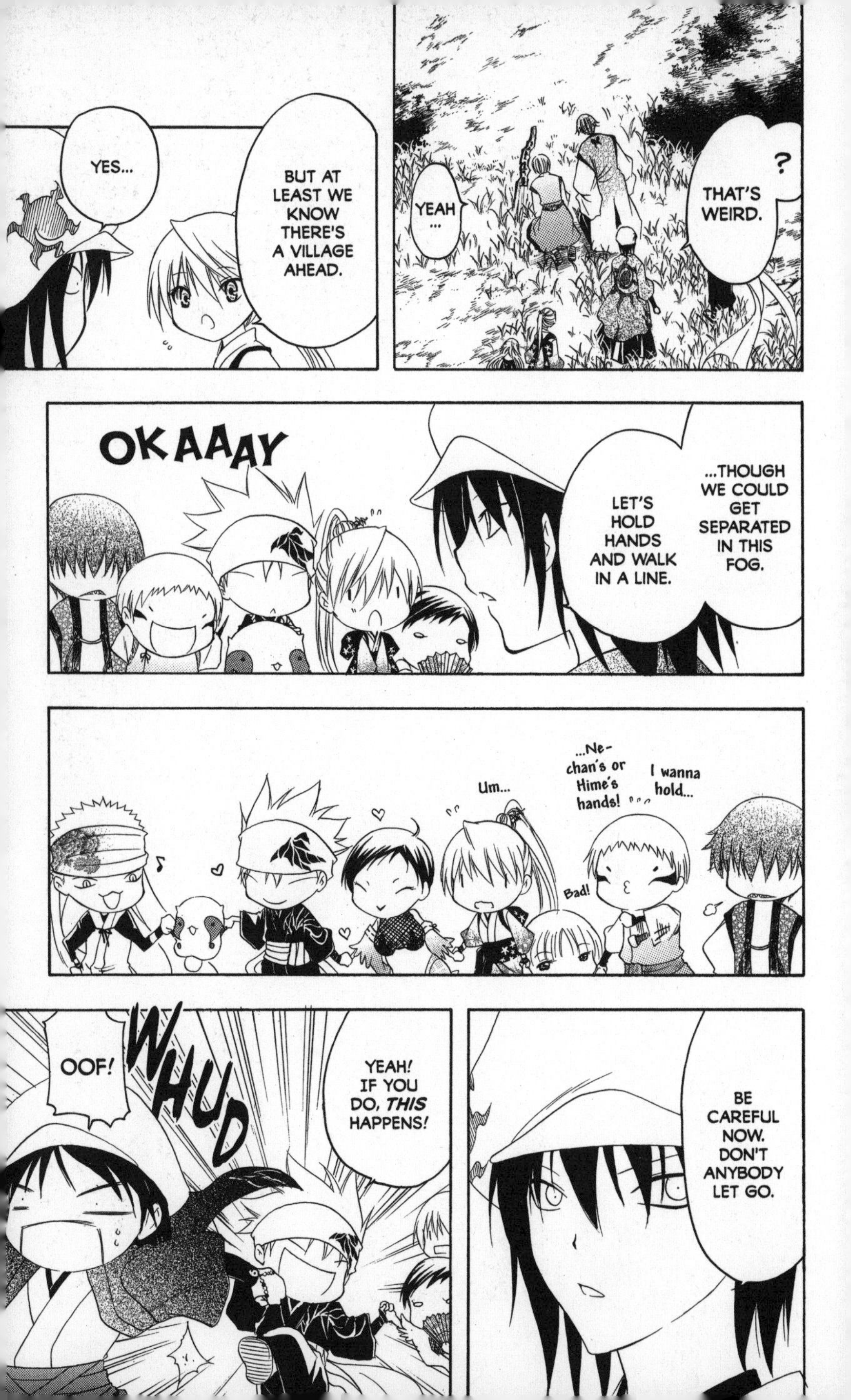
?
THAT'S WEIRD.
YEAH ...
BUT AT LEAST WE KNOW THERE'S A VILLAGE AHEAD.
YES...
...THOUGH WE COULD GET SEPARATED IN THIS FOG.
LET'S HOLD HANDS AND WALK IN A LINE.
OKAAAY
I wanna hold...
...Ne-chan's or Hime's hands!
Um...
Bad!
BE CAREFUL NOW. DON'T ANYBODY LET GO.
YEAH! IF YOU DO, *THIS* HAPPENS!
WHUD
OOF!

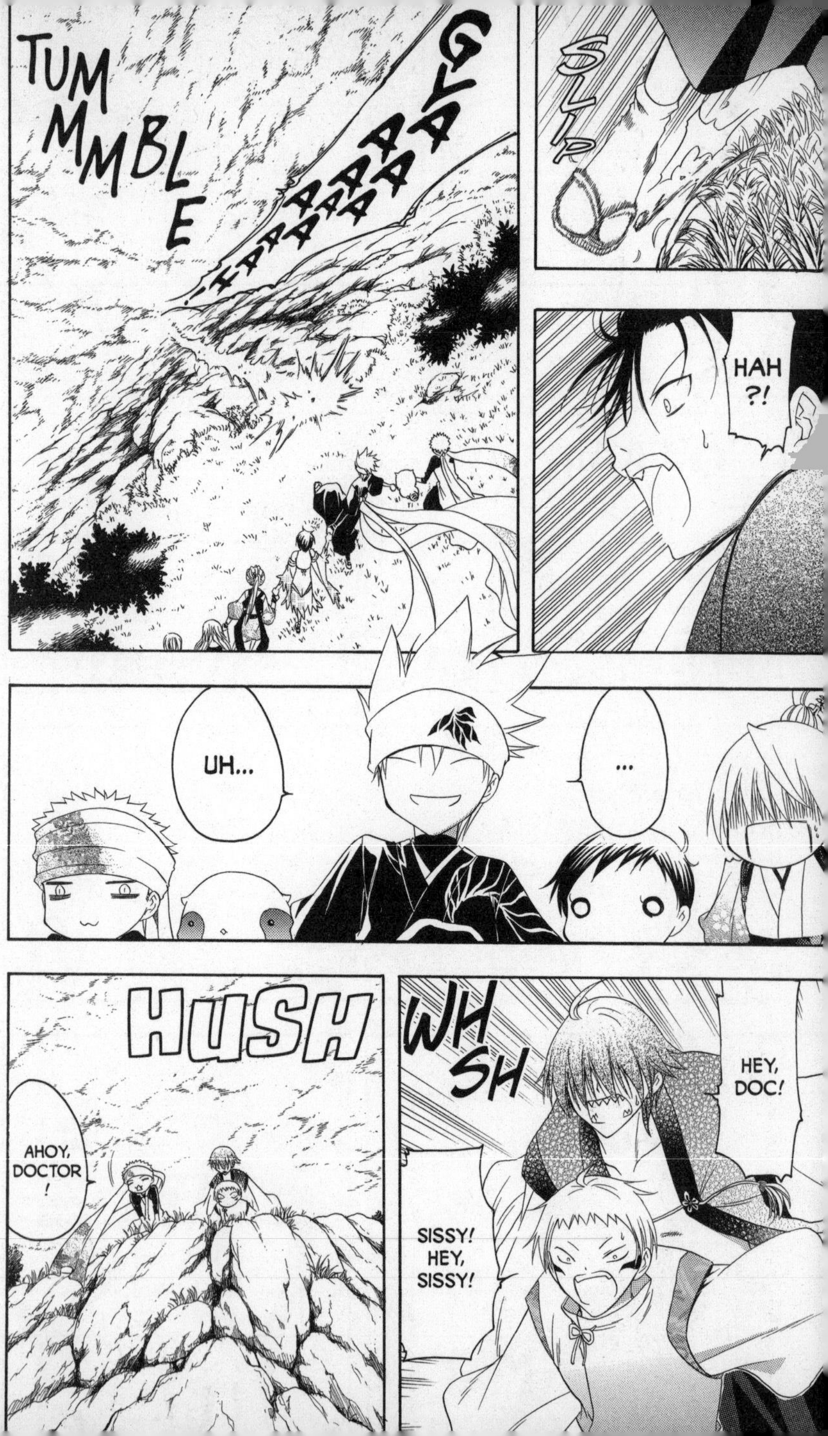

SLIP
HAH ?!
TUMMMBLE
GYAAAAAAAAAAA!
...
UH...
HEY, DOC!
SISSY! HEY, SISSY!
WHSH
HUSH
AHOY, DOCTOR!

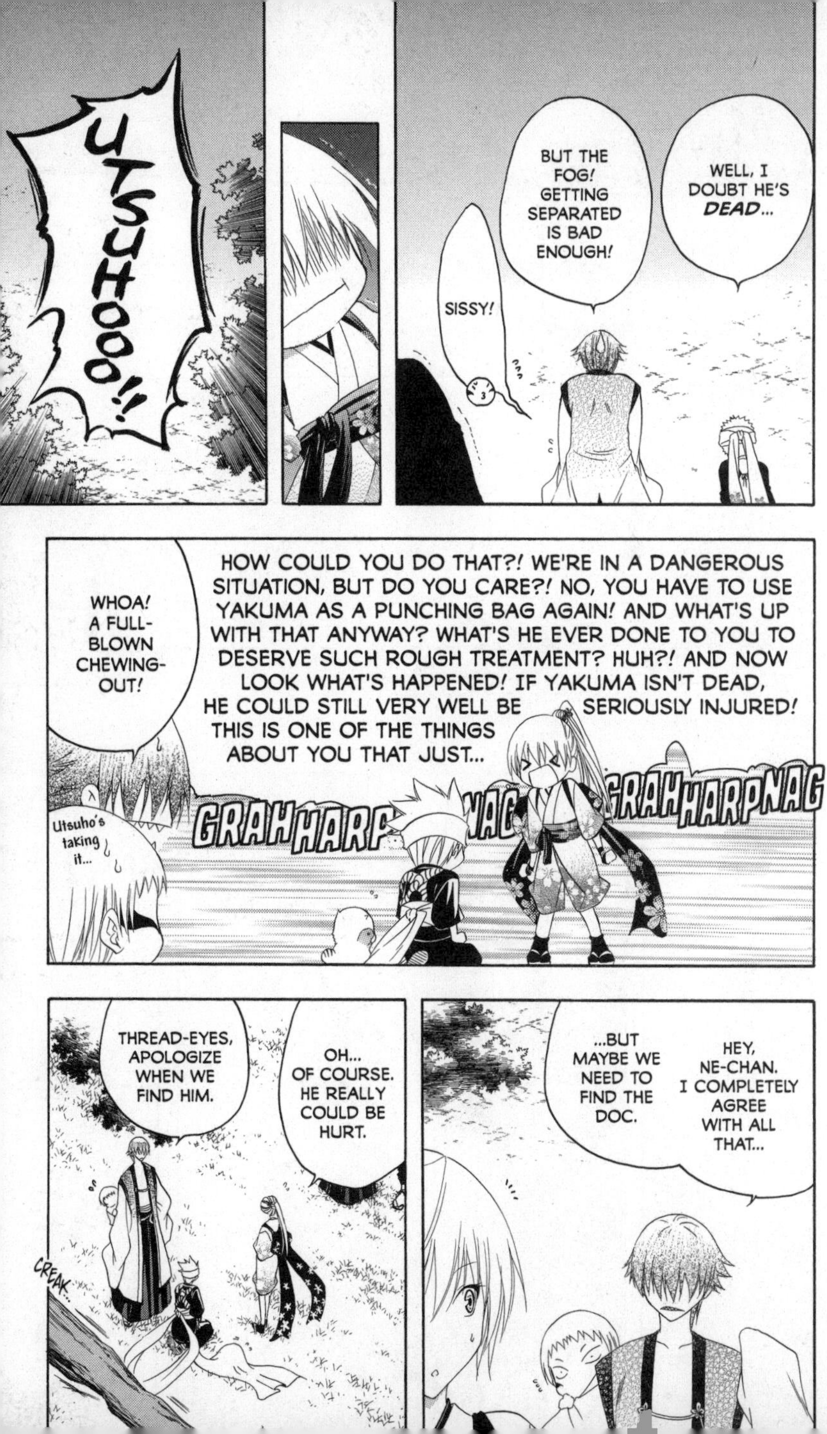
WELL, I DOUBT HE'S DEAD...
BUT THE FOG! GETTING SEPARATED IS BAD ENOUGH!
SISSY!
UTSUHOOO!!
HOW COULD YOU DO THAT?! WE'RE IN A DANGEROUS SITUATION, BUT DO YOU CARE?! NO, YOU HAVE TO USE YAKUMA AS A PUNCHING BAG AGAIN! AND WHAT'S UP WITH THAT ANYWAY? WHAT'S HE EVER DONE TO YOU TO DESERVE SUCH ROUGH TREATMENT? HUH?! AND NOW LOOK WHAT'S HAPPENED! IF YAKUMA ISN'T DEAD, HE COULD STILL VERY WELL BE SERIOUSLY INJURED! THIS IS ONE OF THE THINGS ABOUT YOU THAT JUST...
GRAHHARPNAG
GRAHHARPNAG
WHOA! A FULL-BLOWN CHEWING-OUT!
Utsuho's taking it...
HEY, NE-CHAN. I COMPLETELY AGREE WITH ALL THAT...
...BUT MAYBE WE NEED TO FIND THE DOC.
OH... OF COURSE. HE REALLY COULD BE HURT.
THREAD-EYES, APOLOGIZE WHEN WE FIND HIM.
CREAK...

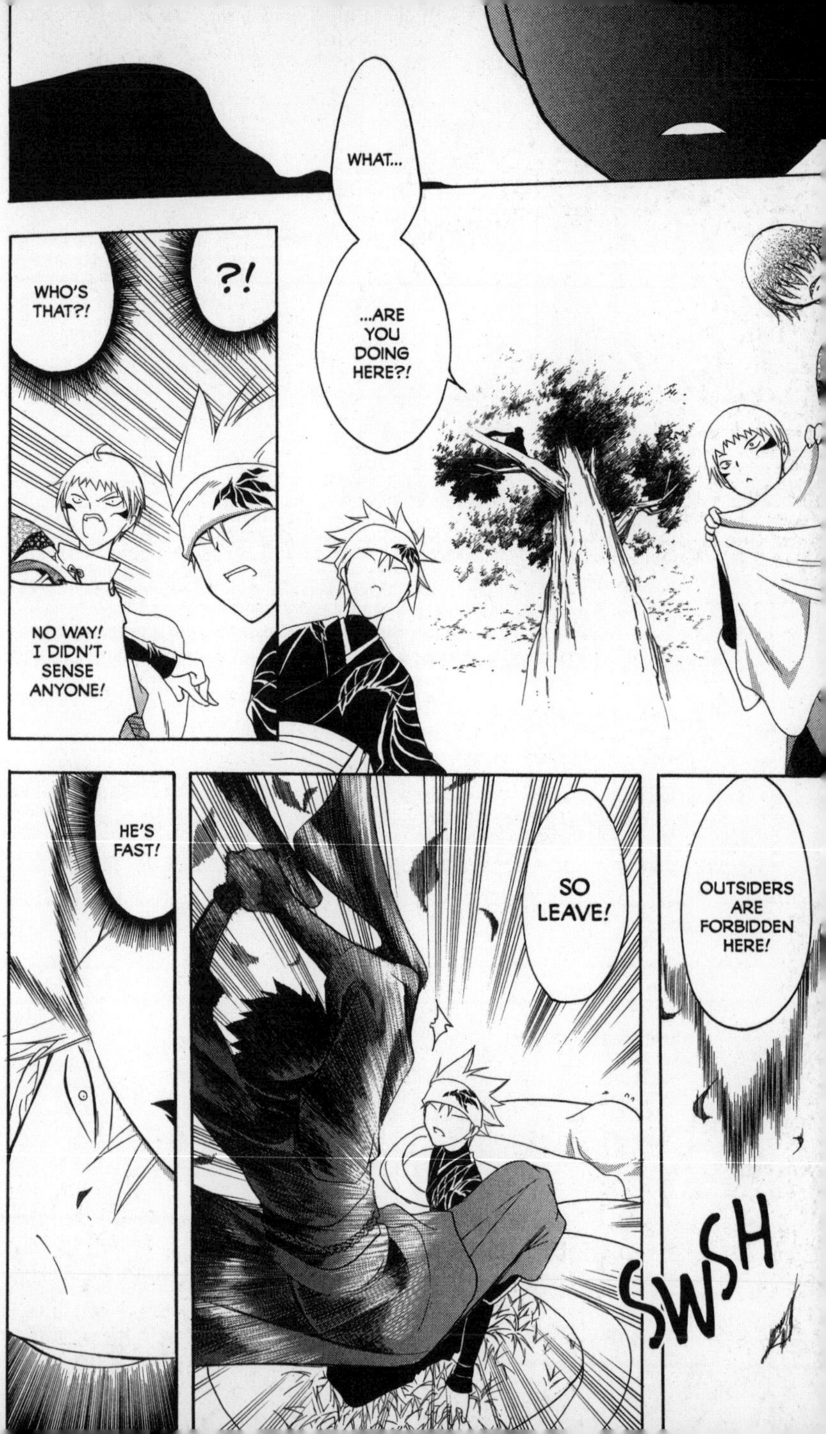
WHAT... ...ARE YOU DOING HERE?!
?!
WHO'S THAT?!
NO WAY! I DIDN'T SENSE ANYONE!
OUTSIDERS ARE FORBIDDEN HERE!
SO LEAVE!
SWSH
HE'S FAST!

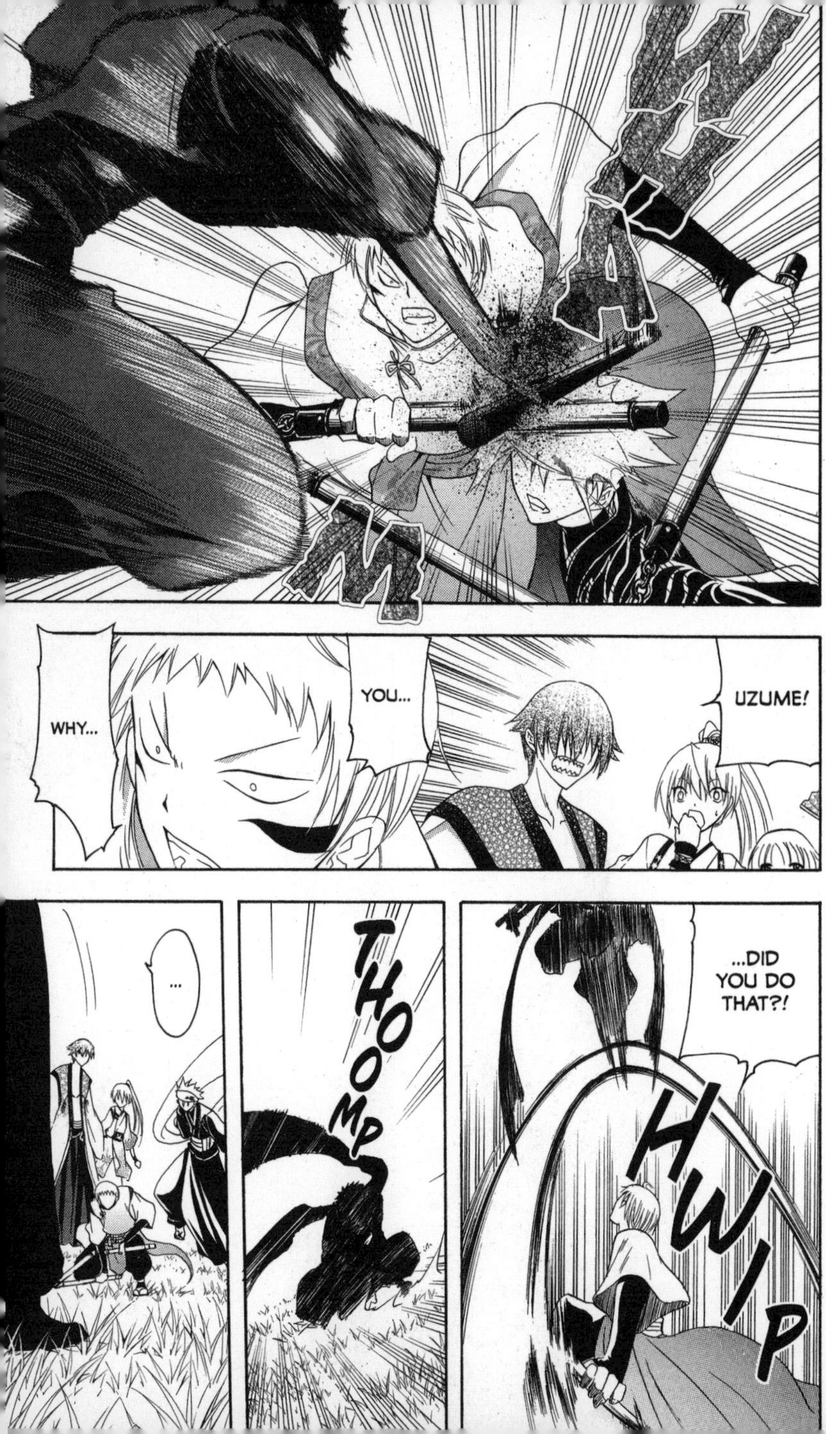
WHAM
UZUME!
YOU...
WHY...
...DID YOU DO THAT?!
HWIP
THOOMP
...

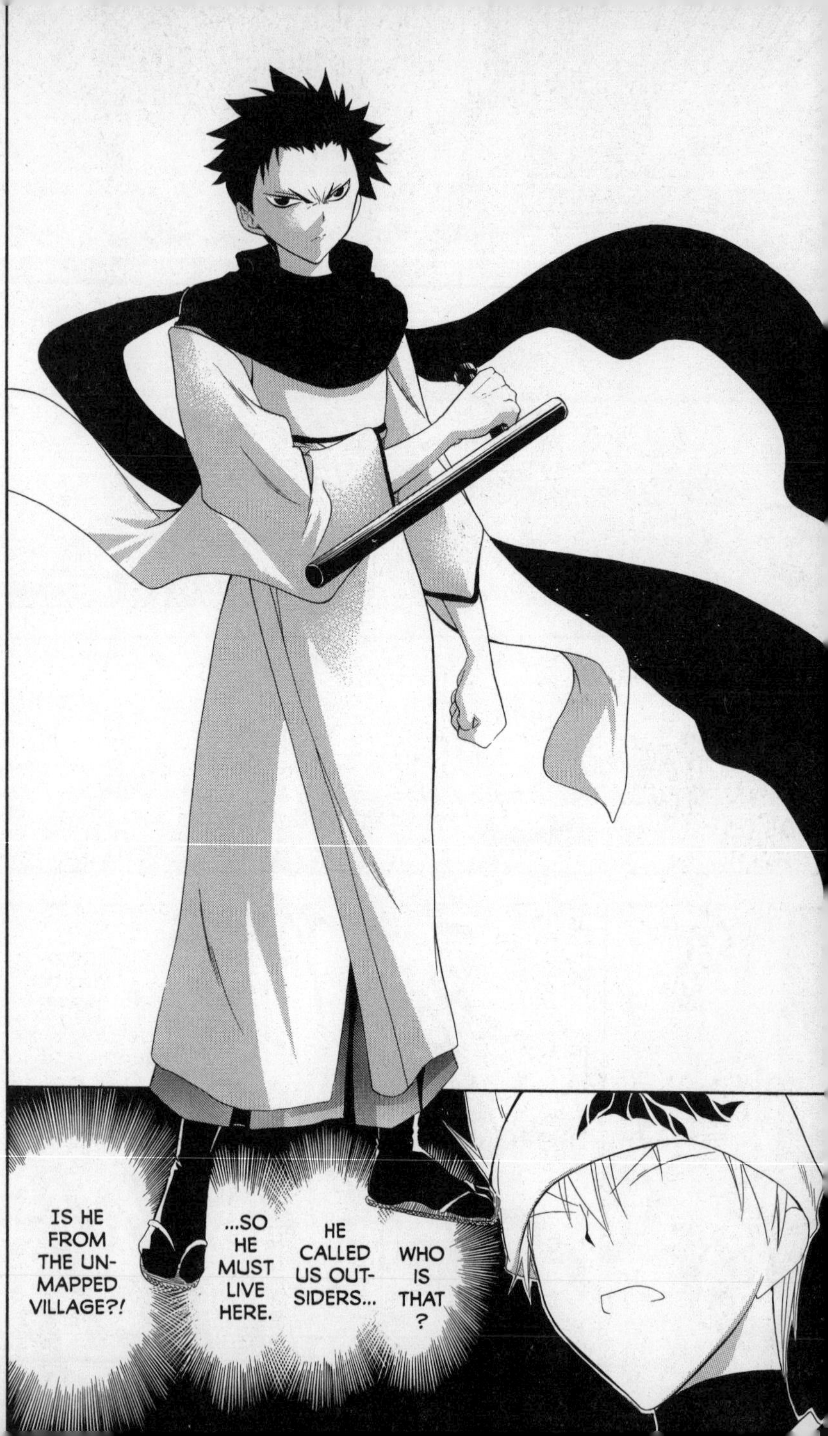
WHO IS THAT?
HE CALLED US OUTSIDERS...
...SO HE MUST LIVE HERE.
IS HE FROM THE UN-MAPPED VILLAGE?!

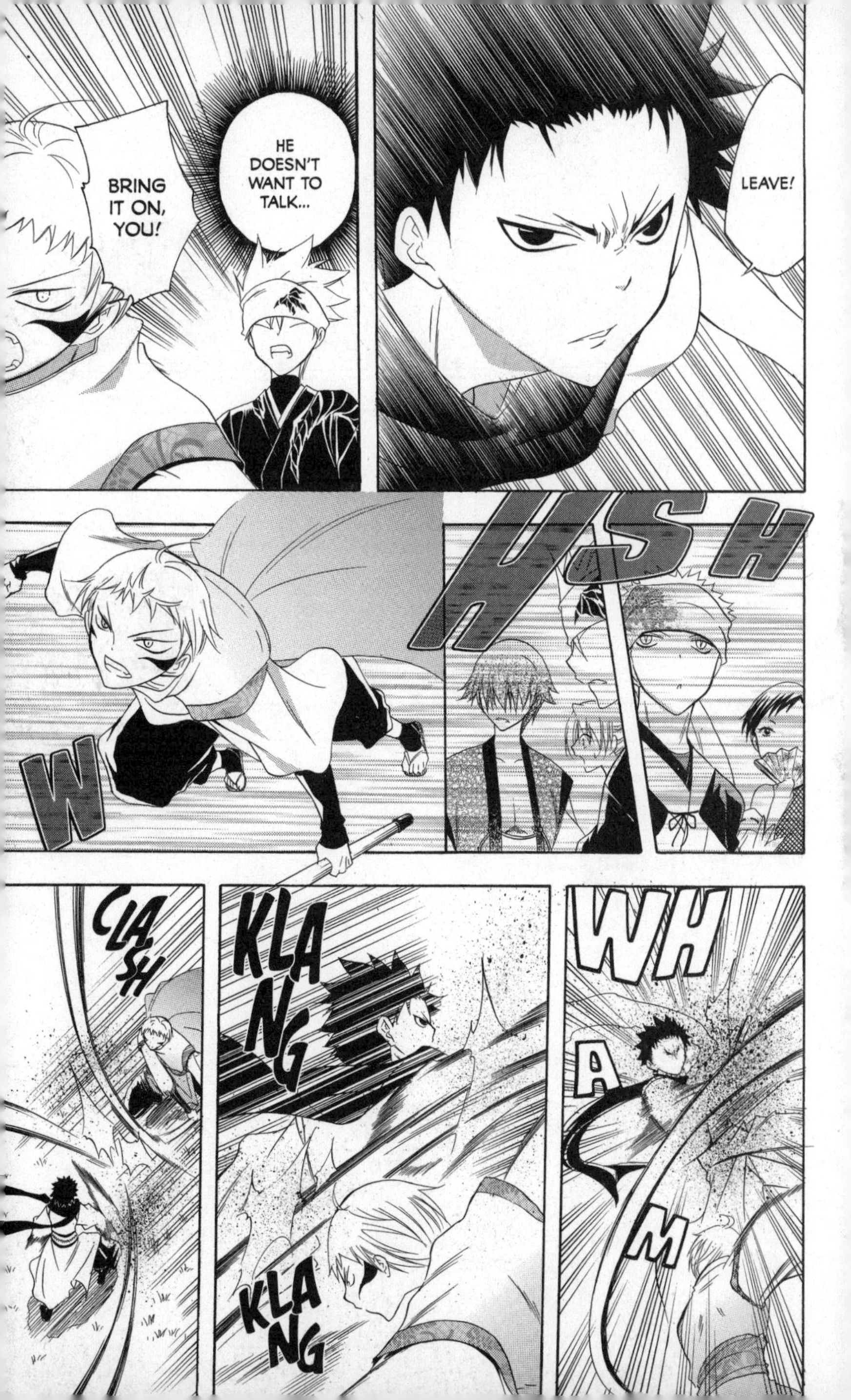
LEAVE!
HE DOESN'T WANT TO TALK...
BRING IT ON, YOU!
WHISH
WHAM
KLANG
KLANG
CLASH

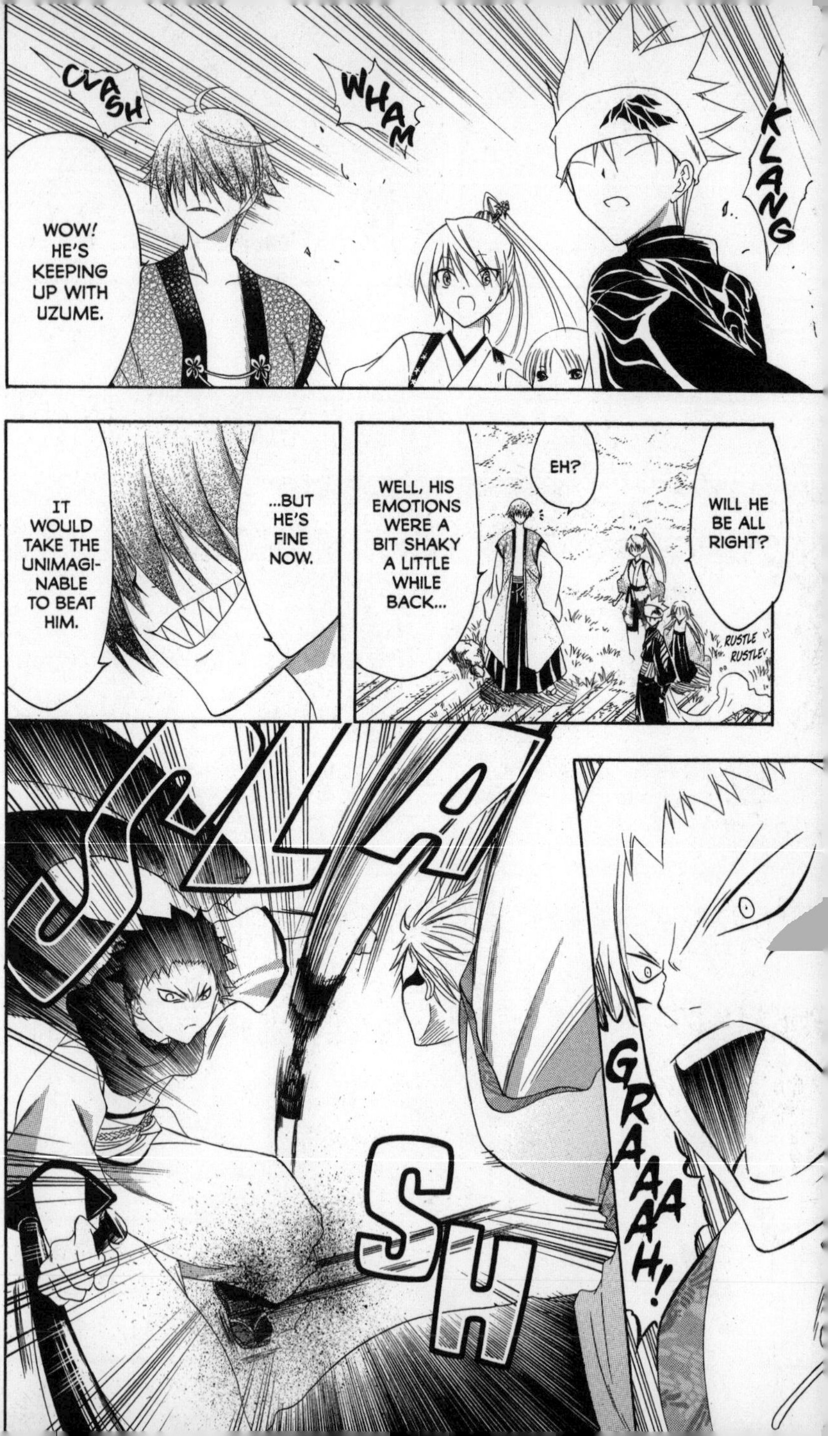
KLANG
WHAM
CLASH
WOW! HE'S KEEPING UP WITH UZUME.
WILL HE BE ALL RIGHT?
EH?
WELL, HIS EMOTIONS WERE A BIT SHAKY A LITTLE WHILE BACK...
RUSTLE RUSTLE
...BUT HE'S FINE NOW.
IT WOULD TAKE THE UNIMAGI-NABLE TO BEAT HIM.
SLA
GRAAAAH!
SH

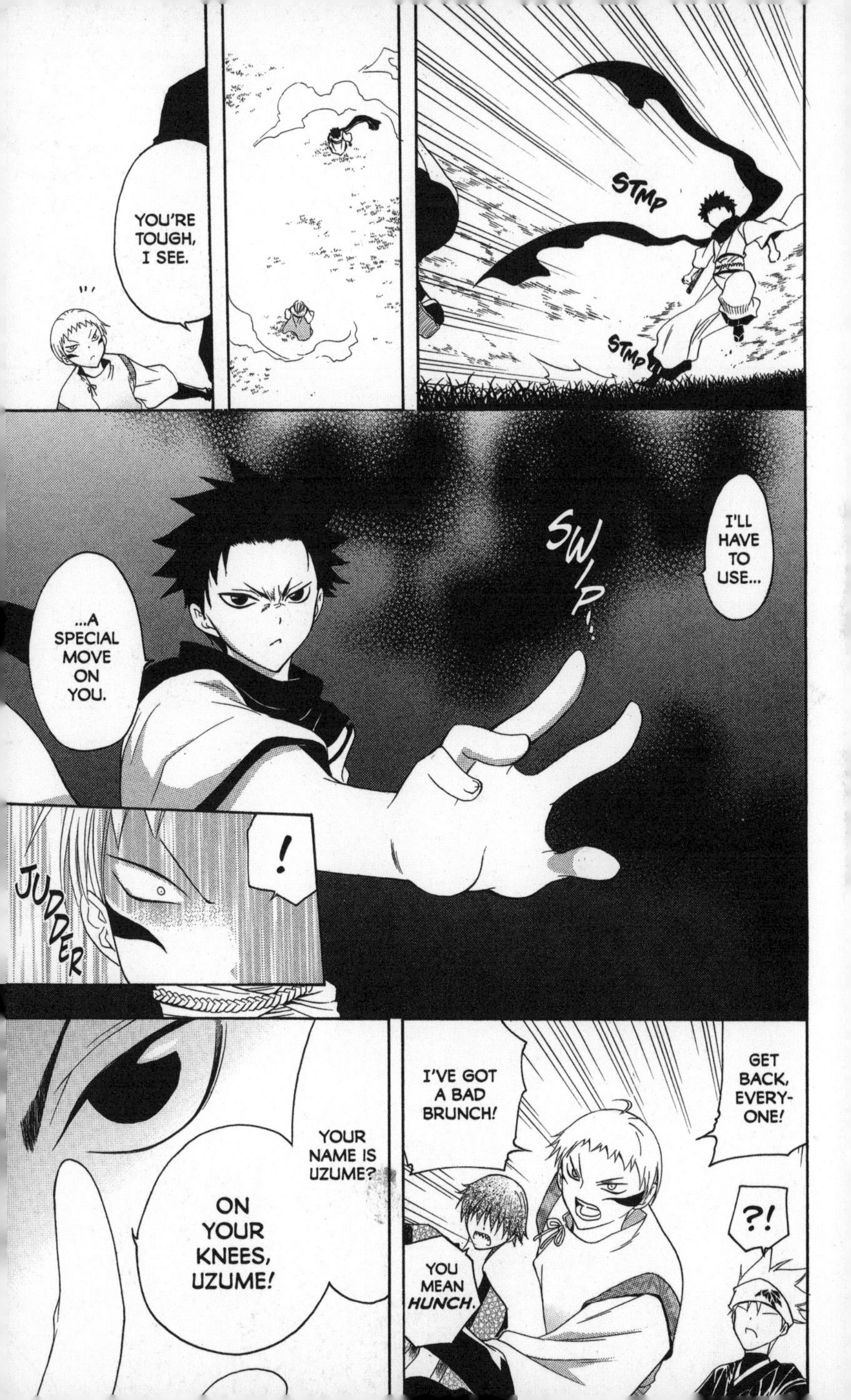
STMP
STMP
YOU'RE TOUGH, I SEE.
I'LL HAVE TO USE...
SWIP
...A SPECIAL MOVE ON YOU.
!
JUDDER
GET BACK, EVERY-ONE!
I'VE GOT A BAD BRUNCH!
?!
YOU MEAN *HUNCH*.
YOUR NAME IS UZUME?
ON YOUR KNEES, UZUME!

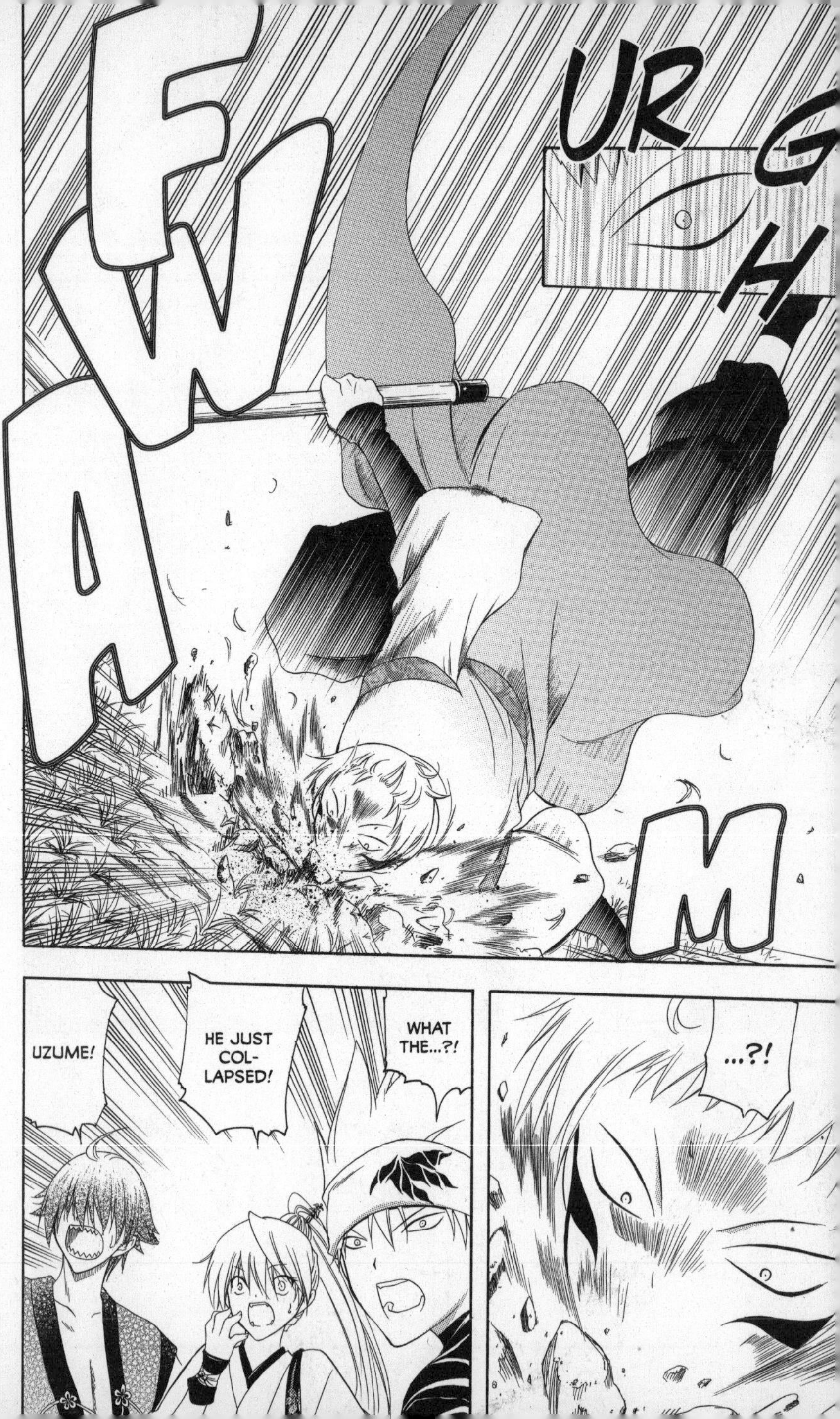
URGH
FWAM
...?!
WHAT THE...?!
HE JUST COL-LAPSED!
UZUME!

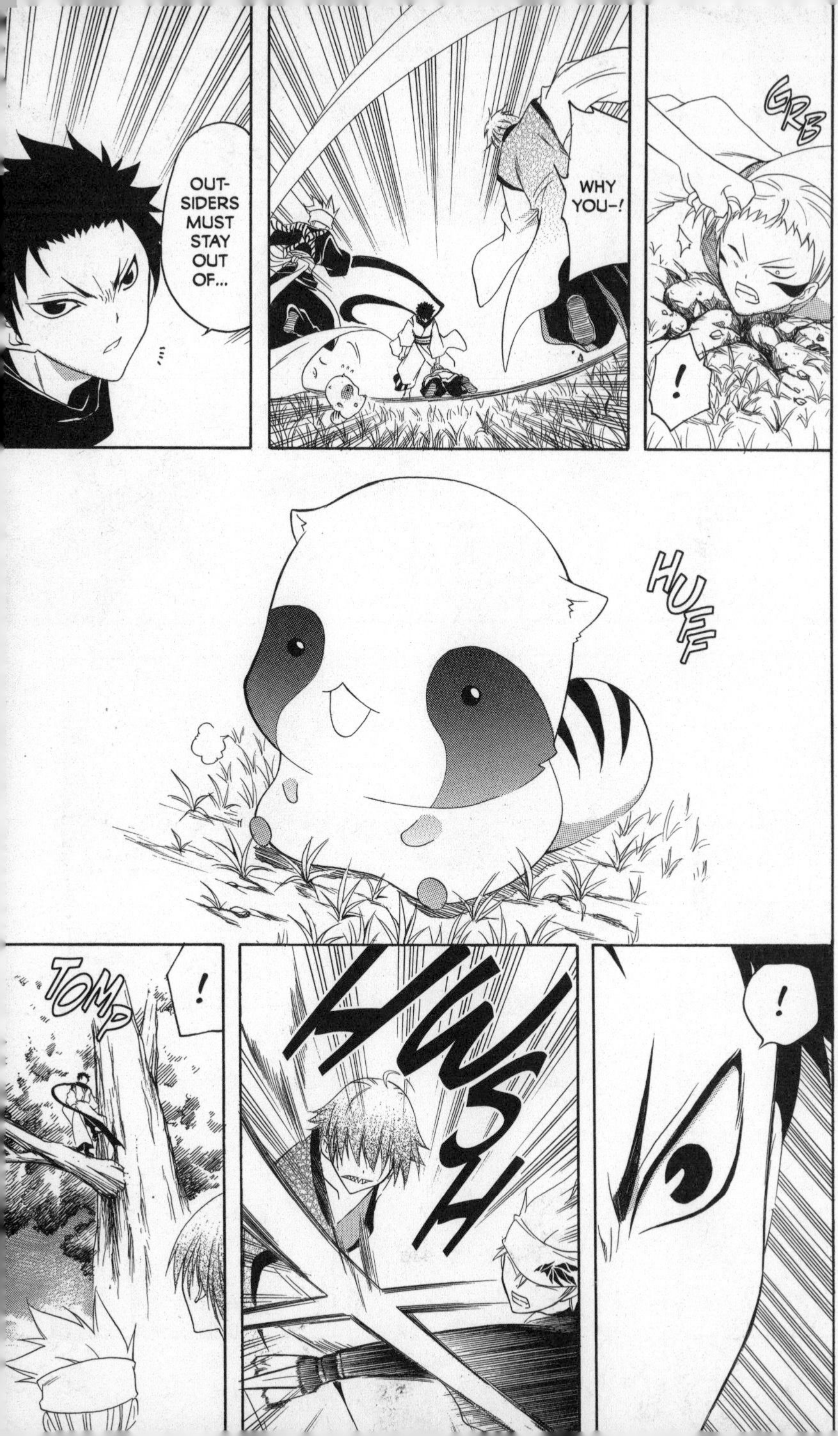
GRB
!
WHY YOU-!
OUT-SIDERS MUST STAY OUT OF...
HUFF
!
HWSH
TOMP
!

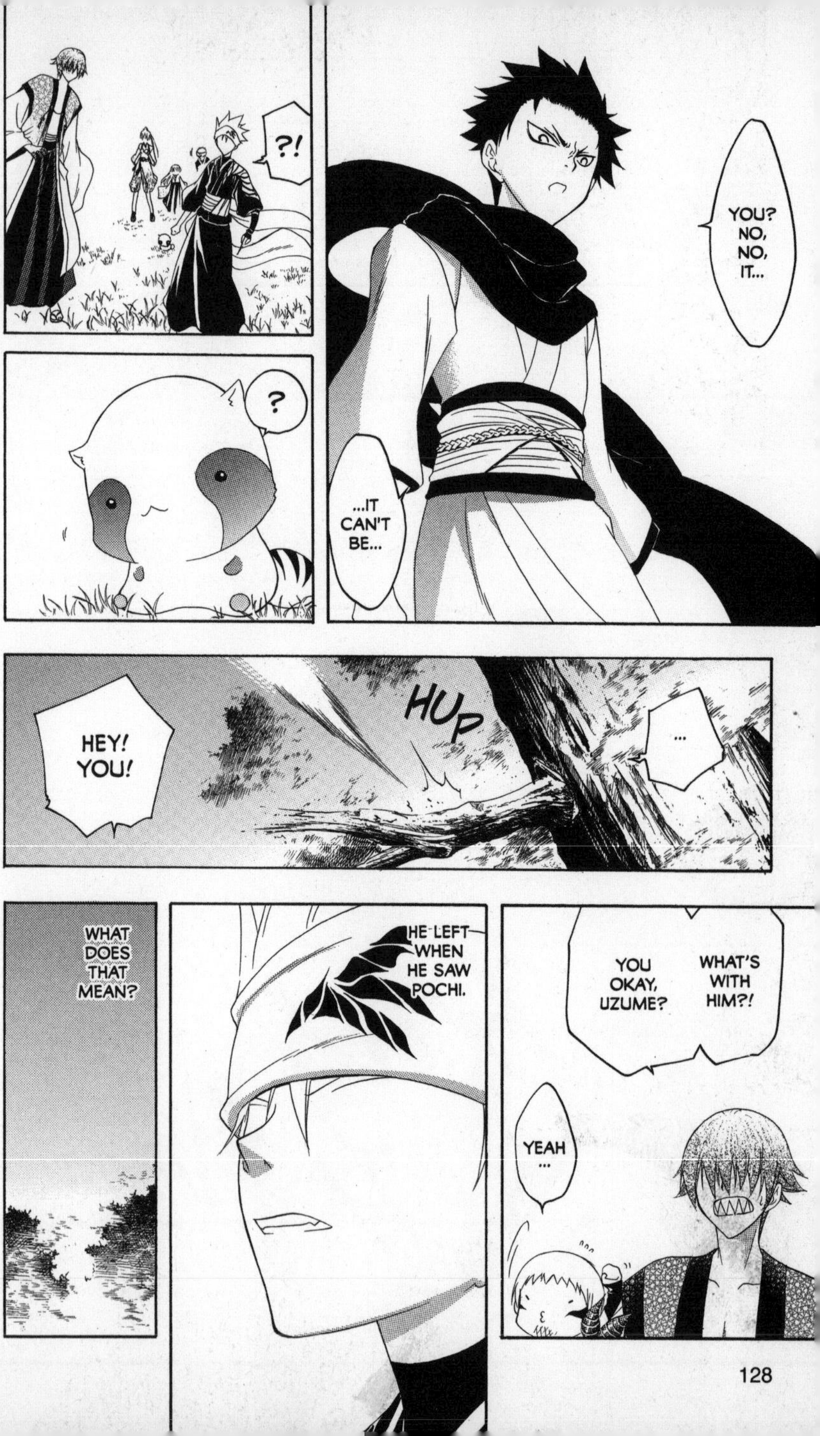
YOU? NO, NO, IT...
...IT CAN'T BE...
?!
?
...
HUP
HEY! YOU!
WHAT'S WITH HIM?!
YOU OKAY, UZUME?
YEAH ...
HE LEFT WHEN HE SAW POCHI.
WHAT DOES THAT MEAN?

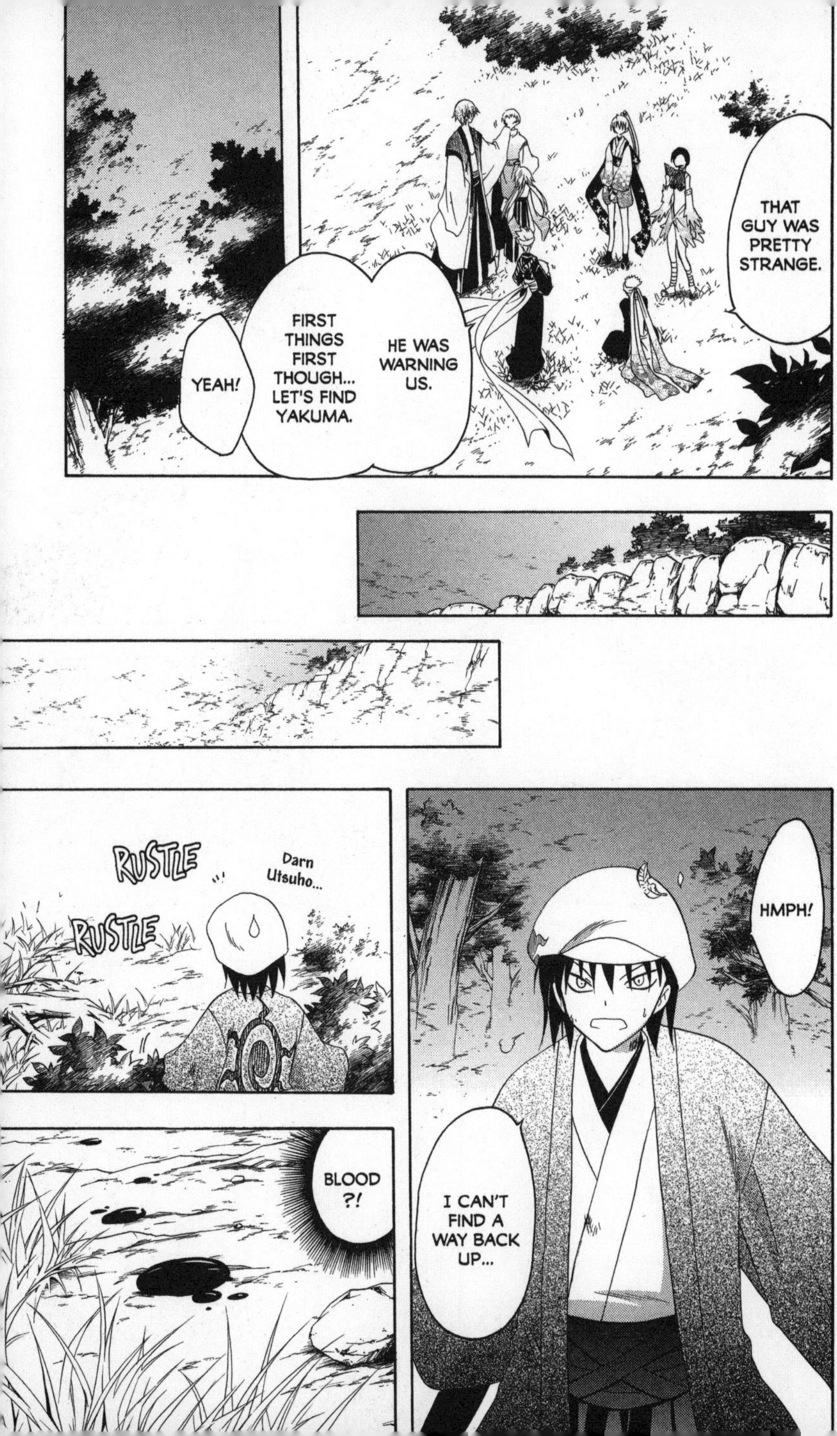
THAT GUY WAS PRETTY STRANGE.
HE WAS WARNING US.
FIRST THINGS FIRST THOUGH... LET'S FIND YAKUMA.
YEAH!
HMPH!
I CAN'T FIND A WAY BACK UP...
RUSTLE
Darn Utsuho...
RUSTLE
BLOOD ?!

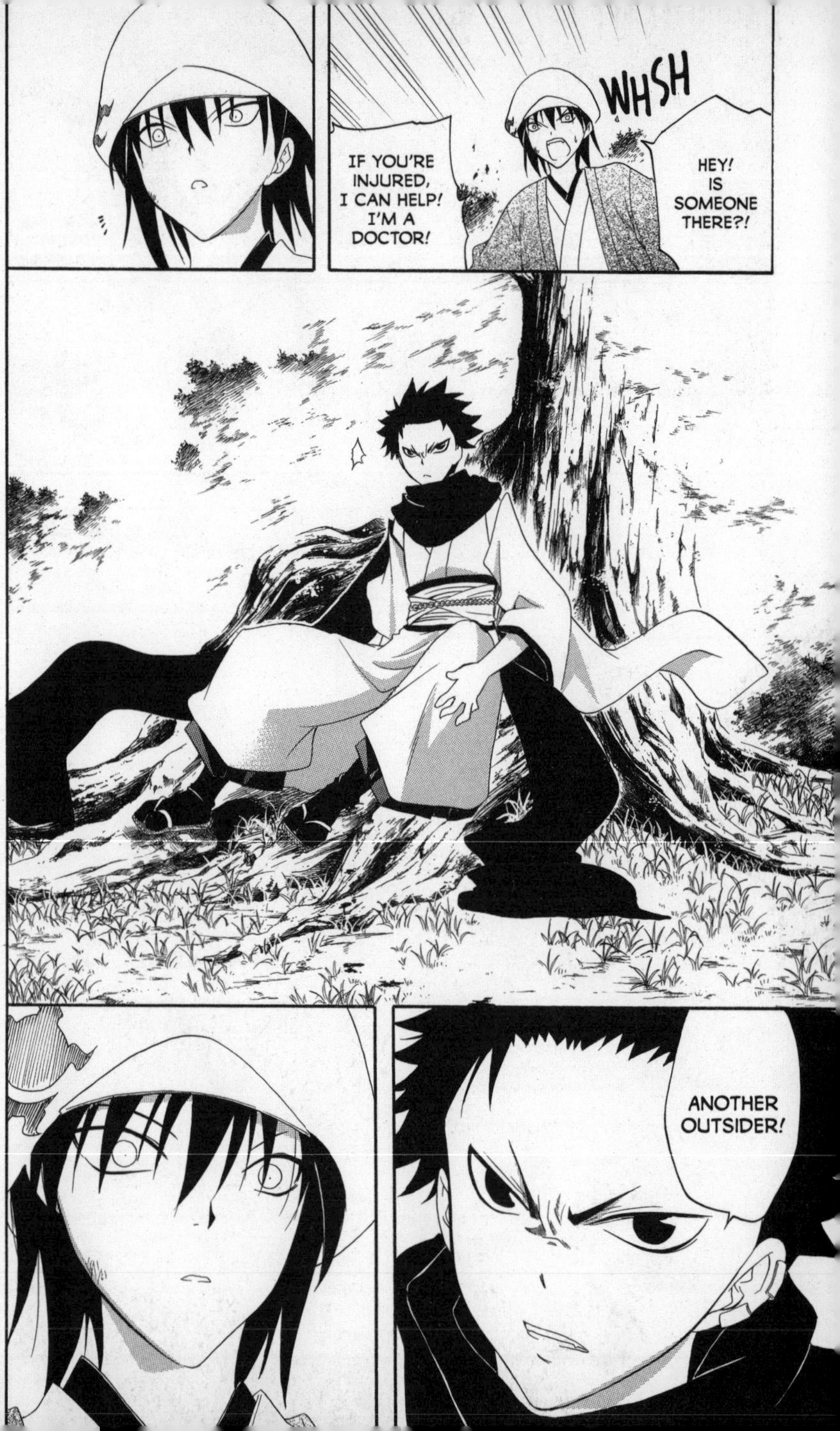
WHSH
HEY! IS SOMEONE THERE?!
IF YOU'RE INJURED, I CAN HELP! I'M A DOCTOR!
ANOTHER OUTSIDER!

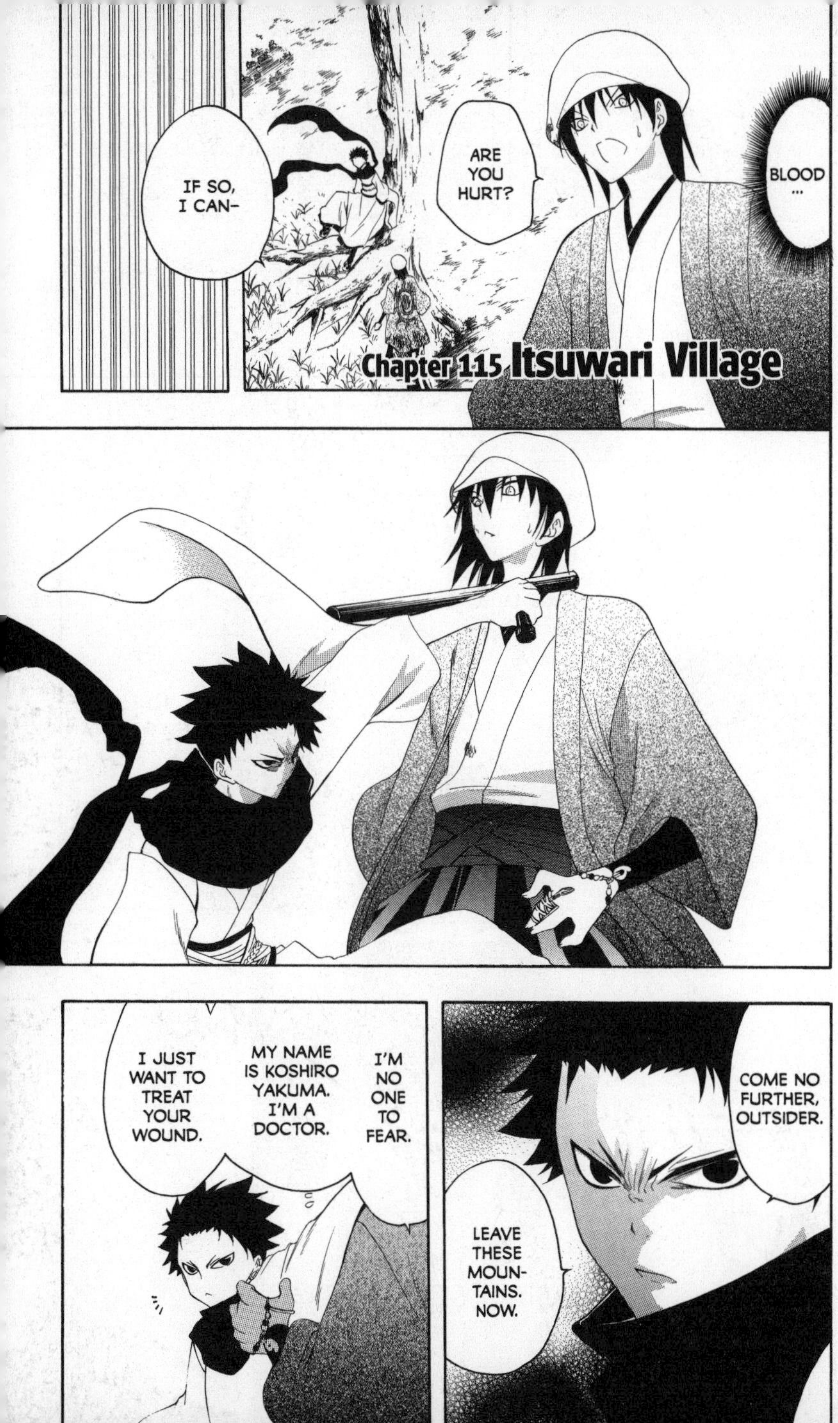
BLOOD...
ARE YOU HURT?
Chapter 115 Itsuwari Village
IF SO, I CAN-
COME NO FURTHER, OUTSIDER.
LEAVE THESE MOUNTAINS. NOW.
I'M NO ONE TO FEAR.
MY NAME IS KOSHIRO YAKUMA. I'M A DOCTOR.
I JUST WANT TO TREAT YOUR WOUND.

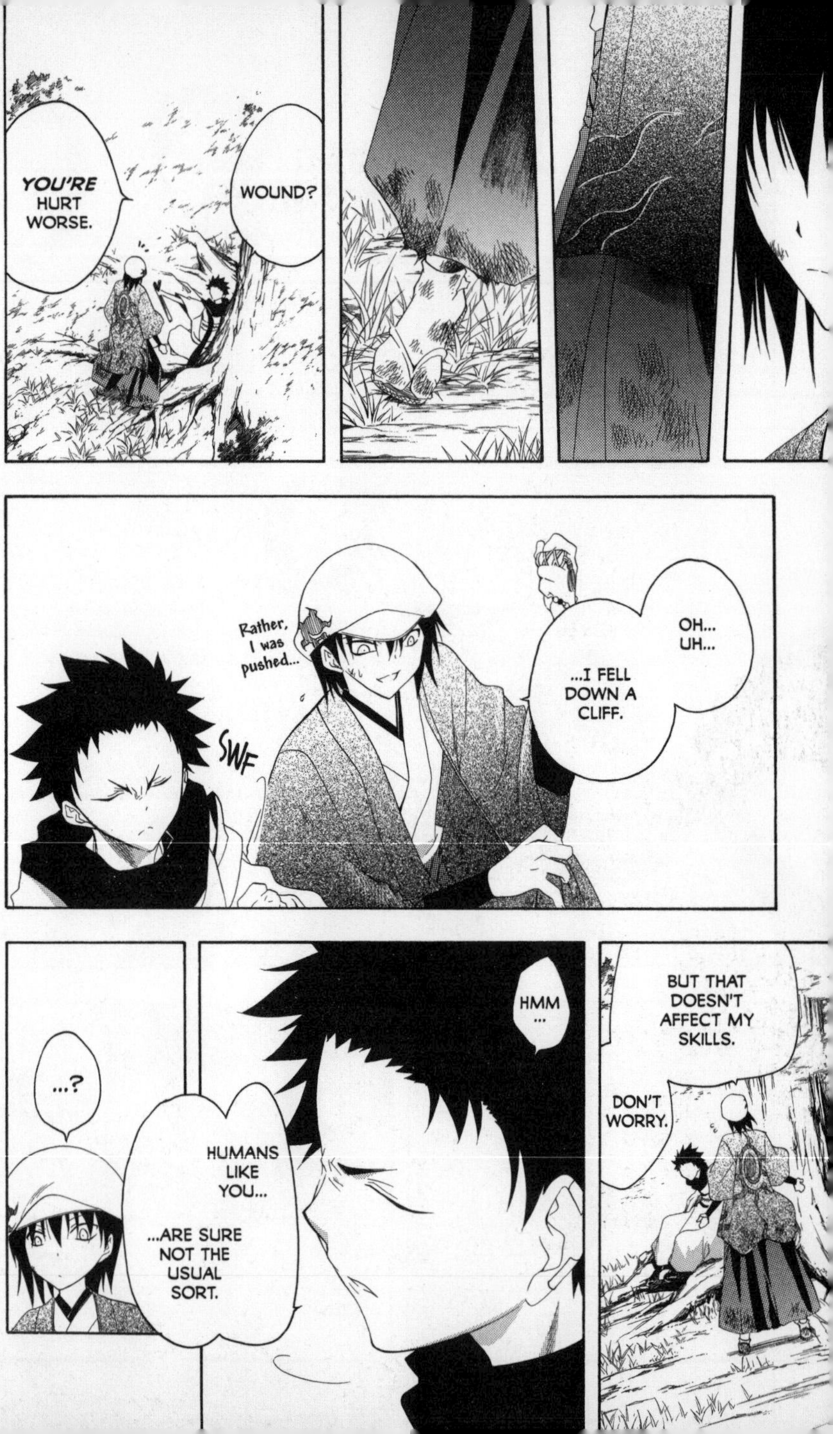
WOUND?
YOU'RE HURT WORSE.
OH... UH...
...I FELL DOWN A CLIFF.
SWF
Rather, I was pushed...
BUT THAT DOESN'T AFFECT MY SKILLS.
DON'T WORRY.
HMM ...
HUMANS LIKE YOU...
...ARE SURE NOT THE USUAL SORT.
...?

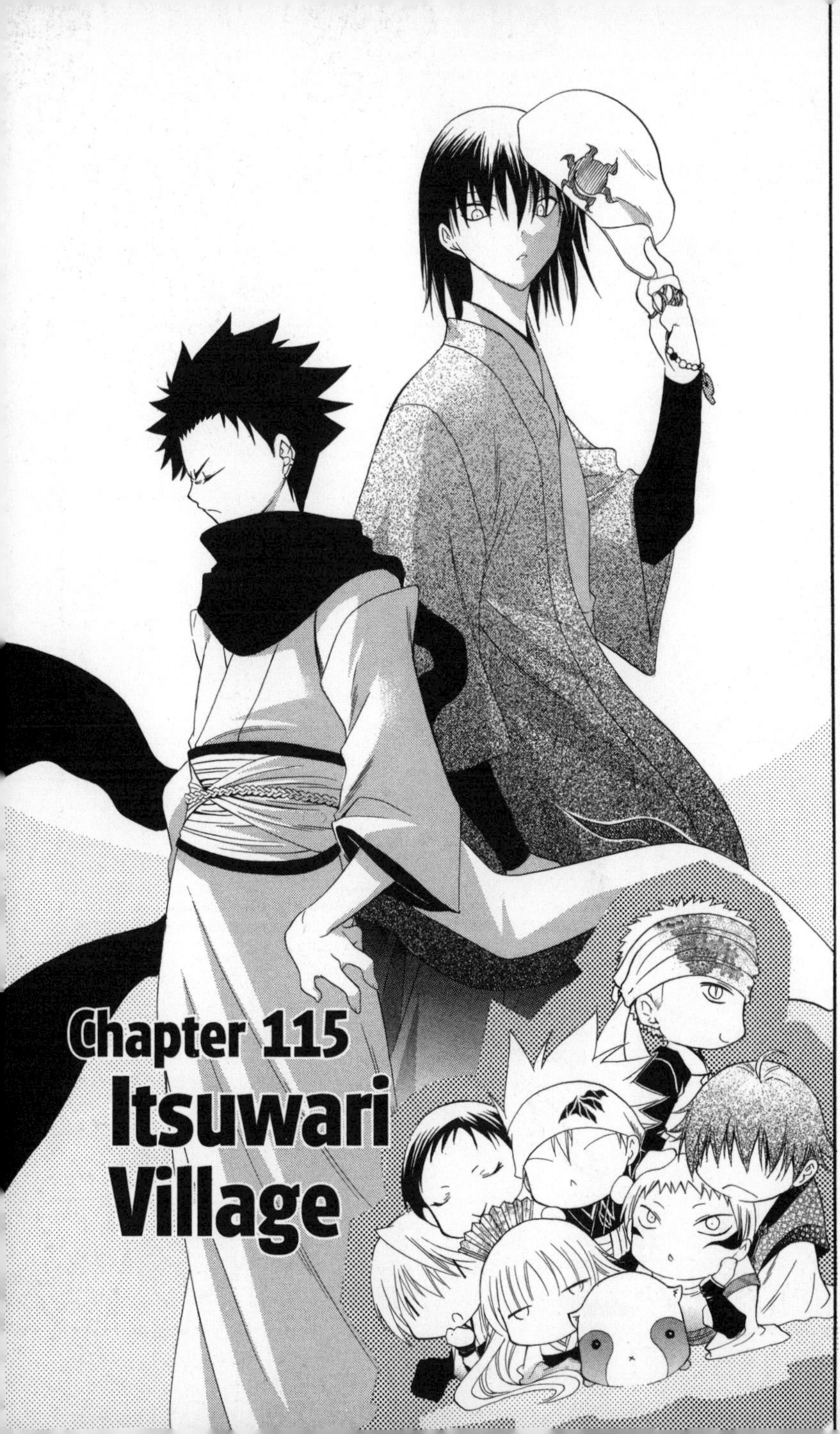
Chapter 115
Itsuwari Village

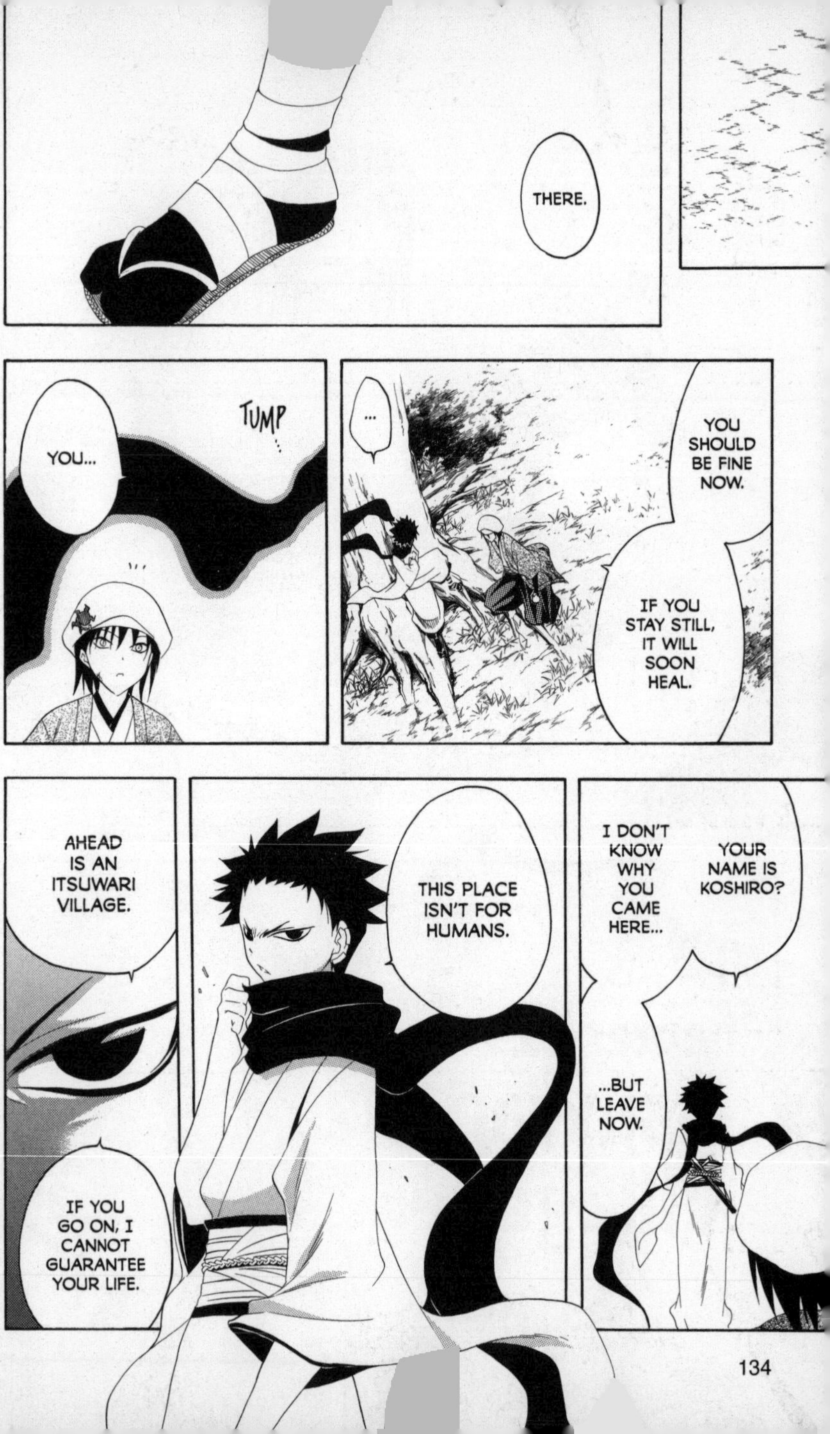

THERE.
YOU SHOULD BE FINE NOW.
IF YOU STAY STILL, IT WILL SOON HEAL.
...
TUMP
YOU...
YOUR NAME IS KOSHIRO?
I DON'T KNOW WHY YOU CAME HERE...
...BUT LEAVE NOW.
THIS PLACE ISN'T FOR HUMANS.
AHEAD IS AN ITSUWARI VILLAGE.
IF YOU GO ON, I CANNOT GUARANTEE YOUR LIFE.

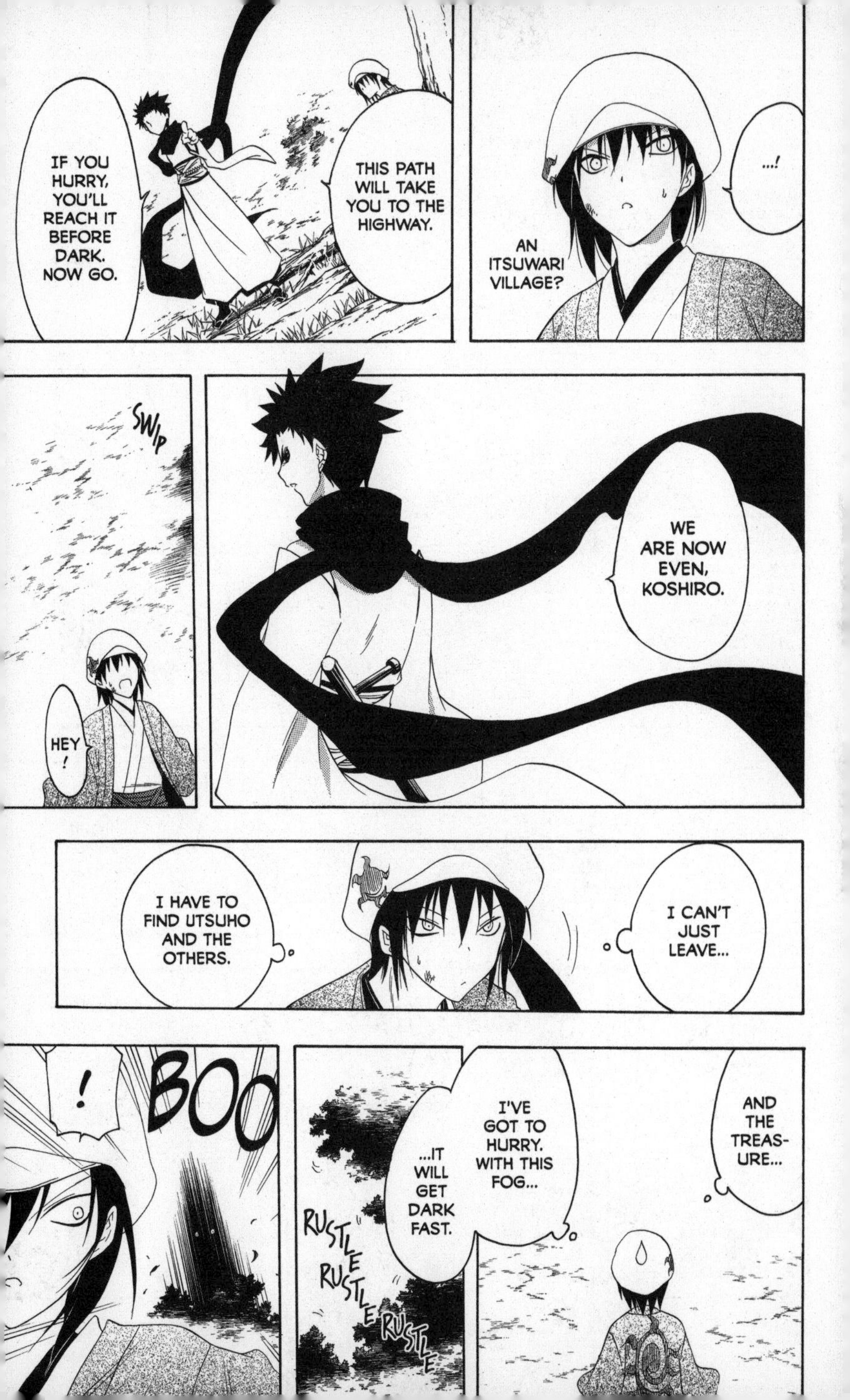
...!
AN ITSUWARI VILLAGE?
THIS PATH WILL TAKE YOU TO THE HIGHWAY.
IF YOU HURRY, YOU'LL REACH IT BEFORE DARK. NOW GO.
WE ARE NOW EVEN, KOSHIRO.
SWIP
HEY!
I CAN'T JUST LEAVE...
I HAVE TO FIND UTSUHO AND THE OTHERS.
AND THE TREASURE...
I'VE GOT TO HURRY. WITH THIS FOG...
...IT WILL GET DARK FAST.
RUSTLE
RUSTLE
RUSTLE
!
BOO

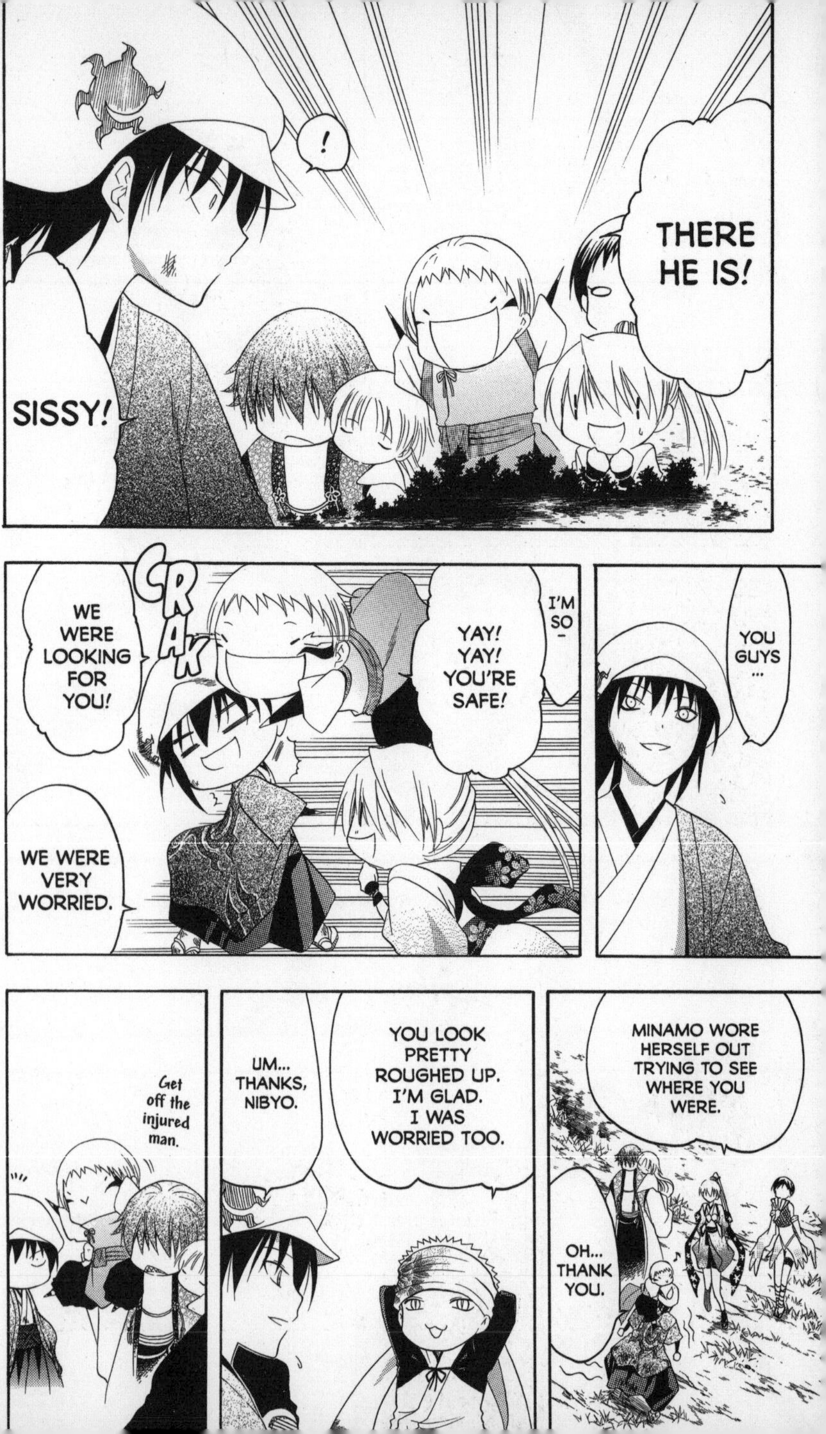
THERE HE IS!
!
SISSY!
YOU GUYS ...
I'M SO -
YAY! YAY! YOU'RE SAFE!
CRAK
WE WERE LOOKING FOR YOU!
WE WERE VERY WORRIED.
MINAMO WORE HERSELF OUT TRYING TO SEE WHERE YOU WERE.
OH... THANK YOU.
YOU LOOK PRETTY ROUGHED UP. I'M GLAD. I WAS WORRIED TOO.
UM... THANKS, NIBYO.
Get off the injured man.

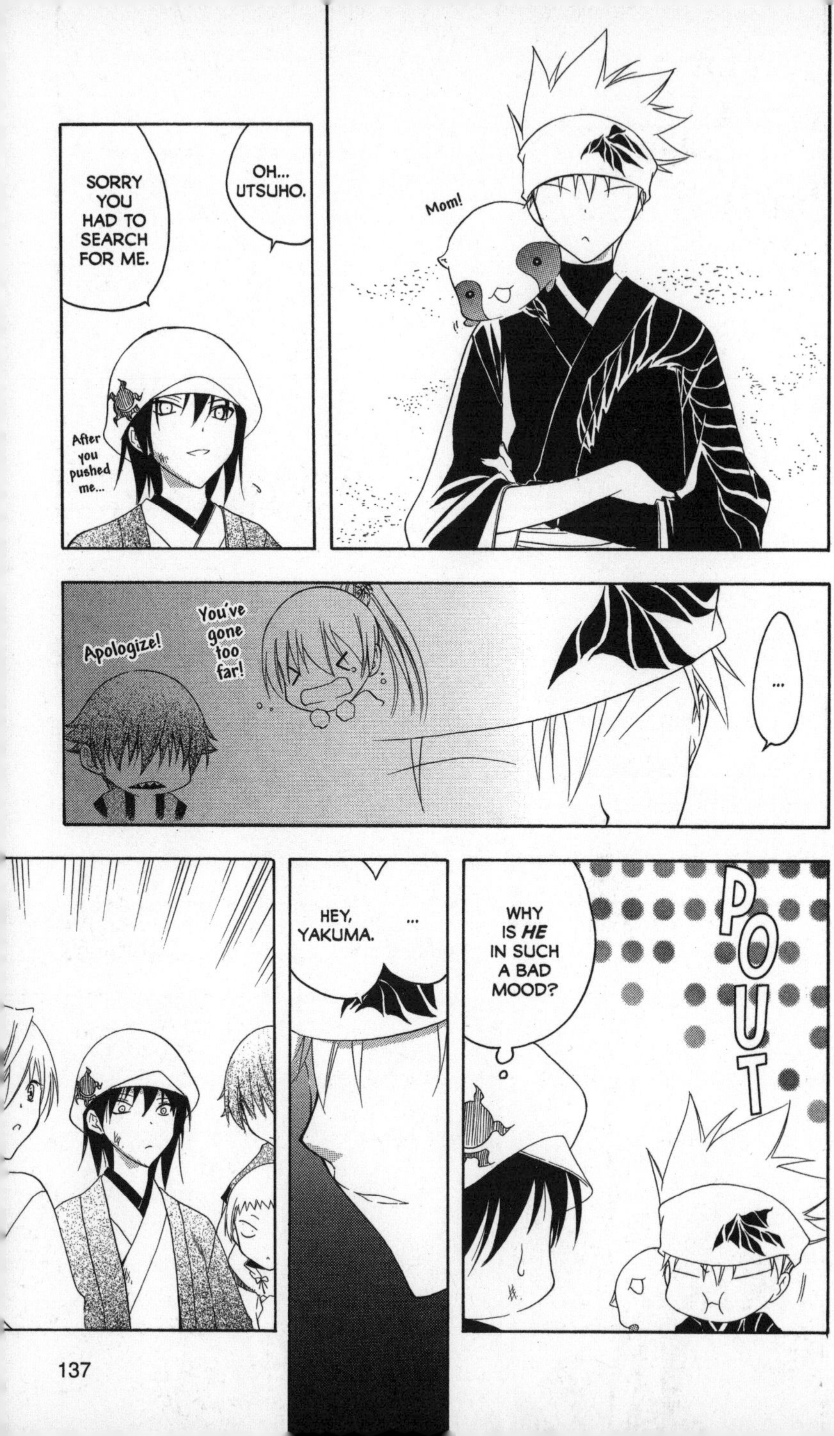
Mom!
OH... UTSUHO.
SORRY YOU HAD TO SEARCH FOR ME.
After you pushed me...
...
You've gone too far!
Apologize!
POUT
WHY IS *HE* IN SUCH A BAD MOOD?
...
HEY, YAKUMA.

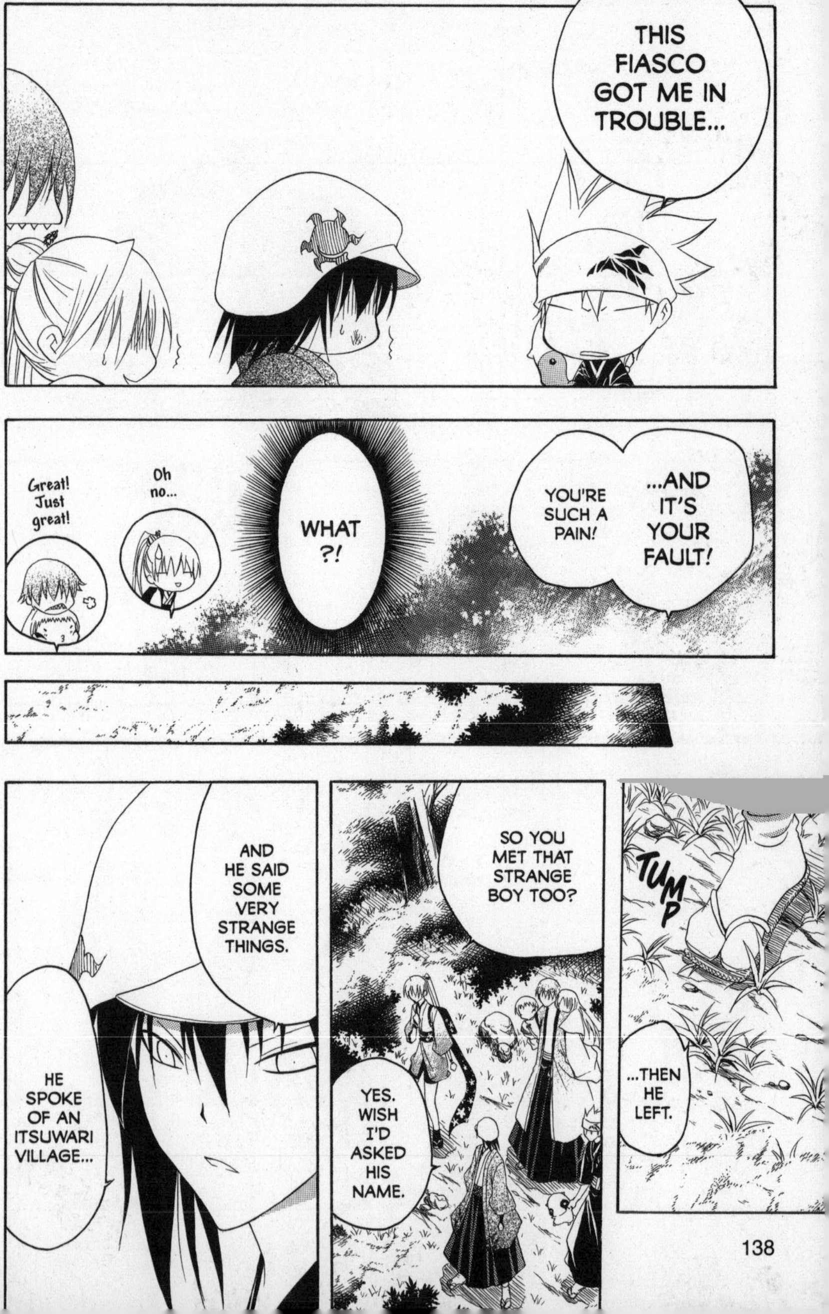
THIS FIASCO GOT ME IN TROUBLE...
...AND IT'S YOUR FAULT!
YOU'RE SUCH A PAIN!
WHAT ?!
Oh no...
Great! Just great!
TUMP
...THEN HE LEFT.
SO YOU MET THAT STRANGE BOY TOO?
YES. WISH I'D ASKED HIS NAME.
AND HE SAID SOME VERY STRANGE THINGS.
HE SPOKE OF AN ITSUWARI VILLAGE...

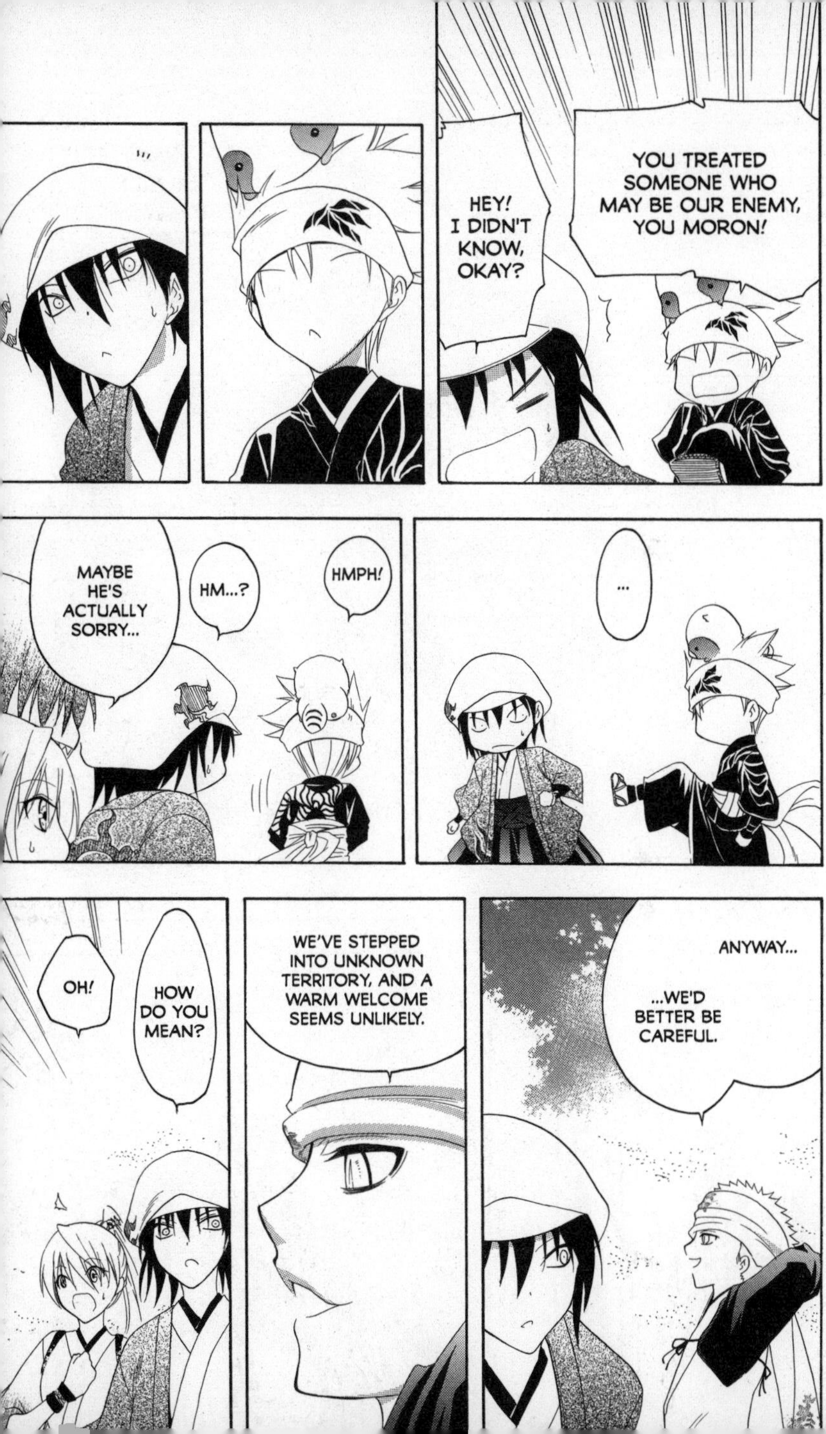
YOU TREATED SOMEONE WHO MAY BE OUR ENEMY, YOU MORON!
HEY! I DIDN'T KNOW, OKAY?
...
HMPH!
HM...?
MAYBE HE'S ACTUALLY SORRY...
ANYWAY...
...WE'D BETTER BE CAREFUL.
WE'VE STEPPED INTO UNKNOWN TERRITORY, AND A WARM WELCOME SEEMS UNLIKELY.
HOW DO YOU MEAN?
OH!

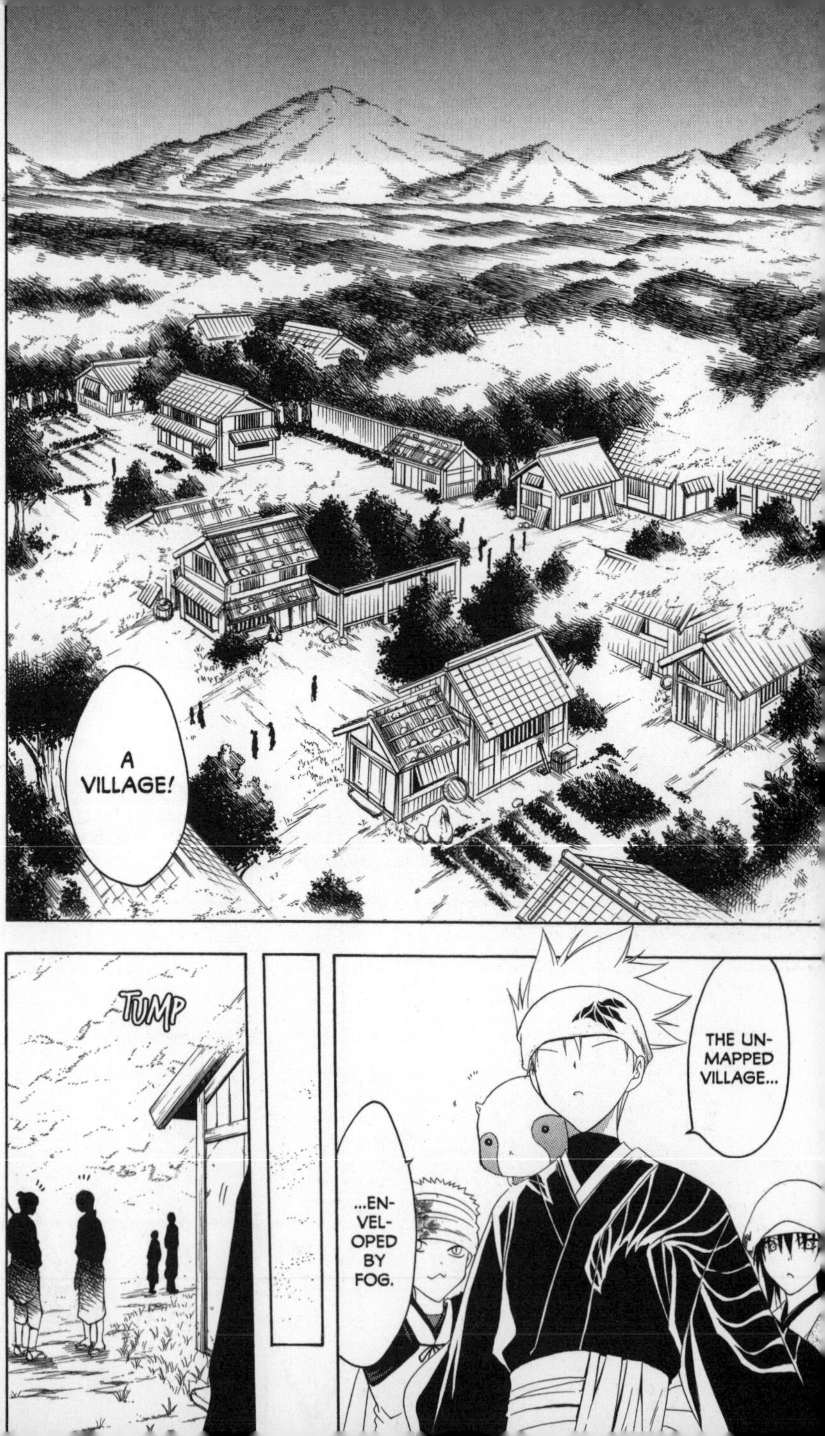
A VILLAGE!
THE UN-MAPPED VILLAGE...
...EN-VEL-OPED BY FOG.
TUMP

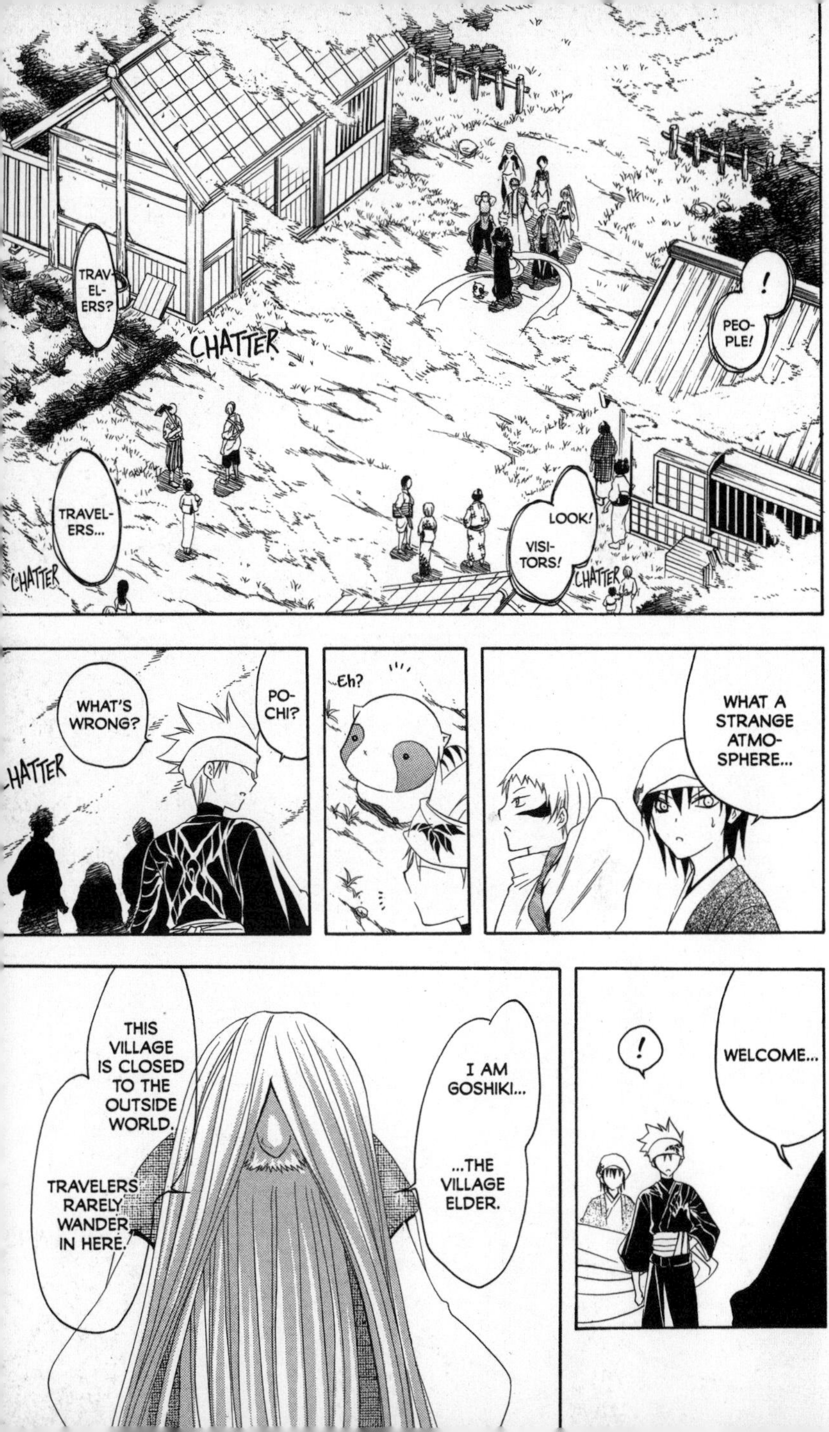
!
PEOPLE!
LOOK! VISITORS!
CHATTER
TRAVELERS?
CHATTER
TRAVELERS...
CHATTER
WHAT A STRANGE ATMOSPHERE...
Eh?
POCHI?
WHAT'S WRONG?
CHATTER
!
WELCOME...
I AM GOSHIKI...
...THE VILLAGE ELDER.
THIS VILLAGE IS CLOSED TO THE OUTSIDE WORLD.
TRAVELERS RARELY WANDER IN HERE.

AL-
READY
...

?

...!

SORRY TO
INTRUDE!

WE WILL
PREPARE
A FEAST IN
WELCOME.

PLEASE,
COME
WITH ME.

YOU
CANNOT
LEAVE
TODAY.

...THE
SKIES
DARKEN.

...IS YOUUU!

EEP
...!

WE WILL
PREPARE
A FEAST IN
WELCOME.

HARDLY
ANYONE
COMES
HERE!

TONIGHT,
WE'LL
HAVE
A FEAST!
A FEAST!

THE
MENU...

ENJOY...

TUNK
...

TNK

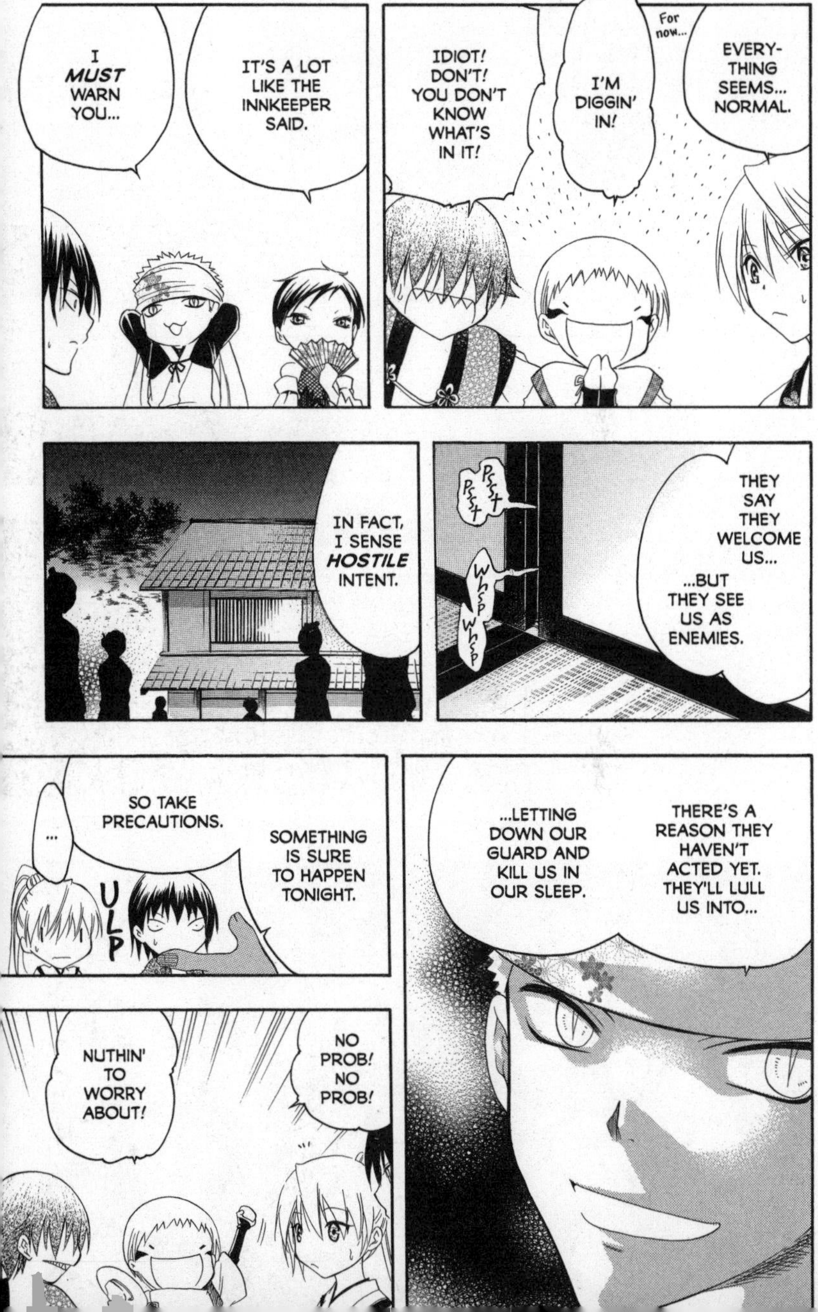
EVERY-THING SEEMS... NORMAL.
For now...
I'M DIGGIN' IN!
IDIOT! DON'T! YOU DON'T KNOW WHAT'S IN IT!
IT'S A LOT LIKE THE INNKEEPER SAID.
I MUST WARN YOU...
THEY SAY THEY WELCOME US...
...BUT THEY SEE US AS ENEMIES.
Pssst Pssst
Whsp whsp
IN FACT, I SENSE HOSTILE INTENT.
THERE'S A REASON THEY HAVEN'T ACTED YET. THEY'LL LULL US INTO...
...LETTING DOWN OUR GUARD AND KILL US IN OUR SLEEP.
SOMETHING IS SURE TO HAPPEN TONIGHT.
SO TAKE PRECAUTIONS.
...
ULP
NO PROB! NO PROB!
NUTHIN' TO WORRY ABOUT!

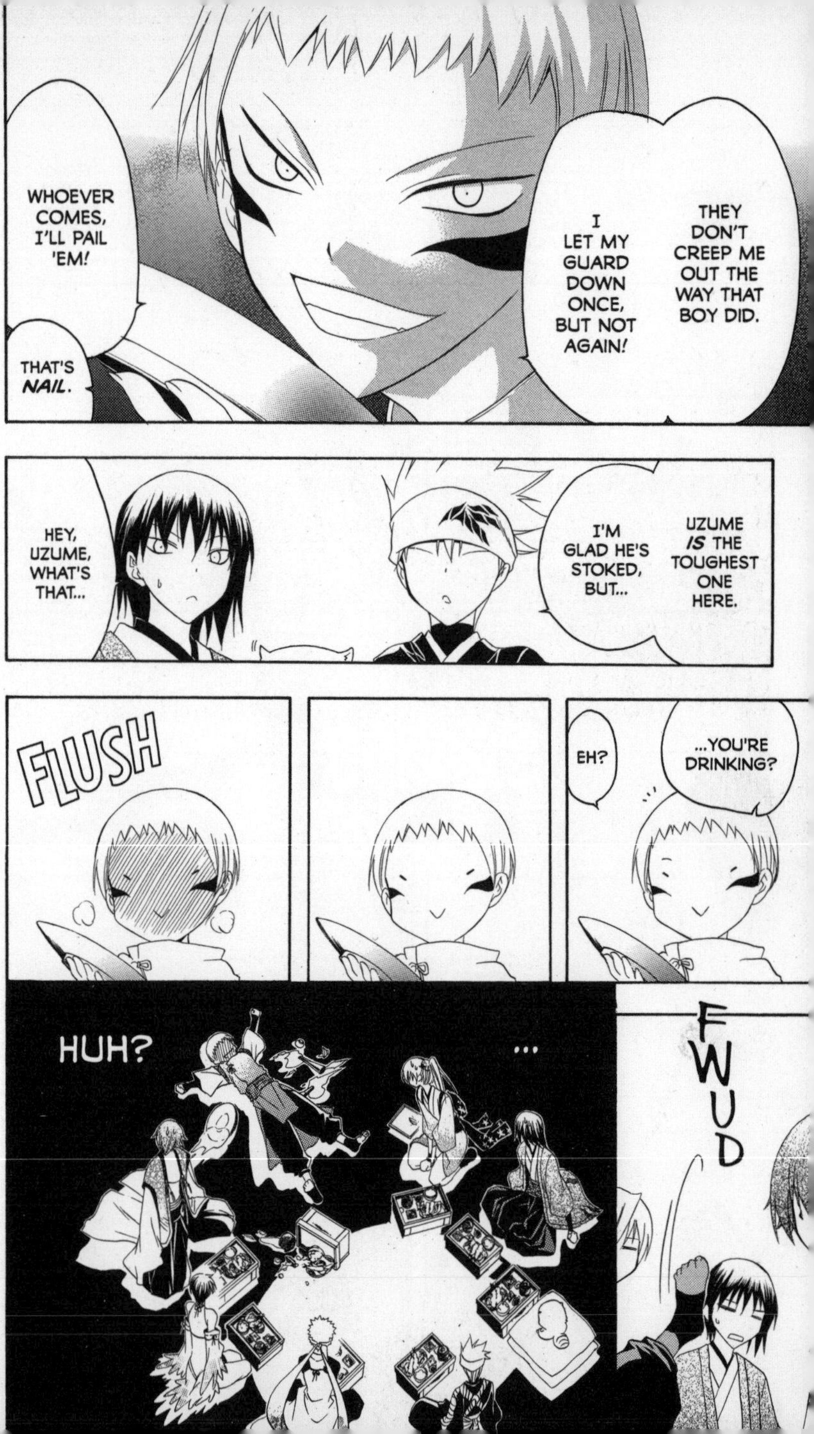
THEY DON'T CREEP ME OUT THE WAY THAT BOY DID.
I LET MY GUARD DOWN ONCE, BUT NOT AGAIN!
WHOEVER COMES, I'LL PAIL 'EM!
THAT'S *NAIL*.
UZUME *IS* THE TOUGHEST ONE HERE.
I'M GLAD HE'S STOKED, BUT...
HEY, UZUME, WHAT'S THAT...
...YOU'RE DRINKING?
EH?
FLUSH
FWUD
...
HUH?

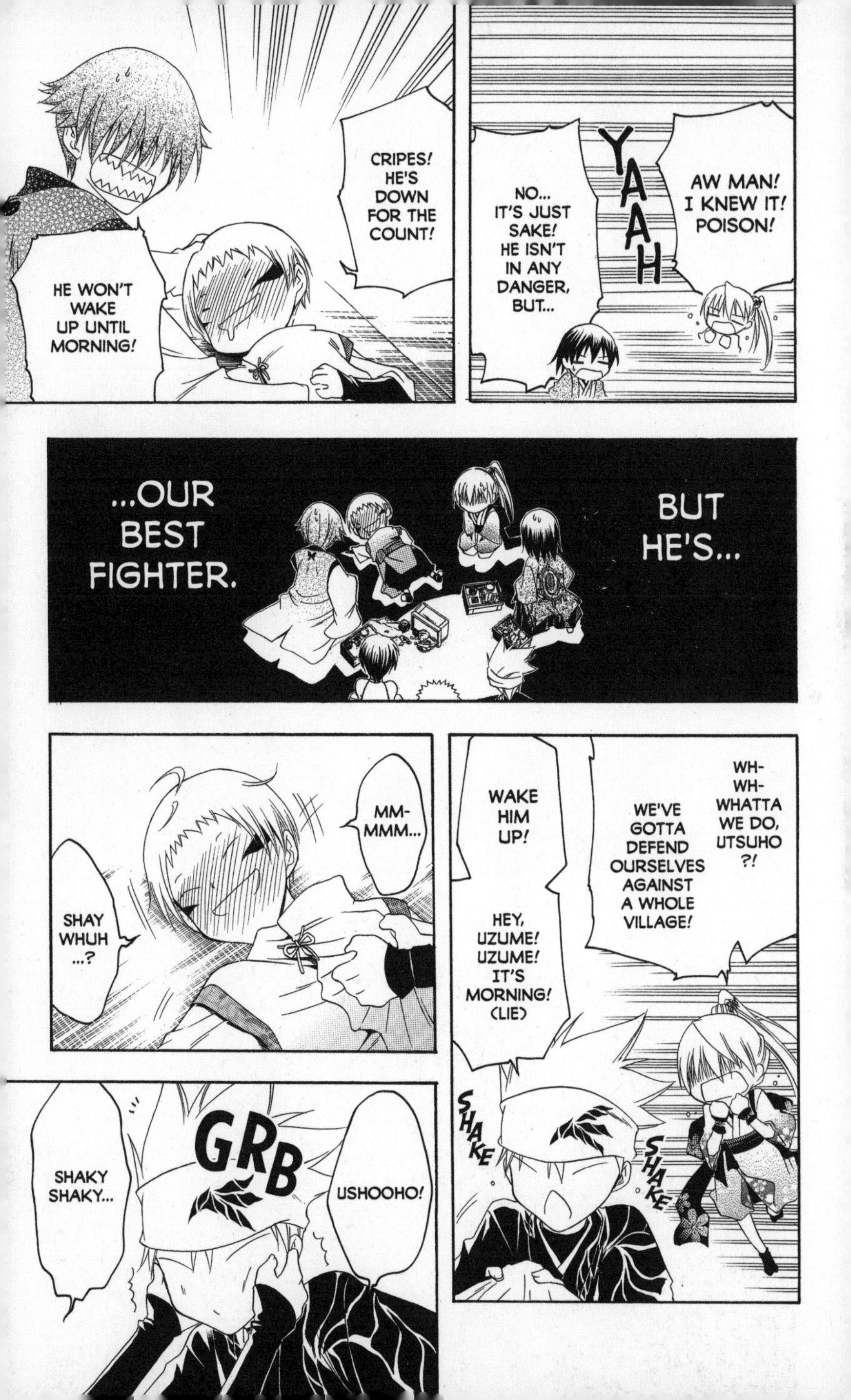

AW MAN! I KNEW IT! POISON!
YAAH
NO... IT'S JUST SAKE! HE ISN'T IN ANY DANGER, BUT...
CRIPES! HE'S DOWN FOR THE COUNT!
HE WON'T WAKE UP UNTIL MORNING!
BUT HE'S...
...OUR BEST FIGHTER.
WH-WH-WHATTA WE DO, UTSUHO?!
WE'VE GOTTA DEFEND OURSELVES AGAINST A WHOLE VILLAGE!
WAKE HIM UP!
HEY, UZUME! UZUME! IT'S MORNING! (LIE)
SHAKE
SHAKE
MM-MMM...
SHAY WHUH...?
USHOOHO!
GRB
SHAKY SHAKY...

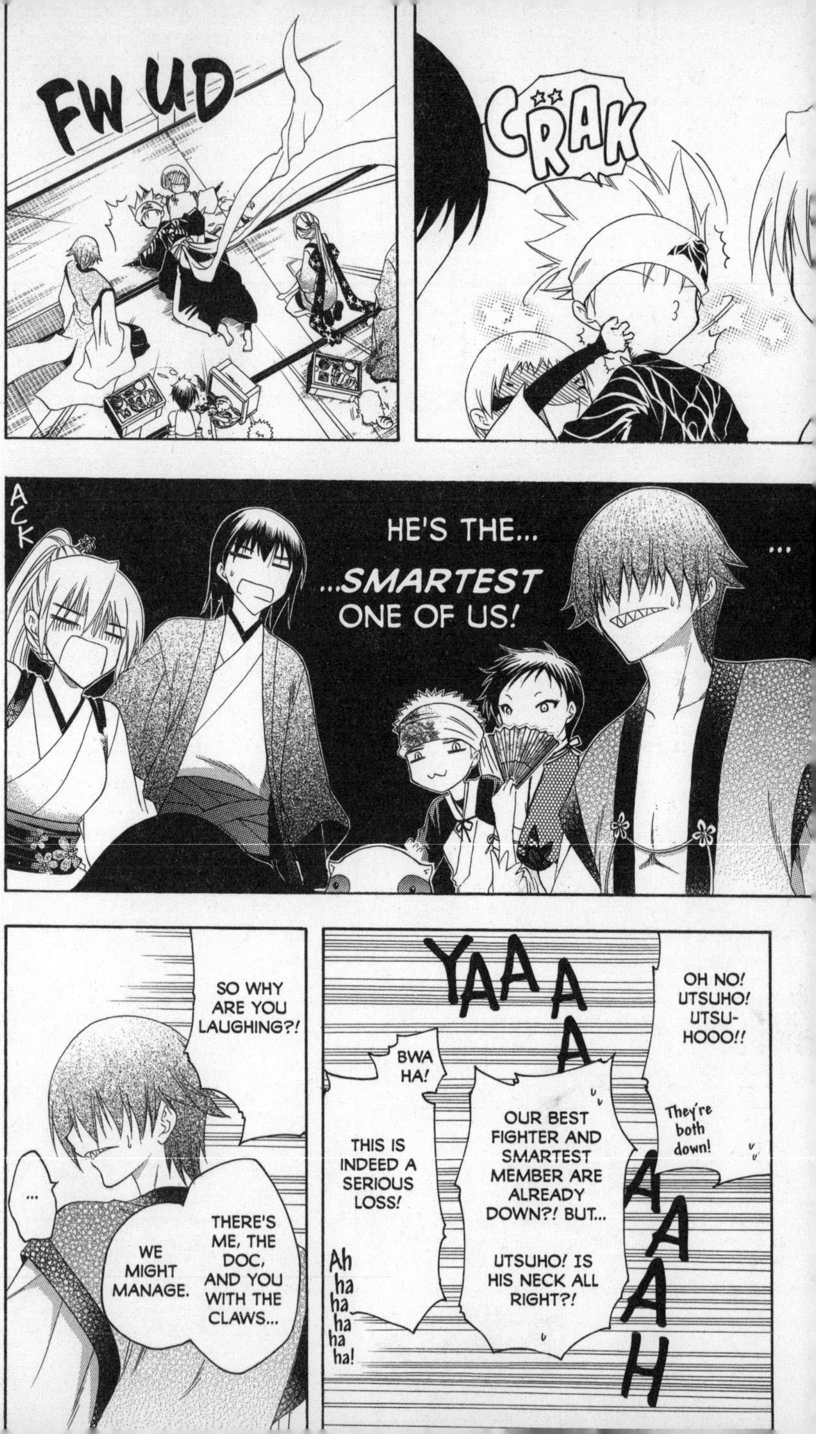
CRAK
FW UD
...
HE'S THE...
...SMARTEST ONE OF US!
ACK
OH NO! UTSUHO! UTSU-HOOO!!
YAAAAAAAAH
They're both down!
OUR BEST FIGHTER AND SMARTEST MEMBER ARE ALREADY DOWN?! BUT...
UTSUHO! IS HIS NECK ALL RIGHT?!
BWA HA!
THIS IS INDEED A SERIOUS LOSS!
Ah ha ha ha ha ha!
SO WHY ARE YOU LAUGHING?!
THERE'S ME, THE DOC, AND YOU WITH THE CLAWS...
WE MIGHT MANAGE.
...

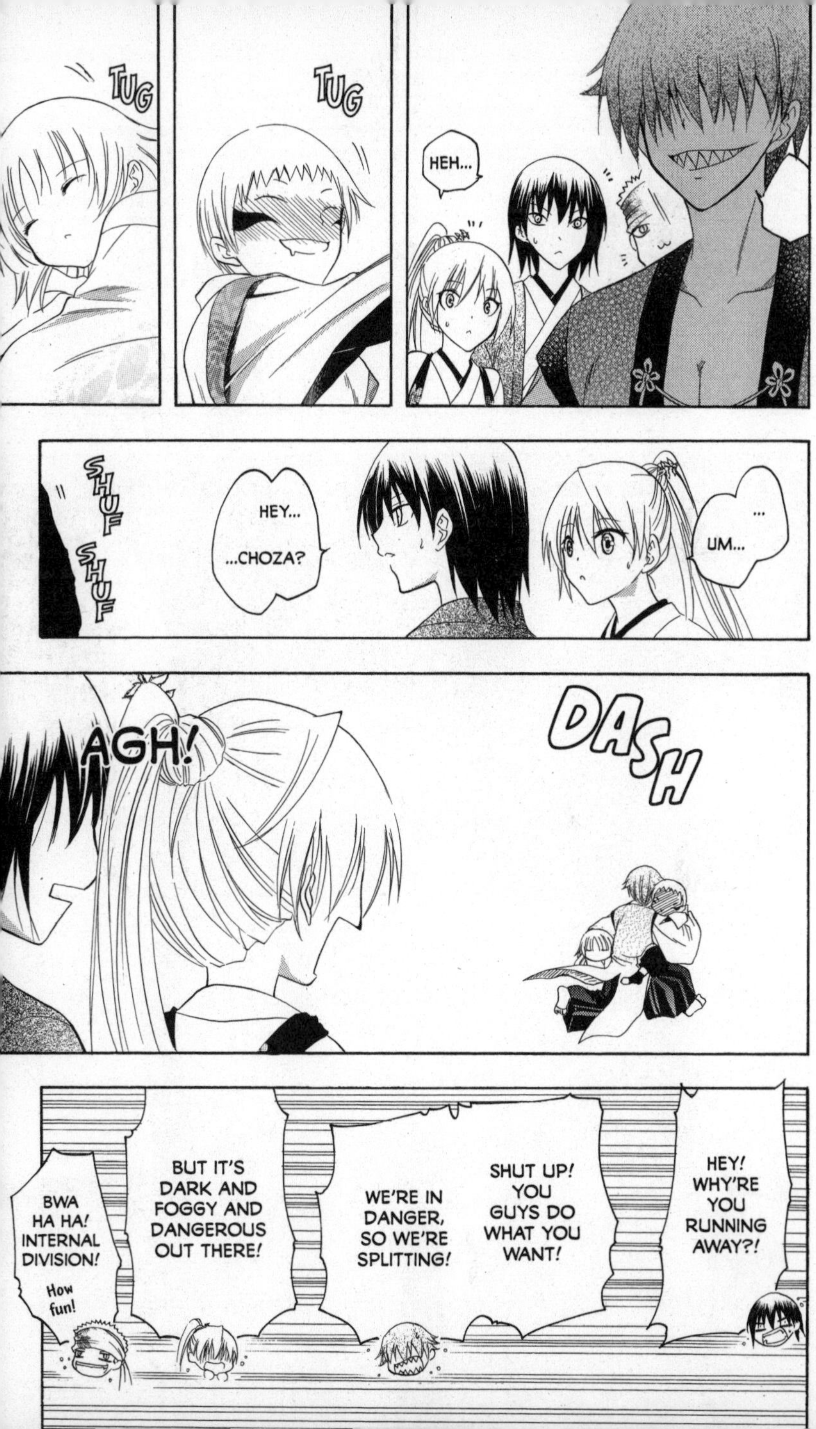
HEH...
TUG
TUG
... UM...
HEY... ...CHOZA?
SHUF SHUF
DASH
AGH!
HEY! WHY'RE YOU RUNNING AWAY?!
SHUT UP! YOU GUYS DO WHAT YOU WANT!
WE'RE IN DANGER, SO WE'RE SPLITTING!
BUT IT'S DARK AND FOGGY AND DANGEROUS OUT THERE!
BWA HA HA! INTERNAL DIVISION!
How fun!

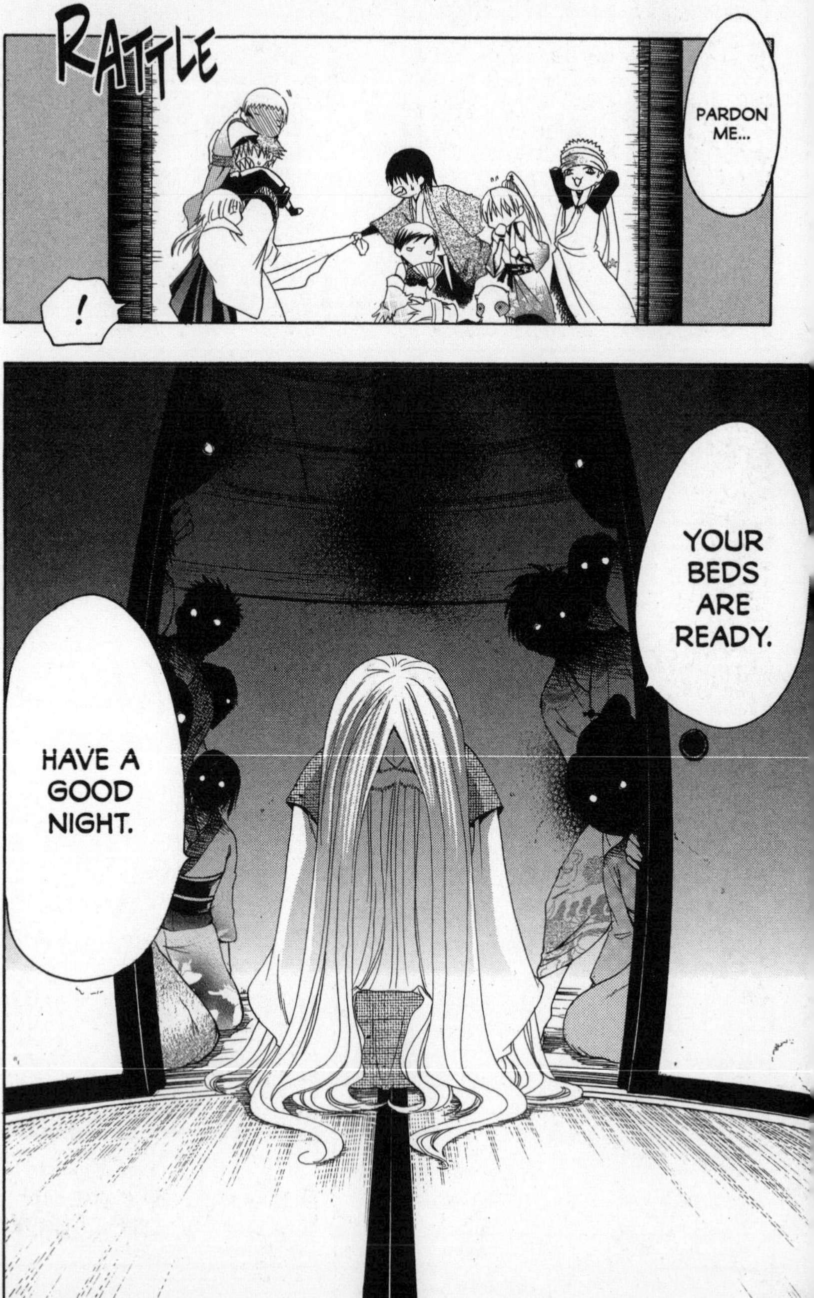
PARDON ME...
RATTLE
!
YOUR BEDS ARE READY.
HAVE A GOOD NIGHT.

Chapter 116 The Village's Secret

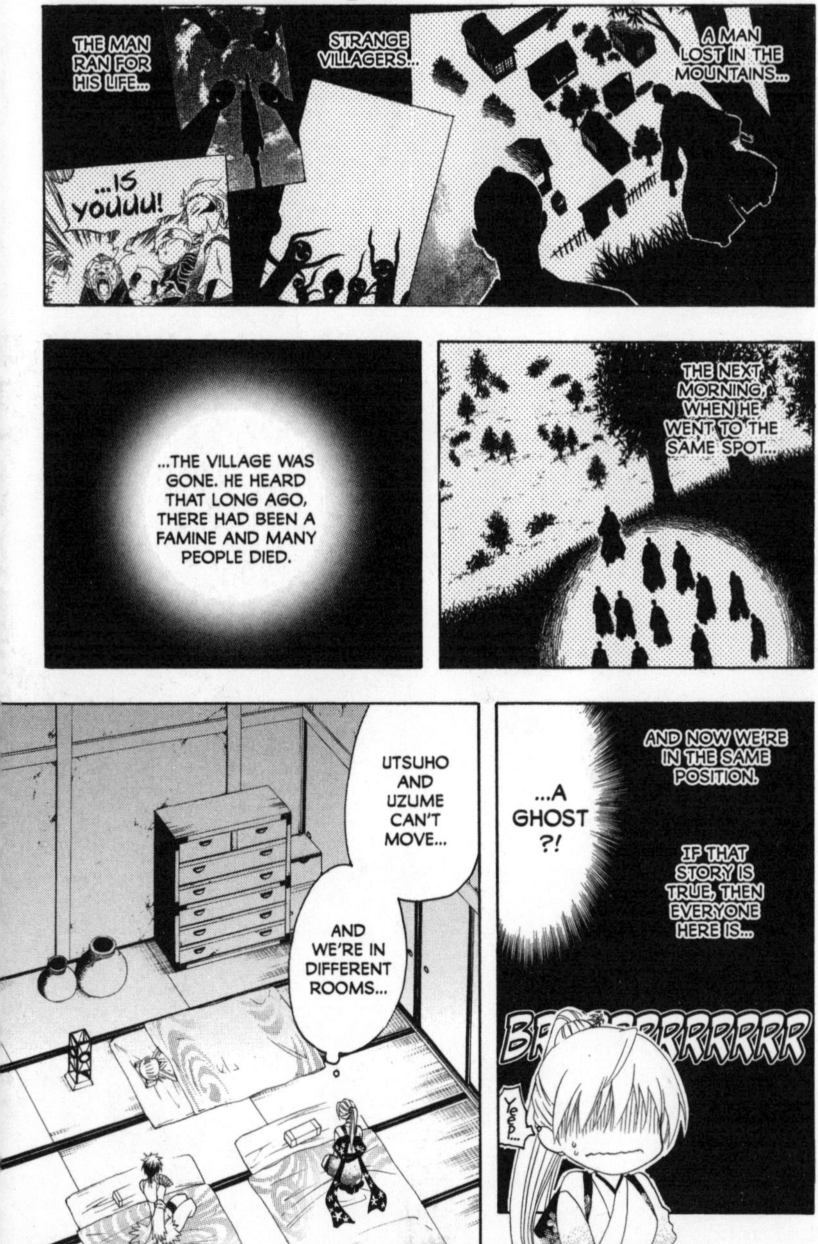
A MAN LOST IN THE MOUNTAINS...
STRANGE VILLAGERS...
THE MAN RAN FOR HIS LIFE...
...IS YOUUU!
THE NEXT MORNING, WHEN HE WENT TO THE SAME SPOT...
...THE VILLAGE WAS GONE. HE HEARD THAT LONG AGO, THERE HAD BEEN A FAMINE AND MANY PEOPLE DIED.
AND NOW WE'RE IN THE SAME POSITION.
IF THAT STORY IS TRUE, THEN EVERYONE HERE IS...
...A GHOST?!
Yeep...
UTSUHO AND UZUME CAN'T MOVE...
AND WE'RE IN DIFFERENT ROOMS...

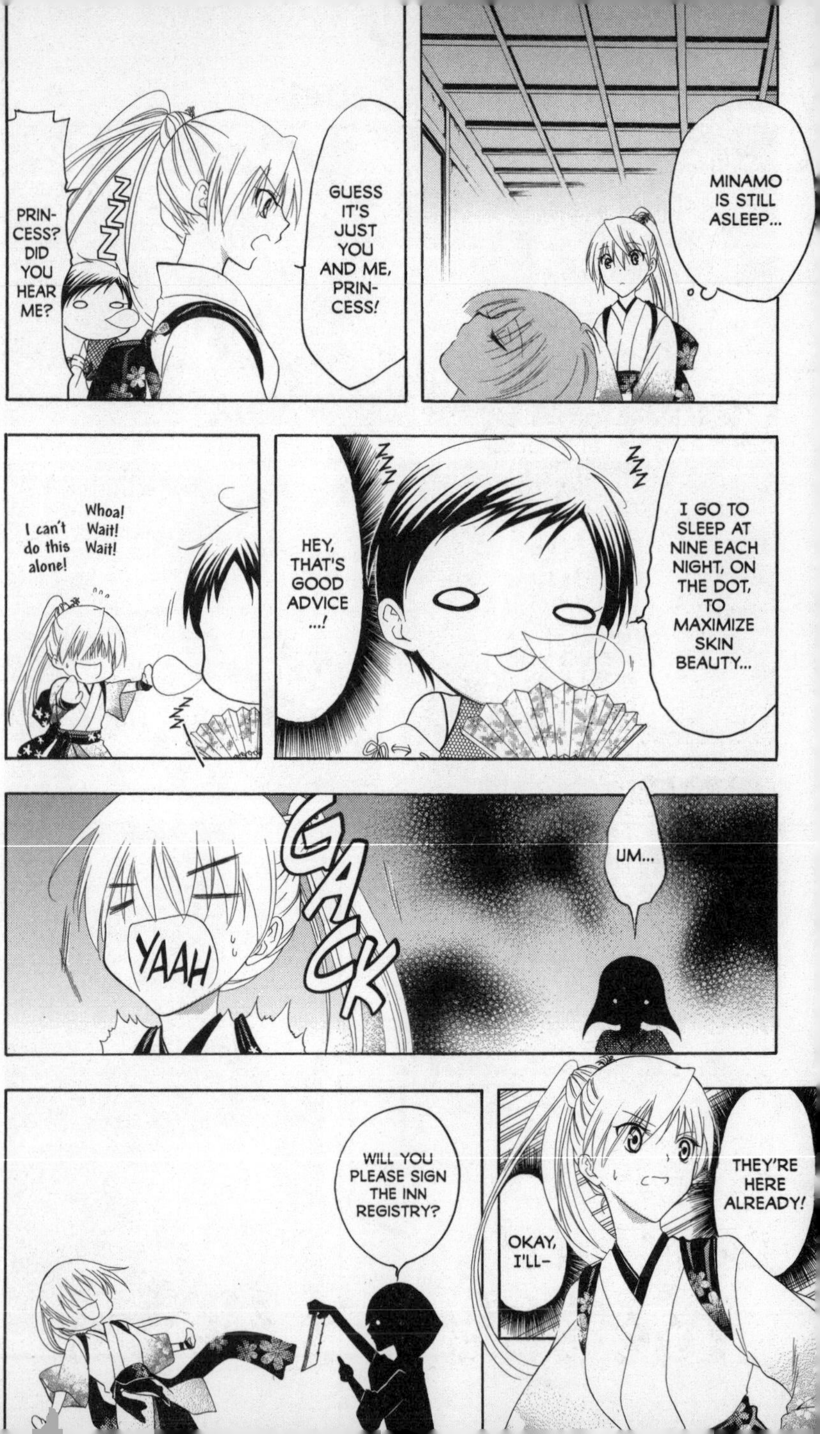
MINAMO IS STILL ASLEEP...
GUESS IT'S JUST YOU AND ME, PRINCESS!
ZZZ
PRINCESS? DID YOU HEAR ME?
I GO TO SLEEP AT NINE EACH NIGHT, ON THE DOT, TO MAXIMIZE SKIN BEAUTY...
ZZZ
ZZZ
HEY, THAT'S GOOD ADVICE ...!
Whoa! Wait! Wait!
I can't do this alone!
ZZZ
UM...
GACK
YAAH
THEY'RE HERE ALREADY!
OKAY, I'LL-
WILL YOU PLEASE SIGN THE INN REGISTRY?

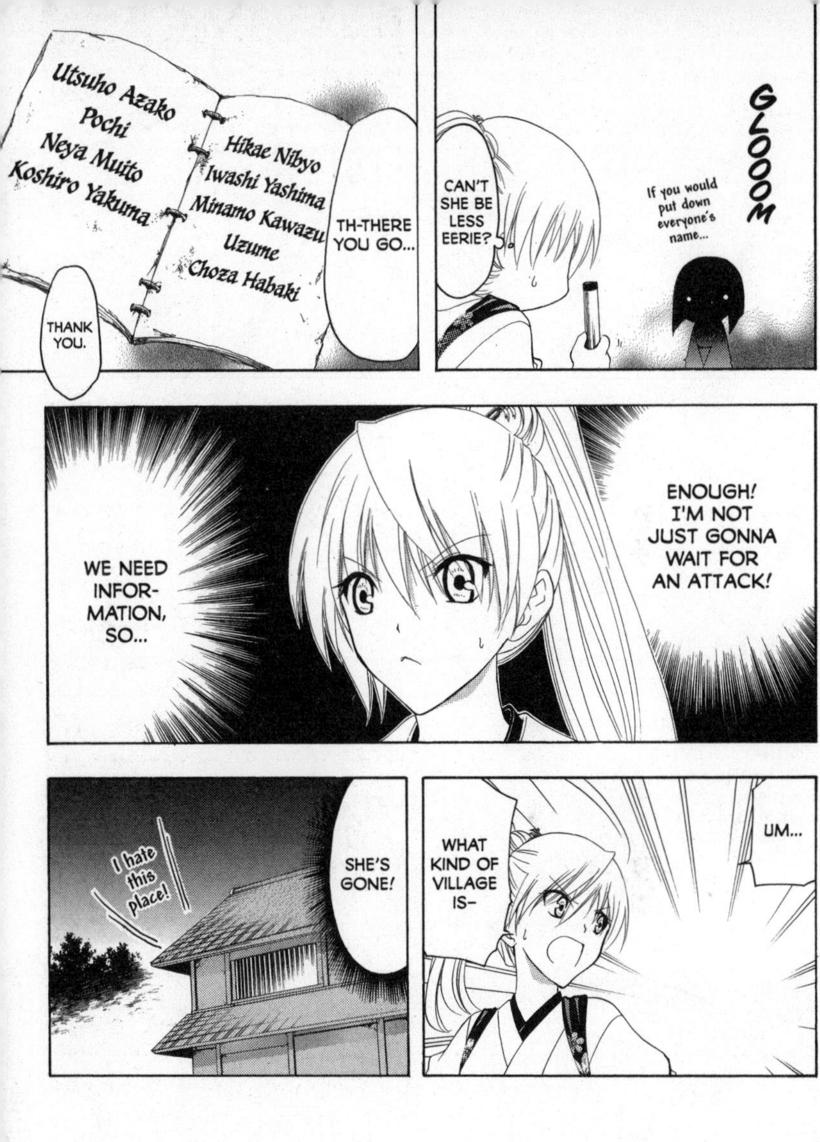
GLOOOM
If you would put down everyone's name...
CAN'T SHE BE LESS EERIE?
TH-THERE YOU GO...
Hikae Nibyo
Iwashi Yashima
Minamo Kawazu
Uzume
Choza Habaki
Utsuho Azako
Pochi
Neya Muito
Koshiro Yakuma
THANK YOU.
ENOUGH! I'M NOT JUST GONNA WAIT FOR AN ATTACK!
WE NEED INFOR-MATION, SO...
UM...
WHAT KIND OF VILLAGE IS-
SHE'S GONE!
I hate this place!

Chapter 116
The Village's Secret

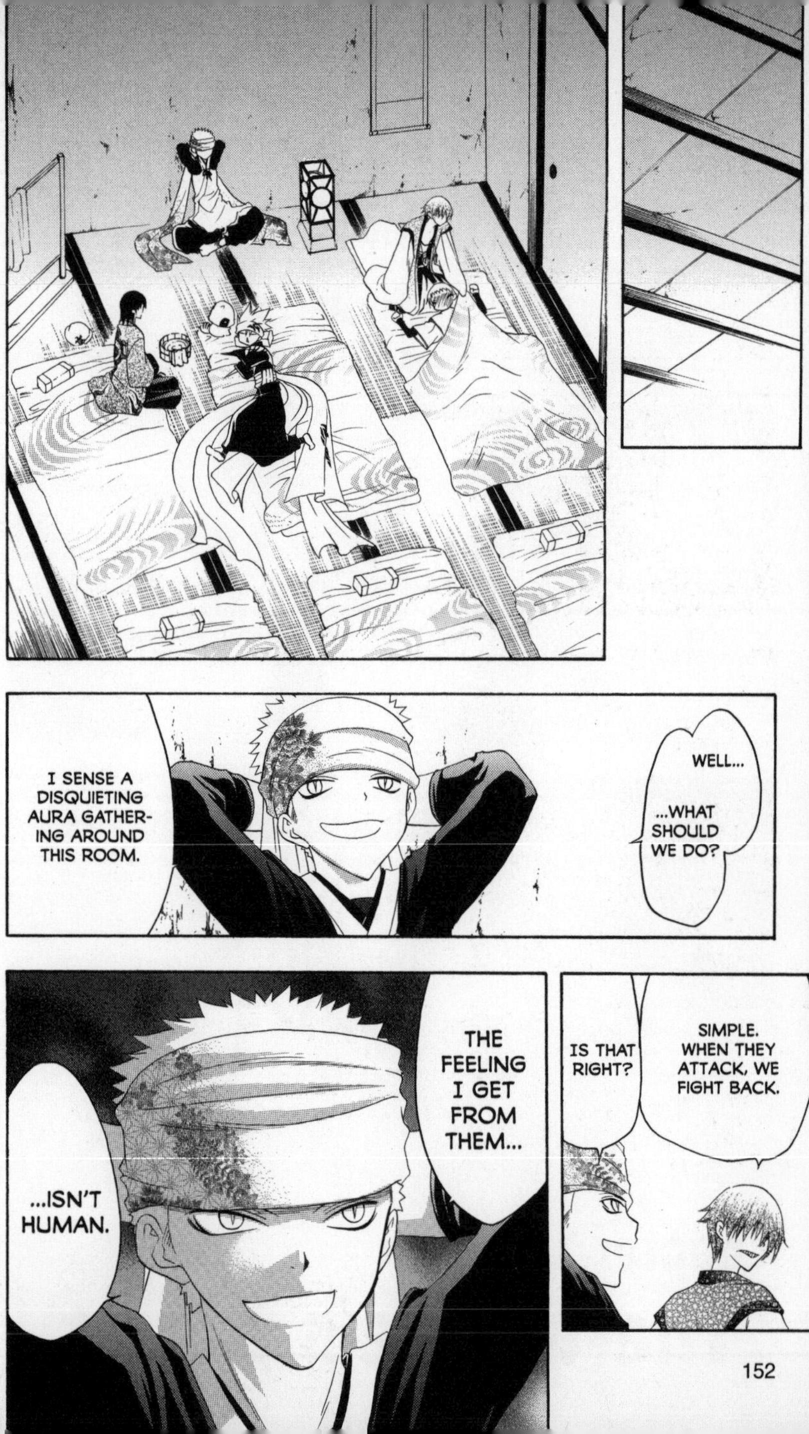
WELL...
...WHAT SHOULD WE DO?
I SENSE A DISQUIETING AURA GATHERING AROUND THIS ROOM.
SIMPLE. WHEN THEY ATTACK, WE FIGHT BACK.
IS THAT RIGHT?
THE FEELING I GET FROM THEM...
...ISN'T HUMAN.

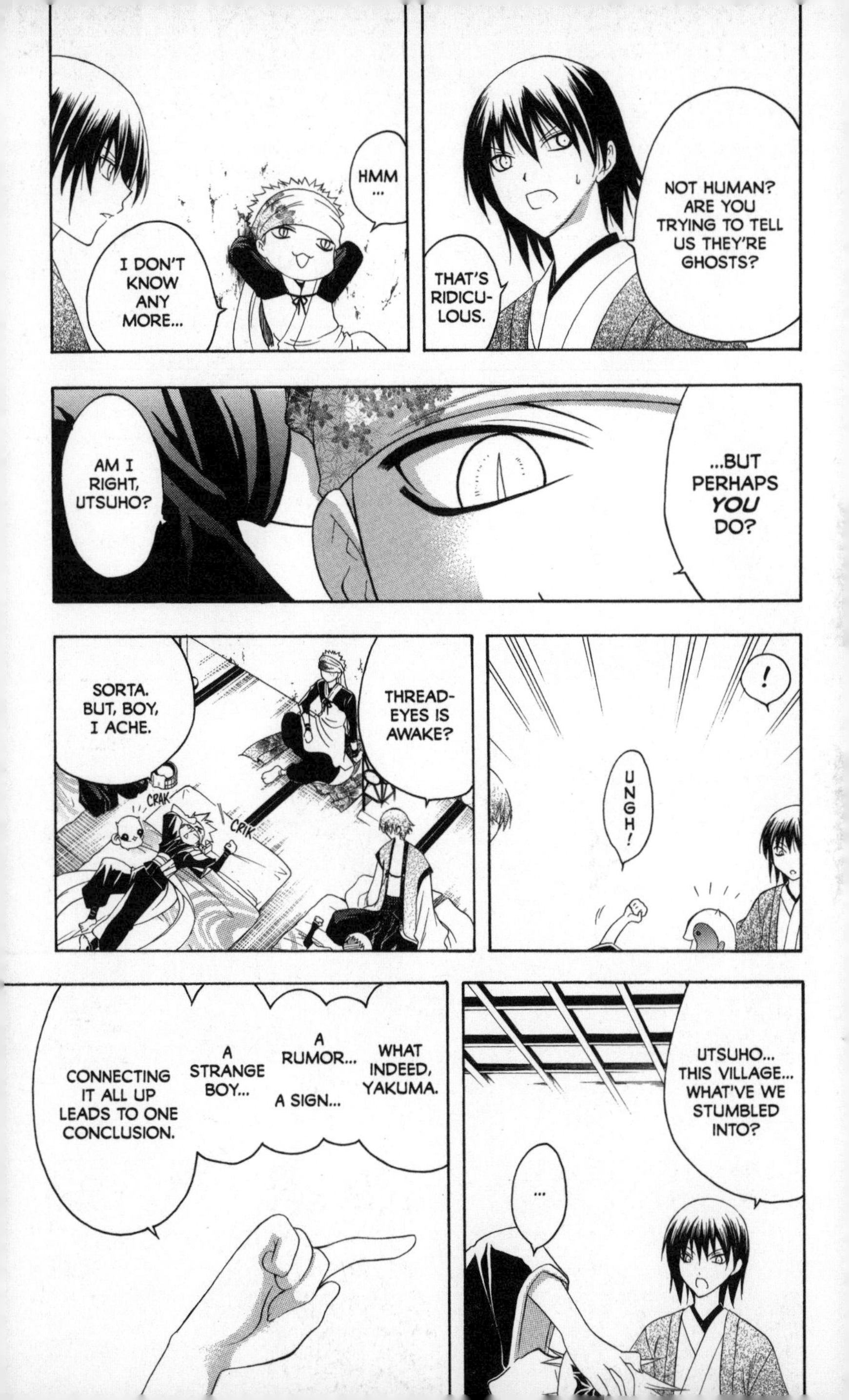
NOT HUMAN? ARE YOU TRYING TO TELL US THEY'RE GHOSTS?
THAT'S RIDICULOUS.
HMM ...
I DON'T KNOW ANY MORE...
...BUT PERHAPS *YOU* DO?
AM I RIGHT, UTSUHO?
!
UNGH!
THREAD-EYES IS AWAKE?
SORTA. BUT, BOY, I ACHE.
CRAK
CRIK
UTSUHO... THIS VILLAGE... WHAT'VE WE STUMBLED INTO?
...
WHAT INDEED, YAKUMA.
A RUMOR...
A SIGN...
A STRANGE BOY...
CONNECTING IT ALL UP LEADS TO ONE CONCLUSION.

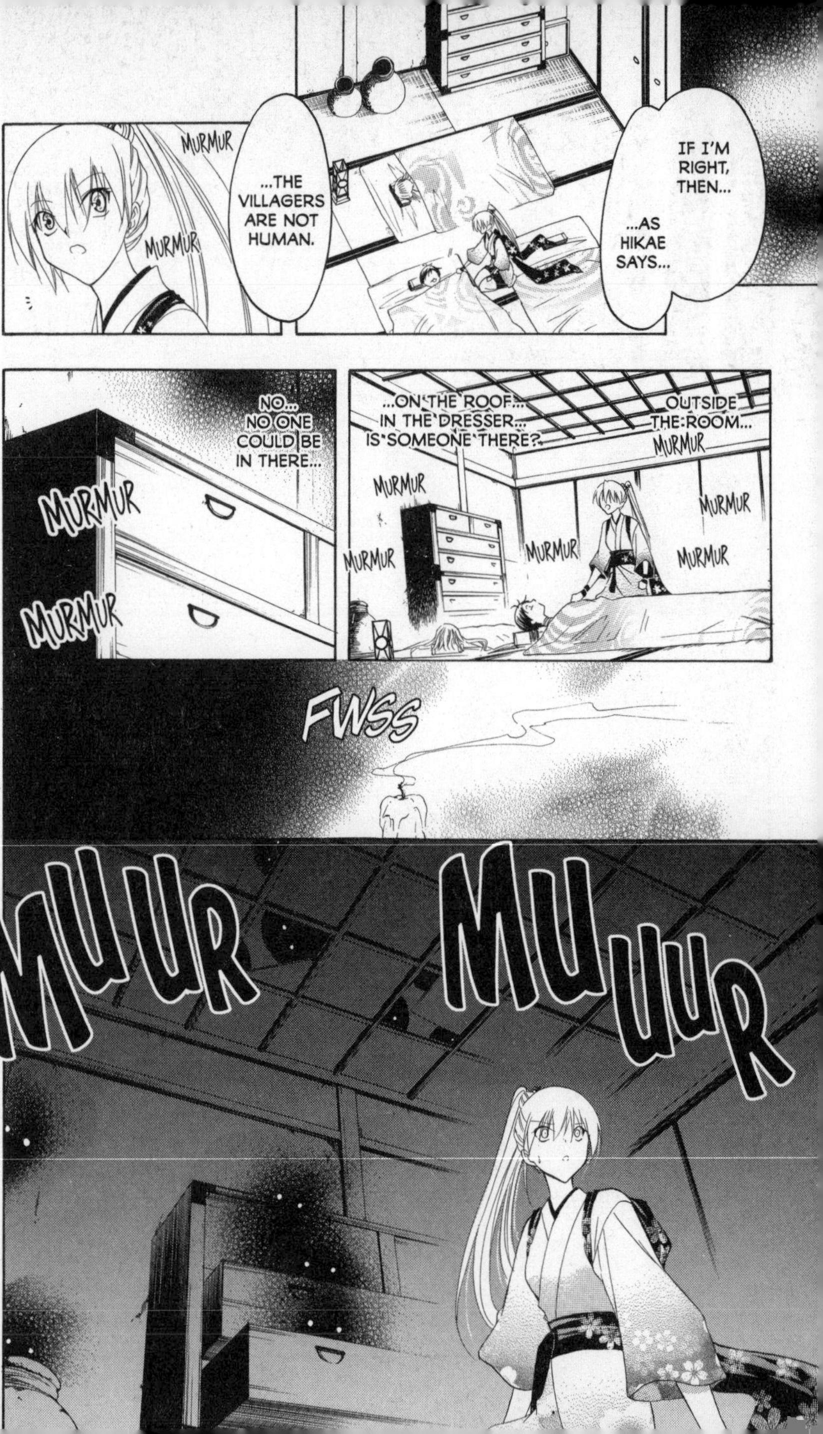
IF I'M RIGHT, THEN...
...AS HIKAE SAYS...
...THE VILLAGERS ARE NOT HUMAN.
MURMUR
MURMUR
OUTSIDE THE ROOM...
MURMUR
...ON THE ROOF... IN THE DRESSER... IS SOMEONE THERE?
MURMUR
MURMUR
MURMUR
MURMUR
MURMUR
NO... NO ONE COULD BE IN THERE...
MURMUR
MURMUR
FWSS
MUUUR
MUUR

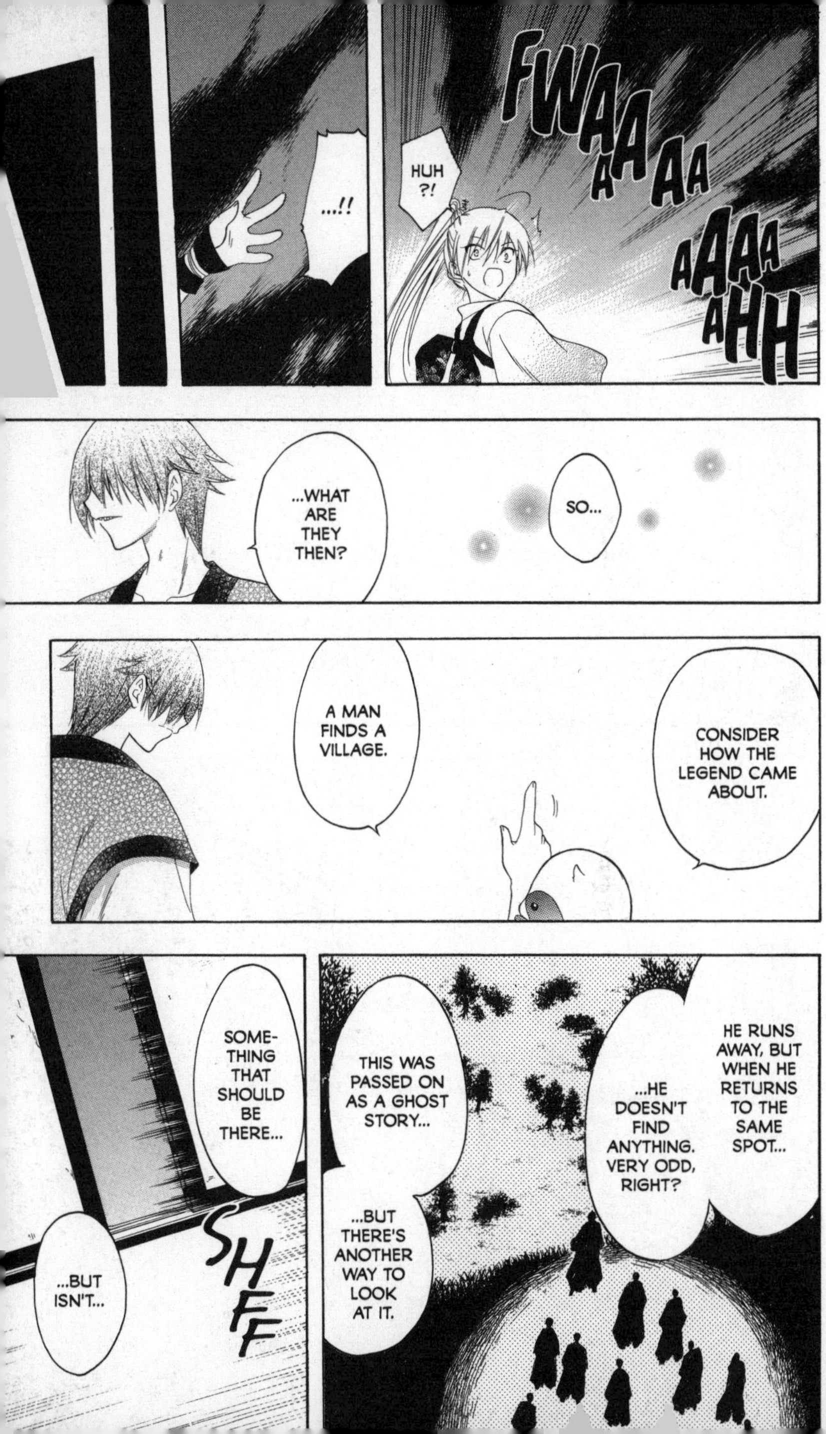
FWAAAAAAAAAAHH
HUH ?!
...!!
SO...
...WHAT ARE THEY THEN?
CONSIDER HOW THE LEGEND CAME ABOUT.
A MAN FINDS A VILLAGE.
HE RUNS AWAY, BUT WHEN HE RETURNS TO THE SAME SPOT...
...HE DOESN'T FIND ANYTHING. VERY ODD, RIGHT?
THIS WAS PASSED ON AS A GHOST STORY...
...BUT THERE'S ANOTHER WAY TO LOOK AT IT.
SOME-THING THAT SHOULD BE THERE...
SHFF
...BUT ISN'T...

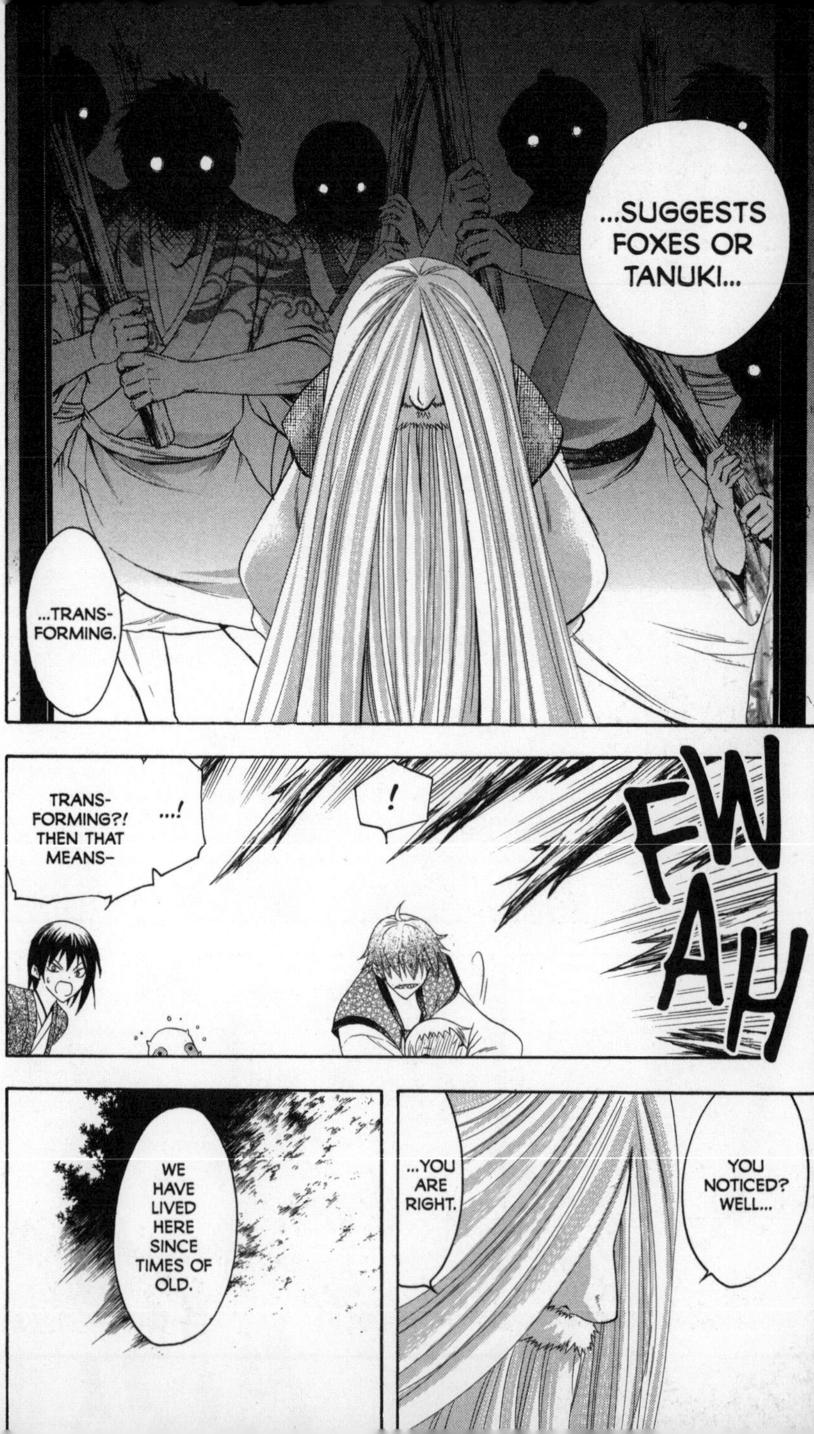
...SUGGESTS FOXES OR TANUKI...
...TRANS-FORMING.
FWAH
!
...!
TRANS-FORMING?! THEN THAT MEANS–
YOU NOTICED? WELL...
...YOU ARE RIGHT.
WE HAVE LIVED HERE SINCE TIMES OF OLD.

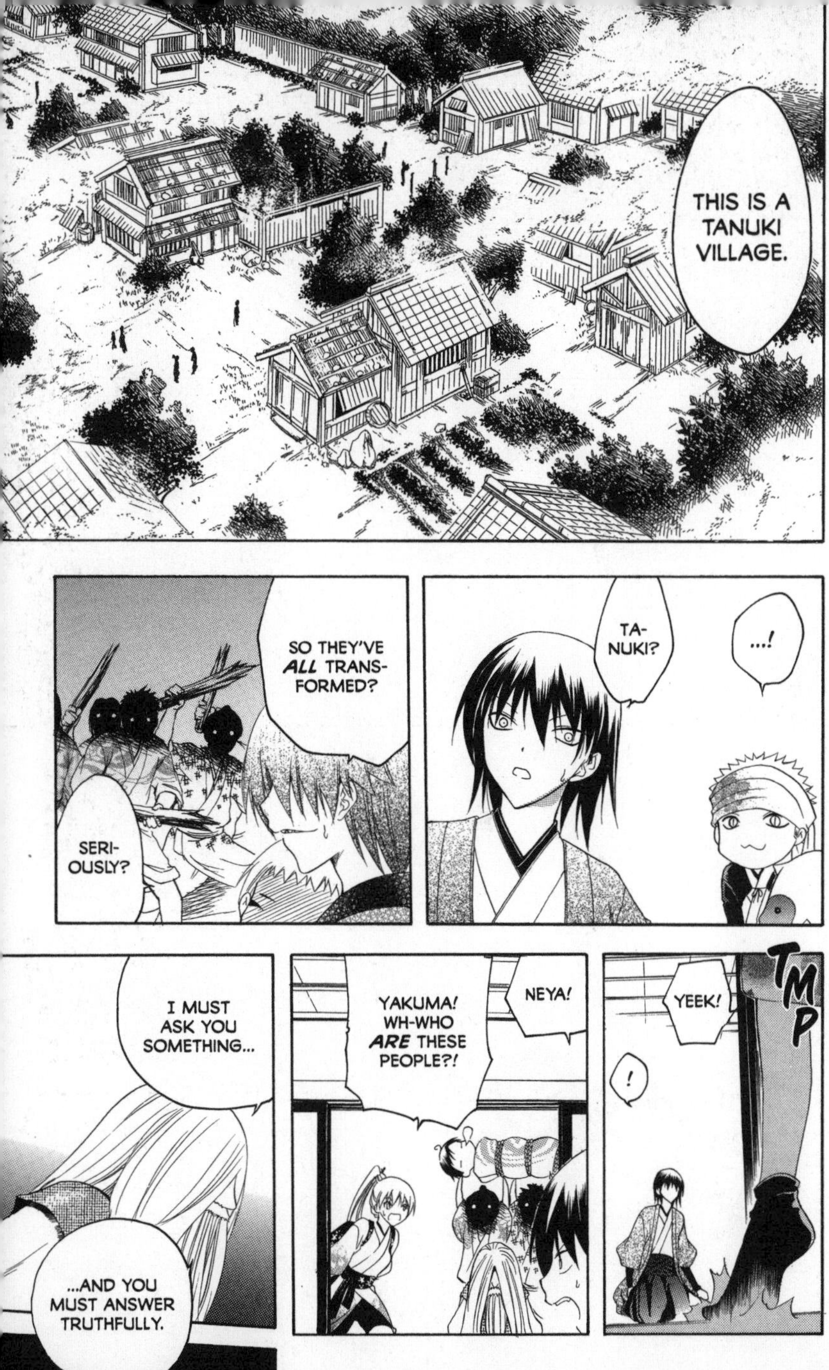
THIS IS A TANUKI VILLAGE.
...!
TA-NUKI?
SO THEY'VE ALL TRANS-FORMED?
SERI-OUSLY?
TMP
YEEK!
!
NEYA!
YAKUMA! WH-WHO ARE THESE PEOPLE?!
I MUST ASK YOU SOMETHING...
...AND YOU MUST ANSWER TRUTHFULLY.

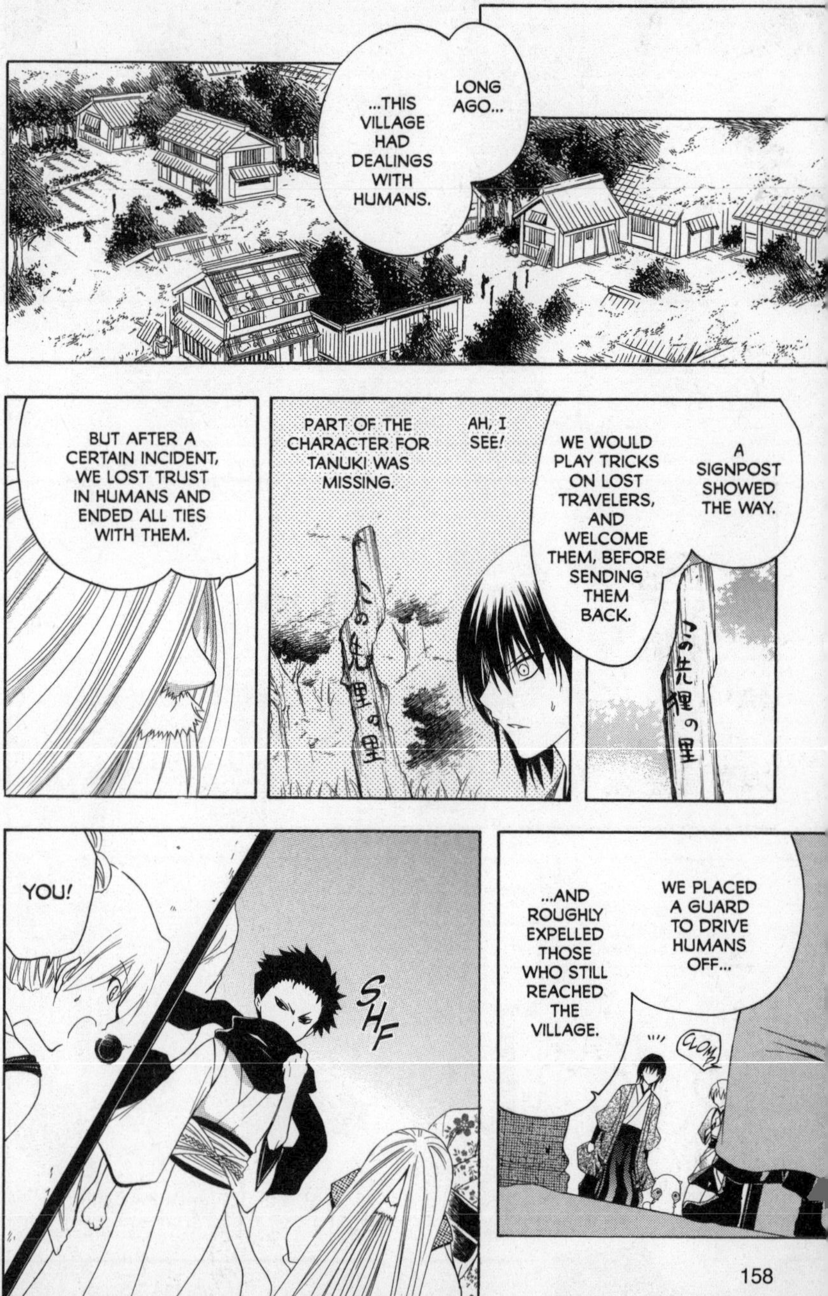
LONG AGO...
...THIS VILLAGE HAD DEALINGS WITH HUMANS.
A SIGNPOST SHOWED THE WAY.
WE WOULD PLAY TRICKS ON LOST TRAVELERS, AND WELCOME THEM, BEFORE SENDING THEM BACK.
この先狸の里
AH, I SEE!
PART OF THE CHARACTER FOR TANUKI WAS MISSING.
BUT AFTER A CERTAIN INCIDENT, WE LOST TRUST IN HUMANS AND ENDED ALL TIES WITH THEM.
WE PLACED A GUARD TO DRIVE HUMANS OFF...
...AND ROUGHLY EXPELLED THOSE WHO STILL REACHED THE VILLAGE.
CLOMP
YOU!
SHF

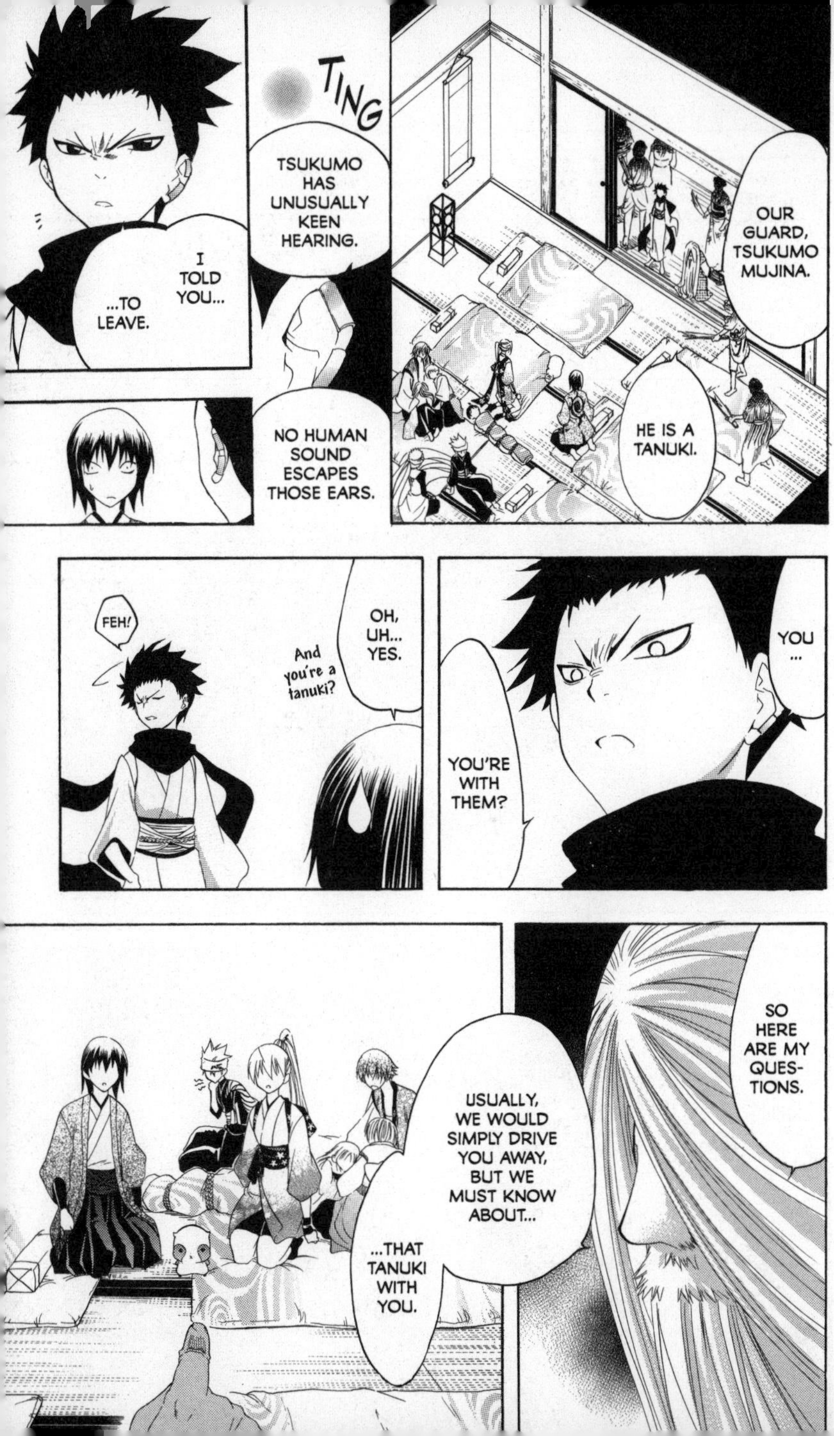
OUR GUARD, TSUKUMO MUJINA.
HE IS A TANUKI.
TING
TSUKUMO HAS UNUSUALLY KEEN HEARING.
I TOLD YOU...
...TO LEAVE.
NO HUMAN SOUND ESCAPES THOSE EARS.
YOU ...
YOU'RE WITH THEM?
OH, UH... YES.
And you're a tanuki?
FEH!
SO HERE ARE MY QUES-TIONS.
USUALLY, WE WOULD SIMPLY DRIVE YOU AWAY, BUT WE MUST KNOW ABOUT...
...THAT TANUKI WITH YOU.

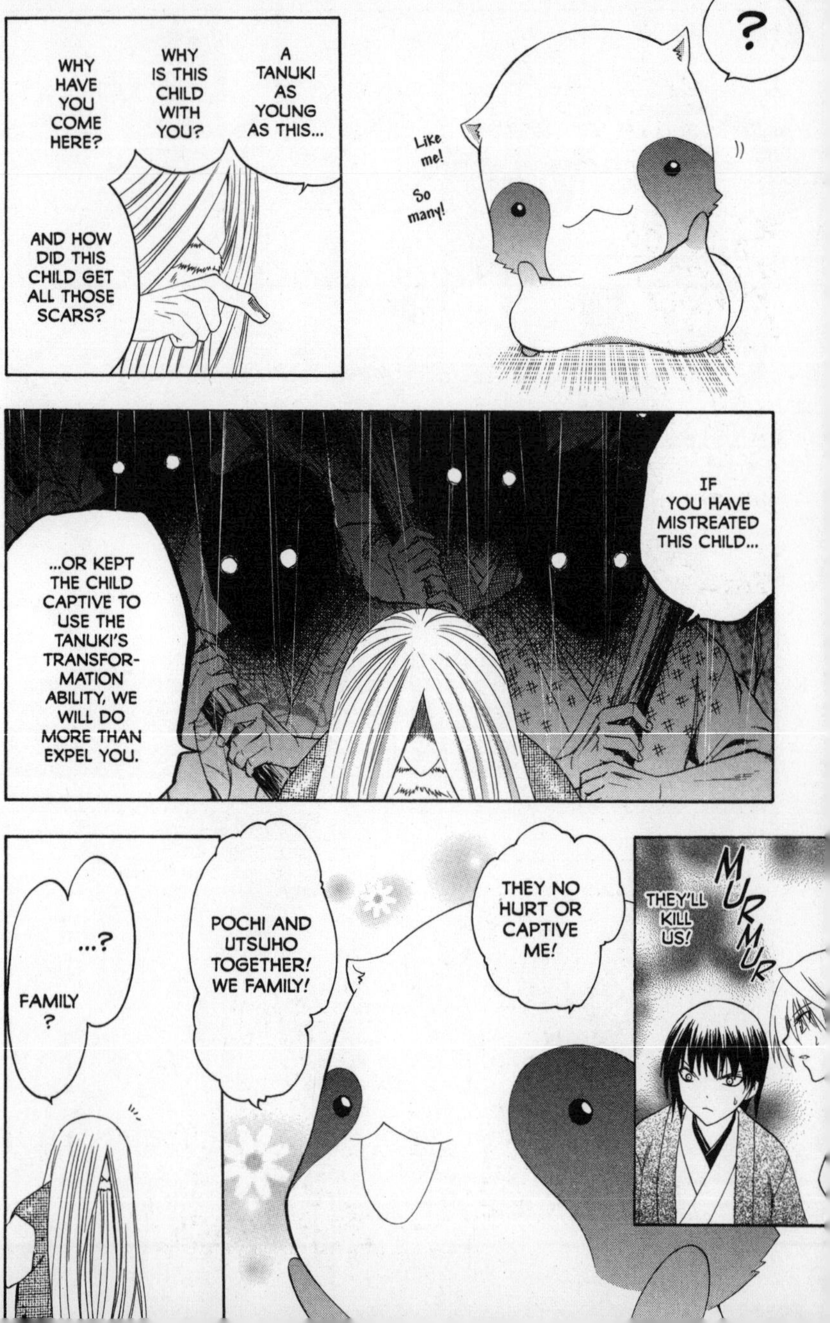
?
Like me!
So many!
A TANUKI AS YOUNG AS THIS...
WHY IS THIS CHILD WITH YOU?
WHY HAVE YOU COME HERE?
AND HOW DID THIS CHILD GET ALL THOSE SCARS?
IF YOU HAVE MISTREATED THIS CHILD...
...OR KEPT THE CHILD CAPTIVE TO USE THE TANUKI'S TRANSFORMATION ABILITY, WE WILL DO MORE THAN EXPEL YOU.
MURMUR
THEY'LL KILL US!
THEY NO HURT OR CAPTIVE ME!
POCHI AND UTSUHO TOGETHER! WE FAMILY!
...?
FAMILY?

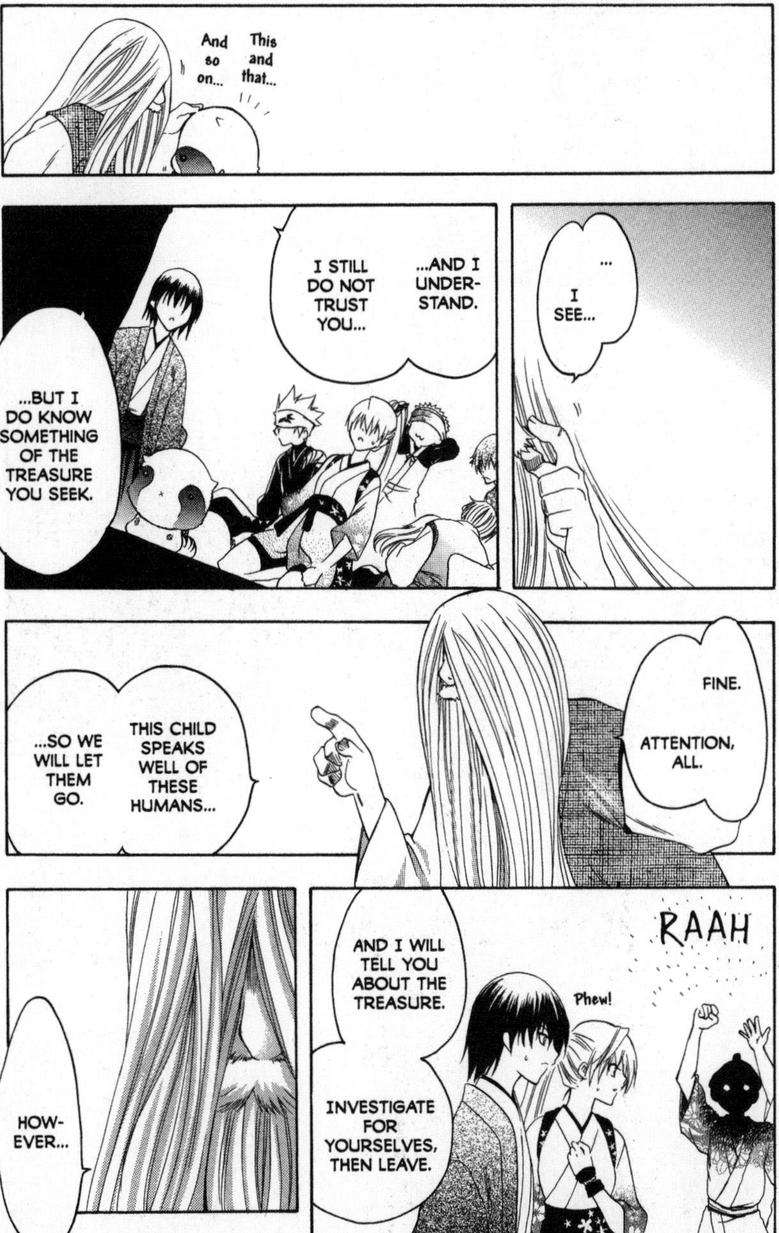
This and that...
And so on...
...
I SEE...
...AND I UNDERSTAND.
I STILL DO NOT TRUST YOU...
...BUT I DO KNOW SOMETHING OF THE TREASURE YOU SEEK.
FINE.
ATTENTION, ALL.
THIS CHILD SPEAKS WELL OF THESE HUMANS...
...SO WE WILL LET THEM GO.
RAAH
Phew!
AND I WILL TELL YOU ABOUT THE TREASURE.
INVESTIGATE FOR YOURSELVES, THEN LEAVE.
HOW-EVER...

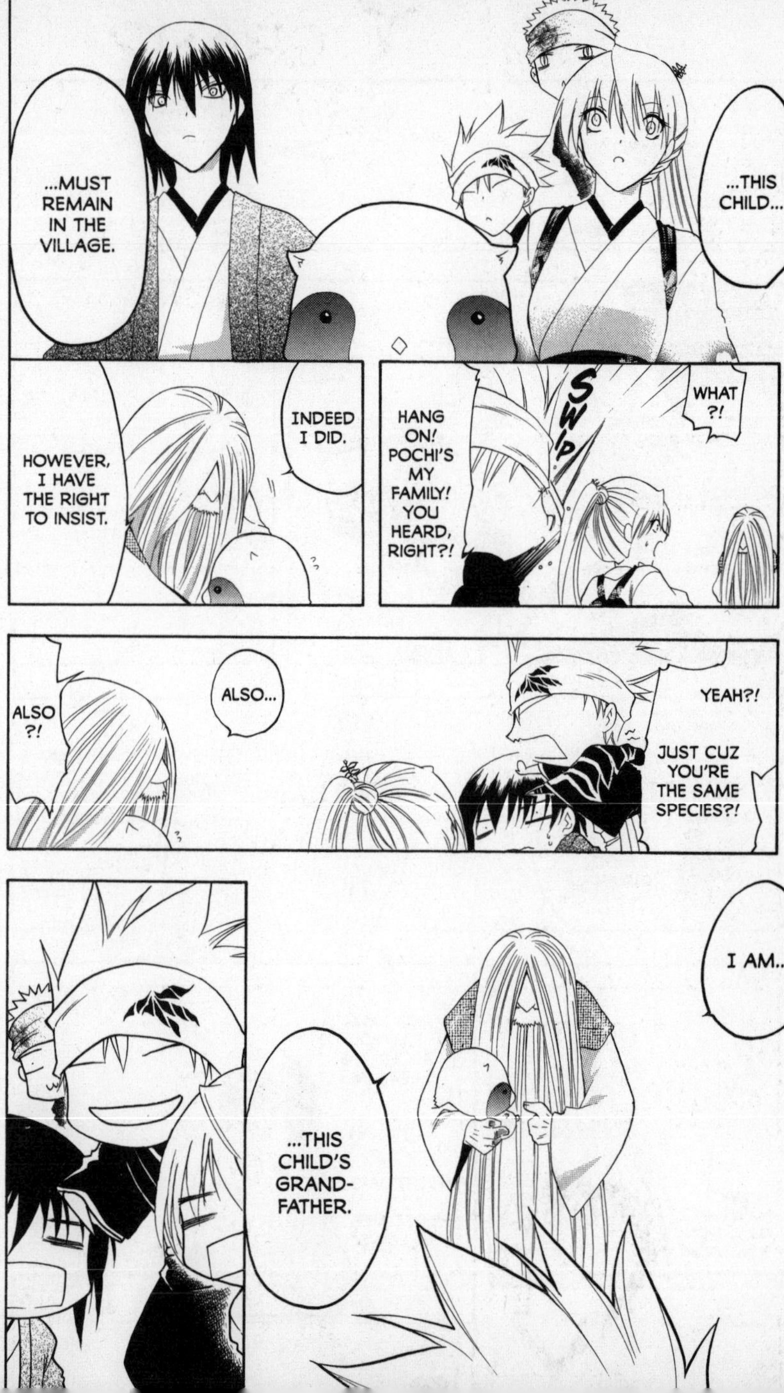
...THIS CHILD...
...MUST REMAIN IN THE VILLAGE.
WHAT?!
SWIP
HANG ON! POCHI'S MY FAMILY! YOU HEARD, RIGHT?!
INDEED I DID.
HOWEVER, I HAVE THE RIGHT TO INSIST.
YEAH?!
JUST CUZ YOU'RE THE SAME SPECIES?!
ALSO...
ALSO ?!
I AM...
...THIS CHILD'S GRAND-FATHER.

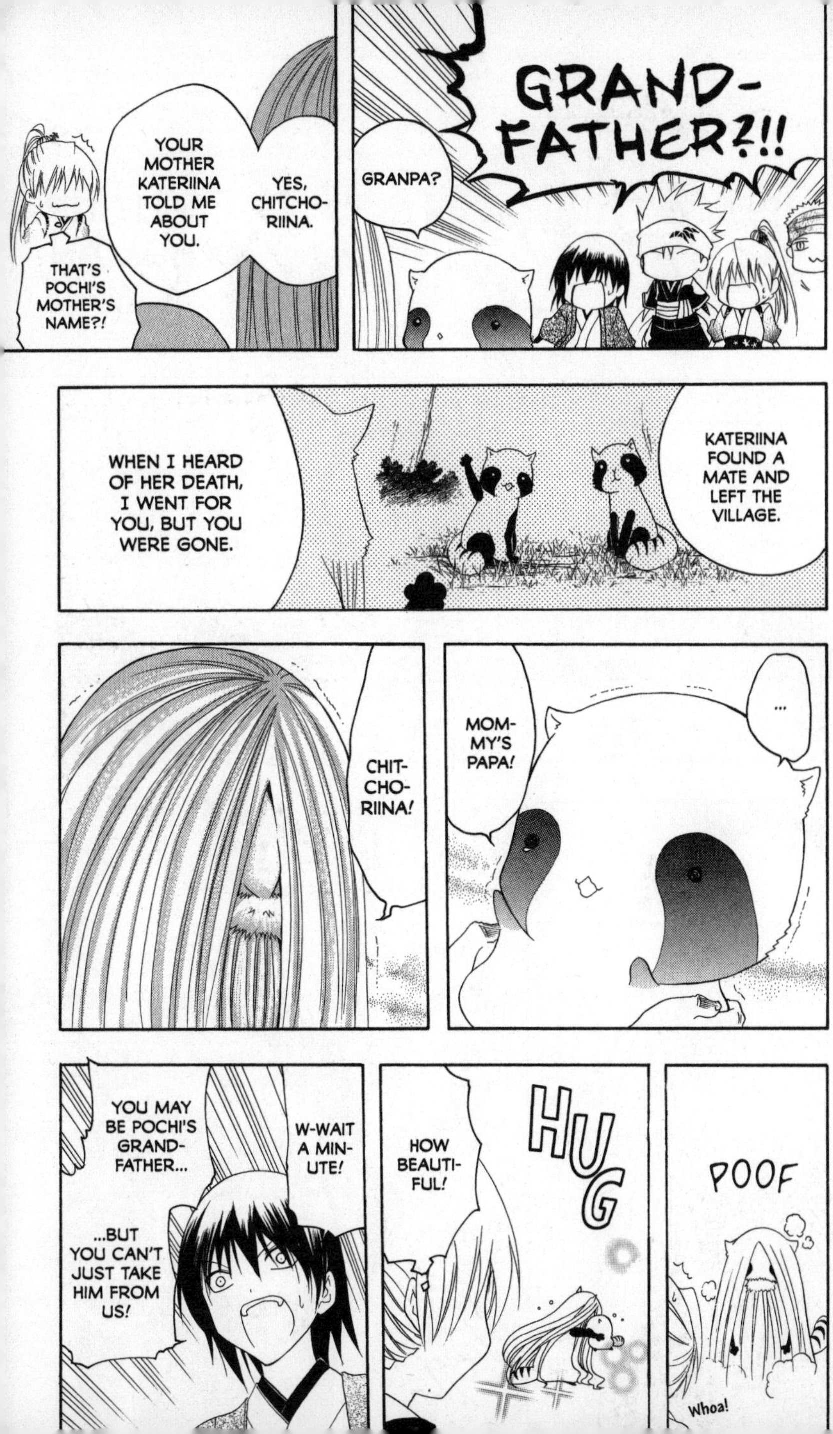
GRAND-FATHER?!!
GRANPA?
YES, CHITCHO-RIINA.
YOUR MOTHER KATERIINA TOLD ME ABOUT YOU.
THAT'S POCHI'S MOTHER'S NAME?!
KATERIINA FOUND A MATE AND LEFT THE VILLAGE.
WHEN I HEARD OF HER DEATH, I WENT FOR YOU, BUT YOU WERE GONE.
...
MOM-MY'S PAPA!
CHIT-CHO-RIINA!
POOF
Whoa!
HUG
HOW BEAUTI-FUL!
W-WAIT A MIN-UTE!
YOU MAY BE POCHI'S GRAND-FATHER...
...BUT YOU CAN'T JUST TAKE HIM FROM US!

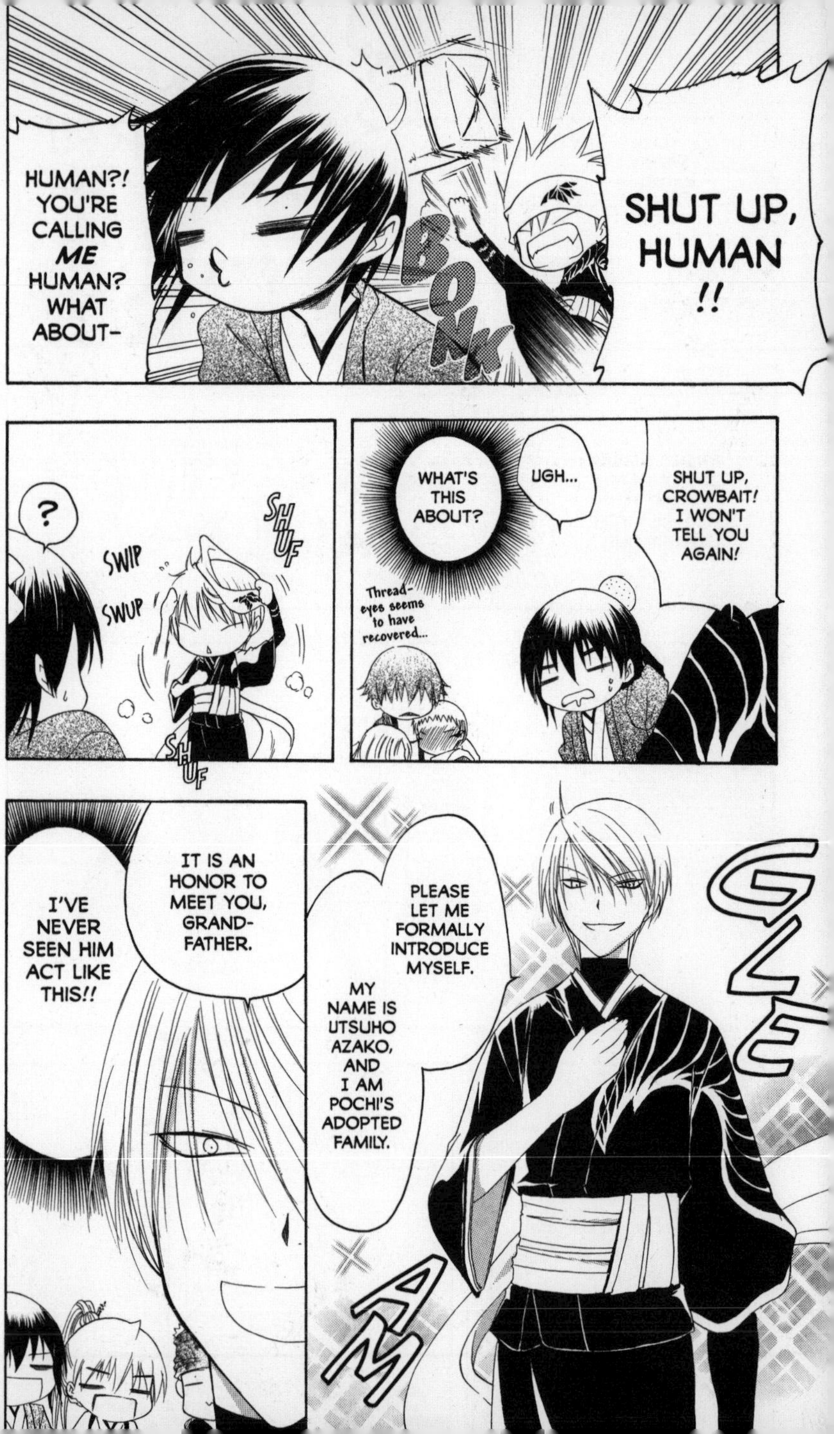
SHUT UP, HUMAN !!
BONK
HUMAN?! YOU'RE CALLING *ME* HUMAN? WHAT ABOUT-
SHUT UP, CROWBAIT! I WON'T TELL YOU AGAIN!
UGH...
WHAT'S THIS ABOUT?
Thread-eyes seems to have recovered...
SHUF
?
SWIP
SWUP
SHUF
GLE
AM
PLEASE LET ME FORMALLY INTRODUCE MYSELF.
MY NAME IS UTSUHO AZAKO, AND I AM POCHI'S ADOPTED FAMILY.
IT IS AN HONOR TO MEET YOU, GRAND-FATHER.
I'VE NEVER SEEN HIM ACT LIKE THIS!!

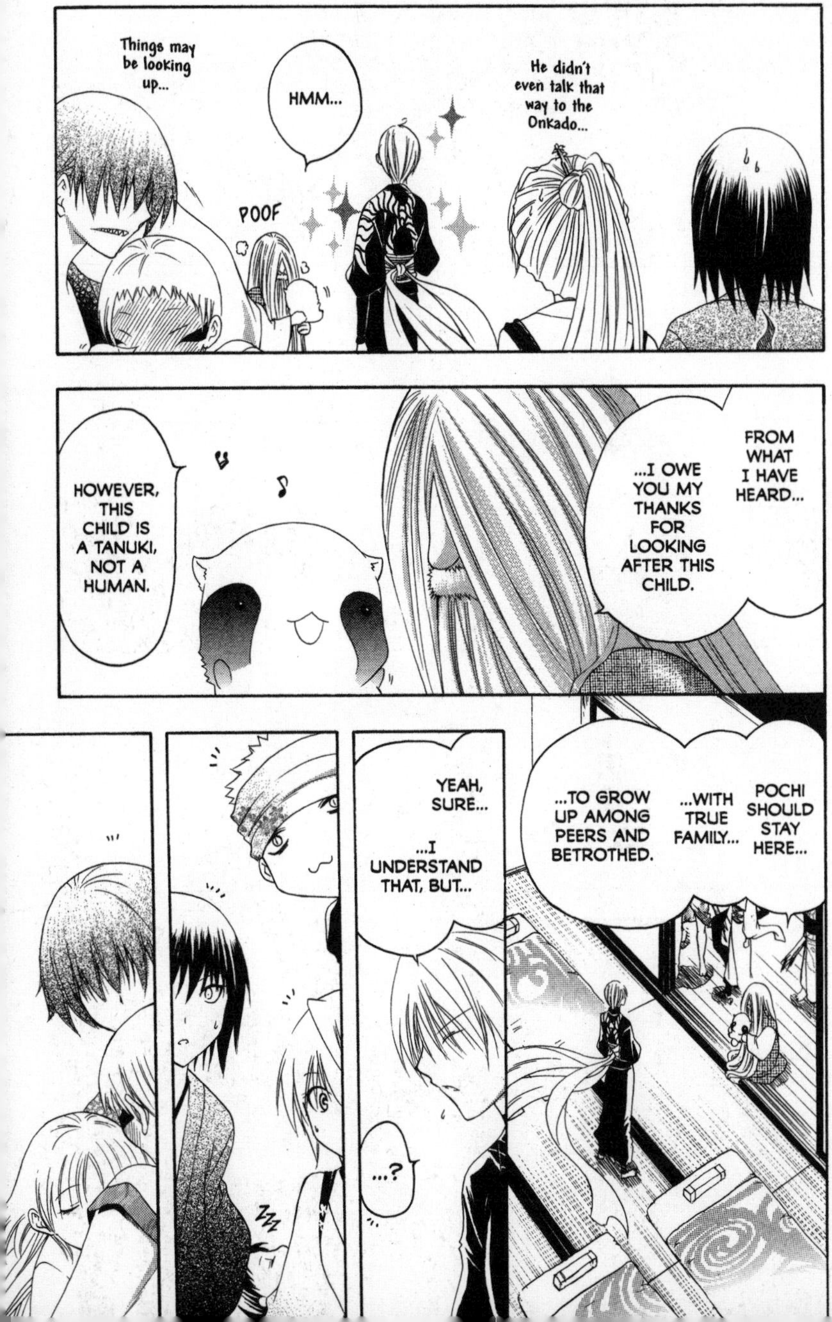
He didn't even talk that way to the Onkado...
HMM...
POOF
Things may be looking up...
FROM WHAT I HAVE HEARD...
...I OWE YOU MY THANKS FOR LOOKING AFTER THIS CHILD.
HOWEVER, THIS CHILD IS A TANUKI, NOT A HUMAN.
POCHI SHOULD STAY HERE...
...WITH TRUE FAMILY...
...TO GROW UP AMONG PEERS AND BETROTHED.
YEAH, SURE...
...I UNDERSTAND THAT, BUT...
...?
ZZZ

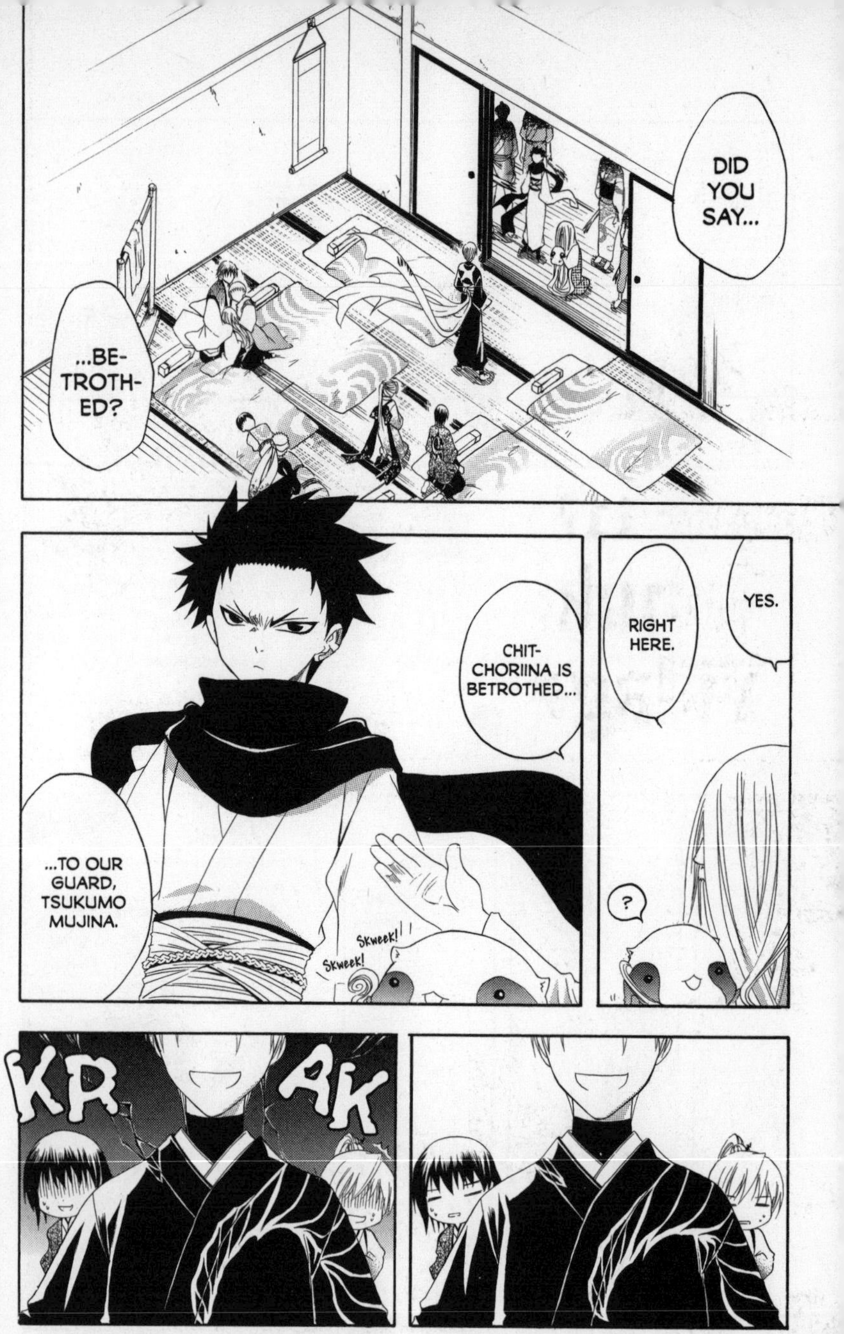
DID YOU SAY...
...BE-TROTH-ED?
YES.
RIGHT HERE.
?
CHIT-CHORIINA IS BETROTHED...
...TO OUR GUARD, TSUKUMO MUJINA.
Skweek!!
Skweek!
KRAK

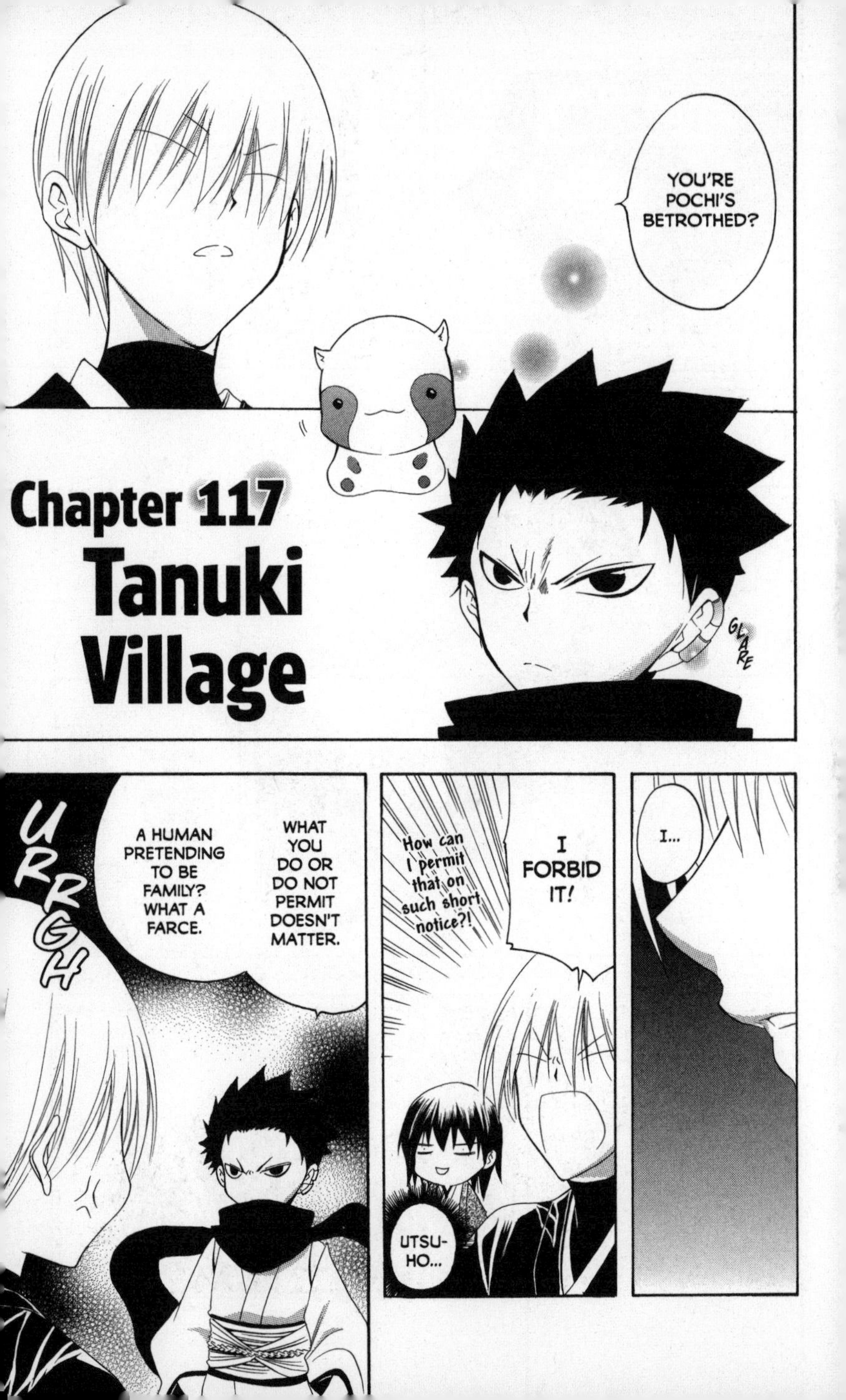
YOU'RE POCHI'S BETROTHED?
Chapter 117 Tanuki Village
GLARE
I...
I FORBID IT!
How can I permit that on such short notice?!
UTSU-HO...
WHAT YOU DO OR DO NOT PERMIT DOESN'T MATTER.
A HUMAN PRETENDING TO BE FAMILY? WHAT A FARCE.
URRGH

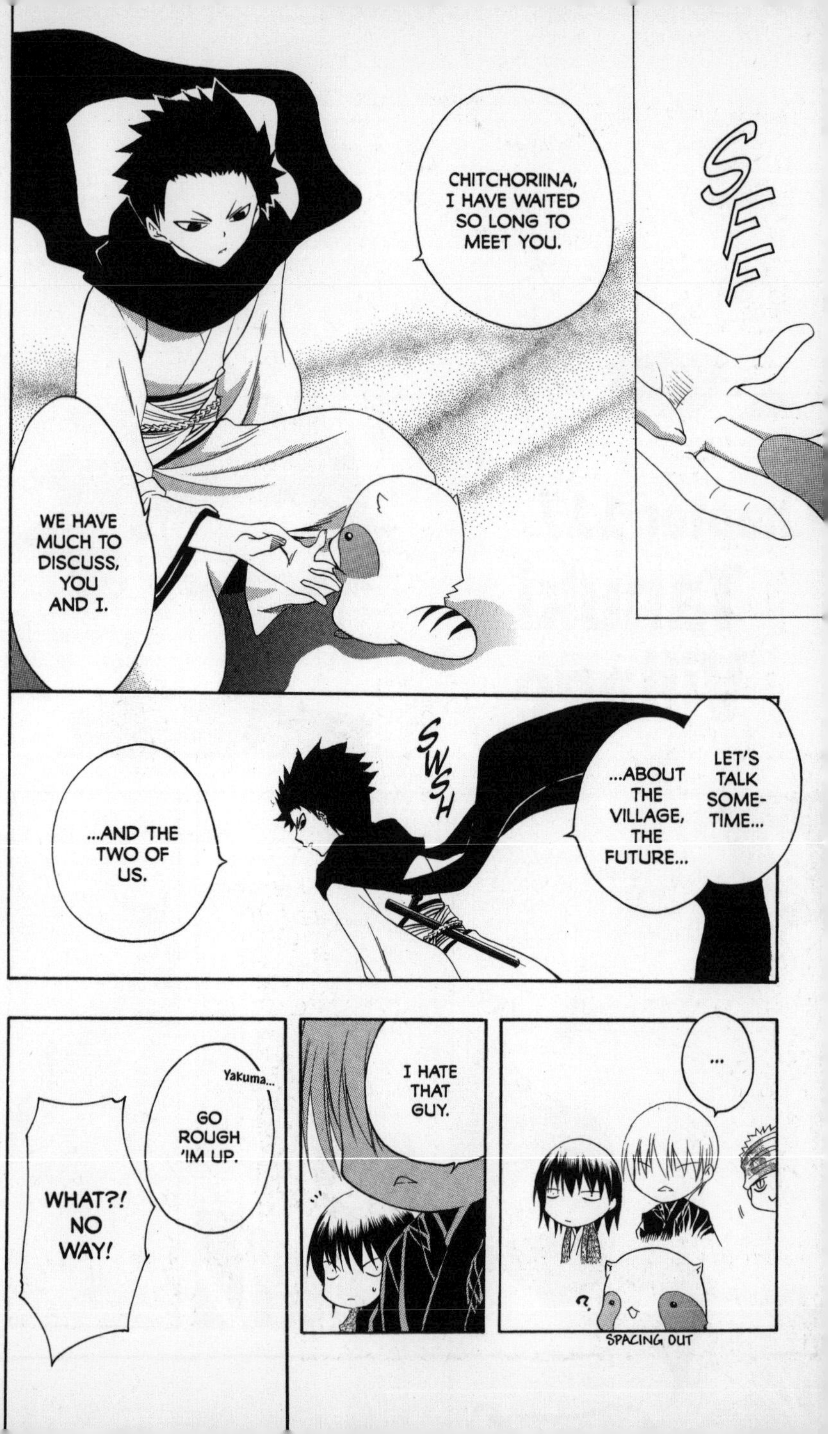
SFF
CHITCHORIINA, I HAVE WAITED SO LONG TO MEET YOU.
WE HAVE MUCH TO DISCUSS, YOU AND I.
LET'S TALK SOMETIME...
...ABOUT THE VILLAGE, THE FUTURE...
SWSH
...AND THE TWO OF US.
...
SPACING OUT
I HATE THAT GUY.
Yakuma...
GO ROUGH 'IM UP.
WHAT?! NO WAY!

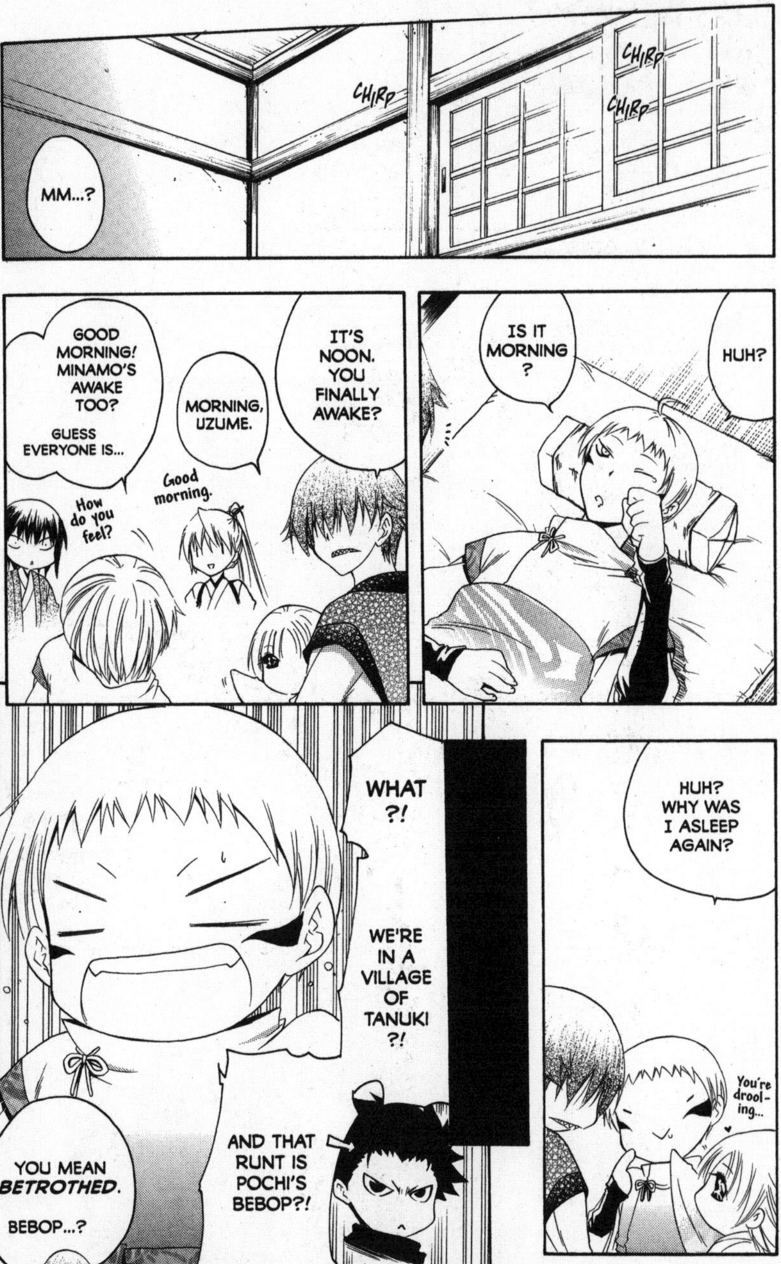
CHIRP
CHIRP
CHIRP
MM...?
HUH?
IS IT MORNING?
IT'S NOON. YOU FINALLY AWAKE?
MORNING, UZUME.
Good morning.
GOOD MORNING! MINAMO'S AWAKE TOO?
GUESS EVERYONE IS...
How do you feel?
HUH? WHY WAS I ASLEEP AGAIN?
You're drool-ing...
WHAT?!
WE'RE IN A VILLAGE OF TANUKI?!
AND THAT RUNT IS POCHI'S BEBOP?!
YOU MEAN ***BETROTHED***.
BEBOP...?

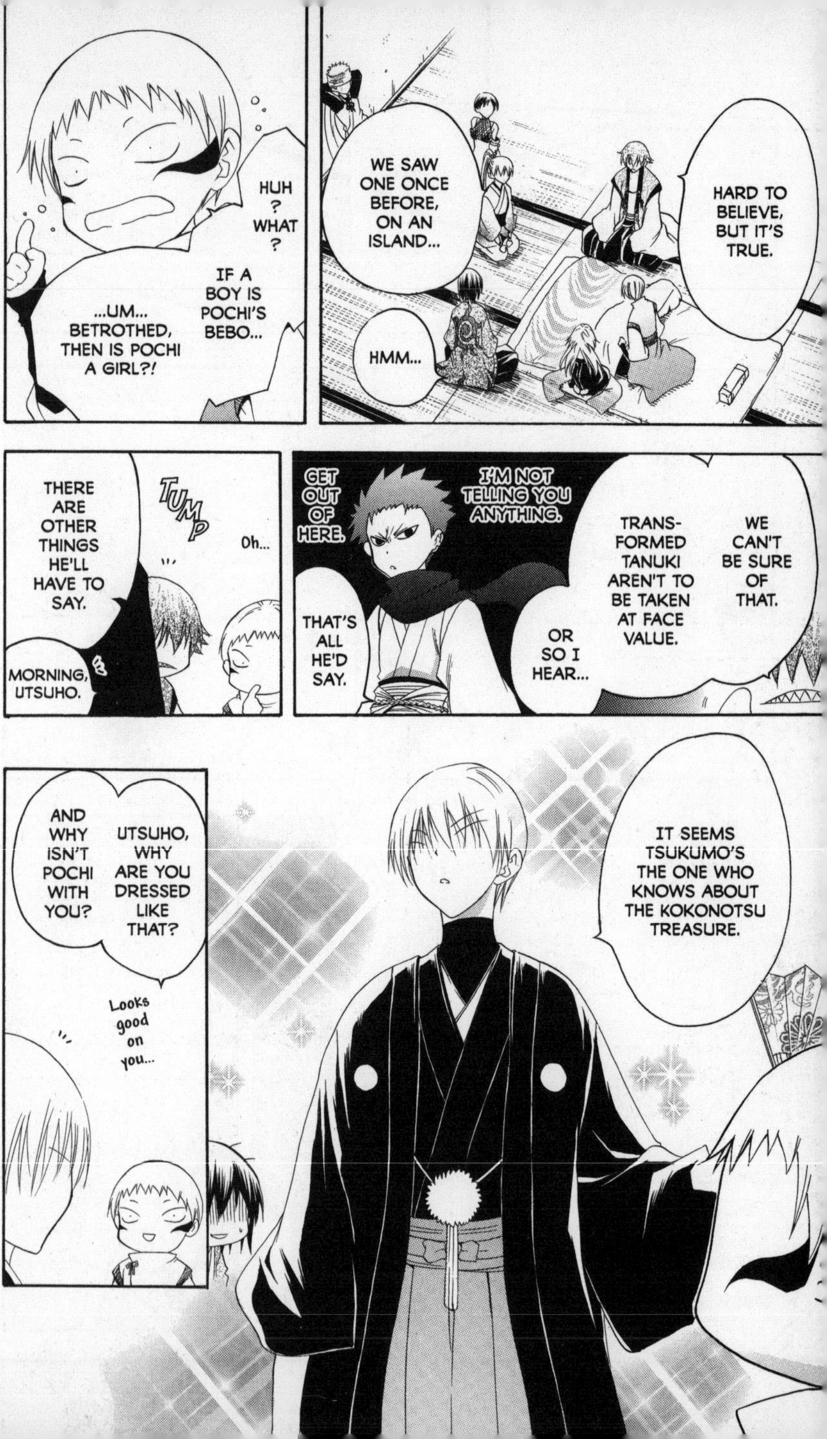
HARD TO BELIEVE, BUT IT'S TRUE.
WE SAW ONE ONCE BEFORE, ON AN ISLAND...
HMM...
HUH? WHAT?
IF A BOY IS POCHI'S BEBO...
...UM... BETROTHED, THEN IS POCHI A GIRL?!
WE CAN'T BE SURE OF THAT.
TRANS-FORMED TANUKI AREN'T TO BE TAKEN AT FACE VALUE.
OR SO I HEAR...
I'M NOT TELLING YOU ANYTHING.
GET OUT OF HERE.
THAT'S ALL HE'D SAY.
Oh...
TUMP
THERE ARE OTHER THINGS HE'LL HAVE TO SAY.
MORNING, UTSUHO.
IT SEEMS TSUKUMO'S THE ONE WHO KNOWS ABOUT THE KOKONOTSU TREASURE.
UTSUHO, WHY ARE YOU DRESSED LIKE THAT?
AND WHY ISN'T POCHI WITH YOU?
Looks good on you...

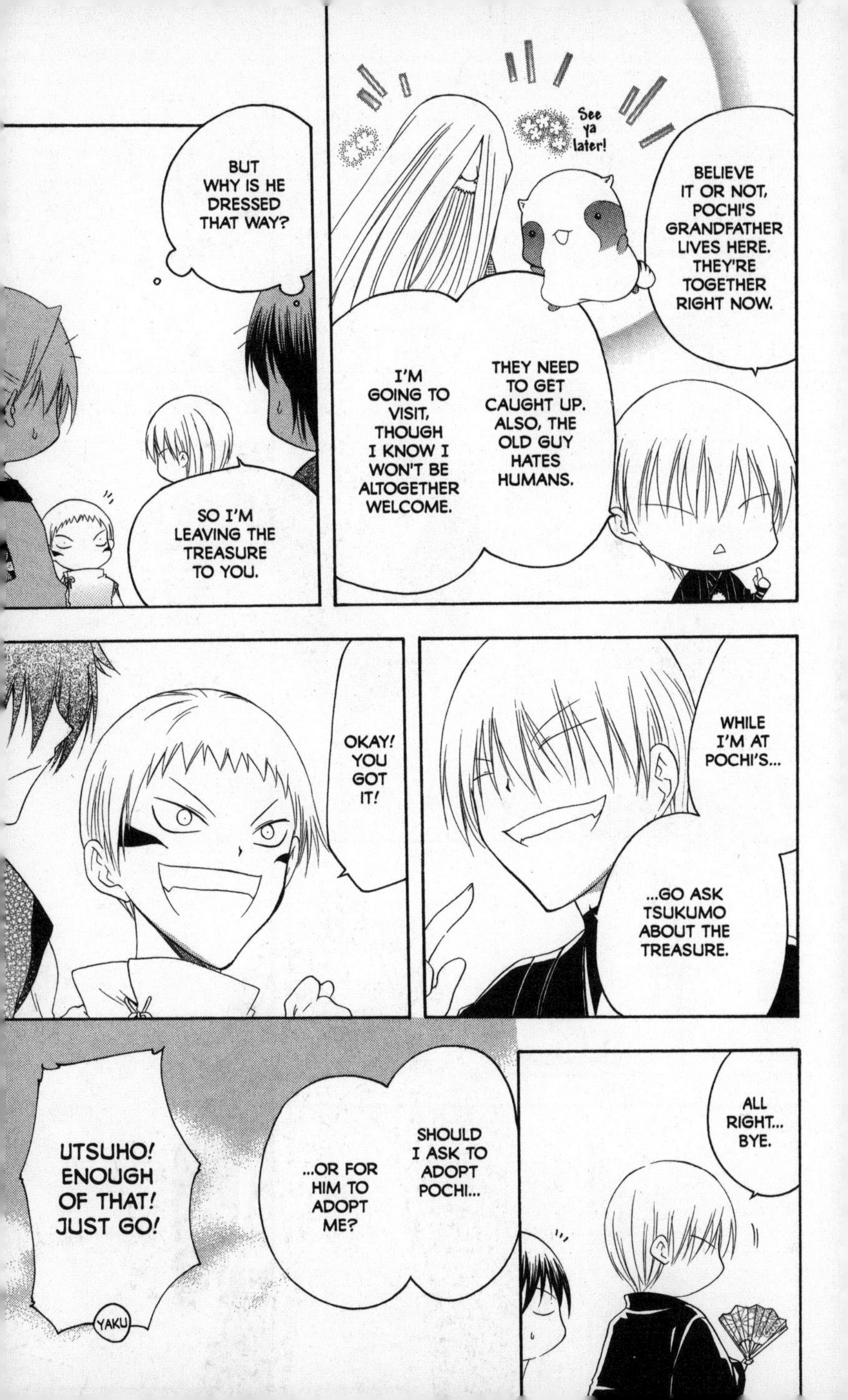
BELIEVE IT OR NOT, POCHI'S GRANDFATHER LIVES HERE. THEY'RE TOGETHER RIGHT NOW.
See ya later!
THEY NEED TO GET CAUGHT UP. ALSO, THE OLD GUY HATES HUMANS.
I'M GOING TO VISIT, THOUGH I KNOW I WON'T BE ALTOGETHER WELCOME.
BUT WHY IS HE DRESSED THAT WAY?
SO I'M LEAVING THE TREASURE TO YOU.
WHILE I'M AT POCHI'S...
...GO ASK TSUKUMO ABOUT THE TREASURE.
OKAY! YOU GOT IT!
ALL RIGHT... BYE.
SHOULD I ASK TO ADOPT POCHI...
...OR FOR HIM TO ADOPT ME?
UTSUHO! ENOUGH OF THAT! JUST GO!
YAKU

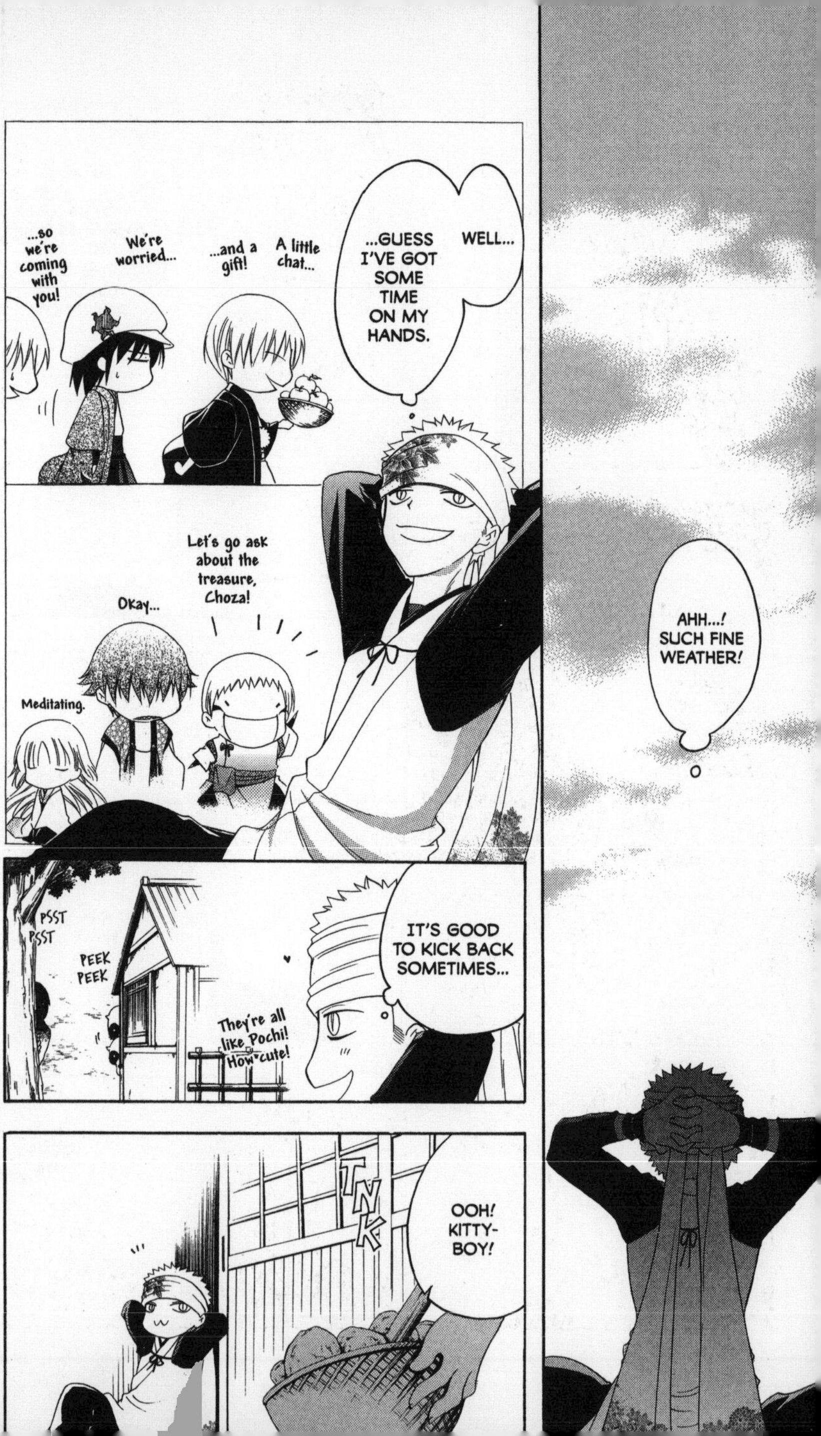
AHH...! SUCH FINE WEATHER!
WELL...
...GUESS I'VE GOT SOME TIME ON MY HANDS.
A little chat...
...and a gift!
We're worried...
...so we're coming with you!
Let's go ask about the treasure, Choza!
Okay...
Meditating.
IT'S GOOD TO KICK BACK SOMETIMES...
They're all like Pochi! How cute!
PEEK PEEK
PSST PSST
OOH! KITTY-BOY!
TNK

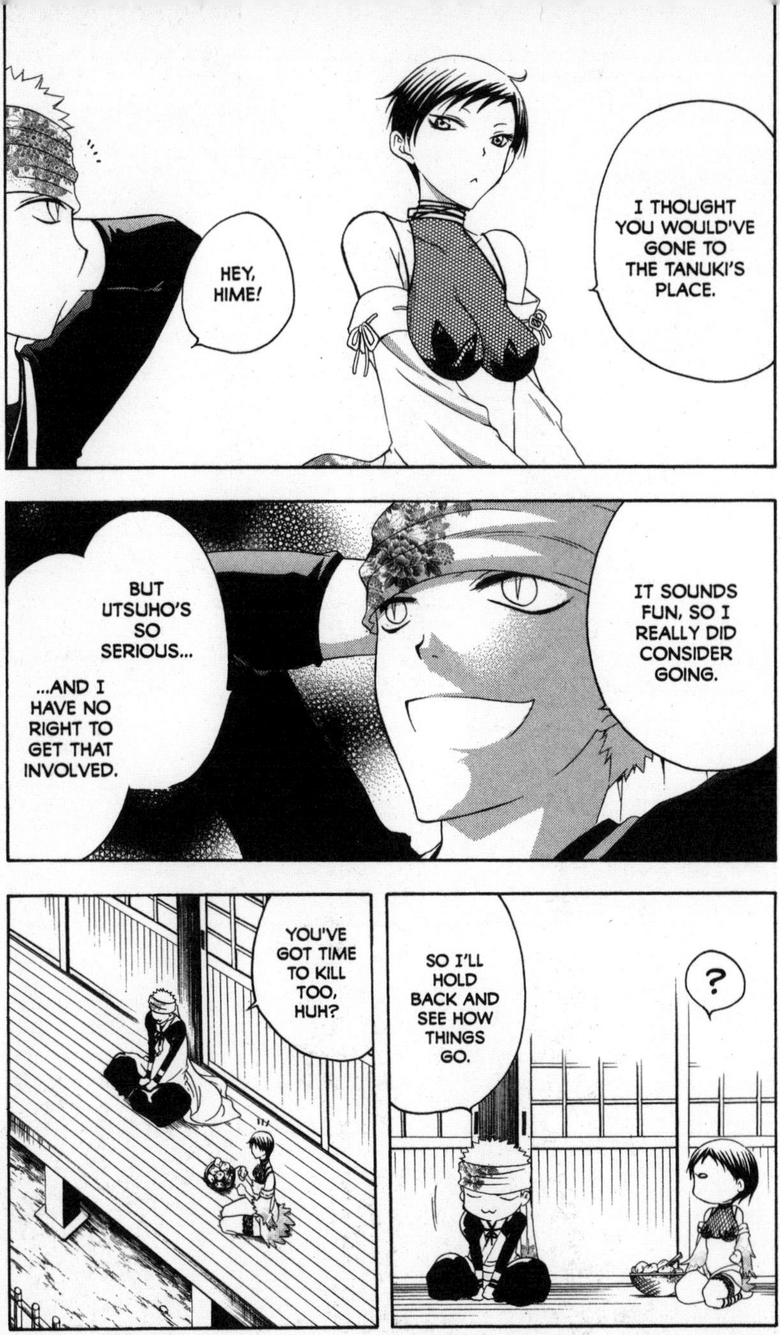

I THOUGHT YOU WOULD'VE GONE TO THE TANUKI'S PLACE.
HEY, HIME!
IT SOUNDS FUN, SO I REALLY DID CONSIDER GOING.
BUT UTSUHO'S SO SERIOUS...
...AND I HAVE NO RIGHT TO GET THAT INVOLVED.
SO I'LL HOLD BACK AND SEE HOW THINGS GO.
?
YOU'VE GOT TIME TO KILL TOO, HUH?

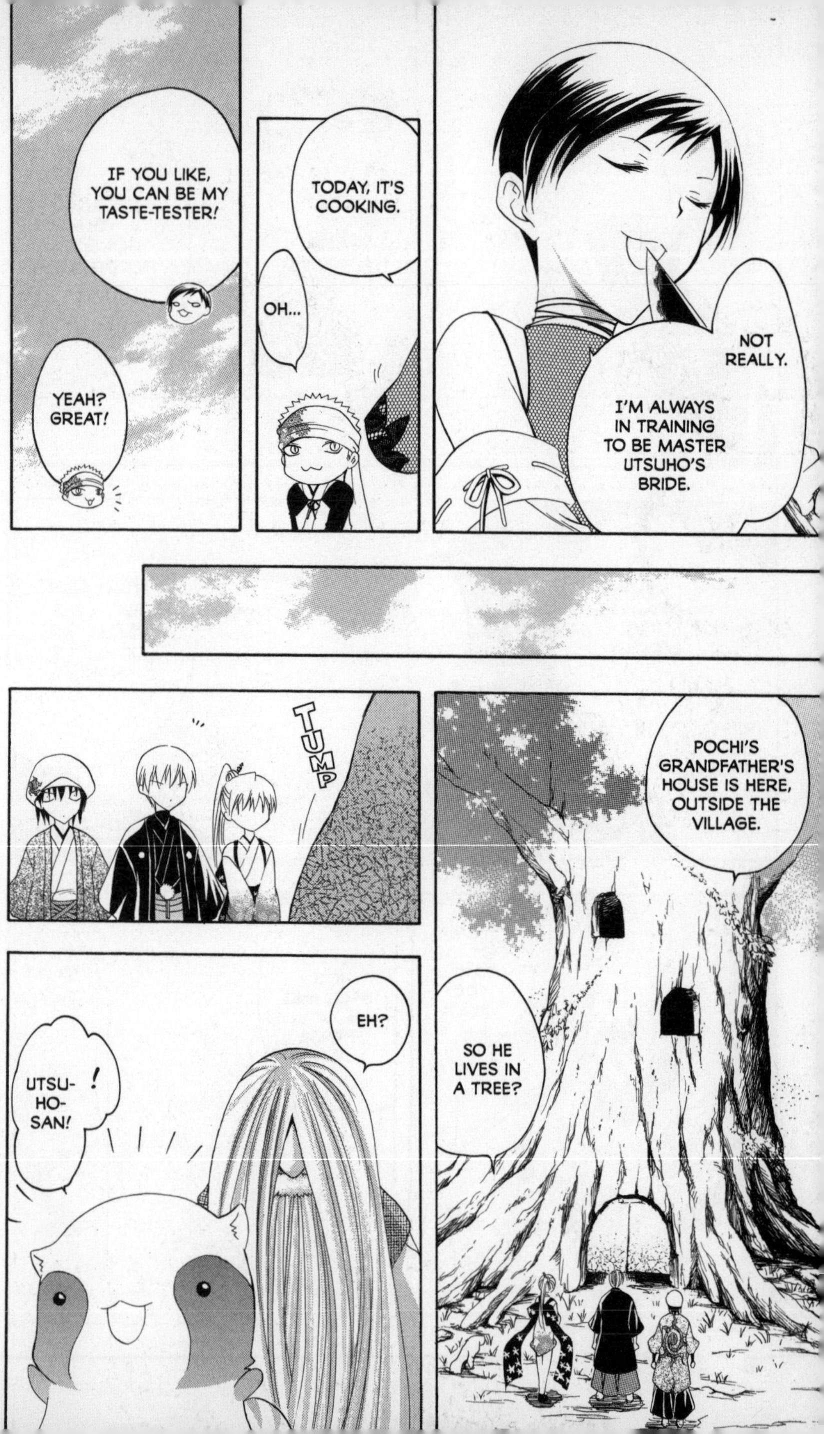
NOT REALLY.
I'M ALWAYS IN TRAINING TO BE MASTER UTSUHO'S BRIDE.
TODAY, IT'S COOKING.
OH...
IF YOU LIKE, YOU CAN BE MY TASTE-TESTER!
YEAH? GREAT!
POCHI'S GRANDFATHER'S HOUSE IS HERE, OUTSIDE THE VILLAGE.
SO HE LIVES IN A TREE?
TUMP
EH?
UTSU-HO-SAN!

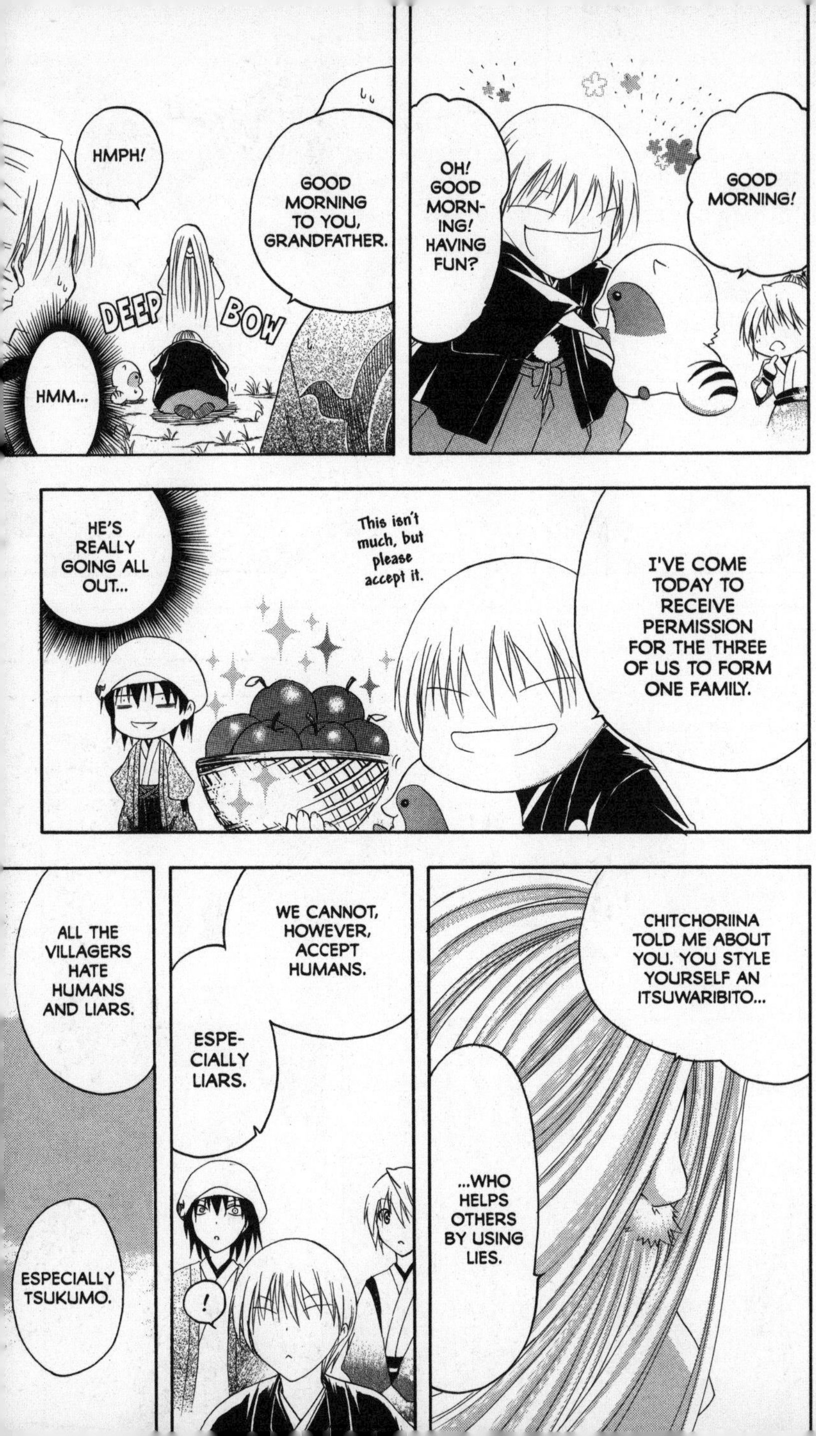
GOOD MORNING!
OH! GOOD MORN-ING! HAVING FUN?
GOOD MORNING TO YOU, GRANDFATHER.
HMPH!
DEEP BOW
HMM...
I'VE COME TODAY TO RECEIVE PERMISSION FOR THE THREE OF US TO FORM ONE FAMILY.
This isn't much, but please accept it.
HE'S REALLY GOING ALL OUT...
CHITCHORIINA TOLD ME ABOUT YOU. YOU STYLE YOURSELF AN ITSUWARIBITO...
...WHO HELPS OTHERS BY USING LIES.
WE CANNOT, HOWEVER, ACCEPT HUMANS.
ESPE-CIALLY LIARS.
!
ALL THE VILLAGERS HATE HUMANS AND LIARS.
ESPECIALLY TSUKUMO.

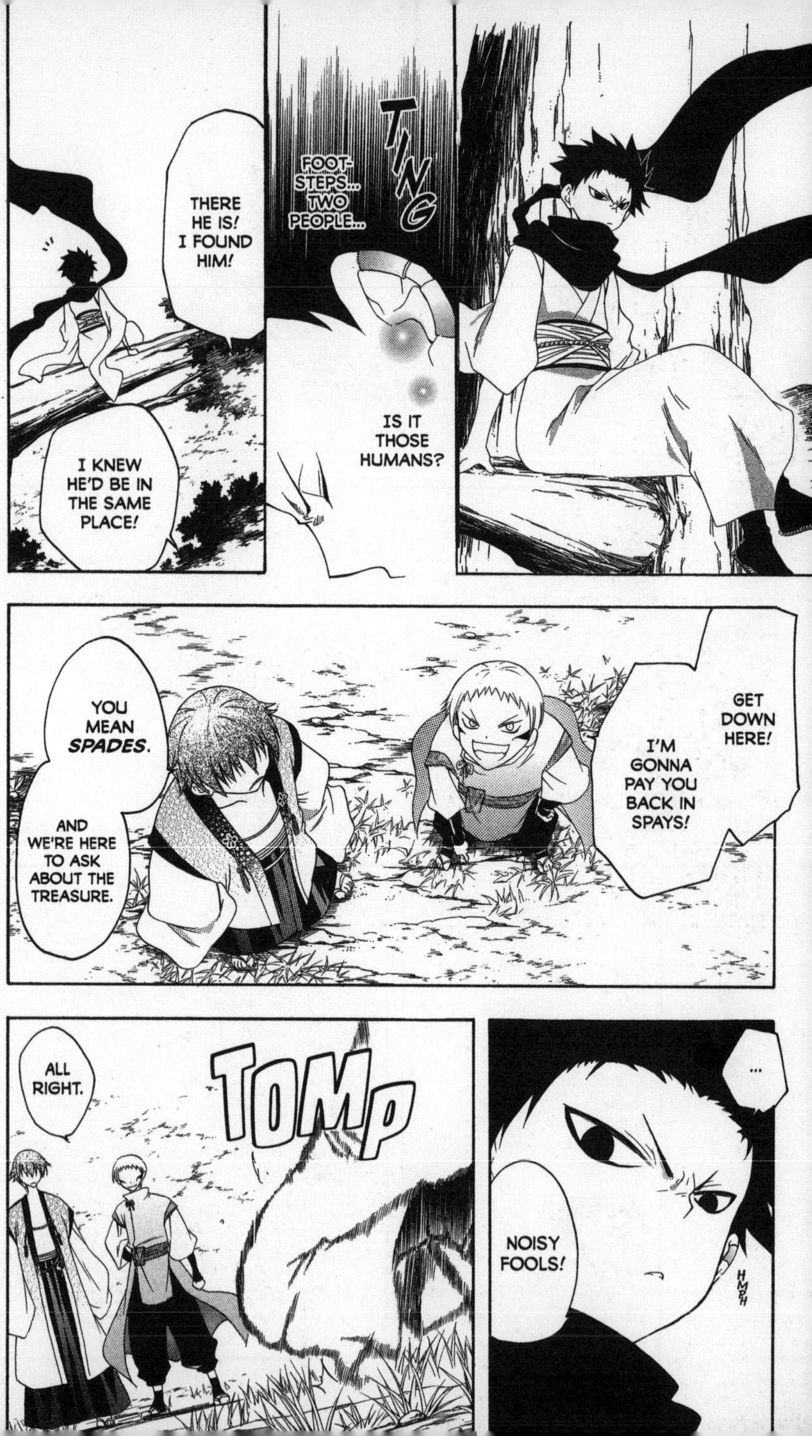
TING
FOOT-STEPS... TWO PEOPLE...
IS IT THOSE HUMANS?
THERE HE IS! I FOUND HIM!
I KNEW HE'D BE IN THE SAME PLACE!
GET DOWN HERE!
I'M GONNA PAY YOU BACK IN SPAYS!
YOU MEAN SPADES.
AND WE'RE HERE TO ASK ABOUT THE TREASURE.
...
NOISY FOOLS!
HMPH
TOMP
ALL RIGHT.

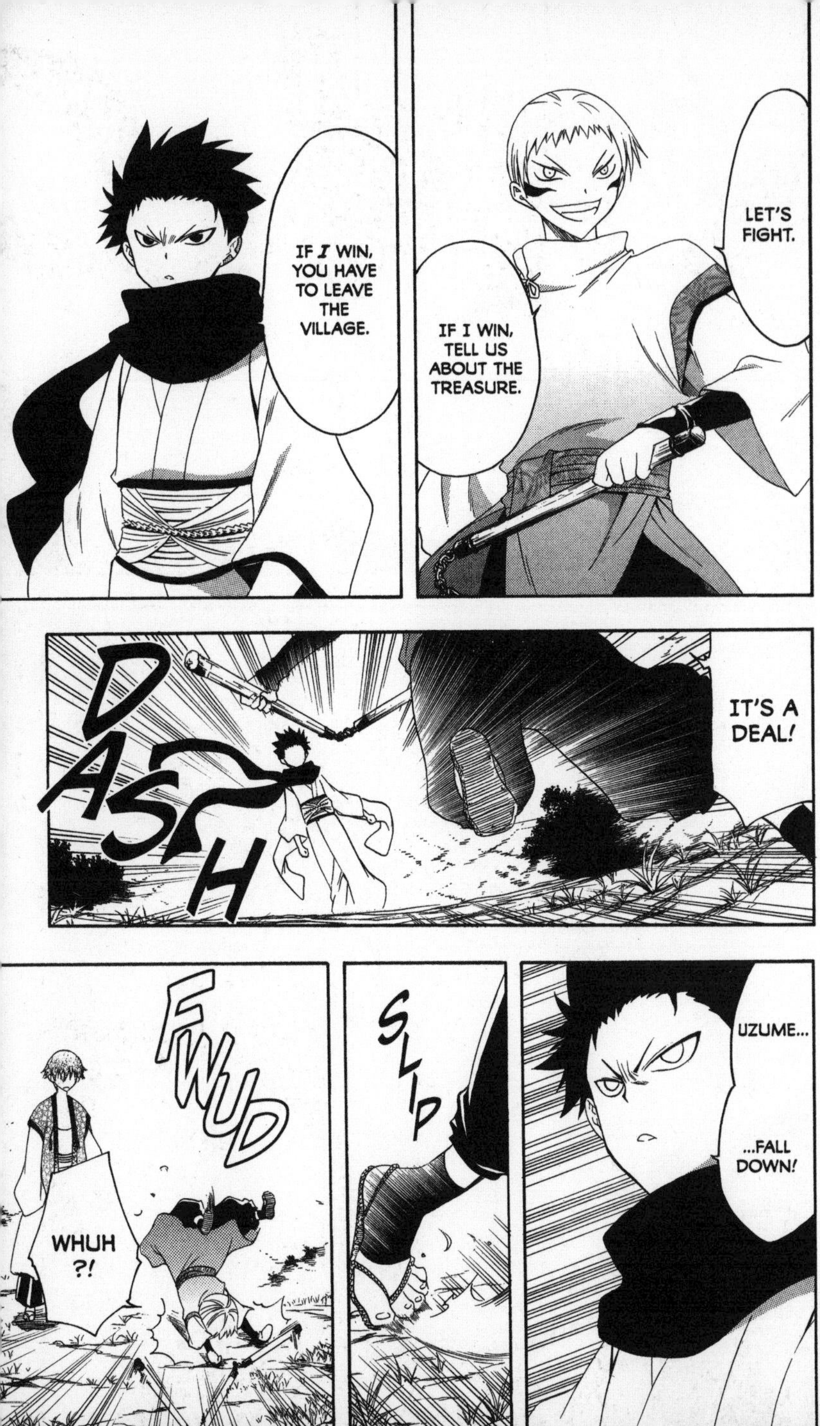
LET'S FIGHT.
IF I WIN, TELL US ABOUT THE TREASURE.
IF I WIN, YOU HAVE TO LEAVE THE VILLAGE.
IT'S A DEAL!
DASH
UZUME...
...FALL DOWN!
SLIP
FWUD
WHUH ?!

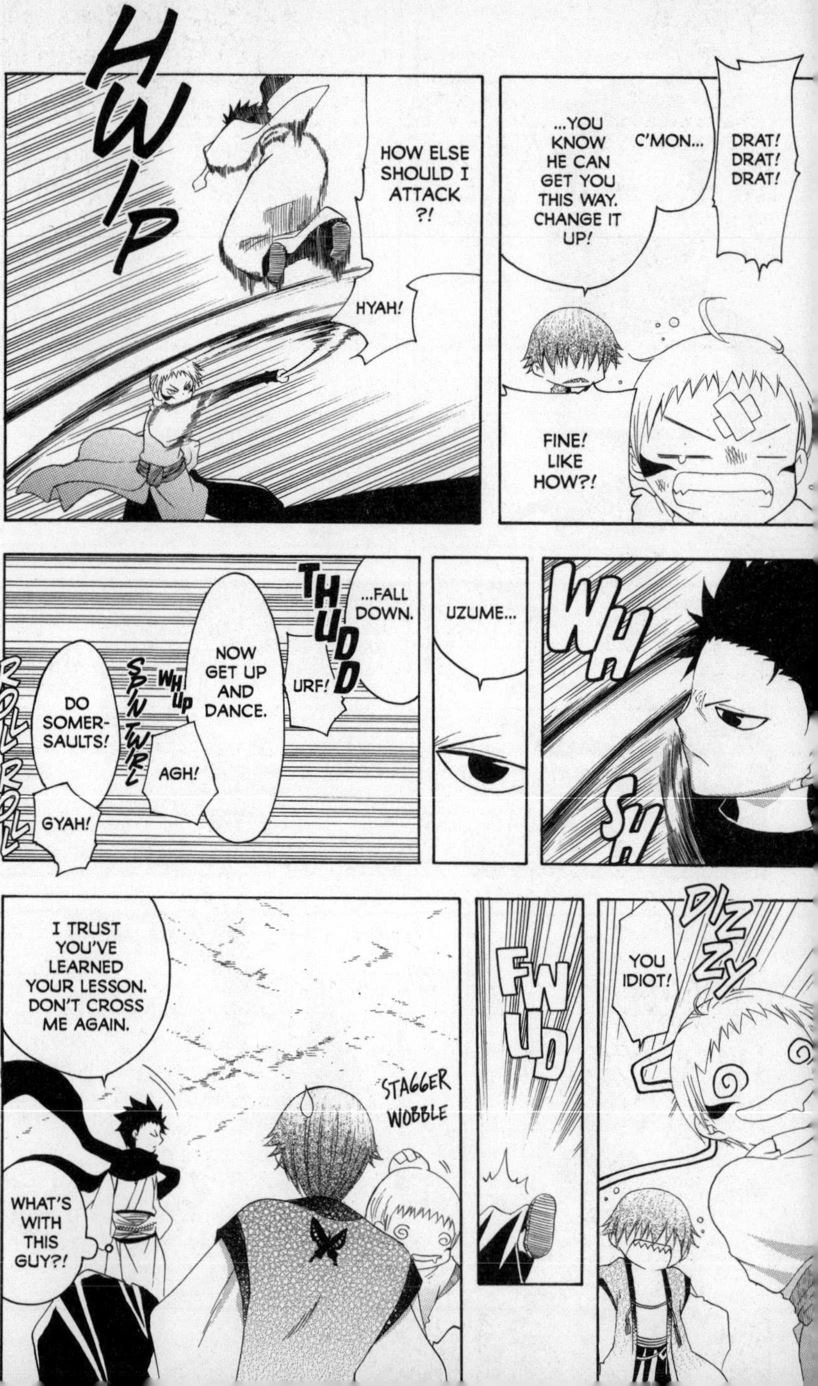
DRAT! DRAT! DRAT!
C'MON...
...YOU KNOW HE CAN GET YOU THIS WAY. CHANGE IT UP!
FINE! LIKE HOW?!
HWIP
HOW ELSE SHOULD I ATTACK?!
HYAH!
WHSH
UZUME...
...FALL DOWN.
THUDD
URF!
NOW GET UP AND DANCE.
SPIN TWIRL
WHUP
AGH!
DO SOMER-SAULTS!
ROLL ROLL
GYAH!
DIZZY
YOU IDIOT!
FWUD
I TRUST YOU'VE LEARNED YOUR LESSON. DON'T CROSS ME AGAIN.
STAGGER WOBBLE
WHAT'S WITH THIS GUY?!

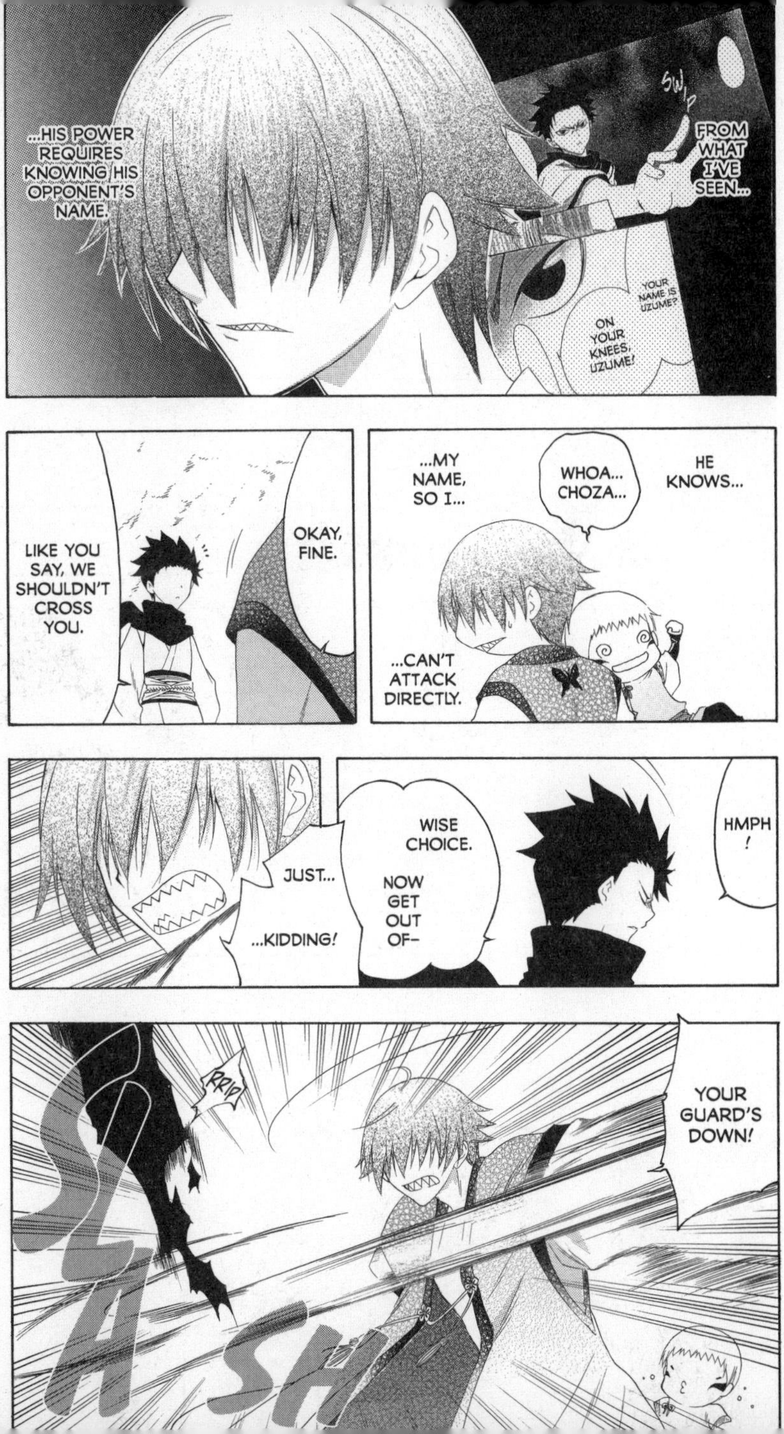
SWIP
FROM WHAT I'VE SEEN...
YOUR NAME IS UZUME?
ON YOUR KNEES, UZUME!
...HIS POWER REQUIRES KNOWING HIS OPPONENT'S NAME.
HE KNOWS...
WHOA... CHOZA...
...MY NAME, SO I...
...CAN'T ATTACK DIRECTLY.
OKAY, FINE.
LIKE YOU SAY, WE SHOULDN'T CROSS YOU.
HMPH!
WISE CHOICE.
NOW GET OUT OF-
JUST...
...KIDDING!
YOUR GUARD'S DOWN!
RRIP
SLASH

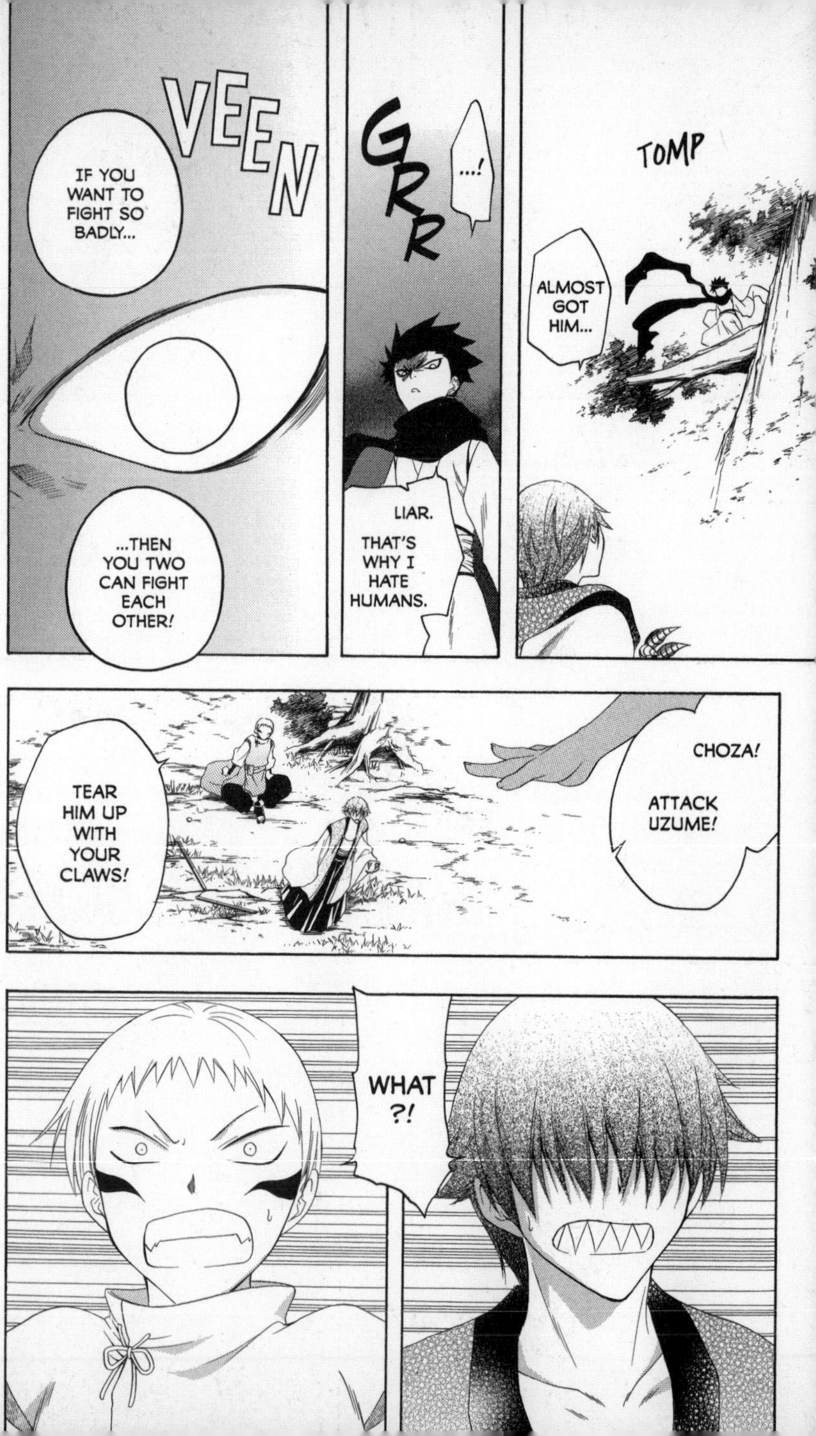
TOMP
ALMOST GOT HIM...
...!
GRR
LIAR.
THAT'S WHY I HATE HUMANS.
VEEN
IF YOU WANT TO FIGHT SO BADLY...
...THEN YOU TWO CAN FIGHT EACH OTHER!
CHOZA!
ATTACK UZUME!
TEAR HIM UP WITH YOUR CLAWS!
WHAT ?!

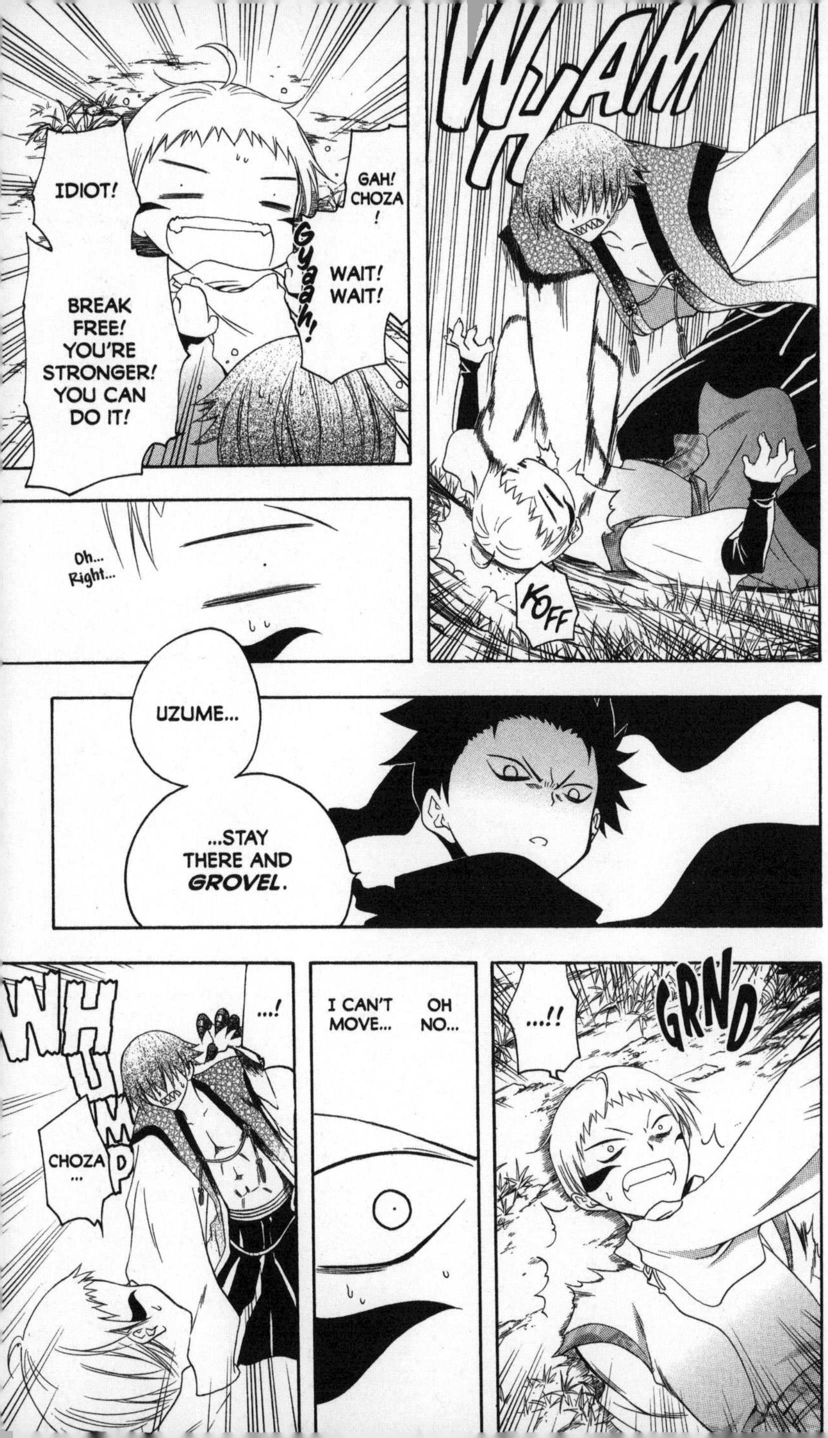
WHAM
KOFF
GAH! CHOZA!
Gyaaah!
WAIT! WAIT!
IDIOT!
BREAK FREE! YOU'RE STRONGER! YOU CAN DO IT!
Oh... Right...
UZUME...
...STAY THERE AND *GROVEL*.
GRND
...!!
OH NO...
I CAN'T MOVE...
...!
WHUMP
CHOZA...

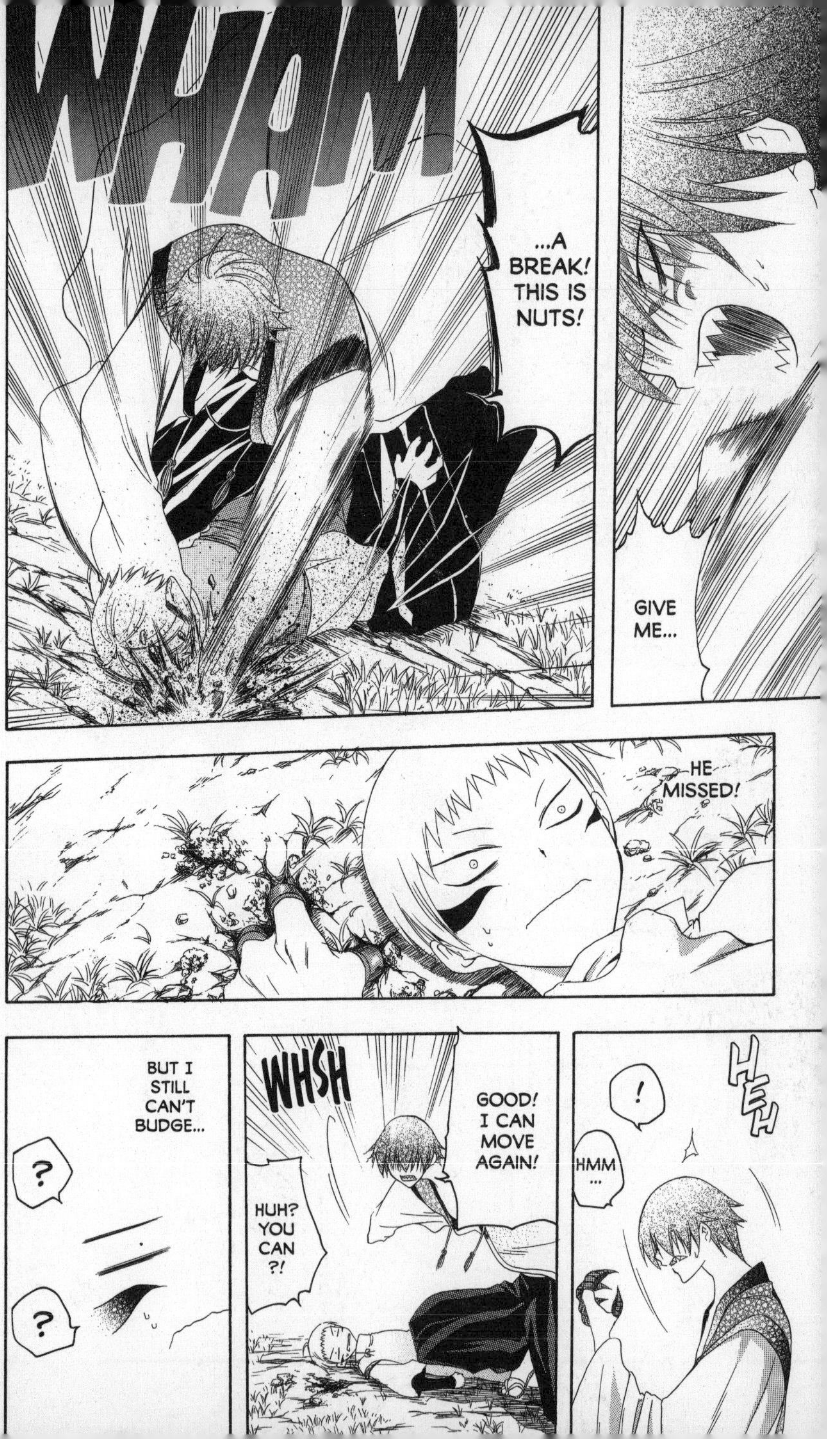
GIVE ME...
...A BREAK! THIS IS NUTS!
WHAM
HE MISSED!
HEH
!
HMM ...
GOOD! I CAN MOVE AGAIN!
WHSH
HUH? YOU CAN ?!
BUT I STILL CAN'T BUDGE...
?
?

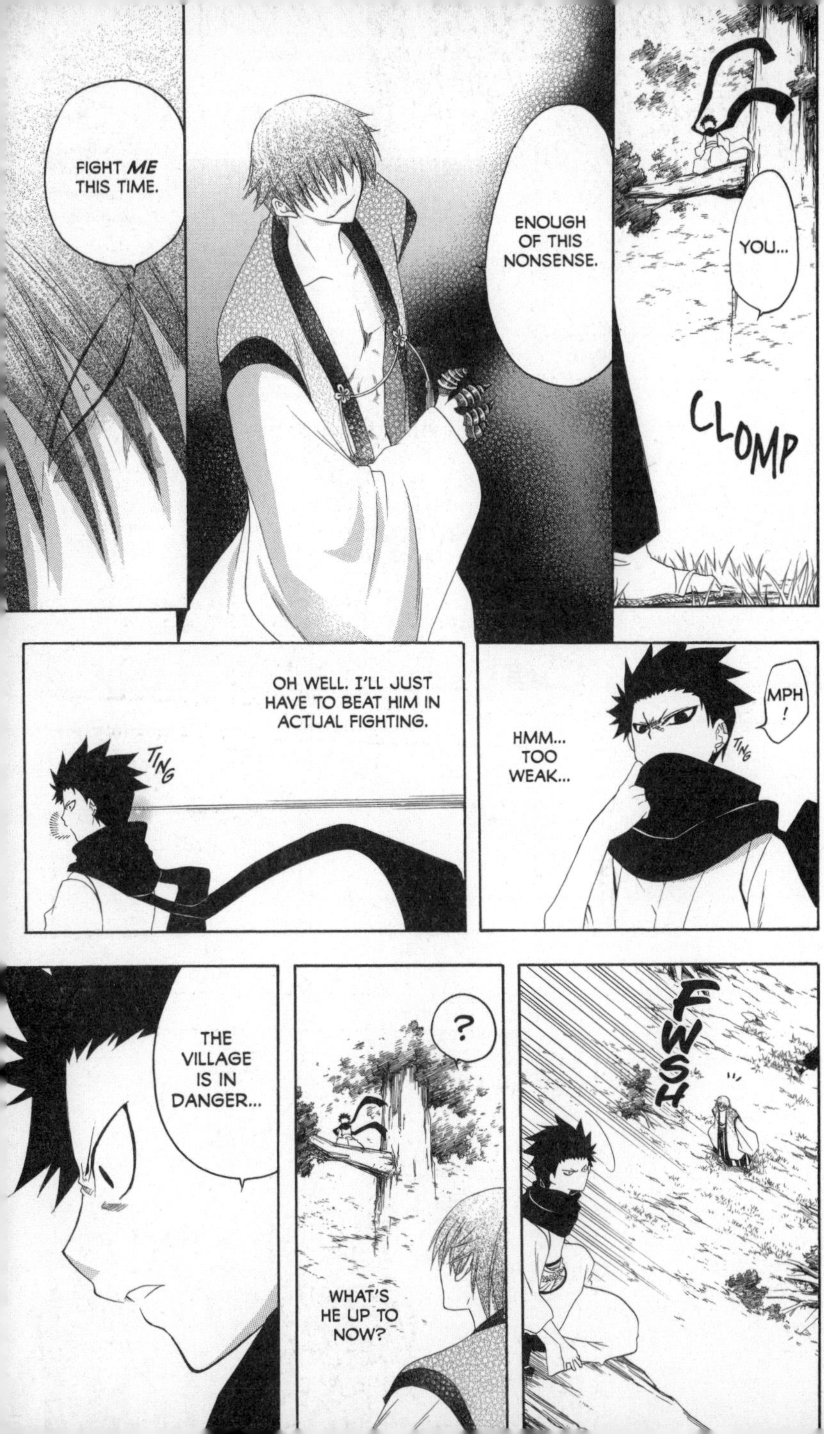
YOU...
CLOMP
ENOUGH OF THIS NONSENSE.
FIGHT *ME* THIS TIME.
MPH!
TING
HMM... TOO WEAK...
OH WELL. I'LL JUST HAVE TO BEAT HIM IN ACTUAL FIGHTING.
TING
FWSH
?
WHAT'S HE UP TO NOW?
THE VILLAGE IS IN DANGER...

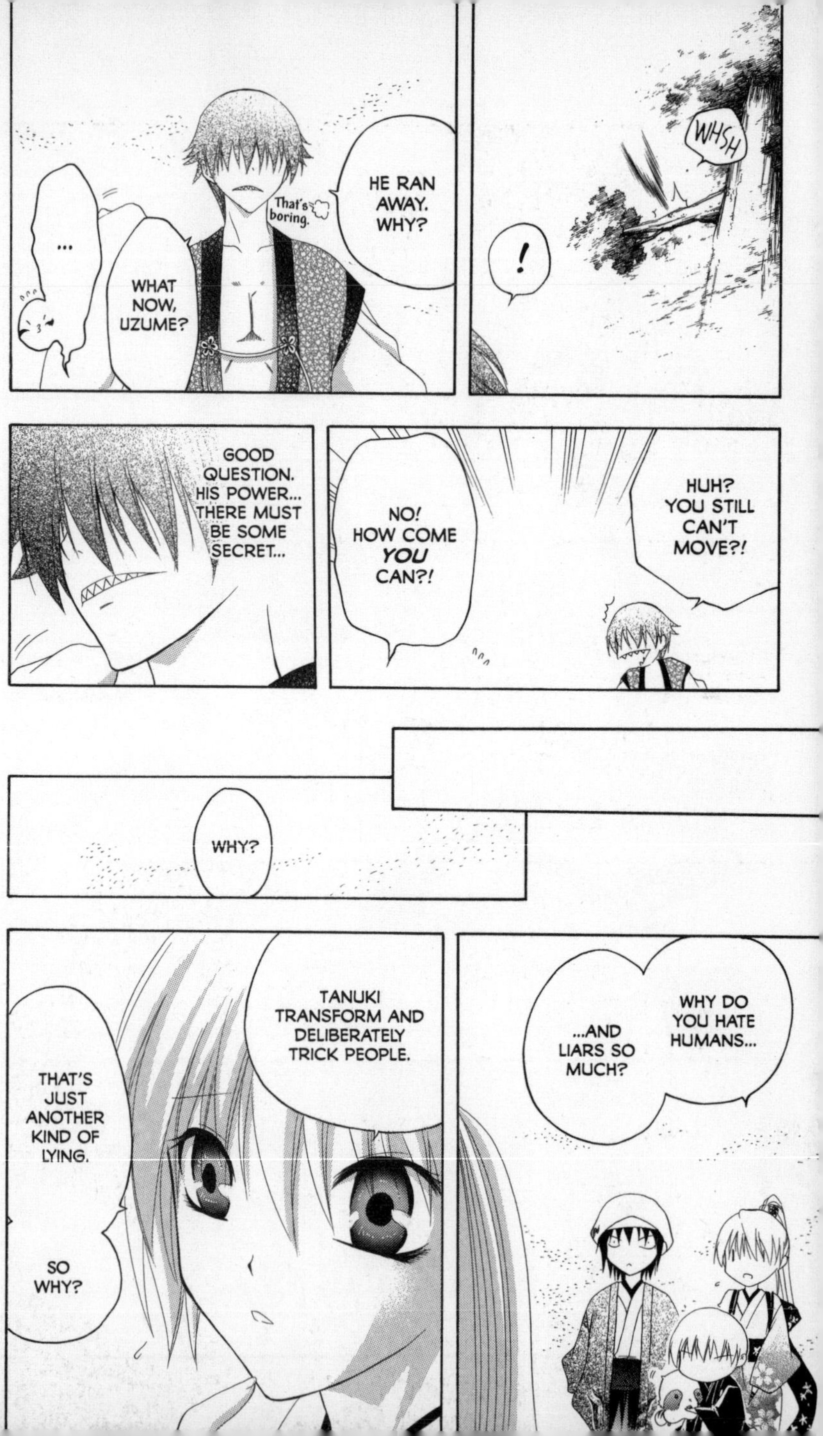
WHSH
!
HE RAN AWAY. WHY?
That's boring.
WHAT NOW, UZUME?
...
HUH? YOU STILL CAN'T MOVE?!
NO! HOW COME *YOU* CAN?!
GOOD QUESTION. HIS POWER... THERE MUST BE SOME SECRET...
WHY?
WHY DO YOU HATE HUMANS...
...AND LIARS SO MUCH?
TANUKI TRANSFORM AND DELIBERATELY TRICK PEOPLE.
THAT'S JUST ANOTHER KIND OF LYING.
SO WHY?

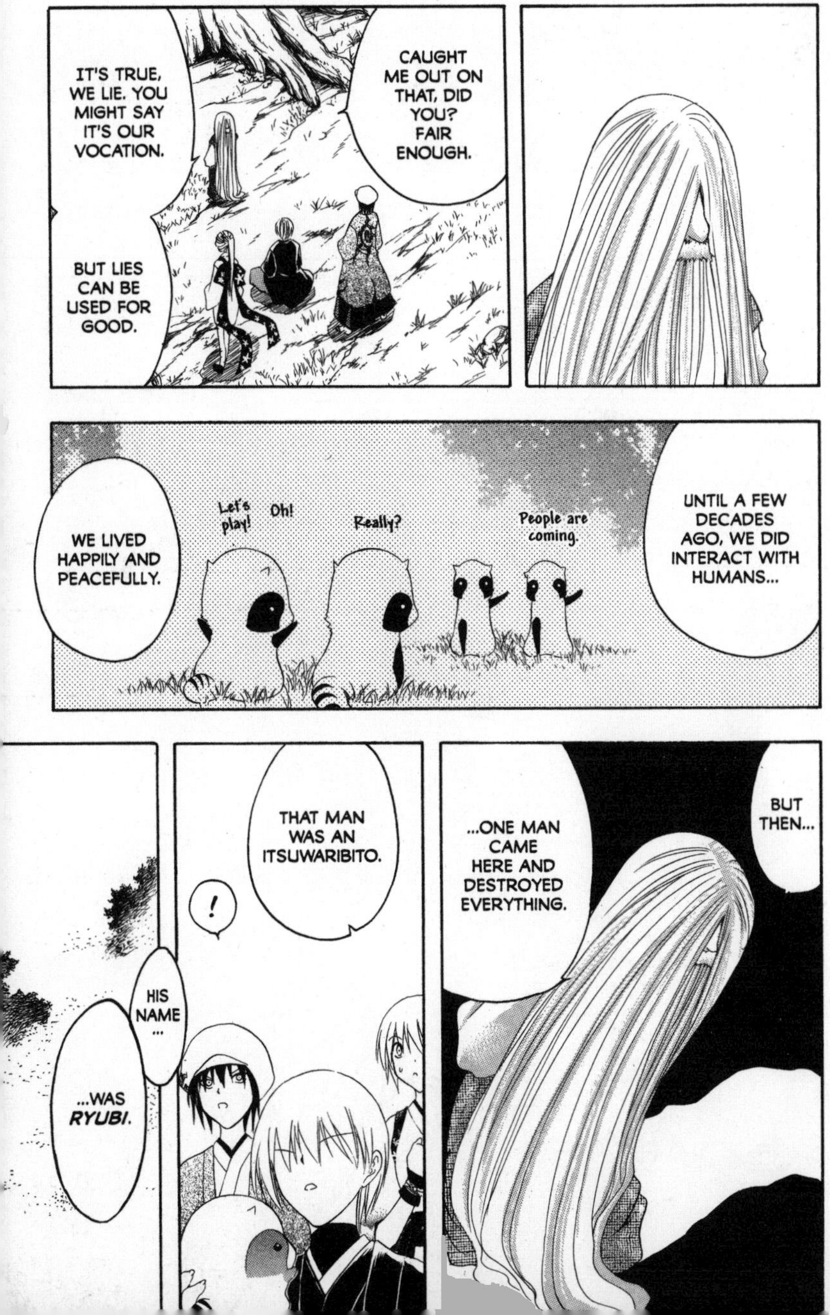
CAUGHT ME OUT ON THAT, DID YOU? FAIR ENOUGH.
IT'S TRUE, WE LIE. YOU MIGHT SAY IT'S OUR VOCATION.
BUT LIES CAN BE USED FOR GOOD.
UNTIL A FEW DECADES AGO, WE DID INTERACT WITH HUMANS...
People are coming.
Really?
Oh!
Let's play!
WE LIVED HAPPILY AND PEACEFULLY.
BUT THEN...
...ONE MAN CAME HERE AND DESTROYED EVERYTHING.
THAT MAN WAS AN ITSUWARIBITO.
!
HIS NAME ...
...WAS *RYUBI*.

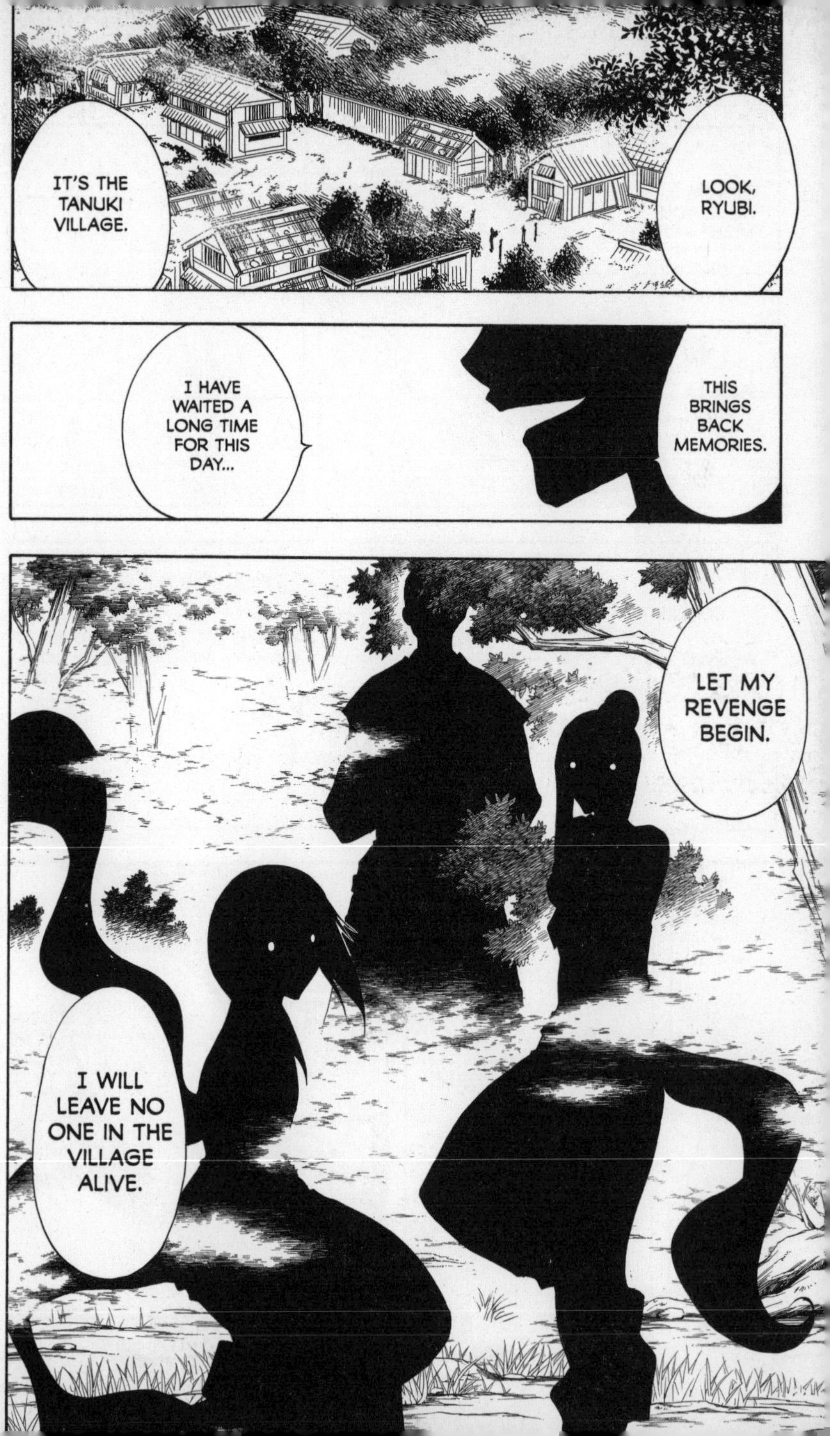
LOOK, RYUBI.
IT'S THE TANUKI VILLAGE.
THIS BRINGS BACK MEMORIES.
I HAVE WAITED A LONG TIME FOR THIS DAY...
LET MY REVENGE BEGIN.
I WILL LEAVE NO ONE IN THE VILLAGE ALIVE.

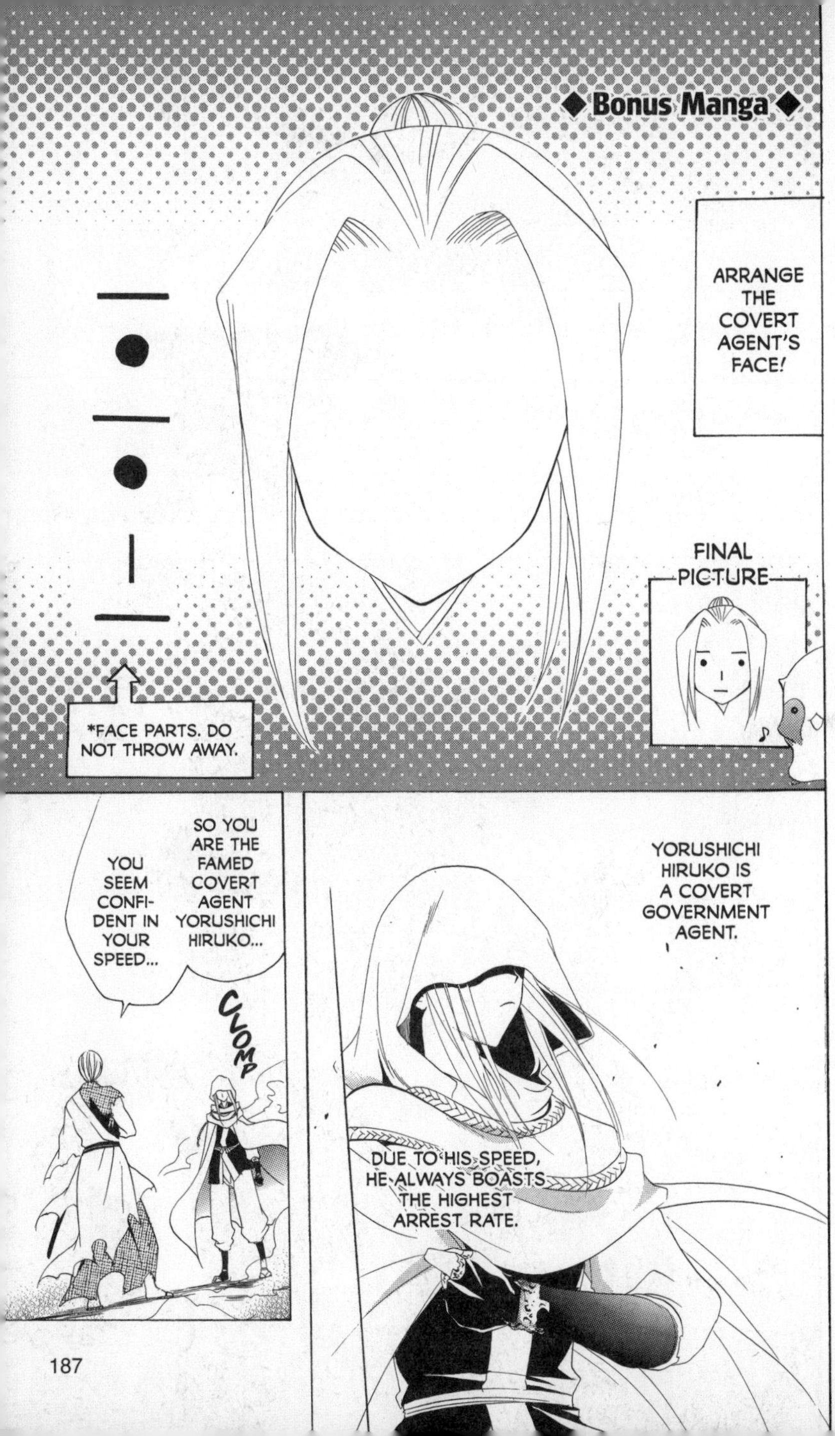
◆Bonus Manga◆
ARRANGE THE COVERT AGENT'S FACE!
FINAL PICTURE
*FACE PARTS. DO NOT THROW AWAY.
YORUSHICHI HIRUKO IS A COVERT GOVERNMENT AGENT.
DUE TO HIS SPEED, HE ALWAYS BOASTS THE HIGHEST ARREST RATE.
SO YOU ARE THE FAMED COVERT AGENT YORUSHICHI HIRUKO...
YOU SEEM CONFI-DENT IN YOUR SPEED...
CLOMP

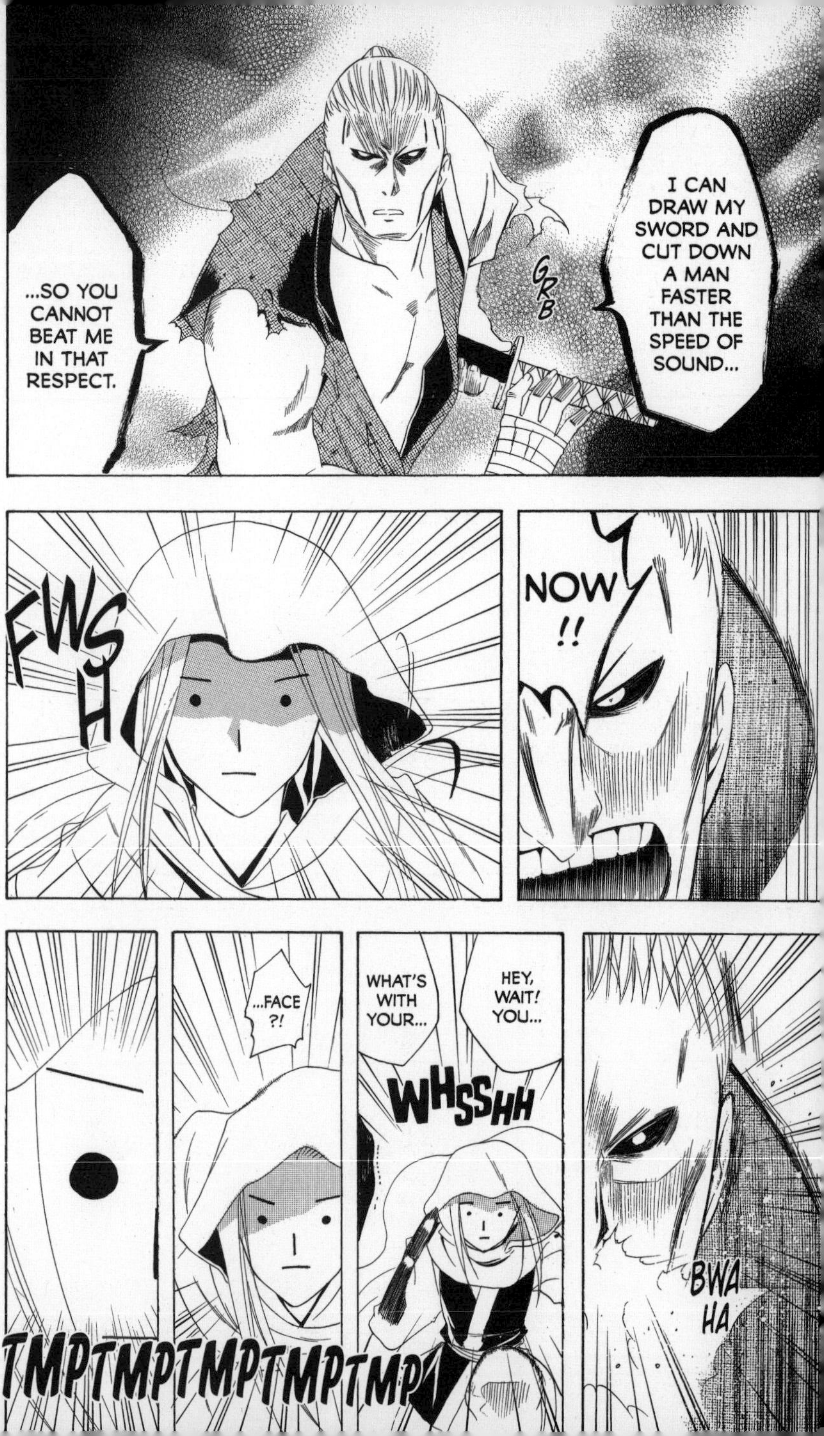
I CAN DRAW MY SWORD AND CUT DOWN A MAN FASTER THAN THE SPEED OF SOUND...
GRB
...SO YOU CANNOT BEAT ME IN THAT RESPECT.
NOW!!
FWSH
BWA HA
HEY, WAIT! YOU...
WHAT'S WITH YOUR...
WHSSHH
...FACE?!
TMPTMPTMPTMPTMP

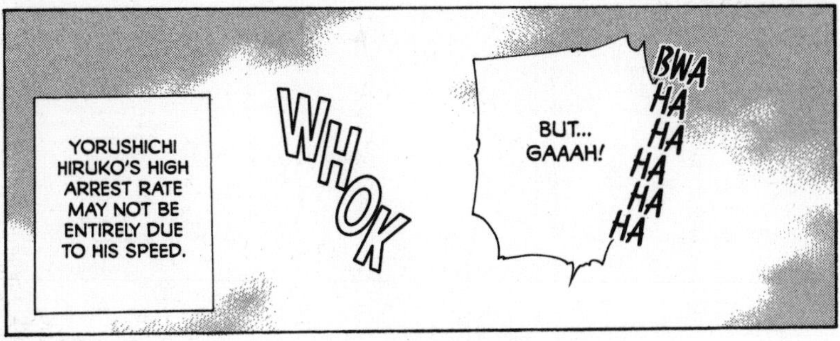
BWA HA HA HA HA HA
BUT... GAAAH!
WHOK
YORUSHICHI HIRUKO'S HIGH ARREST RATE MAY NOT BE ENTIRELY DUE TO HIS SPEED.

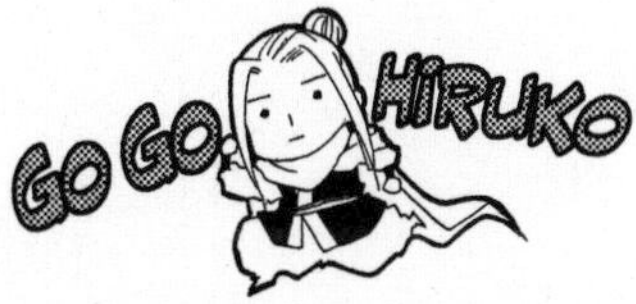
GO GO HIRUKO

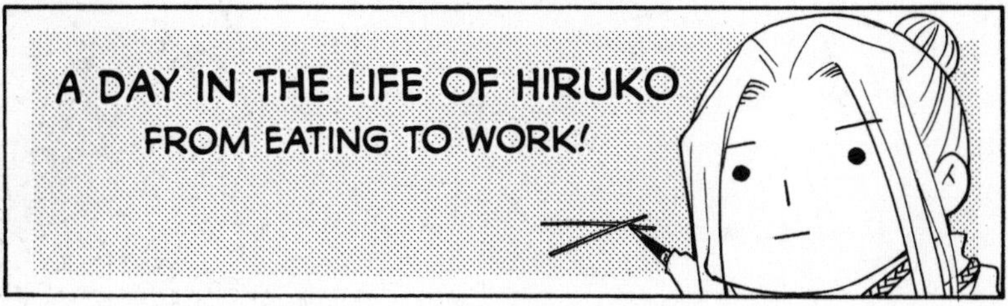
A DAY IN THE LIFE OF HIRUKO
FROM EATING TO WORK!

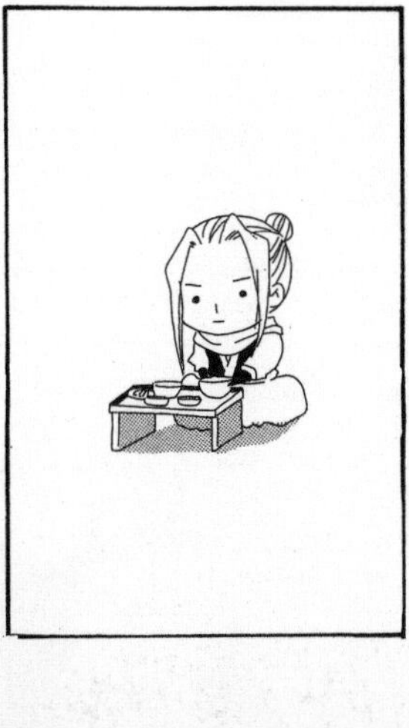

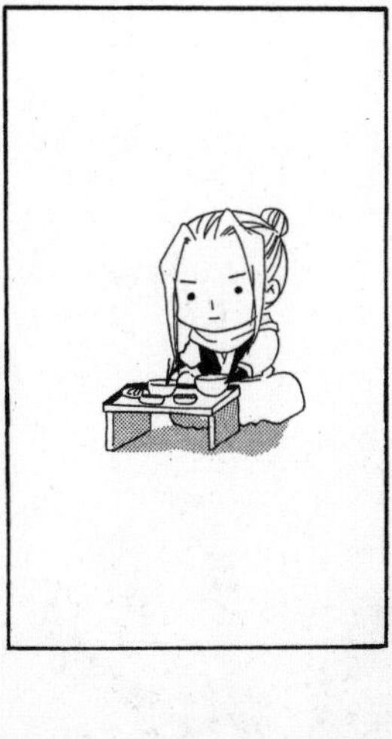

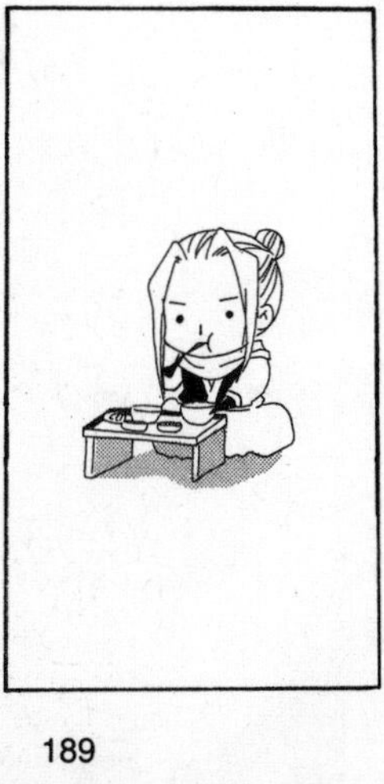

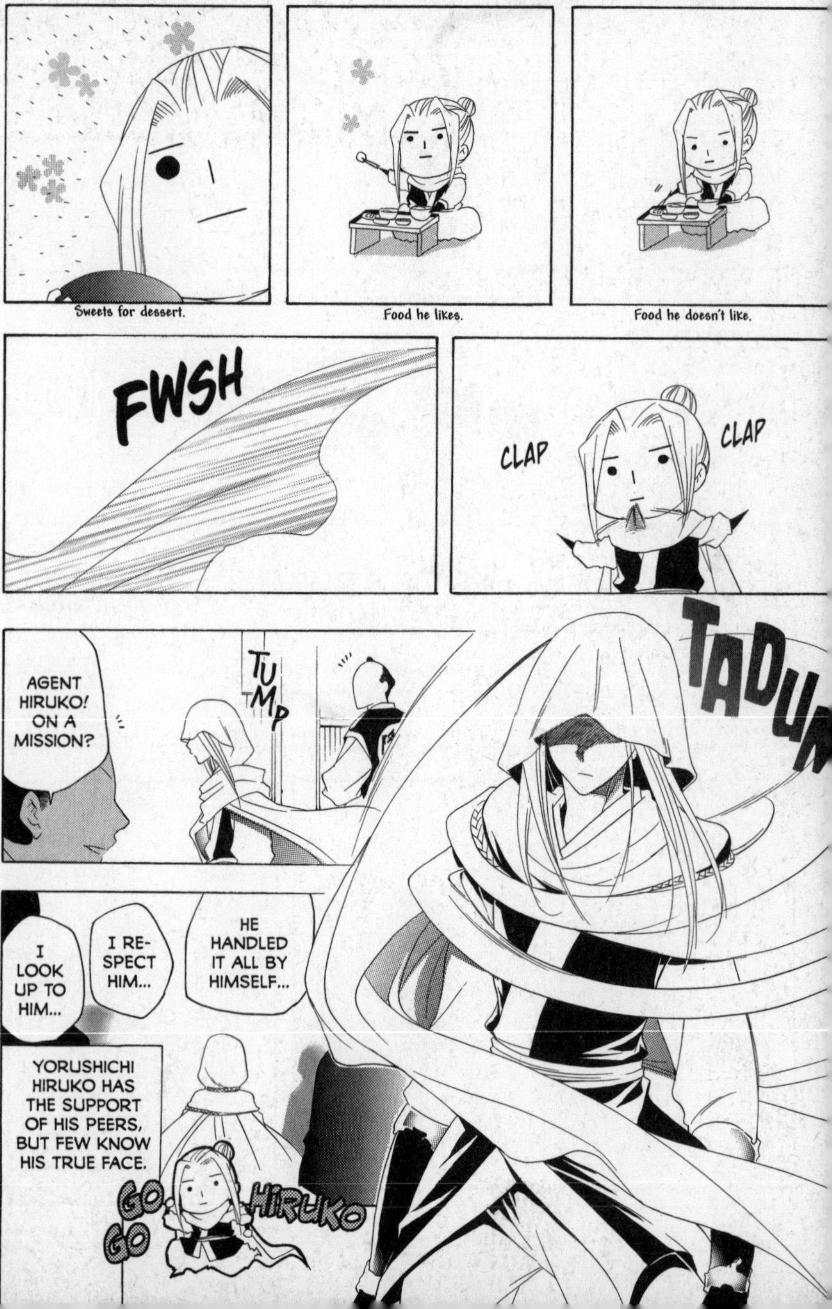
Food he doesn't like.
Food he likes.
Sweets for dessert.
CLAP
CLAP
FWSH
TADU
TUMP
AGENT HIRUKO! ON A MISSION?
HE HANDLED IT ALL BY HIMSELF...
I RE-SPECT HIM...
I LOOK UP TO HIM...
YORUSHICHI HIRUKO HAS THE SUPPORT OF HIS PEERS, BUT FEW KNOW HIS TRUE FACE.
GO GO HIRUKO

ITSUWARIBITO

Volume 12
Shonen Sunday Edition

Story and Art by
YUUKI IINUMA

TSUWARIBITO ◆ UTSUHO ◆ Vol. 12
by Yuuki IINUMA
© 2009 Yuuki IINUMA
All rights reserved.
Original Japanese edition published by SHOGAKUKAN.
English translation rights in the United States of America and Canada
arranged with SHOGAKUKAN.

Translation/John Werry
Touch-up Art & Lettering/Susan Daigle-Leach
Design/Matt Hinrichs
Editor/Gary Leach

Printed in the U.S.A.

Published by VIZ Media, LLC
P.O. Box 77010
San Francisco, CA 94107

10 9 8 7 6 5 4 3 2 1
First printing, August 2014

www.viz.com   WWW.SHONENSUNDAY.COM

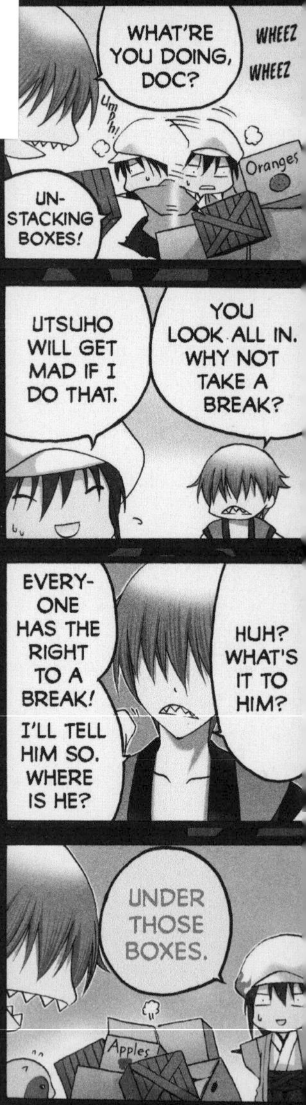
WHEEZ
WHEEZ
WHAT'RE YOU DOING, DOC?
Umph!
Oranges
UN-STACKING BOXES!
YOU LOOK ALL IN. WHY NOT TAKE A BREAK?
UTSUHO WILL GET MAD IF I DO THAT.
HUH? WHAT'S IT TO HIM?
EVERY-ONE HAS THE RIGHT TO A BREAK!
I'LL TELL HIM SO. WHERE IS HE?
UNDER THOSE BOXES.
Apples